SOVEREIGN

ROLAND FLAMINI

SOVEREIGN

ELIZABETH II

and the

WINDSOR DYNASTY

BANTAM PRESS

LONDON · NEW YORK · TORONTO · SYDNEY · AUCKLAND

TRANSWORLD PUBLISHERS LTD
61–63 Uxbridge Road, London W5 5SA

TRANSWORLD PUBLISHERS (AUSTRALIA) PTY LTD
15–23 Helles Avenue, Moorebank, NSW 2170

TRANSWORLD PUBLISHERS (NZ) LTD
Cnr Moselle and Waipareira Aves,
Henderson, Auckland

Published 1991 by Bantam Press
a division of Transworld Publishers Ltd
Copyright © Roland Flamini 1991

A catalogue record for this book is available from the British Library
0593 01834 6

Typeset in Garamond by
Chippendale Type Ltd, Otley, West Yorkshire.
Printed in Great Britain by
Mackays of Chatham plc, Chatham, Kent

For my daughter, Sarah

Acknowledgements

I am indebted to Her Majesty the Queen for permission to quote from her letter to President Ronald Reagan. *Sovereign* is in no way based on special access, but I would be remiss if I did not express my thanks to Sir William Heseltine, Her Majesty's Principal Private Secretary, and to two successive press secretaries at Buckingham Palace, Robin Janvrin first and later Charles Anson for being so responsive to my requests and factual inquiries. In addition, I owe a debt of gratitude to a large number and wide variety of officials, political figures, foreign diplomats and others who shared views and reminiscences, but who wished not to be publicly identified. My thanks to all of them. I would also like to add thanks for their help to Mrs David Bruce, Michael Cole, the late Carlo Ducci, Michael De-la-Noy, Baroness Ewart-Biggs, Baroness Falkender, Joe Haines, Paul Martin, J. A. Mizzi, Catherine Murdock, Chapman Pincher, the late Archie Roosevelt, Selwa Roosevelt, Peter Townsend and Philip Ziegler.

A biography of this kind is bound to pillage the work of a multitude of other writers and diarists. I owe much to all of those whose books, letters and papers are cited in my source notes. I have also benefited greatly from recourse to information available in the United States under the Freedom of Information Act and in this regard I am beholden for their able assistance to the staffs of the National Archives in Washington, and of the presidential libraries listed in the bibliography. My thanks are also due to the Bakhmeteff Archive at the Columbia University Library for access to the papers of Prince Paul of Serbia. A number of other letters from Queen Elizabeth II were also made available to me.

In summarizing them, I hope I have conveyed something of their flavour, and of her perceptiveness and flashes of wit.

I have several professional and private debts. At Delacorte in New York, my editor Patricia Soliman, herself a writer, provided stimulating guidance from the very start of the project, and copy editor Johanna Tani trawled with skill and determination through my unruly manuscript. At Bantam in London, Mark Barty-King and Jennie Bull radiated a reassuring enthusiasm for the idea. Juliet Borowicz read through the finished book with a knowledgeable eye and made many helpful suggestions. I am also indebted to my agents Helen Brann in New York for her encouragement and inspiration, and Murray Pollinger in London for his valuable help. Finally, I owe a further unquantifiable debt of a different kind to my wife, Diane, who knows what it all cost, but whose encouragement never dimmed.

Roland Flamini
Washington DC

Contents

Out of Africa

Treetops. It was hardly a hotel, more a cluster of cedarwood log cabins suspended between heaven and earth in the branches of a giant wild fig tree: a dining room, a small room at the back for the hunter, and a few bedrooms opening on to an observation deck. Thirty feet below was a waterhole on the banks of Kenya's Sagana River, and at night tourists could watch the comings and goings of rhinoceroses, elephants, deer, antelope and warthogs, drinking, splashing, fighting, cooling off after the heat of the day – a microcosm of East African wildlife observed in its moonlit sanctuary. There was neither room nor need for luxury: most visitors stayed at Treetops just overnight.

A white pillowcase fluttered from its roof on the afternoon of 5 February 1952. A party of guests had arrived in the clearing below, and this was a warning of danger at the watering hole. Some forty elephants, frightened and angry, shoved and trumpeted in the water churning up mud. A few feet away from the ladder up to the observation deck stood an old cow elephant with two calves. It might have been more prudent for the new arrivals to have returned to their cars and waited for the elephants to leave. A cow elephant can become angry and charge when disturbed with her young, but she had not scented them – and there were three guns in the party of four men and two women.

After a whispered consultation they decided on a cautious advance across the fifty yards of open ground, covered by one of the rifles. A slim young woman in shirt and slacks led the group. She walked steadily towards the elephants, swung on to the ladder and climbed lightly to the observation deck.

The young woman was Princess Elizabeth, heir presumptive to the British throne, and Treetops was a stopover on her way to Australia with her husband, Philip, Duke of Edinburgh. Before sunset they stood on the deck together fascinated by the scene. An elephant, annoyed by some pigeons, scooped up dust and blew it to scare them away. The cow elephant suckled a calf and a four year old came up to be fed as well. 'Oh, look, it's going to drive the baby away,' Elizabeth said, absorbed. With her cine-camera she filmed monkeys chasing one another across the branches of the Cape chestnut trees, while below a rhinoceros contemplated a delicate snow-white heron perched on one spindly leg at the water's edge.

'I don't want to miss a moment of this,' she said as she trained her camera on two waterbucks locked in fierce battle. 'Is that blood? Do you think it will die?' When tea was brought some time later, she had not moved her camera from filming the wounded waterbuck. 'I think the poor thing is dead,' she said. Jim Corbett, a legendary hunter, was invited to meet her. He hoped the King – George VI – had not caught a cold at London Airport when he saw her off. 'He's like that, never thinks of himself,' she replied softly.

But for his recent serious illness King George would have been at Treetops himself: Elizabeth's tour had originally been planned for him and Queen Elizabeth, and sending his daughter had seemed preferable to postponement or cancellation. When she visited Canada the previous autumn, she had carried the knowledge of the King's precarious condition like a weight on her shoulders. Even now, she still had with her the sealed Accession documents she had originally taken to Canada – papers to be opened only in the event of the King's death. But with her father making such rapid progress they must have seemed superfluous, and she could enjoy what was turning out to be a true adventure. She told Corbett she felt the King had turned the corner when he lifted his walking stick to his shoulder, saying, 'I believe I can shoot now,' a sentiment which the hunter understood.

Her deep affection for her father was evident from the way she spoke of him. So was her pleasure and relief at his recovery, not just because she loved him but doubtless also because his survival bought her precious extra time for living her own life. King George's accession had been the result of an unexpected twist of fate. His elder brother had abdicated: he was next in line of succession, and the Crown had passed to him unsought, unwanted and unwelcome. No such turn of events seemed likely to alter Elizabeth's destiny. Since the age of eleven she had lived first with the possibility and then – when her mother did not give birth to a son – the virtual certainty that she would one day be Queen; and part of the bond between father and daughter was a shared lack of enthusiasm for that prospect.

If King George VI was the reluctant monarch, Princess Elizabeth was his equally reluctant heir. Though she accepted the inevitability of succeeding the King she could hardly be said to have waited for that moment with eager anticipation. She hoped it would come later rather than sooner.

Yet she also shared her father's sense of duty to his country and of obligation to his dynasty. So that when the moment finally came, she slipped naturally into the groove of royal succession. Neither she nor her father echoed the sentiment of Pope Gregory V, who said at his election, 'God has given us the papacy, now let us enjoy it.' No hint of joy or exuberance, and only very rare flashes of humour, were ever allowed to show in Elizabeth's public persona. What was revealed to her loyal subjects was not the portrait of a human being, but rather, the one-dimensional figure of an icon, simple, dignified, dedicated, hardworking, reassuringly unchanging and rather bland.

True enough as far as it went, but what of the woman herself? Her father was a deeply insecure man prone to sudden eruptive rages. He was known to have tantrums in public. Elizabeth didn't even have tantrums in private, but behind her façade of iron self-control the small voice of uncertainty was often at work. As she slowly mastered her awkwardness with people she felt more at ease in her public life, and found her role more enjoyable. And for all her primness, she had – in private – a surprisingly wicked sense of fun and an unexpected talent for mimicry. On one occasion the American film comedian Bob Hope was her guest at lunch at Windsor Castle. As she gave him her standard guided tour of what she regarded as her principal home he remarked that he could stand practically anywhere in the ancient fortress for days just 'soaking up the history'. Yes, Elizabeth replied, Queen Juliana of the Netherlands had said the same thing last week. Then she launched into an imitation of Queen Juliana's accent. 'Suddenly, there was the Queen of England, doing Dutch,' Bob Hope would recall later.

Yet all the time, embedded in her personality was a core of sadness. Hers was the story of a woman who distinguished herself

3

in a role to which she never aspired, and which indeed, since childhood, she had at least occasionally hoped and prayed would be filled by someone else. She would have been happier as a lady of the manor in one of the shires raising racehorses, dogs and children, more or less in that order of importance. Possibly because her first two children were growing up during the demanding early years of her reign, when the time she could devote to them was severely limited, she has always given the impression of detachment from her children.

All public figures lead a double life, but with the Queen the gap between image and reality was wider than usual. This is partly because an extraordinary degree of secrecy surrounded the life she led outside the radius of her public role. She was the first monarch to require members of the royal household to sign a commitment not to discuss their work. The Prime Minister and members of the Cabinet saw the monarch on the basis of confidentiality. Friends who wanted to remain so virtually took a vow of silence. They knew the consequences of indiscretion. When *Time* magazine once asked Walter Annenberg, a former United States ambassador to Britain, about his continued friendship with the Queen, he was quoted as saying, 'One has to be terribly careful or the iron curtain will fall around you just like that.'

Elizabeth's determined defence of her privacy incidentally finds justification in a famous essay on the role and function of the British monarchy by the nineteenth-century journalist Walter Bagehot, who warned against letting 'too much daylight in upon the magic' of the monarchy. If Bagehot had not existed, the Windsors would have had to invent him. From the 1960s, Bagehot collided with the increasingly avid mass media, and the Queen's rearguard action against the press was one of the themes of her reign.

All of which is a long digression from the evening at Treetops when the party had dinner around an unpolished table, sitting on hard benches with cushions only for the women, unaware that fate was about to take a hand in the young Princess's life.

The hosts were Eric Sherbrooke Walker and his wife, Lady Bettie. There was a ripple of excitement when the spirit lamp on which the coffee was being made caught fire and the African servant who had served the simple meal sauntered over with a wet cloth and flapped out the flames. But nothing disturbed the serenity of the evening as the Duke and his wife stood on the balcony until the moon set before going to bed. Corbett, who was eighty, stood guard throughout the night at the top of the ladder with a heavy calibre rifle. While elephants and rhinoceroses cannot climb ladders, terrorists can, and the Mau-Mau terror was just beginning in Kenya.

The Princess was out again a few hours later with her camera and light meter, ready for more wildlife footage. Obligingly, two rhinoceroses sparred against the background of an African dawn. The royal visitors then had a thoroughly English breakfast, and the royal luggage was lowered by rope and packed into the cars for the hour-long ride back to Sagana Lodge, the riverside house that had been a wedding present to Elizabeth and Philip from the people of Kenya. 'It's been my most thrilling experience yet,' the Princess told Jim Corbett. His gallant reply was, 'Ma'am, if you have the same courage in facing whatever the future sends you as you have in facing an elephant at eight paces, we are going to be very fortunate.' Before getting into her car she told him, 'I will come back.' It was a promise she was to keep thirty-one years later.

That afternoon, 6 February, Princess Elizabeth and her husband emerged from a siesta. The day was crisp and clear, and snow-capped Mount Kenya gleamed in the distance. Philip spotted his secretary, Lieutenant Commander Michael Parker, beckoning to him mysteriously from behind some bushes; and, while Elizabeth was asking her former nursery maid and then dresser Bobo MacDonald to order the horses for early next morning, Parker quickly told the Prince that King George VI had died during the night. Philip was stunned. 'He looked as if you'd dropped half the world on him,' Parker said afterwards. Philip broke the news to his wife as she stood in a beige and white summer dress by the Sagana River. For almost an hour members of the household watched them as they walked together, not touching, back and forth along the bank.

King George VI's death from lung cancer occurred at Sandringham House, on the Norfolk coast, in the small hours of the morning. Given that Kenya time was three hours ahead of London time, unknown to herself and those travelling with her, Elizabeth was already Queen as she filmed the early morning activity around the Treetops waterhole. Jim Corbett wrote later, 'For the first time in history a young girl climbed up into a tree one day as a Princess and down from it the next as a Queen.'

When the young Queen returned from her walk and quietly faced her household she was dry-eyed, tense, but in control. Immediately, she began dealing with pressing matters – sending messages of love and support to her mother and sister, notifying the Australian and New Zealand governments of the necessity to cut short her trip and return home, studying the Accession documents she had been convinced she would not need on this journey. Since the paperwork required her signature almost the first decision confronting her was the choice of a name as Queen Regnant. What, her secretary, Colonel Martin Charteris, asked her, would that name be? She answered: 'My own name, of course – what else?'

Well, hardly 'of course'. Her uncle David – the Prince of Wales – was King Edward VIII; her father Albert, Duke of York, became King George VI. As for 'what else', she might have chosen to be Queen Mary III (her third name) in order to avoid confusion with her mother, Queen Elizabeth. Or she could have taken the name of Queen Victoria II, after her revered great-great-grandmother, although she probably saw Victoria as unique in English history. Those who knew the Princess believed that she had given little advance thought to her name as Queen because of the built-in implication of her father's death. The likelihood was, therefore, that her decision to retain her own name was made on the spur of the moment. It was a choice that would certainly have pleased George VI, with its implied tribute to his adored wife.

There was an inadvertent symbolism in the fact that Elizabeth had become Queen while visiting one of the leading colonies. The first two decades of her reign were to be years of divestiture, the break-up of the old British Empire (with Kenya coincidentally supplying the battle cry for the process – '*Uhuru*', the Bantu word for freedom). The loss would be somewhat softened by the emergence of the Commonwealth, and the young Queen, fully grasping its implications, was to devote considerable energy and attention to consolidating this multiracial, voluntary grouping of independent former colonies, and to emerge as its single most important cohesive factor. But the transition from Empire to Commonwealth was only one of the changes confronting Elizabeth as the new monarch. The Britain of 1952 was a country still reeling from the impact of nearly six years of war, a country of social shifts and material deprivations. The scars of the blitz still showed in the cities. Food rationing was still in force. Her father had proved a courageous and inspiring wartime leader: Elizabeth faced the challenge of ensuring that the monarchy, like Britain, could survive the era of radical postwar change.

When George VI found himself catapulted on to the English throne, renounced by Edward VIII in 1937 in order to marry the

American divorcee Wallis Simpson, the deck was hardly stacked in his favour: he was unprepared, uncertain, uneasy – and afflicted with a serious speech impediment and numerous facial twitches as a result of a sickly, repressive childhood under an autocratic father who had little time for any of his sons except his eldest, the Prince of Wales. But aside from his courage, he was blessed with a photographic memory which helped him to master his briefs quickly and effectively, a great deal of sound common sense, a high concept of duty, and a truly remarkable wife. For Elizabeth II, on the other hand, it had been different. Her father had made sure that she did not lack training. She had been studying her future inheritance with him since her late teens, for he wanted her to be thoroughly familiar with the affairs of 'the firm'. To George VI, a practical man, the monarchy was always the family firm.

More prepared she might have been, but for Elizabeth, the time came too soon. Married since 1947, she had two young children and a husband with whom she was in love, and she had looked forward to long years of a settled married life in her father's shadow. Now everything was changed. When Elizabeth appeared for the first time as Queen before her household, Prince Philip stood two paces behind her, which from that moment became his permanent station, at least in public.

Reigning queens of England come to the throne early and depart late. Elizabeth I succeeded her half-sister at the age of twenty-five and ruled for forty-five years. Queen Victoria was eighteen when she followed her uncle William IV, and died sixty-four years later, aged eighty-two. So past history suggested that with the accession of the second Elizabeth at twenty-six, the United Kingdom was on the threshold of another long reign. She was the fourth monarch of the Royal House of Windsor, a name her grandfather King George V had virtually pulled out of the air at the outbreak of the First World War in a discreet papering over of the family's German roots.

The new Queen's German lineage went back to George, Elector of Hanover, who in 1714 became the first Hanoverian king of England. It was Queen Victoria who changed the name from the House of Hanover to Saxe-Coburg-Gotha, family name of her German husband Prince Albert. But names are easier to change than relations, or indeed some other residual family traits. When she became Queen of England, Elizabeth had some sixty German uncles, aunts and cousins, many more than she had British.

Not that there was much that was German about Queen

Victoria's son, the fun-loving King Edward VII, popular despite – or because of – his well-known weakness for fast beautiful women and beautiful fast racehorses, and even less in his successor, George V, who had served in the Royal Navy and brought to the Court the blustery climate of a ship in a squall. The latter's wife, Princess Victoria Mary of Teck, was German-born, however, and spoke English with an accent. Brought up in genteel poverty the youngest daughter of a hard-up nobleman, she came to England as the chosen bride of King Edward VII's son and heir the Duke of Clarence (King Edward was still Prince of Wales at the time). When that son died, the marriage arrangement was simply switched to Edward's next son and heir, Prince George, to whom in due course she bore five sons and a daughter: David, later Edward VIII; Albert (Bertie), later George VI; Henry, Duke of Gloucester; George, Duke of Kent; John, who was an epileptic and died at the age of fifteen in 1919; and Mary, the Princess Royal.

Elizabeth was not quite ten years old when King George V died early in 1936. But Queen Mary survived as the young Elizabeth's mentor in royal matters, dying at eighty-five, just over five months before her granddaughter's coronation. Queen Mary had personified the strength of the Windsor dynasty's women members. Following King Edward VIII's abdication, for example, she wrote to relations urging them never again to see friends of 'Mrs S', in other words, Wallis Simpson. In a letter which she marked 'Read and Burn' she singled out the society hostess Emerald, Lady Cunard, for befriending Wallis Simpson, giving parties in her honour and generally making a great fuss of her. Lady Cunard had greatly harmed Edward VIII, she said, and the royal family were going to ostracize her. She felt society should do the same.

The letter was typical of her toughness and forthright manner, common characteristics among the royal family's women. Elizabeth II's first cousin, the Earl of Harewood, son of Queen Mary's daughter, Mary, described how underneath his mother's gentle nature there was 'a little Hanoverian spleen'. The men, whatever their other qualities, have tended to be judged – and with good reason – as temperamental, insecure, indecisive, or, at least in the case of Edward VIII (or, as he became, the Duke of Windsor) at least, headstrong. The royal women, the mothers, wives and sisters, were controlled, courageous – English roses with petals of stainless steel. To the Duke of Windsor, they – Queen Mary, Queen Elizabeth the Queen Mother, the Queen herself – were the 'ice-veined bitches' who persistently refused to receive his wife into the family, or even permit her to use the title of Her Royal Highness. Yet he never seems to have had the gumption to force a showdown with them.

Elizabeth was born into and brought up in this genetic pattern. Her father taught her a great deal about the work of a constitutional monarch, but as we shall see it was largely from her grandmother that she learned how to be a Queen. And the other lasting influence was her mother.

As monarch, King George V had not been an innovator, yet in a very real sense Elizabeth was the product of an important change in the family rules. Departing from tradition, he allowed the royal princes the option of marrying 'local girls' – the daughters of the English and Scottish nobility – instead of foreign princesses. His son Albert availed himself of this concession – itself, like the change of name, arising out of the hostilities with Germany – to pursue and eventually marry Lady Elizabeth Bowes-Lyon, beautiful, vivacious daughter of the Earl of Strathmore. It was a long, dogged pursuit because everyone was in love with her. A less determined suitor would have been discouraged when Elizabeth rejected his first proposal in 1921. But with true British grit the Duke of York persisted, and on 13 January 1923, the day Elizabeth accepted him, he telegraphed his parents the prearranged signal, 'All right. Bertie.' Which, indeed, it was.

II

Lilibet

Princess Elizabeth, the Yorks' first child, was born at 17 Bruton Street, the London house of the Earl and Countess of Strathmore, her maternal grandparents. At the time, the Yorks lived at White Lodge in Richmond Park, the residence chosen for them when they married by the King and Queen, but it was considered too remote from London for the birth. Indeed, the Yorks hated the place. It was a white elephant, unmodernized and poorly heated, and the young royal couple were desperately lobbying Buckingham Palace for a more suitable Crown property closer to London.

In the event, White Lodge would probably have rendered even more complicated what turned out to be a difficult birth. It was a breech baby. A Caesarean section was performed by the surgeon Sir Henry Stratton at two-forty in the morning of Wednesday, 21 April 1926, after the Duchess of York had been painfully in labour for several hours. Meanwhile, the Duke waited anxiously downstairs with Sir William Joynson-Hicks, the Home Secretary in Prime Minister Stanley Baldwin's Conservative government, for company. The Home Secretary was still required by law to be present at the birth of every royal baby in direct succession to the throne, to testify to the infant's authenticity and to discourage any funny business such as switching babies. Coffee and sandwiches were sent out to reporters waiting in the wet street. The weather had been foul for a week, adding to the atmosphere of national gloom. Britain was in the grip of serious labour unrest, and the threat of a general strike was uppermost in people's minds. But neither the grim economic climate nor the weather could diminish the Yorks' delight at the arrival of their daughter.

At 4 a.m., King George V and Queen Mary were woken up at Windsor Castle and told the news. In the afternoon, they drove to London to see the baby. 'A little darling with a lovely complexion and pretty fair hair,' the Queen wrote in her diary. But she was evidently not overly happy about the sleeping infant's strong Windsor features for she added, 'I wish you were more like your little mother.'

There was also perhaps a hint of disappointment that the child was not a boy. With the Prince of Wales still unmarried and showing no signs of settling down and producing an heir, his brother Albert, Duke of York, was next in line, and the baby princess was therefore the third. Viewed from the dynastic perspective, a male would have been preferable – and indeed even a younger brother of her own would displace her. Which is perhaps why the Duke of York, writing to his mother of his 'tremendous joy' a few days later, is somewhat defensive. 'We always wanted a child to make our happiness complete, & now that it has happened it seems so wonderful & strange,' he told Queen Mary. 'I am so proud of Elizabeth at this moment after all she has gone through during the last few days . . . I do hope that you and Papa are as delighted as we are, to have a grand-daughter, or would you have sooner had another grandson? I know Elizabeth wanted a daughter.' (The King and Queen already had two grandsons, George and Gerald, sons of their daughter Princess Mary, the Princess Royal. They were born respectively in 1923 and 1924.)

The wanted child was breast-fed by her mother and looked after by Clara Knight, who had nursed the Duchess herself and was always addressed as 'Mrs Knight' despite the fact that she was unmarried and remained so all her life. Early in Mrs Knight's long career as a nanny, a child in her firm, unflappable care had reduced the name Clara to 'Alah', and Alah she remained to subsequent generations. Her commanding height helped her put across the point that she stood no nonsense from child or parent. The royal nursery governess Marion Crawford, who was to come later, saw her as 'almost noble-looking'. Alah's under-nurse was twenty-two-year-old Margaret MacDonald. A gardener's daughter from Crowarty, a Scottish Highland village, she was to exert a lifelong influence on the Princess.

The Yorks wanted to name the baby Elizabeth Alexandra Mary after her mother, great-grandmother and grandmother respectively. Queen Alexandra, the Queen Mother, widow of King

Edward VII, had died the previous year. But before the baby could be christened they needed King George's approval – far from a formality, for the King could be very fussy about names. In a letter to his father, Prince Albert made the case for calling his daughter Elizabeth. 'There has been no-one of that name in your family for a long time,' he argued. Yet it was a nice name, and 'Elizabeth of York' sounded especially nice. Prince Albert's choice of Elizabeth reflected his deep feelings for his wife rather than any special admiration for England's Tudor queen. For him, the birth completed the process of emancipation from a domineering father – and he regarded his treasured daughter as entirely his wife's brilliant achievement. He was now the head of his own family unit, and as a mark of his independence he omitted Victoria from the baby's proposed names. Twenty-five years after her death, Queen Victoria's name was still almost mandatory for new-born princesses in Europe, and in not following the form the Yorks were risking a royal storm.

King George noted its absence but, surprisingly, raised no objections. 'I have heard from Bertie about the names,' King George wrote to the Queen. '. . . I quite approve & will tell him so, he says nothing about Victoria. I hardly think that necessary.' When Princess Elizabeth was christened in the private chapel at Buckingham Palace by the Archbishop of Canterbury, Dr Cosmo Lang, on 29 May, the King and Queen were her godparents together with Princess Mary; Arthur, Duke of Connaught, Queen Victoria's last surviving son; and Lady Elphinstone and Lord Strathmore, respectively the Duchess of York's sister and father.

The gold, lily-shaped font was brought from St George's Chapel, Windsor, and the water for the baptism came from the River Jordan in Palestine. The heavy cream satin and lace christening robe had first been worn by Queen Victoria's eldest daughter, and later by King George V and by the baby's own father. The baby, according to Mabell, Countess of Airlie, Queen Mary's lady-in-waiting and lifelong friend, 'cried so much all through the ceremony that immediately after it her old-fashioned nurse dosed her well from a bottle of dill water – to the surprise of the modern young mothers present.' Her uncle, the Prince of Wales, was amused.

Aside from that single lapse, Elizabeth was a remarkably well-behaved baby, and an attractive one. Pink-skinned, fair-haired, she had a well-shaped head and ears and long black lashes. The slate colour of her eyes quickly cleared to a light, bright blue. To a visitor who saw her at eight months sitting up, alert on a couch, she looked like 'a white fluff of thistledown'. In the doldrum days following the General Strike, which had fizzled out by 12 May leaving a bitter mood, the little princess was a welcome diversion for a despondent public. People gathered daily outside 17 Bruton Street, hoping for a glimpse of her as she was wheeled in her pram to Green Park by Alah Knight for her airing. Whenever the crowd was large, Prince Albert instructed the nanny to smuggle her charge out through the back entrance.

She was barely nine months old when her doting parents, at King George's insistence, embarked on a half-year tour of several colonies and dominions, including Australia and New Zealand, leaving her behind with Alah. The prospect of the long trip was daunting to Prince Albert. Extreme nervousness would cause his vocal cords to 'lock' and he would remain openmouthed, unable to say words beginning with certain consonants. Words starting with the letter C were his greatest obstacles. Public speaking was an ordeal for him, and broadcasting sheer torture. Deeply insecure, he would often respond to pressure by flying into a rage, even in public. His staff called these eruptions 'gnashes'. The Prince had consulted more than one speech specialist in an attempt to cure his problem, as later his daughter would take elocution lessons to improve her high speaking voice. In the months before the Yorks' departure he was persuaded by the Duchess to try again, this time with Lionel Logue, a young Harley Street speech therapist. Logue's treatment was designed to build up Prince Albert's confidence, and at the same time correct the physical dysfunction through a series of exercises at which the Prince worked with desperate earnestness for an hour each morning. He was, for example, required to stand by an open window and shout the vowel sounds, to lie on the floor and do breathing exercises to develop his lungs and relax the tension which caused his muscles to spasm and prevented speech from flowing, and to recite tongue-twisters.

The treatment transformed the Prince, who completed the long and arduous tour without a crisis. 'I have so much more confidence in myself now, which I am sure comes from being able to speak properly at last,' he wrote happily to his father after officially opening the new Parliament House in Canberra and addressing a crowd of 20,000 Australians on 9 May. So much confidence that he added impromptu speeches to those already on his schedule. And should he falter, the Duchess of York was there to reassure him with her encouraging smile, as she always would be when he spoke in public. She developed a knack of looking attentively up at him and nodding as he spoke, as if willing him to go on. When, as King, he had to broadcast, she helped him write his speeches and rehearse the consonants he found particularly difficult.

In her parents' absence, the young Princess often brightened the afternoon of her royal grandparents. 'Your sweet little daughter has four teeth now, which is quite good at eleven months old,' the King reported proudly to the Duchess in March. George V lavished on the little Princess the affection he had held back from his own children. A handsome new London home had been found for the Yorks, 145 Piccadilly, close to Hyde Park Corner, into which they immediately moved when they returned on 27 June 1927. Lilibet – as the Princess had named herself – was ensconced with Alah and Margaret MacDonald ('Bobo' to the Princess) in the top floor nursery of the large house with windows overlooking Buckingham Palace across the small triangle of Hamilton Gardens. Every morning, after he had fitted his first cigarette into his holder and checked the weather, the King would take a pair of binoculars and focus on the distant nursery windows of 145 Piccadilly where Princess Elizabeth would wave to her grandfather.

He was brusque with his two grandsons, George and Gerald Lascelles, but Lilibet softened him. The Countess of Airlie said, 'Lilibet always came first in his affections. He used to play with her – a thing I never saw him do with his own children – and loved to have her with him.' In the aftermath of his serious illness from a lung abscess in the winter of 1928, Elizabeth was taken to stay with him at the seaside resort of Bognor, where – the Countess wrote in her diary – 'she made his convalescence . . . bearable to him.' When she was four, the Yorks were offered the dilapidated Royal Lodge in Windsor Great Park as a country house, and the King gave his favourite grandchild a Shetland pony to ride there. The pony kindled her lifelong love for horses, replacing a passion for housework sparked the previous year by the birthday gift of a maid's outfit and miniature dustpan from the Countess of Airlie. The dustpan was discarded; but obsessive tidiness remained as one of the earliest identifiable traits of her character.

For most five-year-old children school begins to widen their horizons beyond the family. Lilibet never attended school, not as an infant or indeed at any age. She was taught to read by her mother, just as the Duchess had been taught by her mother before her. Lilibet was read Bible stories on Sunday, fairy stories and – as the Duchess told Lady Cynthia Asquith – '*Alice [in Wonderland]*, *Black Beauty*, *At the Back of the North Wind*, *Peter Pan*, anything we can find about horses and dogs.' As a child she moved in an environment peopled with grown-ups, and what friends she had of her own age tended to be cousins – the Lascelles brothers and Margaret Elphinstone, the daughter of her mother's sister. In the summer of 1930, however, she acquired a sister, an inseparable (if not always welcome) companion who was to become like a second shadow until she was twenty.

The Yorks' second daughter was born on 21 August 1930, at Glamis Castle, Scottish home of the Duchess. Henry 'Chips' Channon, the American-born Member of Parliament and socialite, visiting it some years earlier, found it had 'an admittedly sinister atmosphere'. According to his diary, the whole castle, with its stories of monsters and ghosts, was 'sinister, lugubrious.' Lugubrious or not, it was where Elizabeth, Duchess of York, grew up and where the family spent August, when the King and Queen were at Balmoral. Compared to Lilibet's birth, this one was plain sailing. But the family, the Yorks included, had been hoping for a boy. Prince Albert and his wife were so sure it would be a boy, they had no girls' names ready. The Duchess proposed Ann Margaret, but King George objected to Ann, so the Yorks settled for Margaret Rose. 'I hope you like it,' wrote the Duchess to Queen Mary. 'I think that it is very pretty together.' Princess Elizabeth promptly announced she would call her sister Bud. 'Why Bud?' asked Lady Asquith. 'Well, she's not a rose yet, is she? She's only a Bud.'

If the Yorks' second child had been a boy, Lilibet would have faded into the background. As it was, Princess Margaret's birth brought her older sister's position into sharper focus. The Yorks had a lot of popular appeal as a family. The Duke and Duchess were young and perceived to be in love. Elizabeth was a fairy-tale child – blond and blue-eyed, and third in the line of royal succession after her uncle and father. The King, after his serious illness, was ageing rapidly: returning from a trip abroad, the Prince of Wales was shocked to find this once overpowering figure 'a little shrunken old man with a white beard.' The Prince of Wales himself was thirty-six and still a firmly entrenched bachelor; and the King's other two sons, Prince Henry, Duke of Gloucester, known in the family as Potty or Glossipops, and Prince George, Duke of Kent, were also unmarried.

At a time when Hollywood movies were taking a firm hold on the public's consciousness, Elizabeth was treated as a film star. Letters from all over the world poured in to Buckingham Palace asking for photographs of 'Princess Betty' the way fan mail arrived at the Hollywood studios for Mickey Rooney and Shirley Temple. Her picture appeared in the papers as often as they could get one. At the wedding of the King's grandniece, Lady Mary Cambridge, granddaughter of the Countess of Athlone, the photographers concentrated on the youngest bridesmaid, who was the five-year-old Princess Elizabeth of York. And at Madame Tussaud's, a new wax statue of the Princess on her favourite pony was the main attraction of the royalty section.

The little Princess herself was not unaware of the attention. She made her first appearance on the balcony of Buckingham Palace at fifteen months in the arms of her mother, when her parents returned from their Australian tour. By the age of three she had been taught by Alah, on instructions from Queen Mary, to stand without fidgeting, to wave sedately at crowds, not to be overwhelmed by photographers, and to control her bladder: if she was able to contain herself during an outing she was rewarded with biscuits when she returned home. On one occasion, when she was at a concert with Queen Mary, she became restless and her grandmother asked if she would prefer to go home. 'Oh no, Granny,' Elizabeth replied. 'We can't leave before the end. Think of all those people who'll be waiting to see us outside.' Such vulgar film star sentiments cut no ice with Queen Mary, brought up in the exigent traditions of Queen Victoria. She immediately ordered a lady-in-waiting to take her granddaughter out by the back way and home in a taxi. But the Princess's parents also harboured a feeling that their daughter was bound for greatness. Prince Albert confided as much to the writer Osbert Sitwell – who noted it in his diary. 'He said, giving me at the same time a very direct look to see if I understood the allusion he was making to Queen Victoria, "From the moment of talking, she showed such character that it was impossible not to wonder whether history would not repeat itself." ' Elizabeth may not have been named after Queen Victoria, but comparisons were to be a recurring theme in her youth. Even Queen Mary was to remark on the resemblance – not, of course, a physical resemblance, but in manner.

Prince Albert was determined that his daughters' upbringing should be the opposite of his own. He had been made to feel secondary to his older brother, precisely because his brother was heir to the throne and he – Prince Albert – was not. It had compounded the misery of his boyhood. His daughters must be able to look upon their childhood as a happy time – 'a golden age', as his official biographer, Sir John Wheeler-Bennett, put it. And, above all, his second daughter would not be made to feel marginal in her own family. So, despite the four years and four months age gap, the two princesses were raised almost as twins, sharing the same nursery, following the same routine, for years studying in the same schoolroom, and often wearing identical clothes. Having her tonsils removed was one of the few things Princess Elizabeth did not do with her sister. 'I had them out when I was very small,' she recalled years later, 'but all I really remember is buckets and buckets of ice cream.'

Though they were often dressed the same, their characters could not have been more different. Elizabeth was quiet, reflective, polite and responsible – with occasional lapses. At a children's party, she spotted a pretty one-year-old, dressed as a fairy, in the arms of a nanny. Elizabeth exclaimed, 'Oh what a lovely fat baby! What is her name?' The nanny replied, 'Raine, Your Royal Highness.' Elizabeth began to laugh. 'What a funny name!' she said, and sped off to play with the older children. Raine Cartland, daughter of romantic novelist Barbara Cartland, grew up to marry an Earl and to become the stepmother of the Princess of Wales.

Margaret was lively, outgoing and wilful. Being almost joined at the hip served only to deepen the contrast between them. Margaret's plaintive appeal 'Lilibet, wait for me' was to echo through Lilibet's youth and reinforce a strong schoolmistress trait in her nature. On the other hand, being forced to live up to standards set by her older sister accentuated Margaret's rebellious streak.

Looking back on 1933, the woman who was governess to the two princesses observed, 'I had the feeling that the Duke and Duchess, most happy in their own married life, were not over concerned with the high education of their daughters. They wanted most for them a really happy childhood, with lots of pleasant memories stored up against the days that might come out, and later, happy marriages.' The governess was twenty-two when she joined the household staff at 145 Piccadilly. Scottish-bred, like the Duchess and the nursery staff, she trained in Edinburgh, and her original intention had been to work for the Yorks for a few months and then return to college to become a child psychologist. Her name was Marion Crawford, and she was to remain with the princesses for seventeen years.

Prince Albert was old fashioned enough to feel that royal princesses did not go to school with ordinary children. His wife, who when she was growing up had briefly attended a day school and had not enjoyed the experience, also saw no reason to inflict it on her daughters. She had an easygoing approach to education. When, for example, it became clear that Princess Elizabeth would never progress beyond the simplest mathematics, it did not trouble her at all. King George V's main concern was about the princesses' handwriting. 'For goodness' sake, teach Margaret and Lilibet to write a decent hand,' he told Marion Crawford. 'None of my children could write properly. They all do it exactly the same way. I like a hand with some character in it.'

Only Queen Mary, who was by temperament more inclined to put a higher value on intellectual discipline, demanded to see the princesses' curriculum. When the governess – by now generally known as 'Crawfie' – sent her a copy she was critical of its emphasis on music, dancing, drawing and singing. Queen Mary, her lady-in-waiting wrote to Crawfie, 'feels that genealogies, historical and dynastic, are very interesting to children, and for [these children] really important.' The Queen also stressed the importance of teaching the princesses about India and the dominions. For Elizabeth's fourth birthday, she had given her a set of building blocks made from fifty different woods from various parts of the Empire.

Family atmosphere, as Crawfie noted, was more important to the Yorks than education. After tea, the family gathered for popular children's card games such as Snap and Happy Families, and following the girls' baths there were free-for-alls and pillow fights on the nursery floor. Then, Crawfie wrote, 'Arm in arm, the young parents would go downstairs, heated and dishevelled, and frequently rather damp,' with the children calling after them 'Goodnight Mummy, goodnight Papa.' As the princesses' interest in horses became known they began to receive toy horses as gifts, and unsaddling them all became a nightly ritual which could not have been more seriously carried out if the horses had been real. There were also dolls to play with – more than one hundred and fifty of them, including some that had belonged to Queen Victoria's children. Only in royal circles could a doll survive so long in one piece. Two French dolls, Marianne and France, had ten sets of gloves, beaded bags, fans, sunshades, tortoiseshell hairbrushes, and tiny made-to-measure shoes. But it was the horses that captured Elizabeth's imagination. She used to tie the cord of her dressing-gown to a knot on her bed and drive an imaginary horse twice round an equally imaginary park before going to sleep.

Horses and dogs. When Lilibet was seven, a breeder of corgis, Mrs Thelma Gray, was invited to bring a basketful of puppies to 145 Piccadilly. The Duke of York chose one named Rozavel Golden Eagle, which became known as Dookie. Then the Duchess acquired another, Jane, and before long a dynasty was started, setting a fashion for these short-legged, bad-tempered Welsh dogs. The corgis were to become for Elizabeth what dwarfs were in the Spanish Court in the sixteenth century, a swarm of them preceding her into a room the way the dwarfs surrounded King Philip II – and, in their own way, misbehaving with the same degree of impunity.

The Yorks' ordered domestic life stood out in sharp contrast to the private lives of the other three royal princes. Prince Henry was a stolid figure with a taste for alcohol that was growing steadily more pronounced. Prince George, handsome and dashing, was the 'black sheep' of the family who had experimented with drugs and was known to be a bisexual. Besides a string of affairs with aristocratic girls, he was rumoured to have had homosexual affairs with an Italian aristocrat and with Noël Coward. When Prince George was killed in a plane crash in 1942, Coward was inconsolable, wept openly at the funeral, and poured out his grief in his diary. Years later, he would strongly imply that they had been lovers. The Prince's taste for low life was well known in London social circles, but when it came to the private lives of the royal princes, the London press exercised considerable self-restraint. George came dangerously close to public scandal on at least one occasion, when he was arrested in the company of a known homosexual in a police raid on a nightclub named The Nut House. He was taken to a police station and quickly released when his identity was discovered. An American woman, Kiki Whitney Preston, introduced him to cocaine and morphine, but by November 1934, he had not only overcome his addiction (albeit temporarily) but redeemed himself in the eyes of the family by marrying – at thirty-two – one of the most beautiful women in Europe, Princess Marina, the dark, twenty-seven-year-old daughter of Prince Nicholas, younger brother of King George of Greece.

As for the Prince of Wales, the princesses' Uncle David, he was the double bane of the royal Court and the establishment. The death of his father and the prospect of his consequent accession to the throne was their nightmare. His Assistant Private

Secretary, Alan 'Tommy' Lascelles, confided to the Prime Minister, Stanley Baldwin, that, because of his employer's 'unbridled pursuit of wine and women, and whatever selfish whim occupied him at the moment,' he, Lascelles, couldn't help thinking sometimes when the Prince was out riding that 'the best that could happen to him and to the country, would be for him to break his neck.' To which Baldwin replied, 'God forgive me, I have often thought the same.'

There is no evidence that this furtive little chat was anything more than wishful thinking, but the key point about it is the date. The meeting was in August 1927, and it shows the heir to the throne was already on a collision course with the Court – and, indeed, with members of his own staff – because of his private life almost a decade before his affair with Wallis Simpson forced the crisis that led to his abdication. Some felt that the Prince of Wales had long had misgivings about becoming king, and was subconsciously in the frame of mind to abdicate when his grand passion for Wallis Simpson forced him to make the choice. Lascelles claimed that the Duke of York had revealed to him a telling remark by his older brother: 'It was never in my scheme of things to be King of England.'

Years later a writer who had known Lascelles well was to describe him as a man 'of the highest moral principles who tended to judge other people by his own standards, and usually found them wanting.' By 1929, Lascelles had found the Prince's behaviour too much for his upright nature and he quit the royal service. Persuaded to return as Assistant Private Secretary to George V in 1935, he not only survived the Abdication but was ultimately to become Private Secretary to King George VI and later to serve the latter's daughter Elizabeth in the early years of her reign in his own straitlaced, uncompromising manner.

To the princesses, their golden-haired Uncle David was a favourite visitor who regularly filled their nursery with his charming presence. He would play games with them, and a favourite was Winnie-the-Pooh. Sitting in front of the fire, the Duchess of York would read them a story. When she had finished, the two princesses and their uncle would have to mime the characters in the tale. One afternoon at 145 Piccadilly, Queen Mary was roped in to play a dressing-up game – but one with a royal twist. In the game, the princesses, in various guises, pretended that they were being presented at Court. Lilibet and Margaret Rose entered – the former in male clothing. Queen Mary enquired, 'Whom do I have the honour of receiving?' Replied Lilibet: 'Lord Bathtub and Lady Plug.' How did they think of two such names? the Queen wanted to know, managing to keep a straight face. They hadn't, the princesses explained. While they were dressing, Uncle David came in. The princesses told him they needed new names and he immediately came up with 'Lord Bathtub and Lady Plug'.

Ironically, Elizabeth knew little, if anything at all, about the scandalous relationship that was to change radically the course of her own life. Superprotective where their family life was concerned, the Yorks would have been careful not to discuss the Prince of Wales's affair with Mrs Simpson in front of their daughters. Prince Albert would have concealed from Elizabeth his growing alarm that gossip about the heir to the throne and his married mistress, repeated in the American and European press (but not in the British newspapers because of an agreed blackout by Fleet Street proprietors), was damaging the prestige of the Crown across the Empire. She was spared the royal family's mortification at seeing the Prince of Wales with Wallis Simpson at Ascot, at parties, and even at the state ball on 14 May 1935, marking King George V's Silver Jubilee. The princesses would surely have noticed that their uncle's visits were less frequent without being aware of the reason. Uncle David stayed away partly to avoid the Duchess of York's growing opposition to Wallis Simpson, and partly because of the lady's demands on his attention, and ultimately also because on 20 January 1936, he had succeeded his father as King and Emperor.

Two months earlier, Prince Henry had married Lady Alice Montagu-Douglas-Scott, daughter of the Duke of Buccleuch, one of Britain's richest peers, and the King had watched admiringly as his beloved Lilibet, in her bridesmaid's dress designed by Norman Hartnell – the first of many dresses Hartnell was to create for her as Princess and Queen over fifty years – solemnly followed the bride. It was one of his last appearances outside the immediate family circle. His weakening state cast a shadow over the traditional family Christmas at Sandringham; and when, in the second week of January, Elizabeth returned there the King was dying. She was taken in to say goodbye, and found him sitting drowsily propped up in bed in an old Tibetan dressing gown, a gift from an early tour of India. It was the first time she had seen the approach of death, and she looked very unhappy when she left for home with her sister.

On Monday, 20 January, Lord Dawson of Penn, the King's physician, told Queen Mary that her husband had lapsed into unconsciousness and was beyond hope. To spare the nation, her family, and the King himself a long death agony, the Queen gave Dawson permission to terminate the King's life. She had first consulted her four sons, who had been called to the King's bedside, but the decision was her own. Dawson gave the King a morphine-based injection, and death came shortly afterwards, the physician having timed the end so that the official announcement would make the first edition of *The Times*. 'We family dined alone & then went to G[eorge]'s room at intervals & at 5 to 12 my darling husband passed peacefully away – my children were angelic.' Thus did the Queen record the moment of his death. When word reached the dining room Queen Mary, correct as always, even in her moment of grief, rose to her feet and kissed the hand of her eldest son. The manner of George V's death remained a family secret until it was revealed by Lord Dawson's biographer thirty years later.

Three months later, Elizabeth met Wallis Simpson for the first and (until thirty-one years later) only time, at the Royal Lodge. One April afternoon, King Edward VIII – as he now was – and Wallis drove from Fort Belvedere, his own country house as Prince of Wales, to show off his new American station wagon, then a novelty in Britain. While the King, Wallis and the Yorks were having tea in the forty-foot-long green-panelled salon designed by the Regency architect Jeffry Wyatville for King George IV, Elizabeth and Margaret Rose entered with Marion Crawford, 'both so blonde, so beautifully mannered, so brightly scrubbed that they might have stepped from the pages of a picture book,' as Wallis put it years later in her autobiography. They kissed their Uncle David warmly and he in turn introduced them to Wallis simply as 'Mrs Simpson'. The Princesses shook hands politely, Margaret staring at the King's companion with open curiosity, and then went and helped themselves to orange juice. The atmosphere in the room, Marion Crawford noted, 'was not comfortable'. Wallis Simpson had a 'distinctly proprietary way of speaking to the new King.' She drew him to a window and lectured him about how the landscaping in the Yorks' garden could be improved. The Yorks showed considerable forebearance, but presently, the Duchess cut through Wallis's speech (rather icily, the royal governess thought) saying, 'Crawfie, would you like to take Lilibet and Margaret into the woods for a while?' As they left the house, Princess Elizabeth asked curiously, 'Who *is* she, Crawfie?'

The tension had transmitted itself to Elizabeth, but she received no explanation from her governess. Recalling the incident more than twenty years later, Marion Crawford could not remember 'what I said or how I slurred the awkward moment over.' When the family met for dinner that evening the memory of the visit hung in the air, but it was not mentioned. Perhaps because the Duke and Duchess clung to the hope that somehow disaster could be averted, the royal sisters were shielded from the truth, so Elizabeth and Margaret were left to the mercy of their youthful anxieties.

That a family drama was unfolding involving their Uncle David was clear to both princesses – but what? Conversations would suddenly stop when they entered the room. An invitation to the children to have tea at Fort Belvedere was not taken up, on some pretext they found hard to understand. On his visits, now few and far between, Uncle David himself never referred to his problems. Still less did he mention Wallis Simpson. But the princesses could not have failed to notice the change in him. Instead of his usual cheerfulness, he seemed distracted, making plans with the princesses, and then forgetting them.

Preparations were going ahead for his coronation. The new King was still a dashing, popular figure with the British public, which so far had little inkling of the mounting differences between him and his family, his Court and his Prime Minister. For his family, the main concern was his obsessive attachment to the woman his mother had called an 'adventuress', now on the point of divorcing her second husband. But even without the Simpson factor, the Court had its hands full coping with his whims and changes. Under George V and Queen Mary life had proceeded at the stately pace of a Haydn string quartet, within the framework of a royal calendar which altered little from one year to the next. Edward VIII came to the throne determined to be what he called 'an up-to-date King'. To the staff of dyed-in-the-wool traditionalists he inherited from King George, his style was as dissonant as twelve-tone music.

His trio of Secretaries – Lord Wigram, Sir Alec Hardinge and Tommy Lascelles – became the guardians of orthodoxy fighting against the King's erratic behaviour. They blamed Wallis, with whom the King continued to spend a great deal of his time, for many of his faults – particularly what they saw as his declining interest in his responsibilities. Meanwhile, the Yorks were increasingly becoming the symbols of tradition and continuity in the monarchy. For example, when King Edward spent the last two weeks of September at Balmoral, and Wallis was among the guests, he did not invite King George V's close friend the Archbishop of Canterbury, who, in the old days, had been a regular visitor. So the Duchess of York stepped into the breach and invited him to stay at Birkhall, the Yorks' house on the Balmoral estate, telling him when he left that he must come again next year, 'so that the links with Balmoral may not be wholly broken.' There was no doubt who was upholding the standards of the old Court.

On 20 October, Prime Minister Baldwin – the same Baldwin who a decade earlier had hoped that the Prince of Wales would break his neck – went to Fort Belvedere and warned the King that his open relationship with Wallis Simpson was assuming the proportions of a public scandal. After that interview, Major Alec Hardinge, the King's Private Secretary, visited 145 Piccadilly and warned the Yorks that Wallis's divorce petition was scheduled to be heard on 27 October, and that the possibility of abdication could no longer be ignored. As Hardinge had already discussed the problem with the Prime Minister, it seemed likely a consensus was emerging in official circles that a marriage between the King and Wallis Simpson had to be stopped at all costs. Prince Albert 'was appalled and tried not to believe what he had been told.' He was appalled for several reasons, but primarily because, whatever happened, the monarchy must not be damaged and his family name dragged through the mud; and second, because of the – to him – terrifying prospect that he might have to succeed his brother.

In King George V's scheme of things, the heir to the throne was in a category of his own among the king's sons. Singled out for special attention from an early age, and especially following his investiture as Prince of Wales when he was eighteen, he received training in being a monarch – talks with his father on state matters, travel in what was then the Empire, meetings with statesmen. It was not thought necessary to have a backup, and to King Edward's brothers, the business of kingship was *terra incognita*. To Prince Albert, hampered with his stammer, the prospect of stepping into his brother's shoes was doubly forbidding. But events were moving inexorably towards that conclusion.

In November, Edward told Baldwin that he sought Cabinet approval to marry Wallis Simpson. At this point the issue took on a constitutional dimension. For Edward to have contemplated such a step without the requisite approval would have precipitated the resignation of the government and a grave constitutional crisis. After three weeks of discussions, with King Edward remaining obdurate in his intention of marrying Wallis, and Prince Albert, the Prime Minister and others trying unsuccessfully to warn him of the consequences of his intentions, three options remained which

Baldwin telegraphed to the prime ministers of the dominions (Canada, Australia, New Zealand and South Africa) for their reaction: '(i) Marriage of His Majesty to Mrs Simpson, she becomes Queen. (ii) King's marriage to Mrs Simpson without his abdication but on the basis that she should not become Queen [in other words, a morganatic marriage]. (iii) A voluntary abdication by King in favour of Duke of York.

But one consequence of Mrs Simpson's divorce was that the British press at last broke its silence. On 3 December the papers published reports of the constitutional crisis over the King's wish to marry Mrs Simpson. There was no groundswell of opposition, but public sympathy was not with the King in his desire to marry a twice-divorced American. The reaction of dominion premiers to Baldwin's telegram was mixed, with New Zealand strongly opposed to marriage and the others cool to the idea. So the King faced the choice of renouncing his love or his throne.

From November, 145 Piccadilly was unwillingly a maelstrom of activity. 'Important people came and went,' Marion Crawford would write later. 'The Prime Minister, Mr Baldwin, assorted bishops and archbishops . . . all looking anxious and harried.' Still, the Yorks did not spell out the situation to their daughters. But now the princesses glimpsed newspaper posters out of their car window; and the tenseness at home did not escape ten-year-old Elizabeth. For days she asked, 'What is happening to Uncle David?' On one occasion, she met her father in the entrance hall returning from a visit to his older brother. He brushed straight past her into the drawing room where the Duchess was waiting. She could hear him behind the closed door having a 'gnash', and the low, murmuring tones of her mother's voice trying to calm him down. That it had something to do with her uncle's marrying was clear. But who? And why was everybody so gloomy about it? Deprived of real answers, she was forced to fall back on speculation. In answer to one of her sister's incessant questions, she said: 'I think Uncle David wants to marry Mrs Baldwin, and Mr Baldwin doesn't like it.'

On 10 December – a Thursday – she at last learned the truth. At 7 p.m. the King asked his brother to meet him at Fort Belvedere, and the Duke of York heard at firsthand that Edward VIII intended to abdicate. 'I could see that nothing I said would alter his decision,' the Duke wrote in his diary. 'His mind was made up. I went to see Queen Mary & when I told her what had happened I broke down & sobbed like a child' – much to the

Queen's embarrassment because Walter Monckton, the King's legal adviser, was also present. Then the Duke went home to break the news to his wife. According to early biographies, the Duchess of York tiptoed into the nursery and gently explained to her daughter what had happened. Crawfie, on the other hand, says it was she who – on instructions from the Duchess – told the Princess about the Abdication. In reality, Elizabeth heard it from a footman at her home. She was indeed in the nursery when she heard noises of people cheering outside the house. What was it all about? She went down and asked the footman. From him she learned that Uncle David had abdicated and Papa was king. She rushed upstairs to relay this sensational news to Margaret.

Margaret considered the situation. 'Does that mean that you will have to be the next queen?' she asked. 'Yes, some day,' Lilibet replied. Margaret said, 'Poor you.' Later, the princesses appeared at a window to wave to the crowd outside – the first of many such appearances.

III

Heir Presumptive

Edward VIII reigned for 327 days before giving up his throne and his country for the woman he loved. It was the fairy tale of Prince Charming gone sour: in this version, the prince left the Palace instead of bringing the fair maiden to live there with him happily ever after. On 12 December, as the former monarch was still on his way to exile, Prince Albert left 145 Piccadilly as Duke of York to attend his Accession Council and returned as George VI, King of England. He was two days away from his forty-first birthday. Crawfie had primed the princesses to greet their father with a curtsy when he came home, but the new Queen said no. She would not allow formality to undermine the family atmosphere.

A new King had been proclaimed, but the Abdication was an earthquake that had shaken the British monarchy to its foundations, and there were fears in political circles that the whole system could still collapse under the strain. These fears were partly the result of residual doubts about the new monarch's capacity for kingship, his ability to restore public confidence, which was his most urgent task. Small, thin, intense, Prince Albert had always had something of the image of the weakling in the Atlas body-building advertisements, the one who has sand kicked in his face; and many now questioned whether he was physically and mentally robust enough to survive. 'There's a lot of prejudice against him,' Baldwin explained to the Countess of Airlie a few days after the Abdication. 'He's had no chance to capture the popular imagination as his brother did. I'm afraid he won't find it easy for the first year or two.'

Many of these doubts were shared by the King himself, and he did not hide them from his relations. 'This is terrible, Dickie,' he said miserably to his cousin Lord Louis Mountbatten, who was grandson of Queen Victoria's second daughter, Alice, and was always known in the family as Dickie. 'I never wanted this to happen. I'm quite unprepared for it . . . I've never seen a State paper. I'm only a naval officer. It's the only thing I know about.' It has long been said that serious thought was given to passing over the Duke of York in favour of one of his younger brothers. But considering the calibre of Prince Henry and the murky past of Prince George, to say nothing of the Duke of York's own close association with Alec Hardinge and other figures in the Court, this seems unlikely, and there is anyway no evidence to support the story. In time, the new King would come to be appreciated as a decent, hardworking, dutiful, considerate man, not unsympathetic towards human failings. But as 1936 drew to a close, it was the popularity of his young family that made the difference. All the public admiration for Princess Elizabeth helped the transition to gain broad acceptance. It fell to Crawfie to explain to the Princess her position as heir presumptive to the throne, and also how it would change if the Queen had a son, who would automatically become the heir apparent, and the next king. On learning this, Elizabeth included in her nightly prayers a request to God to send 'a little brother'. In reality, however, there was little likelihood of her prayers being answered. After the birth of Margaret Rose, the Queen's gynaecologists had warned her that another pregnancy would endanger her life.

In short, father and daughter were locked into their destinies, and on 15 February the family moved to Buckingham Palace, known to the royals as Buck House. 'At 145 Piccadilly . . . we had been a small, utterly happy family,' Crawfie recalled. 'Now we were separated from one another by interminable corridors.' The eighteenth-century palace is a rambling edifice of large state rooms, damask-lined salons and long, echoing corridors – so vast, that a footman spent an entire day each week winding up and servicing all its clocks and a vermin man fought an endless battle against mice. To make the magnificence more habitable, the Queen introduced homely touches into the royal living quarters, for example bringing in her own four-poster bed, and her kidney-shaped dressing table with its satin skirt. The princesses had their own wing, where Elizabeth continued to share a bedroom with Bobo MacDonald – a practice begun at 145 Piccadilly for space reasons, continued at Buckingham Palace for companionship in the new surroundings, and not terminated until the Princess was in her early teens, long after she had become accustomed to sleeping at the Palace, and even longer after she had dispensed with the need of a nursery maid. Margaret shared her room with Alah.

Before the Abdication there had been a lengthy haggle over money. King Edward wanted a royal title and compensation for relinquishing ownership of the Windsor properties, Balmoral Castle in Scotland and Sandringham House on the Norfolk coast, together with all their contents. Buckingham Palace and Windsor Castle are Crown property to be occupied by the reigning monarch, so they were not in dispute. Prince Albert agreed that his brother should become His Royal Highness the Duke of Windsor, and should receive a guaranteed annuity of £25,000 – reduced after subsequent very bitter negotiations to £21,000, and granted on condition that the former King 'gave an undertaking not to return without [the monarch's] consent.'

The royal couple who had once complained about being forced to live in unmodernized, dilapidated White Lodge, and had even been briefly homeless, now had no shortage of housing. They spent Christmas at Sandringham, and journeyed by royal train to Balmoral each August. Balmoral, a baronial castle on the River Dee with turrets, battlements and crenellations, looks like something out of *Macbeth*, but isn't. Glamis Castle, where Queen Elizabeth grew up, has genuine links with Macbeth, one of whose titles was Thane of Glamis. Balmoral, where Scottish pipers marched ceremonially around the table playing the bagpipes during dinner, was built by Queen Victoria and Prince Albert.

In the final analysis, the public crisis of the Abdication faded rapidly away without triggering the upheaval the pessimists predicted. The family trauma was more deeply felt, and Uncle David's act of folly would cast its shadow over the House of Windsor for many generations to come. The gist of what the princesses were told at the time was that 'Poor Uncle David' had decided to step down because the woman he wanted to marry was not suitable to be queen. After 1936 the subject was not mentioned again in front of them for years.

Elizabeth and Margaret Rose kept their ears open and pooled their information, as they did on most things. But Elizabeth did not learn of her favourite uncle's marriage to Wallis Simpson on 3 June 1937 until some years later. To the royal family, Wallis was the villainess of the piece: she had played covertly for high stakes, always aiming at the Queen's crown. When that strategy failed, she still held out for marriage because she knew that without marriage there would be no security.

Queen Mary and Queen Elizabeth were her bitterest enemies, the latter holding her responsible for forcing the burden of the monarchy on her unprepared, insecure, beloved Bertie, which was ultimately to contribute to his early death. Queen Elizabeth's hatred was passed down through the Windsor generations. Discussing Wallis Simpson with a girl friend years later, Prince Charles, Princess Elizabeth's oldest son, remarked, 'She's a dreadful woman.' How did he know? the friend wanted to know. How well had he known her? 'I know because my grandmother says she was,' Prince Charles replied.

The princesses were encouraged to look forward, not backward. Occasionally, however, Elizabeth could not resist wondering what life was like outside the confines of her world. 'As a child,' Elizabeth was to confide to the Florentine artist Pietro Annigoni when he was painting her portrait in 1955, 'I used to look out of these windows at the people and the cars. They all seemed so busy. I used to wonder what they were doing and where they were going and what they thought about outside the Palace.' These were the tall windows of the Yellow Room at Buckingham Palace, overlooking the front courtyard and, beyond that, the white monument to Queen Victoria and the Mall. Other children were especially fascinating to her, as Marion Crawford was to recall in her offending (but by no means offensive) book. To Elizabeth they were 'like mystic beings from a distant world.' She and her sister would have loved to speak to them and make friends, 'but this was never encouraged,' Crawfie continues. 'I have often thought it a pity.' Their Swedish and Danish cousins rode bicycles in the streets, mixing freely with their subjects; the English royal family has always viewed this relaxed approach to the monarchy as bad for the mystique. The princesses lived in a more controlled environment.

Occasional forays were arranged into the outside world, but always under careful supervision. Crawfie did attempt some unofficial outings, such as when she took the princesses incognito for a ride on the London Underground from Piccadilly to Tottenham Court Road, but such adventures were quickly discouraged. The more typical excursion involved several grown-up minders, including the governess and a detective, and sometimes the Queen herself. Occasionally, instead of the princesses venturing into the outside world, the outside world was brought to them, and the formation of the First Buckingham Palace Company of the Girl Guides in the spring of 1937 was a case in point.

Princess Elizabeth had for some time shown interest in becoming a Girl Guide, partly as a way of increasing her contact with girls her own age. Had she remained Elizabeth, daughter of the Duke and Duchess of York, she would have joined one of the two thriving Girl Guide Companies in the central London area. As heir presumptive, the Queen decided Lilibet no longer had that option. Instead the Queen 'suggested' to the Chief Guide, Olave Baden-Powell, the formation of an autonomous Palace company; and the First Buckingham Palace Company came into being consisting initially of fourteen Girl Guides with Violet Synge, a tall, Eton-cropped Guide leader with wide experience, as its captain. There were eventually four patrols, and Princess Elizabeth was assistant patrol leader of Kingfisher Patrol. Her patrol leader was also her second cousin, Patricia Mountbatten, elder daughter of Lord Mountbatten. The other Guides were the daughters of family friends, or members of the Royal household, such as Libbie Hardinge, Margaret Elphinstone and Judy Legh, whose father was Lieutenant Colonel Sir Piers (Joey) Legh, Master of the King's Household.

Inevitably, Princess Margaret Rose also wanted to become a Girl Guide, but Violet Synge ruled that at six she was too young. Couldn't she 'stretch a point'? Crawfie asked her. The Girl Guides considered the question. Then a company of Brownies was formed for the younger Princess consisting of two members: Margaret Rose and an even younger friend. As the Guides and the two Brownies were taking the Promise (or Oath of Allegiance) together, Margaret Rose asked Violet Synge, 'Did you know some people don't believe in Jesus?' and she demanded to know why. The Guide captain replied tactfully, 'You had better ask Crawfie.' Elizabeth's attempts to widen her circle of friends through the Guides clearly had limited results, but Guiding remained an enjoyable experience for her. A round garden teahouse became the company's clubhouse, and most of the activities were held in the vast grounds of Buckingham Palace, with the King as an occasional spectator. He sometimes even joined in the singsongs, especially in singing 'Under the Spreading Chestnut Tree', which was his favourite. But it was a gentler, more rarified version of real life. The normal rough-and-tumble of the Girl Guides was not replicated in the First Buckingham Palace Company, nor was the movement's

31

declared purpose of mixing children from all walks of life. Violet Synge noted to the Chief Guide that all her Guides drove out of the Palace in Rolls-Royces, 'while I,' she added, 'attach myself in my Morris Minor.'

Elizabeth worked on her First Class Award with typical dedication. For her Nature Badge she made a study of the flora and fauna of Windsor Great Park, noting her observations in her round, childish hand on pages torn from an exercise book. She put out food for the birds, and then wrote descriptions of the ones that flew down to eat it. She noted that some trees at Windsor had 'strange-shaped growths'. One looked like a bust of Queen Victoria, and another was just like 'a creature with blubbly lips'. But the coveted First Class Award eluded her because she consistently flunked the Needlewoman's Badge which she needed to qualify. In this respect she differed from her father who did needlepoint as a hobby and embroidered some fine chair seats in his day. In the end, she transferred to the Sea Rangers along with the rest of the company. The Sea Rangers did not do needlework.

But that was in the future: Guiding, in the spring of 1937, took second place to preparing for the Coronation ceremony of King George VI and Queen Elizabeth. To emphasize continuity following the Abdication, the same date was kept that had originally been set for the coronation of King Edward VIII – 12 May. Coronation souvenir manufacturers, who had already produced piles of cups and saucers, tankards, scarves and ashtrays with King Edward's blond handsome head and the monogram EVIIIR, switched quickly to items carrying the picture of the new King and Queen. The new royal couple themselves had to take a crash course in the long, complicated ancient ritual, and to familiarize his daughters with the ceremony they were to attend, the King prepared for each of them a book of its rites and history, bound in red leather. So while the King and Queen rehearsed with the Archbishop of Canterbury and other dignitaries, 'day after day in our schoolroom,' wrote Marion Crawford, 'I read their father's Coronation story to the Princesses.' For visual aid, they had a thirty-foot-long Victorian panorama of the coronation of King George IV unearthed for them by Queen Mary. Sandwiched between the lessons were dressmakers' fittings of the princesses' coronation robes, and a visit to the Royal Mews – the Palace stables, coach houses, and homes of the coachmen and grooms – for an all-important seasickness test. Lilibet and Margaret Rose clambered into the painted well-sprung coronation coach which

Crawfie and an equerry then shook vigorously from side to side for several minutes to ensure that when they rode home from the ceremony in Westminster Abbey with their parents, the two girls would not be sick.

The whole panoply of aunts, uncles and cousins unfolded as Europe's royalty poured into London for what was to be their last great gathering before the outbreak of the Second World War. There were Uncle Charles (King Haakon of Norway); Uncle Gustav and Aunt Louise of Sweden; Uncle George and Aunt Sophie of Greece; Uncle Paul, the King of Greece's brother; Aunt Marie of Rumania (the Rumanian Queen Mother); the dashing cousin Paul of Serbia and his Greek wife, Princess Olga; Aunt Ena (Victoria Eugenie) of Spain; non-relations such as Aunt Wilhelmina of Holland, her daughter Crown Princess Juliana and her husband, Bernhard, known as Bernilo (he was universally popular with the royal family, she generally disliked because they found her affected as well as overly domineering towards her husband), plus, of course, platoons of Hesses and squads of Saxe-Coburg-Gothas all related through 'Gangan Victoria', as she was known to the British royal family. The talk among the European royals was dominated by events in Spain – in the throes of civil war – and Germany. But there was time to speculate about a husband for King George's serious eldest daughter, Elizabeth, who would one day inherit the richest monarchy in the world.

On the night of 11 May, the object of this speculation peered from behind the curtains at the crowd already gathered in front of Buckingham Palace, seated on the steps of Queen Victoria's monument, and lining the pavements of the Mall. 'Will they sit out there all night just to see Papa?' was her surprised comment. In time, even larger crowds would spend the night in the rain to cheer her.

She was awakened at 5 a.m. by the band of the Royal Marines marching to take up its position near the Buckingham Palace gates. 'I leapt out of bed, and so did Bobo,' Elizabeth remembered in an account of the day's activities written for her parents and preserved in the archives of Windsor Castle. 'The band was playing right across from my window. Margaret and I put on our dressing gowns and shoes and Bobo made me put on an eiderdown as it was cold and we crouched in the window looking on to a cold, misty morning . . . Every now and then we were hopping out of bed to look at the bands and the soldiers, and then hopping in again.' At seven-thirty, the princesses bathed and donned their high-waisted dresses of creamy white lace worn over silken slips. Elizabeth was to have worn a train, but her younger sister threw a tantrum, insisting that she have one too. Faced with the danger of Princess Margaret Rose tripping over a train in the middle of Westminster Abbey, ankle-length frocks were made for both sisters. From their shoulders hung ceremonial cloaks in royal purple, fringed with ermine. On their heads were simple coronets specially made for them by the same jeweller who designed their mother's crown.

For the first time, Elizabeth was attended by her own lady-in-waiting, who carried the Princess's little coronet on a silk cushion, and in Westminster Abbey took precedence over all the other royal ladies. After a fleeting visit to see their parents resplendent in their Coronation robes, the two sisters departed for the Abbey (forty minutes before the royal procession) in a large coach with their aunt, the Princess Royal, and her son Viscount Lascelles. 'Four hours,' Lilibet told the fussing Crawford as the latter saw her off at Buckingham Palace. 'That's how long we shall be at the Abbey. I do hope Margaret can keep awake.'

But Margaret Rose did stay awake. Sitting with her sister in the royal box beside Queen Mary, who appeared in stately grandeur with a five-strand diamond choker around her neck, and every inch of her white gown ablaze with jewels, the little Princess behaved far better than could be expected of a six-year-old. There was some squirming, wriggling and yawning, but Elizabeth – closely engrossed in her copy of the Order of Service – only found it necessary to nudge her into silence a few times. The ceremony, which has changed little in a thousand years, was a dazzling choreography of mitred clergy and coroneted nobles in which the dominant colours were gold and crimson. Despite the recent traumas, the rite was beautiful and moving, and at the moment when the Crown of St Edward the Confessor, the Crown of England, was placed on the head of George VI all thoughts of the crisis were forgotten in the solemnization of his kingship.

The ceremony differed from its predecessors in that in the King's Coronation oath the general reference to ruling 'the British Dominions beyond the Seas' for the first time specifically mentioned Canada, Australia, New Zealand, the Union of South Africa and the 'Empire of India'. It was a change designed to reflect the growing independence of Britain's dominions, and it foreshadowed the emergence of the even more independent postwar Commonwealth. As the service went on, Margaret was not alone in betraying signs of restlessness. 'At the end the service got rather boring as it was all prayers,' Elizabeth wrote later. 'Granny and I were looking to see how many more pages to the end and we turned one more and then I pointed to the word at the bottom of the page and it said "FINIS". We both smiled at each other and turned back to the service.'

The two princesses rode back to Buckingham Palace with the King and Queen through streets lined with troops and packed with cheering crowds. It was 5 p.m. when the Coronation coach, with its panels painted with seascapes, passed through the gates into Buckingham Palace. The King went up to the second floor and, wearing the Imperial Crown, led his wife by the hand on to the balcony. For a moment he stood motionless, staring out at the immense gathering of people. Then, with a smile, he gave a rather hesitant wave. The cheers rose to a roar. Later, when the King had gone inside, the crowds broke the police barriers and surged towards the Palace railings. They chanted, 'We want George', 'We want the King'. The BBC sound engineer, on hand to record the Coronation address later, heard King George mutter, 'The King wants his dinner.'

For weeks afterwards, Princess Margaret's favourite game was coronations. The crown was made of paper, a ruler did service as the sceptre and a rubber ball as the orb. Margaret herself was alternately the King or the Archbishop of Canterbury, with Elizabeth reluctantly joining in. Since her father's Coronation, Crawfie claimed later to have noted, Lilibet had become more reserved. Margaret, on the other hand, was emerging as a spirited personality with a quick, comic wit and an exhibitionist streak. Both girls were Shirley Temple fans; they saw her films several times in the palace film theatre and had written fan letters to the child star in Hollywood. But it was Margaret who learned the songs and the dance routines and could do a clever imitation of the star's piping voice and sugary manner.

Dancing lessons at Madame Vacani's school were a must for all London society children – girls and often also boys. In the case of the princesses, however, the school came to them. Miss Betty Vacani held her classes in a room at Buckingham Palace. While Elizabeth worked diligently at her dance steps – recalled the princesses' French teacher, who watched their lessons – Margaret was 'quicksilver'. She was equally adept with wisecracks. For example: 'Nothing is impossible if you try hard enough,' Crawfie told the princesses one day in typical governess-speak. 'Try putting toothpaste back into the tube,' was Margaret's prompt retort.

The King was amused by his younger daughter's irreverence. She used her wit and comic talents to get what she wanted from him, but he liked her cheerful disposition, and spoiled her terribly. It made him smile to hear her singing at the top of her voice somewhere in the depths of the Palace. But her precocity, her bossy manner with subordinates, and her temper tantrums did not make her popular with the household staff. Margaret's antics often embarrassed Elizabeth. 'Stop her, Mummy. Oh, please stop her!' she would plead when Margaret was being more than usually outrageous. When Elizabeth tried to take a hand in correcting her sister, there were battles in the schoolroom. Squeaks of 'Beast!' and 'Cow!' would erupt, and then the admonishing Scottish voice of Crawfie: 'Girrrls! Girrrls.' Sometimes Elizabeth went public with their youthful differences. As when – at the outbreak of the war – she took part in the BBC's highly popular programme *Children's Hour*. After saying a few words to the children of Britain and the Empire, she went on, 'My sister is by my side, and we are both going to say goodnight to you. Come on, Margaret, you behaved very badly today and you don't deserve to speak, but say goodnight.' When the programme was aired the BBC deleted Elizabeth's rebuke, and Margaret, who was then aged ten, pronounced her first public sentence: 'Goodnight and good luck to you all.'

But if Margaret was too rebellious, Elizabeth could sometimes come across as over-responsible. On one occasion, shortly after the Coronation when many members of the invited foreign royalty were still at Buckingham Palace, she admonished her governess: 'Crawfie, I saw you pass King Haakon yesterday, and you didn't curtsy.' Crawfie remembered passing a tall, distinguished-looking man in the garden. His face had seemed familiar, but she had not been able to place him. It was highly unlikely that the Scandinavian monarch had protested the omission, but Crawfie dutifully expressed her regret to her young charge and asked her, 'What do you think I should do? Shall I send him a note?' No, replied the Princess, 'That's not necessary. I'll explain to him.' She did, too.

A year after moving into Buckingham Palace, the princesses' lives had settled comfortably into a routine that could hardly be called strenuous. They rose at 7.30 a.m., had their breakfast in the nursery at 9.00 a.m. and then joined their parents at their own breakfast. Lessons, with Crawfie teaching both girls, began at 10.00 a.m. in the schoolroom adjoining the third-floor nursery. Margaret's formal schooling lasted one hour each day – until 11.00 a.m., when 'the music started' – the in-palace way of referring to the daily ceremony of the Changing of the Guard, which the princesses occasionally liked to watch from their window. Elizabeth stopped at 12.30 p.m. From 2.00 p.m. to 4.00 p.m. there were lessons in swimming, dancing, deportment and, occasionally, elocution. Afternoon tea at 4.15 was a family ritual in the drawing room with the King and Queen, who tried never to allow their schedule to interfere with their family life. Queen Elizabeth tried to spend time with the princesses between 5.00 p.m. and 7.00 p.m., although the King could not always be present. Alah still dressed them identically whenever possible, and had running battles with Crawfie when the latter – an energetic walker and fitness buff – allowed them to over-exert themselves in the grounds of Buckingham Palace, or Balmoral.

A start was also made on Elizabeth's preparation for kingship. '*Mon metier à moi est d'être Roi*', Edward VII once declared: but there are no textbooks on the metier, the profession of being king. George VI's characterization of the monarchy as 'the family firm', implies a more collective effort. But as Managing Director of the House of Windsor Ltd he was in the best position to train his designated successor. So, at the age of twelve, when most girls have no more on their minds than dolls, clothes and homework, the Princess most days joined her father on his early morning walk in the grounds of Buckingham Palace when he would talk to her about the business of the day. Queen Mary also took a hand in broadening Elizabeth's horizons, leading her and Margaret on cultural visits to famous London landmarks and institutions. Setting an exhausting pace, she showed them the Bank of England, the Tower of London, and various galleries and hospitals. The purpose was not merely to see the sights but also to gain experience in the way royalty behaved on such visits.

Unlike their predecessors, the King and Queen did not believe in keeping their family hidden from visitors, and the princesses were exposed to a continuous procession of politicians, dignitaries, clergy and foreign relatives. The usual procedure when there were guests for lunch was for the princesses to make their appearance for dessert. Lord Killearn recalled that when, as British ambassador in Cairo, he lunched with the King and Queen at Buckingham Palace the princesses 'came in with the coffee,' sat on either side of their mother, and ate little piles of sugar crystals. After lunch, the focus of interest was a newly installed television set (this was 1938!) which the King had no idea how to work, much to the amusement of his daughters. When Killearn (who was then Sir Miles Lampson) left, the 'little girls were sent ahead to open the door.' Things were even more relaxed at Balmoral where Killearn spent the night in September 1938 and played a raucous game of cards after dinner with the Queen, Lord Elphinstone (the Queen's brother-in-law), and Princess Elizabeth.

At Windsor, the princesses were included at a lunch at which the guests included the United States ambassador Joseph P. Kennedy and his wife, Rose, Neville Chamberlain, the Prime Minister, and Lord Halifax, the Foreign Secretary. 'The princesses,' Rose Kennedy would later recall, 'were in rose dresses and checked blouses, red shoes with silver-coloured buckles, white socks, and necklaces of coral and pearl. Princess Margaret had a ribbon in her hair.' Princess Elizabeth, then thirteen, sat between the Prime Minister and Joe Kennedy. 'I suppose this was regular procedure – associating with older people even when she was very young,' mused Rose Kennedy. Very useful, of course, but it restrains 'the natural inclination of a normal youngster . . . towards fun and frolic.'

Rose Kennedy was also present when the Queen launched the liner *Queen Elizabeth*. 'Little Princess Margaret Rose saw me in the group,' she noted, 'smiled, told Princess Elizabeth, who immediately told the Queen, who looked over and bowed.' About the same time Princess Elizabeth met another member of the Kennedy clan who, years later, was to make a brief reappearance in her life. 'Was at tea with the Princess Elizabeth, with whom I made a great deal of time,' wrote Jack Kennedy of the meeting. What the heir to the British throne thought of this brash twenty-one-year-old American who was clearly trying to impress her is not known.

Though the King and Queen were relaxed about Elizabeth's formal education in other respects, they felt she needed a good grounding in constitutional history. An ordinary student would have been assigned Warner and Marten's *History of England*. The Princess went straight to the source: she began to take twice-weekly tutorials from one of the book's two authors. Henry Marten was mildly eccentric: he had a pet rook which used to perch on his shoulder, and a weakness for sugar lumps, which he ate in between nibbling absentmindedly at his handkerchief. He had spent his life at Eton first as a boy, then as a master, and then as Vice-Provost, and, out of habit, he would sometimes address the Princess as 'Gentlemen', as if he were in an Eton classroom. Elizabeth already had a keen interest in British history. She had devoured the popular books provided by Crawfie, and Marten deepened that fascination. He had a natural teacher's skill for capturing a student's attention and stimulating him (or, in this case, her) to think. To interest his new pupil in the complex pattern of royal relationships through the ages he devised a game played with coloured counters, each with the name of an English king or queen and their children through the ages. Counters representing kings were coloured red, queens were blue, princes brown, princesses yellow, with other colours for lesser royals. The aim of the lotto-like game was to fit each counter on to its appropriate square on a number of boards.

Sometimes Marten went to Windsor Castle or Buckingham Palace. But often the Princess would drive to Eton with Crawfie and sit in his book-filled study while he discoursed about British rule in India, the Church and Parliament or Queen Victoria. The Princess took notes in an Eton College exercise book and afterwards wrote essays, with varying degrees of success. There were occasions when her work was returned with an N, a Marten marking which stood for Nonsense.

He would seize on any occasion to develop a theme. Once, Elizabeth mentioned that she had been chased by a swarm of bees. 'I wonder whose bees they were,' the historian mused.

'I have no idea,' replied the Princess. 'Just anybody's I suppose. Aren't they?'

'If they have any owners, those owners have rights,' Marten went on. 'And so has the owner of the property on which they swarm. I think we ought to think about those rights . . . ' This started a lesson on the law of ownership, its origins in Roman times, and the law in modern times.

Girl Guiding remained an enduring interest for Princess Elizabeth. She liked the group activity with her peers, and she liked Violet Synge, whom she found a sympathetic listener. During the royal family's seasonal migrations to Sandringham and Balmoral, Elizabeth wrote Violet Synge chatty letters, addressing her as 'Dear Captain', and ending with jokey made-up signatures such as 'Despasia' and 'Globigerinous'. As the letters, full of news of her holiday activities, were written on Sandringham or Balmoral notepaper anonymity was clearly not intended: the pseudonyms were a private joke. But Elizabeth's friendship with the Guide leader was no joke to Crawfie.

The royal governess, who can scarcely be said to have been modest about her position, had not liked being rebuffed over admitting Princess Margaret to the Guides, and had regarded Violet Synge with suspicion ever since. Now she resented her influence over the princesses.

But events in the world were soon to take a hand in the lives of the princesses and those around them: 1938 was the year of the Munich Agreement, the commitment secured from Adolf Hitler by Neville Chamberlain that was supposed to guarantee 'peace in our time.' When she heard there would be no war, Elizabeth's reaction was 'How disappointing!' She was probably reflecting the prevailing sentiment in the royal household, which was dominated by an old-fashioned military hierarchy. As a group, they were out of sympathy with Chamberlain's efforts to secure peace through a policy of appeasing Hitler and Mussolini.

Life at Buckingham Palace was lived to a background of regimental bands and the stamping of soldiers' feet. Senior Palace staff tended to be discreetly headhunted from what Lady Elizabeth Longford, an earlier biographer of Queen Elizabeth, calls 'the magic circle' of interlocking families with long-standing royal connections. In less poetic terms, the members of the King's household were chosen from the same tribe, with preference given to its warriors. The Private Secretaries, equerries and aides-de-camp were former or serving officers from one of the seven regiments of the Household Division, the socially acceptable Grenadier, Coldstream, Welsh, Scots and Irish Guards and the two Cavalry Regiments – that is, the Life Guards and the Blues. Soldiers had the merit of good grooming, punctuality and deep loyalties. Tommy Lascelles and Joey Legh were former officers in the Coldstream Guards; Hardinge had served in the Grenadiers. It went beyond regular royal service. Young Guards subalterns were pressed into service to partner the princesses at tea, and ride with them at Windsor, so that for the princesses the Guards represented not only the staff but social friendship as well. The King – a Navy man himself – did not find the preponderance of Guards officers surrounding him entirely to his liking, and neither did the Queen, who complained to a friend that the royal household needed 'a little leaven to the Guards officer mixture who are the King's private secretaries.' But the magic circle was so entrenched that the King found the state of affairs hard to change; and the pedigree of key household members did not alter appreciably until well after his death.

The Munich Agreement was short-lived, and as 1939 dawned

Europe was once again on the brink of war. Despite the prospect of real danger, the King and Queen on 5 May sailed from Southampton on the liner *Empress of Australia* for a seven-week tour of Canada and the United States. The visit to America was at the invitation of President Roosevelt. Convinced that a conflict between Britain and Germany was inevitable in the long run, Roosevelt intended his meeting with the King and Queen as a gesture of public support even though isolationist sentiment in America was strong. For King George VI, the trip was a test in many respects. He was the first reigning British monarch to set foot in the former American colony. There was continuing American sympathy for the Duke of Windsor, who had maintained a high profile since his abdication, visiting both the United States and Germany and making friendly overtures towards the Nazi regime. So the King's visit was shaping up as a test of his royal mettle.

Queen Elizabeth was later to say that 'the tour made us'. It gave the King's confidence a welcome boost, enhanced his international reputation, and broadened his outlook. It also made him determined to cut back on Court ceremonial. 'There must be no more high-hat business,' he told one of his advisers during the tour, 'the sort of thing my father and those of his day regarded as . . . the correct attitude – the feeling that certain things could not be done.' Court protocol was relaxed as a result, although no substantive changes were introduced in the royal household. But at Marlborough House, Queen Mary's residence across the street from St James's Palace, the old standards were rigidly maintained. Joe Kennedy was among the foreign envoys never invited to dine there because they drew the line at wearing the old Court dress, including knee breeches, on which Queen Mary insisted. Social climber though he undoubtedly was, Kennedy refused to wear breeches even though it meant passing up the coveted invitation. 'I'd offend folks in America' was his explanation.

On 22 June 1939 Elizabeth and Margaret were taken by destroyer to meet up with their returning parents for a homecoming celebration at sea. For Princess Elizabeth it had been the longest separation from her parents since their tour of Australia and New Zealand, when she was nine months old. Lunch on board was a happy family occasion. The King led the singing of 'Under the Spreading Chestnut Tree', and 'The Lambeth Walk'. London's welcome of its King and Queen was no less cheerful, mixed with a strong sense of relief that they were back safely in such dangerous times. Thousands crowded the Mall, singing 'God Save the King' and 'Land of Hope and Glory'. The King and Queen and the two princesses appeared on the balcony of Buckingham Palace, and the singing changed to 'For He's a Jolly Good Fellow'. When the royals went inside the crowd refused to disperse, and the King and Queen stepped out again. Harold Nicolson who witnessed the homecoming procession from a stand reserved for Members of Parliament in front of the House of Commons recalled that the King 'wore a happy schoolboy grin. The Queen was superb. She really does manage to convey to each individual in the crowd that he or she have had a personal greeting.' She was, he went on, 'one of the most amazing Queens since Cleopatra.'

In their morning walks among the rhododendrons that were the King's special delight in the Buckingham Palace grounds, Elizabeth was no doubt given a first-hand account of his American trip and his meeting with President Roosevelt, with whom he felt he had developed a good relationship. If George VI had suffered from being kept on the periphery of the monarchy by his father, the same was not going to be true of his daughter. Lisa Sheridan, a photographer who received several assignments to take pictures of the royal family during this period, noted the 'particular bond of understanding between the King and Princess Elizabeth,' how he made 'a point of explaining everything he can to her personally . . . I saw them looking at papers on his desk . . . Later, when they went into the garden together, her arm went spontaneously around his waist and he pulled her towards him . . . I suppose theirs is a special intimacy, more deep than perhaps is usual in the ordinary family.' Elizabeth's relationship with her father was deepening into a mature understanding. She admired his strong sense of duty, and his capacity for hard work. Like him, she was not imbued with a gregarious spirit, and strangers could find conversing with her heavy going. On their weekend at Windsor Castle, Joe and Rose Kennedy were walking through Windsor Great Park and – according to Rose – 'ran into Princess Elizabeth hiding behind the shrubs. She had on a pink coat and was hatless and she smiled at us.'

A visitor to Windsor Castle once came upon the King discussing the contents of an official document with Elizabeth, while her younger sister sat silently knitting. Silent knitting was uncharacteristic of Margaret, but the scene said much about the relative situations of the two sisters and the impact on their respective personalities: Elizabeth preparing to be Queen, Margaret living in her shadow. In an earlier age, Margaret would in due course have been at the top of the list of Europe's marriageable princesses. She would probably have married a king or crown prince. But the Second World War and a changing world shut off even that option in her future. The closeness of the two Windsor sisters only served to emphasize the contrast in their destinies, the one clear-cut, pre-ordained; the other uncertain. Sibling rivalry ran amok, fuelled by their opposite characters. The more Elizabeth played the big sister, the more unruly Margaret became. Shouting 'Don't be a limpet, Margaret,' from the water as her younger sister hesitated on the edge of the swimming pool was not the best form of encouragement for a six-year-old. In their worthy effort to create a family atmosphere and to avoid shutting out Princess Margaret as George VI had himself felt shut out, the King and Queen ended up with one rather prim daughter and one rebellious one. Subsequently, while the life of the first daughter followed its programmed course loaded with a sense of purpose, the second zigzagged erratically – and frequently unhappily – towards middle age, cushioned from worse disaster by her royal status.

Margaret said later that the young princesses had no sense that theirs was a lonely life. But it is hard to miss what has never been experienced. They had few friends of their own age, and none that were close. The distance was always there. Margaret used to like to watch children walking past Buckingham Palace and showed great interest in their clothes. Lilibet longed to have a bicycle. But in the absence of a bicycle there were always horses. The indispensable Marion Crawford says Elizabeth's 'first love of all was undoubtedly Owen the [Buckingham Palace] groom, who taught her to ride' and for years, Owen's word was law. This admiration was a natural extension of her passion for horses. In her eyes, Owen was a sort of honorary horse. The toy horses of her girlhood, complete with removable saddles and blankets, remained lined up in a long row outside her room until she left the Palace to get married, and two large rocking horses flanked the door outside her father's study, and the princesses would rock on them while the King worked at his desk.

By the time she reached her early teens, Elizabeth was already both a very good rider and becoming knowledgeable about the finer points of equestrian pursuits. She took an interest in her father's racehorses, and those who knew her say that she was happiest when riding, or in the stables talking to horses. Lonely children lavish love and care on their pets. The corgis got some of Elizabeth's affection, but the horses got most. In later life, she would say that all the happiest memories of her childhood were associated with Windsor Castle and the Great Park, where she had the greatest pleasure horse riding.

IV

The House of Windsor at War

In the summer of 1939, Europe was living on borrowed time. Austria had been annexed, Czechoslovakia invaded. The Munich Agreement was consigned to the scrap heap of history, and Britain had been committed by Neville Chamberlain's public guarantee to aid Poland in the event of a German attack – which now seemed increasingly imminent. On 22 July, the royal yacht *Victoria and Albert* dropped anchor in the Dart River and the Royal Naval College at Dartmouth received a visit from its most distinguished living alumnus, King George VI. He had not returned to the college since his cadet days twenty-seven years earlier, and his arrival with the Queen and the two princesses could not have been worse timed. Dartmouth was afflicted with a double epidemic of both chicken-pox and mumps, and most of the cadets were confined to the sick bay with one illness or the other. So while the King went on a nostalgic tour of the establishment, gleefully looking himself up in the *College Punishment Book*, the two princesses were confined to the Captain's house and garden to reduce the risk of infection, and various senior cadets who had escaped the epidemics kept them entertained, playing croquet with them. Among these was Prince Philip of Greece, nephew of their Uncle Dickie Mountbatten, and the princesses' third cousin.

He was tall, eighteen years old, extremely blond, and had smiling good looks. He was a frequent visitor to Broadlands, the Mountbattens' Hampshire home, which Elizabeth knew well, and to his aunt Princess Marina of Kent's Buckinghamshire home at Coppins Iver, where Elizabeth had also stayed, yet this was apparently their first meeting. Crawfie, in attendance as usual, found him 'rather offhand in his manner'; and when he played tennis while the princesses watched, the governess thought he 'showed off a good deal'. But Crawfie was not a thirteen-year-old princess leading a sheltered existence. 'How good he is, Crawfie!' Elizabeth whispered to her as Prince Philip sailed over the tennis net. 'How high he can jump!' Miss Crawford admits that 'the little girls were much impressed' – and especially the elder girl. Lord Mountbatten, a guest of the Royals on the yacht, noted that the following afternoon, 'Philip came back on board the V & A for tea and was a great success with the children.'

In his naval officer's uniform, with the white collar-tabs denoting his cadetship, Prince Philip must have cut a dashing figure. The Princess, Mountbatten observed, 'stared at him . . . and followed him everywhere.' When the *Victoria and Albert* sailed from Dartmouth, it was with an unofficial escort of boats belonging to the college. Gradually, so the legend goes, the swarm thinned out as the boats began to turn back, until just one determined rower was left. It was Prince Philip of Greece, who had to be ordered back by an officer on the royal yacht.

Commenting on the meeting, Mountbatten's official biographer wrote, 'It is hard to believe that no thought crossed [Mountbatten's] mind that an admirable husband for the future Queen Elizabeth might be readily available.' By 1940 this possibility was being discussed in the Greek royal family, and it is equally hard to believe that Mountbatten was not actually behind it. The girl who shared lemonade and ginger nuts with Philip was, according to her governess, at an 'awkward and leggy age, rather large-mouthed.' Moreover, Crawfie's description of the two princesses, aged thirteen and almost nine, as 'little girls' reflects not only how they were still considered and treated by the King and Queen, and in consequence by the royal household, but also how they looked. At Dartmouth, they wore identical powder-blue berets, with short curly bobbed hair showing underneath, and powder blue double-breasted coats. On their feet were ankle-length white socks, and white strap shoes. The tendency to dress the two princesses in matching outfits like twins went beyond the prevailing fashion and was to persist until Princess Margaret rebelled against it in her teens. Up to that point, however, it was the standard practice: in 1939, the two princesses wear identical outfits in forty-two out of forty-nine published pictures of them together in the London popular press.

If their daughter's admiration for Prince Philip registered with the King and Queen, it probably caused mild amusement, and perhaps reminded them that their Lilibet was no longer a 'little girl'. But as the last summer of peace drew to a close more important issues occupied the King's attention. When war was declared on 3 September, the family was, as usual for that time of the year, at Balmoral, where the King not only liked to shoot grouse but ate it every night for dinner during the season. The King and Queen returned immediately to London, leaving the princesses at Balmoral.

In October, Elizabeth wrote to Violet Synge that for greater security, they had decamped to Birkhall, the smaller house close to Balmoral Castle where they had gone as small children; 'but it's a secret,' she added. Violet Synge had become an army nurse and Elizabeth said she could imagine her riding about on her bicycle. The First Buckingham Palace Company of the Girl Guides was an early casualty of the war. It was disbanded when its Guides were dispersed, some being evacuated to North America, and others to the country. But, as Elizabeth told its former captain, a nucleus of the company had regrouped at Birkhall (the Hardinges, for example, were neighbours) and had established contact with the local Balmoral Girl Guides. The 'Royal' Guides had tried to teach them some scouting games, but Princess Elizabeth – accustomed to the staidness of the Palace group – found the local Guides an undisciplined lot.

The Princess spent her fourteenth birthday not at Birkhall but at the Royal Lodge, Windsor, where she was within reach of her parents. The Germans had stepped up their aggression to full pitch. Norway and Denmark had been occupied, and King Haakon forced to escape to England, where George VI had given him refuge at Buckingham Palace. On 10 May 1940, Hitler's ground and air forces invaded the Netherlands, Belgium and Luxembourg. Queen Wilhelmina of the Netherlands also fled to England along with Crown Princess Juliana, and her two granddaughters Princess Beatrix and the newly born Princess Irene, who was immediately christened in Buckingham Palace Chapel, as Elizabeth and Margaret had been.

By 15 May, the German army had outflanked the supposedly impregnable French Maginot Line and the advancing British and French armies, and nothing now stood between the Germans and Paris. In England, Neville Chamberlain, too, was outflanked. In the Commons, members of his own Tory Party voted with the

Labour opposition to defeat the Government over the issue of its conduct of the war, and the Prime Minister was forced to resign. Chamberlain's resignation saddened the King, who liked and respected him, and who was reluctant to face the inevitable choice of his successor, Winston Churchill. The King had not forgiven Churchill for his support of King Edward VIII, and shared the widely held view of him as a dangerous political maverick. A great wartime partnership, therefore, began with resentment on the King's side, and a certain cavalier attitude towards the sovereign on Churchill's. Princess Elizabeth, doubtless identifying with her father's feelings, was also sorry to see Chamberlain go, her earlier opposition to his appeasement policy forgotten. 'My eldest daughter told me', the Queen wrote to the departing Prime Minister, 'that she and Margaret Rose had listened to [the broadcast of his resignation] with real emotion – In fact, she said, "I *cried*, Mummy".'

The first of the new Prime Minister's many challenges in his five years in office was the withdrawal of British troops hemmed in at Dunkirk. In the aftermath of the historic retreat across the Channel, a German invasion of Britain was considered imminent, and the royal family's security suddenly became a pressing issue. Some ministers suggested that, for safety, the princesses should be evacuated to Canada. Queen Wilhelmina and Princess Juliana had already gone there, as had the children of the Norwegian and Danish royal houses. It made sense to send the heir to the throne out of the war zone in order to ensure that the throne would continue once Hitler had been defeated. But the King, backed by Churchill, refused to consider it. 'I strongly deprecate any stampede from this country at the present time,' Churchill wrote. The Queen, who practised using a pistol every morning, had the last word on the subject. 'The children could not go without me, and I could not possibly leave the King,' she said.

Instead of Canada, the princesses moved to Windsor Castle, which was to be their home for the five years of the war. What Princess Margaret later called 'a pathetic attempt' was made to render the castle more secure against possible attack. 'They dug trenches and put up some feeble barbed wire,' the Princess recalled, 'and the feeble barbed wire, of course, wouldn't have kept anybody out but it kept us in.' For a while, the fear of a possible snatch by German paratroops was so real that the princesses were not allowed to venture outside castle grounds. In the nursery in the massive Brunswick Tower the princesses kept packed suitcases ready for a quick dash to Liverpool where, according to an invasion contingency plan, a fast frigate of the Royal Navy would be waiting to whisk them across the Atlantic to safety. Elizabeth could no longer go to Eton for her lessons with Henry Marten. Instead Marten came to the castle where, in lieu of the attacking bees, he used developments in the war to illustrate his lessons. But as winter came and the invasion did not materialize, the siege mentality relaxed and the princesses' area of free movement was enlarged to include Windsor Great Park. Wherever they went, though, the princesses were shadowed by a picked escort of the Guards, and an armoured car.

The Palace made a point of telling the world that Elizabeth had given up learning German and had taken up Spanish instead and – a gesture to the Americans – was also studying the history of the United States. In reality, Elizabeth had never made any real effort to learn either German or Spanish, but since the King and Queen's trip to the United States, Marten had been asked to include some tutorials on American history.

Elizabeth was a wartime teenager. She was exposed to most, if not all, of its fears and privations. But, confined to Windsor Castle, she had less opportunity to experience its hard-edged, often bizarre lighter side. Like all British children she took an avid interest in the war's progress. Along with her younger sister – and, indeed, her grandmother Queen Mary – she knitted socks and scarves for the servicemen, collected tinfoil and scrap iron for the war effort, and kept to food rationing, which included two vegetarian days a week. To cope with clothes rationing, the Queen had several of her dresses cut down for Elizabeth. 'Margaret gets all Elizabeth's clothes then,' the Queen told Queen Alexandra, wife of King Peter of Yugoslavia, 'so with the three of us we manage in relays.'

Elizabeth was not troubled at having to wear her mother's hand-me-downs. One trait she did not share with her father and mother was their fastidiousness about clothes. The King would spend hours with his tailor and had his suits fitted again and again, and the wartime clothes shortage was for him a real hardship. Her mother loved floating outfits in pink and baby blue. Elizabeth could not understand this. Although she appreciated good clothes, she was not fashion conscious; she did not have a particularly good dress sense, nor was she – unlike other members of her family – interested in ceremonial clothes. In other words, she did not possess the royal family's flair for dressing up.

Besides, hand-me-downs appealed to her frugality. She would

smooth and fold the wrapping paper from her presents, rolling up the ribbon for future use. This was no doubt due to the dominant Scottish influence in the nursery. But it was also a clue – a signal of her lifelong self-discipline and passion for orderliness. Her books were ranged in perfect order of size, and she took pains to align her shoes exactly parallel. She would even sort out according to size the coffee sugar crystals her parents gave her as a treat after lunch.

In May 1941, Hitler ordered the Luftwaffe to begin nightly raids against London. Night after night throughout the summer the bombers came, dropping their bombloads on civilian targets, and each day revealed fresh scenes of devastation. The worst raid was on 7 September. The sky was thick with enemy planes, in an attack lasting several hours, and London's rescue resources were stretched to breaking point. The previous day, the British cabinet had decided that it could not continue to function effectively in the capital and would have to move its operations to Scotland, along with the King and Queen. But 7 September was Hitler's last all-out bid to destroy London. Convinced that the Royal Air Force had an unlimited supply of Spitfires and Hurricanes with which to defend the city, he abandoned the blitzkrieg strategy and the night attacks suddenly stopped. The German air build-up in western France was ordered east ready for his next – and ultimately disastrous – offensive: the invasion of Russia.

Two days later, on 9 September, the King visited the East End of London, where the damage and loss of life had been particularly heavy. He spent the whole morning in this densely populated, working-class area, clambering over the rubble in the streets to inspect the damage and talk to the homeless. In the afternoon of the same day, a bomb fell on Buckingham Palace, lodging itself under the stone steps outside the Regency Room on the north side just below the King's study, where he was working at the time, and failed to explode. That night, however, the device went off, shattering window panes on that side of the Palace and damaging the swimming pool. The King and Queen, who spent their days at Buckingham Palace and drove to Windsor Castle every evening to sleep, were not in the building at the time of the explosion. But on 12 September the King and Queen narrowly missed death when a German aircraft deliberately bombed Buckingham Palace in a daytime raid, flying straight down the Mall at the façade in a daring low-flying attack. The bombs missed the Palace and fell in the grounds, destroying the chapel. Two fell in the quadrangle, thirty yards away from where the King and Queen were sitting in the former's little sitting room talking to Hardinge. As the bombs exploded, he wrote in his diary, 'We looked at each other, & then went out into the passage as fast as we could get there . . . We all wondered why we weren't dead. Two great craters had appeared in the quadrangle.' The King spoke of 'a new bond' with Londoners who were being rendered homeless daily. The Queen said, 'I'm glad we've been bombed. It makes me feel I can look the East End in the face.'

But another thing that the royal family and Londoners had in common in the early days of the blitz was the general inadequacy of their air-raid shelters. Londoners took refuge from the bombing in the Underground stations: at night, when the trains stopped running, the platforms became teeming public dormitories. The shelter at Buckingham Palace at the time was a maid's room below street level. It had been reinforced with timber and divided into cubicles both for privacy and to reduce the danger from blast. The furniture inside consisted mainly of overstuffed settees on which the King and Queen sat during air raids, and there were fire buckets in the corners. At Windsor Castle, the shelter was in the basement. Bobo MacDonald and Alah were entrusted with bringing the princesses down to it the moment the warning siren sounded, and they were met at the shelter entrance by Sir Hill Child, the Master of the Household, as if they were arriving for an official reception.

The first time the air-raid alarm sounded, it was the middle of the night. Sir Hill was there and waiting: but no princesses arrived. Marion Crawford ran up to the nurseries to investigate and found Alah putting on her uniform and the princesses dressing. 'We're dressing, Crawfie,' said Princess Elizabeth. 'We must dress.' But Crawfie shouted, 'You are not to dress. Put a coat over your night clothes at once.' In the shelter, while Elizabeth read a book, and Margaret slept on Crawfie's knee, Sir Hill remonstrated with Alah. 'You must understand the princesses must come down at once,' he told her. 'They must come down whatever they are wearing.' At 2.00 a.m. the all-clear sounded. Sir Hill Child bowed to Princess Elizabeth. 'You may go to bed, ma'am,' he said. Court ceremonial was never totally abandoned, even in air-raid shelters.

Later, as the raids dragged on and increased in intensity, bunk-beds were installed in the shelter and the princesses took down some of their books and possessions. Several bombs fell around Windsor Castle, causing the shelter to shake, but no harm ever

51

came to Elizabeth and Margaret. To relieve the tedium of confinement at Windsor, the princesses appeared in a Christmas play together with children from Windsor Great Park school, which was attended by sons and daughters of the King's tenants. The play was called *The Christmas Child*: Elizabeth was proficient as one of the Three Kings, and Margaret very touching as a little girl who had no Christmas gift: the King and Queen wept when Margaret sang 'Gentle Jesus'.

King George, who died a little every time he had to make a speech, and who broke out in a cold sweat at the very thought of having to make a broadcast, was amazed at his daughters' performances. Margaret revealed a distinct talent. Elizabeth – and this was perhaps more important in his eyes – showed herself capable of overcoming her natural reserve and holding her own in front of an audience. So the Christmas pantomime at Windsor became a regular fixture throughout the war. Well-known fairy stories, such as *Cinderella* and *Sleeping Beauty*, were reworked for the princesses to star in by H. I. Tanner, a local schoolmaster, who one year also cobbled together a rollicking satire called *Old Mother Red Riding Boots*.

Elizabeth was usually cast as the principal boy. Margaret tended to have the title role. In the 1941 production of *Cinderella*, Margaret was Cinderella, and Elizabeth, in a white wig and breeches, Prince Florizel. In *Sleeping Beauty*, a year later, Elizabeth would again be the prince, and her sister the sleeping princess. But the pantomimes became progressively more ambitious, with printed programmes, and music provided by members of the band of the Grenadier Guards. In *Old Mother Red Riding Boots*, cast, stage crew and helpers totalled eighty-three people, not counting the nineteen-piece Guards orchestra.

Elizabeth's particular perspective on the war included the exploits of one midshipman in His Majesty's service. Writing to Churchill to thank him for birthday roses when she turned fifteen, she said, 'I'm afraid you have been having a worrying time lately, but I'm sure things will begin to look up again soon.' Churchill's most recent worry had been the evacuation of British and Allied troops stranded on the Greek beaches in the wake of the Italian invasion. About 45,000 had been successfully withdrawn despite heavy bombing, but another 11,000 had to be left behind. The progress of the Greek fighting had also been Elizabeth's personal worry because Prince Philip was serving on HMS *Valiant*, which was in the thick of it. She corresponded regularly with Prince

Philip. They exchanged what King George VI's official biographer called 'cousinly letters'.

When her first lady-in-waiting was appointed in Elizabeth's middle teens to help with her correspondence, her parents observed that most of it seemed to be either to or from Prince Philip – clearly a good-natured dig at the Princess for she had no intention of delegating these letters to her lady-in-waiting. In any case, she liked dashing off handwritten letters, and was to retain this personal touch even in later, busier years.

Whatever Elizabeth's own feelings about Philip were at the time, Greek royal circles were already talking of their marriage. Chips Channon, in Greece on a special mission for the British government, recorded in his diary a revealing conversation with Prince Philip's aunt, Princess Nicholas. She told him, Channon wrote, that '[Philip] is to be our Prince Consort, and that is why he is serving in [the British] Navy.' Princess Nicholas was the Duchess of Kent's mother and had just returned from a trip to England where she had stayed with her daughter and son-in-law. Her statement to Channon suggests that there had been family talk of a match between Elizabeth and Philip. Indeed, from the standpoint of the hard-up and politically insecure Greeks, a marriage into the House of Windsor, the wealthiest and most entrenched in Europe, was devoutly to be wished. Moreover, though Philip was no catch financially, he was royal and shared with Elizabeth a common descent from Queen Victoria.

The Greek royal house was of Danish origin. Prince William of Denmark, who himself belonged to the German family of Schleswig-Holstein-Sonderburg-Glucksburg, was set up by the European powers as King George I of Greece. His younger son, Prince Andrew, married Princess Alice of Battenberg, daughter of Prince Louis of Battenberg. Prince Louis himself was the husband of Queen Victoria's granddaughter, Victoria of Hesse. Born in Germany he had joined the British navy and risen to the top rank of First Sea Lord, but was forced to resign following a smear campaign because of his German origins. It was Prince Louis who changed the family name to Mountbatten and who first bore the title of Marquis of Milford Haven. Philip was born in Corfu to Prince Andrew and Princess Alice, the youngest of five children, in 1921. But his life very nearly began in tragedy. In 1923, a revolutionary council seized power in Greece. Prince Andrew, who served in the Greek army, was made a scapegoat for Greek military failures against Turkey. He was tried for treason and would have been executed were it not for the intervention of King George V of England, and the timely presence of a Royal Navy ship in Athens to carry the family off into exile. Philip travelled in a cot made from a fruit crate.

Such talk was all grist to the marriage rumour mills in the royal houses of Europe, but if it reached the ears of George VI at that time, he certainly brushed it aside as premature. The King was to find it hard to come to terms with his daughter's marriage when it happened six years later: in 1941, the very idea would have been out of the question.

At forty-six, he was shouldering the awesome responsibility of a country at war, and the burden was not making him any more outgoing or communicative, even with his brothers. Prince George, who saw him often, complained that he was 'always amiable but not forthcoming and one has to worm things out of him.' Only with his wife and daughters did he feel able to drop his guard. Queen Elizabeth he regarded as his partner, and she was the object of his deep devotion. Margaret was a precocious child who amused him with her lively antics. Elizabeth was becoming a close companion who shared the same interest in horse racing and shooting. The King was a first rate shot and, with his encouragement, Elizabeth was becoming a good shot. Margaret, on the other hand, showed little interest in shooting. Like the King, Elizabeth particularly enjoyed deer stalking – in the wet Scottish weather a tough sport requiring tracking skill, and a true hunter's determination and killer instinct.

At Balmoral, King George and his daughter would set out early on a cold morning with their ghillies. The damp seeping through their clothing, they crawled all day through the heather in search of their elusive quarry. On one occasion, Elizabeth, out walking in the hills around Balmoral with Marion Crawford, spotted a stag in the distance. 'Let's stalk it,' Elizabeth said to the governess, who had never before stalked anything wilder than the Palace corgis. 'I'll show you how it's done.'

For half an hour they struggled up a hill through thick bracken to where the stag had been spotted. There was no animal in sight, but Elizabeth suddenly said, 'I smell it!' As they crawled forward on their stomachs, the governess was too worried about being bitten by a snake to reflect on the idea of the Princess picking up the scent of an animal the way the animal could pick up hers. Moreover, Elizabeth was quietly rebuking her for making too much noise. At length, they rounded a craggy shoulder and there he was – a truly regal animal. Elizabeth's face was 'transfigured', Crawfie recalled. 'I could see then what an ecstasy it was for her to stalk a stag and come up to him at last.' Usually, the ecstasy culminated in shooting the animal dead, but on this occasion the Princess had no gun with her and had to be content with watching her quarry make his escape.

As Elizabeth was at the time approaching her sixteenth birthday, she was being prepared for her confirmation by the Dean of Windsor, Canon Crawley. Inevitably, Margaret was, too, and the Canon noted that while Elizabeth took her preparation very seriously, Margaret's approach was more flippant. In March 1942 the two princesses, looking very grave under their small white net veils, were confirmed by Archbishop Lang in St George's Chapel, Windsor. There was no question which sister was the focus of the family's attention. Queen Mary came to Windsor from Badminton, the home of the Duke of Beaufort, where she had been a reluctant evacuee since the outbreak of the war, to see her granddaughters for the first time in a year. She found 'Lilibet much grown, very pretty eyes and complexion, pretty figure,' as she wrote to her last surviving sister-in-law, Princess Alice, Countess of Athlone. 'Margaret very short, intelligent face but not really pretty.' Queen Mary's lady-in-waiting, Lady Airlie, described Elizabeth's confirmation in her diary without even mentioning Princess Margaret at all.

On her sixteenth birthday the following month Princess Elizabeth's presents included a single pearl, which was her father's annual gift to her – and an élite regiment of the British army. The King appointed her Colonel-in-Chief of the Grenadier Guards, and on 21 April, she took the salute at a parade of 634 officers and men drawn from the eight wartime battalions of the regiment. Pinned to her halo beret she proudly wore the regimental badge in gold, a grenade. In peacetime the scene would have blazed with the scarlet of the guardsmen's tunics, but they wore their battle dress, and flat caps instead of the bearskin busbies.

It was – appropriately – the first official engagement the Princess had ever undertaken. Appropriate because her connection with the Grenadiers was to be one of the longest personal associations with any British institution. The most familiar image of Elizabeth as Queen is the photograph of her riding sidesaddle in the uniform of one of the regiments of the Brigade of Guards at the annual ceremony of Trooping the Colour. And doubly so because her colonelcy of the Grenadiers was the start of a long interest in the military. She approached what was in reality a nominal role with the same thoroughness that she did everything else. On her periodic inspections of 'her' regiment she insisted on seeing everything, including the horses' teeth. Once, during a parade, she stopped in front of a soldier and reprimanded him for untidiness. The incident caused embarrassment because the Guards do not admit to anything short of perfection in drill and turnout, and a senior officer suggested that a greater use of tact would be helpful. But generally, the Grenadiers could do no wrong in her eyes. When she was married, some of the many food parcels sent to her by wellwishers, especially from the United States, were pilfered by the soldiers who unloaded them. 'Were they Grenadiers?' Bobo MacDonald asked her. 'Certainly not,' Elizabeth snapped back. 'Grenadiers would never do such a thing!'

As the war dragged on and the danger became more commonplace, the princesses' confinement to Windsor Castle was occasionally brightened by a quick trip to London or elsewhere, usually in the company of the King and Queen. On a visit to a Royal Air Force station, they climbed inside a Hudson bomber and sat in the pilot's cockpit. Even more exciting was the afternoon spent at Denham Studios, outside London, where Noël Coward was directing, and starring in, the wartime Royal Navy epic *In Which We Serve*. Besides the King and Queen and the princesses, the visitors included the Mountbattens, Lord Louis, Edwina and daughters Patricia and Pamela: the film was loosely based on Lord Mountbatten's exploits as a destroyer captain. They watched Coward film a scene of the evacuation of Dunkirk in a howling wind; and though the swaying of the simulated ship's deck under their feet made the princesses slightly seasick, to Noël Coward – meeting them for the first time – they seemed 'thrilled and beautifully behaved'. The princesses seemed less thrilled at a poetry reading organized by Edith and Osbert Sitwell for the benefit of the Free French. Sitting on either side of their mother, they dutifully listened to verse readings by John Masefield, T.S. Eliot, Vita Sackville-West, Edith Sitwell, Gordon Bottomley, and others.

But it could be equally exciting to stay at home in Windsor with other members of the First Buckingham Palace Company of Sea Rangers and do a commando course devised and supervised by the physical training instructor of the Grenadier Guards, learning to scale walls, cross chasms, and swing on ropes. Sometimes, it was too exciting, for a new kind of danger now threatened from the skies. The V2 flying bomb, or 'doodlebug', was the precursor of the modern guided missile. This deadly weapon flew shrieking overhead until its propelling motor went dead and it plunged silently to earth, most often on civilian housing. Since the Germans could only launch it in the general direction of London, and not guide it to a specific target, the strategic use of the flying bomb was limited; and its main purpose was to demoralize the population. Though many such bombs fell around it, Windsor Castle miraculously escaped a direct hit. In the summer of 1942, however, the King and Queen and the two princesses had a close call.

It happened while Princess Elizabeth's company of Sea Rangers was spending a few days under canvas in the grounds of Frogmore, an attractive Georgian house down the hill from Windsor Castle, with a large winding lake suitable for boating. As the girls pitched their tents, soldiers from the princesses' escort of Grenadier Guards dug a deep trench nearby as shelter from air raids. It remained unused until the last afternoon of the camp when the King and Queen were the girls' guests for tea. Without warning, a doodlebug suddenly roared overhead. Everyone – the King and Queen, the princesses – everyone raced unceremoniously for cover, diving into the trench. Then the roaring ceased. Heart-stopping seconds of silence that seemed more like hours followed: then came a shattering roar as the device exploded on the Great West Road, the main London-Windsor highway a few miles away. Though the account of the incident – in the log of Elizabeth's own Kingfisher Patrol – makes light of the inherent danger, the royal family had had a narrow escape, and the Sea Rangers quickly dismantled their camp and headed for home.

As 1943 dawned, the tide had turned in the Allies' favour. In the Middle East, General Bernard Montgomery had repulsed Field Marshal Erwin Rommel at El Alamein and was pushing the Afrika Korps back north across the desert to Libya and the sea. The invasion of Sicily was imminent. But at home there were still plenty of reminders that the war was not yet won. The doodlebugs were an ever-present menace. Shortages of food and clothing – especially the latter – added to the discomfort. Every day brought news of friends and relatives missing in action: the princesses' own cousin George, Viscount Lascelles, was a prisoner of war. And royals from German-occupied Europe continued to find refuge in England, bringing the princesses into contact with some of their many Balkan relations. Among these was King Peter of Yugoslavia, twenty-year-old grandson of Queen Marie of Rumania, King George V's formidable first cousin, known in the family as 'Missy'. Elizabeth and Margaret met Peter when he brought his fiancée, the striking Greek Princess Alexandra, to Windsor to introduce her to the King, who was the young monarch's godfather. In fact, prompt action by Prince Albert – as he then was – at Crown Prince Peter's christening in 1923 had probably saved his life. During the long ceremony, the doddery Serbian Orthodox Patriarch dropped the infant into the baptismal font and, while everyone else was paralysed with shock, the infant's British godfather had quickly fished him out of the water.

Now King Peter again needed to be saved, in the metaphorical sense. Both his mother and the Serbs in his government-in-exile were opposed to his marriage to Princess Alexandra and he was hoping for the King and Queen's support. George VI's personal view was that a decision to go against Serbian wishes would be divisive at a time when the King should concentrate on unifying his exiled countrymen – advice which must have stirred memories of his own brother's abdication. But at the same time he took his responsibilities as *Koum* (Serbian for godfather) seriously and felt obliged to back his godson. In the course of this discussion the young princesses arrived and curtsied to King Peter. 'Another cousin for you,' said the Queen, introducing Princess Alexandra by her nickname, 'Sandra'. And as Alexandra remembered it, 'Lilibet, so markedly the elder sister, said at once, "I hope you will be very happy, Cousin Sandra." Immediately Margaret said primly, in exact repetition, "I hope you will be very happy, Cousin Sandra." ' Then Elizabeth said, 'Come on, Margaret,' and the girls trotted out of the room, returning presently followed by a footman carrying four small bowls. With great precision the bowls were set down on the floor a little way from the low tea table, and the princesses carefully portioned out dog food in each one. 'Ready,' sang out Margaret, and Elizabeth, giving a final inspection, nodded. At their call, four corgis appeared and converged on the food. Princess Alexandra recalled, 'Not until the dogs were eating happily did the girls come to have their own tea.'

On that occasion, the princesses wore identical dresses, which was becoming a bit of a joke in London social circles. On 19 May, when they accompanied the King and Queen to St Paul's Cathedral for a *Te Deum* to celebrate the Allies' victory in Africa, Chips Channon noted that the two were 'dressed alike in blue, which made them look like little girls.'

Slowly, however, King George's elder daughter was shedding the chrysalis of Lilibet and becoming Elizabeth (although personal letters to friends of her parents who had known her as a child would continue to be signed 'Lilibet' even after she turned fifty). One clue to her growing up was her blossoming friendship with Prince Philip. 'Who do you think is coming to see us act, Crawfie?' she asked before the Christmas pantomime, which was *Aladdin*, in 1943. Answering her own question, she said, 'Philip.' She was pink-cheeked with excitement. She had the title role. Prince Philip sat in the front row and rolled in the aisle at the dreadful anti-Japanese jokes. 'The pantomime went off very well,' Crawfie wrote six years later. 'I have never known Lilibet more animated. There was a sparkle about her none of us had ever seen before.' Considering the time lag, Crawfie could have been perceptive in hindsight, but Elizabeth was not a good dissembler and would have found it hard to conceal her true feelings from her governess.

When, early in 1944, King George of Greece quietly approached George VI on his cousin Philip's behalf, it was the knowledge of Lilibet's feelings that stopped her father short of an outright refusal. According to Harold Nicolson, who was well in with the Palace, 'The [royal] family were at first horrified when they saw that Philip was making up to Princess Elizabeth. They felt he was rough, ill-mannered, uneducated and would probably not be faithful . . . ' Prince Philip – then aged twenty-three – did not fit the mould of the princesses' Guards officer friends, who tended to be the sons of aristocratic British families. He was independent-minded, outspoken, slightly raffish, and not overly gifted with social graces. The fact that he was also exceptionally handsome, tall, blond, blue-eyed and very charming was not necessarily in his favour as far as the King and Queen were concerned. Nicolson mentions doubts about Philip's possible fidelity. And King George would not have been the first father to be suspicious of the intentions of a very handsome man who chased his very serious and not exactly beautiful daughter.

In short, the King and Queen hardly considered Philip of Greece an acceptable suitor for Elizabeth. But who *would* be? This was one question to which the King and Queen had different answers. George VI had grown up in a family where the tradition was to marry foreign royalty. When it came to finding an appropriate spouse, nationality mattered less than royal blood. His mother was German, his grandmother Danish; six of his eight great-uncles and great-aunts had married Germans, and his great-grandmother's husband had also been German. In his generation, one of his brothers had married a Greek. His multinational relations, besides Germans, included Greeks, Rumanians, Bulgarians, Danes, Swedes, Spaniards, Norwegians and a few surviving Russians. It was only during the First World War, with the traditional source of suitable husbands and wives obviously cut off, that his father had widened the field and allowed the royal children to marry into English (i.e. non-royal) families, thus opening the way for Prince Albert's own marriage to Lady Elizabeth Bowes-Lyon. Though the tradition of royals marrying other royals appealed to George VI, his non-royal wife can hardly be said to have shared his enthusiasm. Queen Elizabeth never felt completely at home with the cross-fertilization of cultures and nationalities in her husband's family. Scottish to the core, she may have set her heart on an English or Scottish husband for Lilibet, such as the dashing Hugh Euston – later the Duke of Grafton – who had for a time been one of the Guards officers in the princesses' bodyguard at Windsor Castle. Another officer who was to remain a lifelong friend as well as a member of the household was the handsome, affable Lord Rupert Nevill. So in reality one of Philip's drawbacks as a potential husband was simply that he was a foreigner at a time when the royal family, despite centuries of German blood, were being very British. This was ironic, for although his first languages had been Greek and German, he had from boyhood shown a preference for England, and his English relatives, and a determination to be, and sound, British.

It is not far-fetched to think that the King and Queen's reservations were at least partly prompted by the reputation of Prince Philip's father. Shortly after going into exile, Prince Andrew and Princess Alice separated. The Prince lived first in Paris and then in Menton, in the South of France; his wife, who had become deaf and had taught herself to lip-read in several languages, moved first to Geneva and then back to Greece. She started an order of Greek Orthodox nuns, and always wore a short nun's habit and headdress. The irreverent Chips Channon described her as 'eccentric to say the least.' As for Prince Andrew, Channon added, he 'philanders on the Riviera.' At his father's, Philip would later recall, there was always 'a silver bucket of something on ice.' The young Prince spent his boyhood shuttling between his estranged parents in their two contrasting lifestyles, but strongly resembled his father in looks, sharp wit and forthright, positive temperament.

The doubts about his education were rooted in English prejudice rather than reality. Because Philip's parents were hard up, his mother's older brother, the Marquis of Milford Haven, paid for him to go to Cheam preparatory school with his own son David, who was two years older. From there, however, he transferred to Dr Kurt Hahn's school, Salem, on the estate of his sister, Theodora, who married the Margrave of Baden. If Eton aspires to produce leaders of men, Hahn's aim was to go one better and provide young men with the intellectual and physical equipment to be 'philosopher-kings'. When the Nazis closed down Salem, the Jewish educator moved his school to Gordonstoun, in Scotland, and Philip went with it. He did well in both the extremely demanding class curriculum and the equally tough sports standards. But, though based in Scotland, Gordonstoun, with its high-minded German refugee headmaster, remained in many people's minds a 'crank school' – an institution out of the mainstream of the public school tradition.

If he owed his looks to his father, Philip inherited from his mother's family an interest in the sea. Like his maternal grandfather and two uncles before him, he entered the Royal Navy, graduating in the top five of his class at Dartmouth Naval College. By 1941, he was a second lieutenant, but there was an obstacle to further advancement. If he wanted to make the Royal Navy his career, he needed to obtain British nationality – a tall order because the war had blocked all applications for naturalization. His uncle, Lord Mountbatten, was attempting to secure his nephew's British citizenship. The fact that Mountbatten had stepped in as Philip's guardian following the death of his brother the Marquis was not a plus in the royal family's view. The King's second cousin had enemies in the royal household. He had been a close friend of Edward VIII until the abdication when he had transferred his friendship to the new King and his family. He certainly was not popular with the Queen who felt that he was pushing the romance between Elizabeth and Philip in order to advance his family's interests.

Not that it needed much pushing. By Elizabeth's eighteenth birthday, there were signs that the couple were not waiting for any parental green light. At about the same time that Elizabeth began at last to sleep in a room on her own, Philip's photograph appeared on her mantlepiece. What would 'people' say, Crawfie wondered. For 'people' read the King and Queen. Elizabeth's reply was 'a smile full of meaning' – whatever that is. Princess Margaret, from whom few secrets were possible and who was herself quite fond of

61

the Prince, said, 'I'm sure she likes him, Crawfie.' She did. Queen Alexandra and King Peter of Yugoslavia met Elizabeth and Philip walking with the royal corgis in Windsor Great Park. The couples waved to each other, but continued on their separate ways. After that, Alexandra says in her memoirs, they saw 'Philip and Lilibet several more times . . . and now they were, quite definitely, holding hands.' Coppins, Marina of Kent's home in Iver, Buckinghamshire, became a frequent meeting place, away from the court officials, Princess Margaret's overdeveloped curiosity, and the King and Queen. When she confirmed these meetings between her nephew and the Princess to a relation, the Queen said she hoped Philip 'wasn't just flirting'. Marina replied, 'I suspect his flirting days are over. I think he would be the one to be hurt now if it was a flirtation, but Lilibet would never treat anyone's affection lightly, she's much too sincere, and Philip knows that . . . I think those two are more serious about each other than even they've realized.' The knowledge that the Queen was nervous about the way things were going was not likely to worry Princess Marina unduly. She regarded herself as 'real' royalty and remained somewhat aloof from the English royals, and is said to have referred to Queen Elizabeth and the Duchess of Gloucester as 'those common little Scottish girls.'

Having got over the initial shock, the King found much to admire in Prince Philip and quite quickly reversed his earlier poor opinion of him. The Queen, however, did not join the Prince Philip fan club; and both she and her husband felt that – as the King put it bluntly to Mountbatten – 'We are going too fast.' To Queen Mary, the King explained, 'We both think [Elizabeth] is too young for that now, as she has never met any young men of her own age . . . I like Philip. He is intelligent, has a good sense of humour & thinks about things in the right way . . . We are going to tell [King] George [of Greece] that P[hilip] had better not think any more about it for the present.'

What George VI surely meant was that Elizabeth lacked experience in romantic relationships, not having had any other attachment that was remotely comparable. For in reality, the two princesses were not short of young male company at Windsor Castle. Senior boys from Eton and junior officers from the Guards were in frequent attendance. 'The right kind' of young officers were invited to tea dances. But the atmosphere on such occasions could be stiff, and many of the officers found it an ordeal to dance with Margaret and Elizabeth. Elizabeth did not find it easy to put her partners at their ease, and Margaret got a kick out of mischievously leading the young men on until they committed some *faux pas*, such as calling her by her name instead of 'Ma'am', and then publicly snubbing them. This amused the King, but a courtier recalled that Margaret 'was a wicked little girl ... she really was maddening very often ... but Princess Margaret was very attractive, collected the men better than [Elizabeth] did. She played the piano, amused people for whole evenings. [The royal family] spoiled her. They adored her; the King used to look at her as if he couldn't believe anybody could be so much fun.'

It took a bold young quasi-foreigner with considerably less reverence for British royalty to stir the emotions of young Lilibet. By the end of 1944, speculation about a romance between Elizabeth and Philip had begun to appear in the press and the Princess found herself the target of a new kind of public attention. When she visited a factory outside London the factory girls shouted 'Where's Philip?' Elizabeth was shaken. When she told the story to her governess later, she was still distressed. 'Oh, Crawfie, it was horrible,' she said. For the first time, she realized the extent to which her feelings for Philip were public property – the extent to which she was public property. She began to dread visits to factories and shops, and any exposure to the public which could so easily puncture her fragile composure. 'The heart of a princess is shy and as easily hurt as any other girl's heart,' Marion Crawford noted. The incident also brought home the sheer vulnerability of her position. Her love for Philip was public knowledge: but he had not yet made known his feelings to her? How could she be sure he felt the same way about her? And what if he did not? But the girls calling for Philip also introduced the unwelcome notion that other girls might find him attractive. Already, she was – in a sense – having to share him with Margaret, for he squired both sisters to dances. Though Margaret was a sixteen-year-old schoolgirl, she went about with as much freedom as her almost twenty-one-year-old sister. The King and Queen, observed Marion Crawford, 'did not find it easy to forbid their younger daughter to do what she wanted.'

V

Marriage and Motherhood

For his daughter's eighteenth birthday, the King invited the cast of a popular wartime BBC radio comedy show called *ITMA* to give a performance at Windsor Castle. ITMA stood for 'It's That Man Again', and the man in question was its star, radio comedian Tommy Handley. *ITMA* was the royal family's favourite radio show. They listened to it religiously every Wednesday evening. The King enjoyed inviting comedians to give 'Royal Command Performances' at Windsor Castle, and would afterwards swap funny stories with them – the bawdier the better. He enjoyed telling jokes himself, and did it well, as did his daughters – especially Margaret.

There was also an outsize birthday card signed by all her former fellow Sea Rangers. For the princesses had outgrown girl-scouting, and the Windsor Company had been disbanded. When, later, the Girl Guides' most distinguished member succeeded to the throne, the organization went to considerable lengths to retrieve all the records and correspondence connected with the First Buckingham Palace (later Windsor Castle) Company. Letters were written to successive organizers who had been connected with the group in its seven years existence, and to some former Guides, requesting that any patrol log-books, documents, and any correspondence by the princesses which happened to be in their possession be handed over to the Chief Guide. The bulk of the material was put in the Guides' archives at their headquarters across the street from the Royal Mews at Buckingham Palace. However, some letters from Elizabeth and from Margaret were immediately placed under lock and key in the Chief Guide's office.

Among the guests at the Princess's eighteenth birthday party was the usual complement of young officers. But there was also a Royal Air Force Battle of Britain hero, somewhat older than the rest, who had recently been appointed equerry to King George. He found Elizabeth 'shy, occasionally to the point of gauchness, and this tended to hide her charm. When it shows through it is with a touching, spontaneous sincerity.' Like the King, Elizabeth had no small talk, which could lead to awkward pauses. At the same time, her fourteen-year-old sister seemed to him 'unremarkable – except when she came out with some devastating wisecrack; then, to her unconcealed delight, all eyes were upon her.'

The equerry was Group Captain Peter Townsend, a distinguished member of 'The Few', the fighter pilots who had borne the brunt in the aerial defence of London. He had flown over five hundred missions, and had been shot down twice, once in the English Channel from which he had been fished out by a trawler. By the time he gave up counting in the Battle of Britain, he had personally shot down eleven enemy aircraft. He had been assigned to Buckingham Palace on temporary duty as aide to the King because George VI wanted first to honour the service which had saved the nation, and then to make a modest dent in the preponderance of aristocratic Guards officers on his staff. Not that Townsend, thirty-one years old and with lean, intense good looks, was exactly a son of the people. His father had been a senior colonial official; he himself had been educated at a public school – though a minor one – and, by coincidence, his uncle happened to be the intellectual Labour politician, Hugh Gaitskell, who became leader of the party in the 1950s. But so close was the magic circle, that the appointment of this middle-class air force officer was a breakthrough. George VI's experiment in democracy got off to a promising start: Townsend quickly gained the King's confidence and his initial three-month appointment became a permanent position lasting nearly ten years. It was then that the choice backfired: Townsend – by then a divorced man – and Princess Margaret fell impossibly in love.

There was, of course, little thought of this when Townsend met the King for the first time in the summer of 1943. Joey Legh – known to his friends as Babe – had warned him in advance, 'When you go in to see the King he might become agitated and start shouting at you. The only thing to do is to keep calm until it blows over.' At the time, of course, the King's gnashes were a Palace secret unknown to the general public, but the secret was soon revealed to Townsend in its full, intimidating force. For when the King was angry, his prominent blue eyes would take on an alarming glare and he would rant loudly with complete disregard for his surroundings. In due course, Townsend developed a knack for coping with these spectacular outbursts, partly because of his deep affection for the monarch. The most skilful at calming him down, however, remained the Queen. She would talk to her husband in a soft, soothing voice as if she were quieting a frightened horse. On one occasion, as the King raged at a helpless member of his staff, she held his pulse in her fingers and, with a smile, began to count – tick, tick, tick. King George began to laugh, and his mood immediately changed.

Queen Elizabeth rarely lost her temper – and never in public. She had managed the feat of establishing her own strong personality without seeming to appear in competition with her husband. Though wartime Britain saw the King and Queen as a team her public image was quite separate from the monarch's. Her smile and charm seemed inexhaustible. Her exotic pastel-coloured dresses, her feathers and fox furs, appeared to have come out of an early Thirties time capsule rather than a wardrobe. But her obvious disregard for shifting fashions added to her popularity. Her unchanging style made her seem somehow more dependable: people always knew what to expect. In a very real sense, she saw herself as the King's partner, but she never overtly interfered in matters of state. Courtiers who knew that she was capable of holding strong views were rarely able to determine the extent of her influence on the King's thinking on a particular issue, but had no doubt that such influence was there. According to one royal biographer, Tommy Lascelles, who by the time Princess Elizabeth was eighteen had succeeded Alec Hardinge as Private Secretary, 'found her a rival and sometimes obstructive influence in all that touched the Sovereign.'

It was especially the Queen who continued to have doubts about the growing romance between Elizabeth and Philip of Greece. In August 1944, Mountbatten approached the King and Queen again on the subject. Their reaction can only be interpreted as playing for time. They agreed that Mountbatten should fly to Cairo to seek King George of Greece's approval that Philip should become a British subject. This step was, after all, important for the young Prince's service career. However, Mountbatten was not authorized to discuss a possible marriage. 'I am sure this is the best way of doing this particular operation, don't [sic] you?'

the King wrote to his cousin, 'though I know you like to get things settled at once, once you have an idea in mind.' In Cairo, Mountbatten went for a walk around the British embassy garden with his nephew. 'Philip entirely understood that the proposal [regarding his citizenship] was not connected with any question of marrying Lilibet,' Mountbatten reported to Philip's mother, his sister, Princess Alice, on 28 August, ' . . . though there is no doubt that he would very much like to one of these days.'

Then Mountbatten went for another stroll in the garden, this time with the King of Greece, who was living in Egypt as a refugee from his German-occupied country. Mountbatten told the monarch that with the death of the Duke of Kent in an air crash in 1942, King George VI and the Duke of Gloucester were the only two surviving males in the British royal family, and if Philip would accept British nationality, he would be an additional asset to the British royals and a great help to them in carrying out their royal functions. The Greek royals were not taken in by this explanation. They were fully aware, as Crown Princess Frederika (wife of King George's brother Crown Prince Paul) told the British ambassador, that what was really behind it was the possibility of a marriage to Princess Elizabeth. But Philip's family may also have realized that, in view of the British royal family's evident lack of enthusiasm, their best course was patience, letting love take its course. 'The best hopes are to let it happen – if it will – without parents interfering,' Mountbatten wrote to Princess Alice. 'The young people appear genuinely devoted and I think after the war it is very likely to occur.'

Meanwhile, the young people themselves continued to see each other whenever possible. In the autumn of 1944, Philip was invited to Balmoral. His wardrobe was so meagre that he had to be lent a pair of plus fours to wear for stalking. Despite the frequent house parties, the King and Queen tried hard to create an informal family atmosphere at their Scottish home. The 'astonishing affection' in the family was very evident, according to Peter Townsend, 'perpetual currents of it flowed between father and mother, sister and sister, between parents and daughters and back again.' In the hall of the great house stood a large, green baize-topped table and on it was always a large jigsaw puzzle. Anyone could try his hand, but the real addicts were the King and Princess Elizabeth. At dinner, the protocol was to converse with one neighbour for half the meal, and then turn to the other, following the Queen's cue. Afterwards, there were cards or parlour games, notably 'The

Game', a form of charades in which one team thinks of a phrase or expression which a member of the opposing side must then act out for his or her teammates. Newcomers were always surprised at the enthusiasm and almost adolescent sense of fun with which the Queen took part in the proceedings.

When Elizabeth turned eighteen, the Cabinet asked the King to consider nominating her Princess of Wales. The title Prince of Wales, of course, is traditionally conferred on the male heir to the throne. It proved a popular idea, particularly in Wales, but the King rejected it. 'How could I create Lilibet Princess of Wales,' he wrote, 'when it is the recognized title of the wife of the Prince of Wales? Her own name is so nice, and what name would she be called by when she marries, I want to know.' The King seemed unprepared, or unable, to accept that Elizabeth could be Princess of Wales in her own right. In his view, the title of Princess of Wales belonged exclusively to the wife of the Prince of Wales, a somewhat narrow argument, and one that did not seem to have been properly thought through. It was as if the King had not in his own mind completely ruled out the possibility of having a male heir and did not want to pre-empt the title. In the autumn of 1943, he had amended the Regency Act of 1937 so that Elizabeth would come of age at eighteen instead of attaining her majority at twenty-one. She was then eligible to become a member of the Council of State. Composed of senior members of the royal family the Council takes over the monarch's responsibilities when the latter is out of the country, or is incapacitated. The purpose of the change, the King explained to the Cabinet at the time, was to give the Princess 'every opportunity of gaining experience in the duties which should fall upon her in the event of her acceding to the Throne.'

In the event? True, if the Queen had given birth to a son, the infant prince would have taken Elizabeth's place in the line of succession. But it was a highly improbable 'if'. King George was then forty-nine; the Queen was forty-four and had long ago been advised not to have any more children. Clearly, the King – or his advisers – were being extra cautious.

The King also informed the Cabinet that Elizabeth would not be going to college, nor would she be serving in any of the woman's armed forces. Although she would ordinarily have been drafted at eighteen, the King argued that she was too busy preparing for her future responsibilities. But he had reckoned without his daughter's single-minded pursuit of her objective. Elizabeth yearned to join the service. She wanted to be part of the war effort, to be part of the action as millions of Britons were. As Philip was. And she wanted to get out of the Palace. So she argued and cajoled until the King finally agreed to allow her to join the Auxiliary Territorial Service, the women's unit of the British army, known as the ATS. Her own first choice was the Royal Navy, but that was not practical in the context of the kind of service envisioned by her parents. Moreover, her Aunt Mary, the Princess Royal, was Colonel-in-Chief of the ATS, which guaranteed that – as with the Girl Guides – a controlled environment could be created for the Princess, leaving out some of the less agreeable aspects of military life.

Princess Elizabeth's stint in the Army had parallels with the war-time service careers of many Hollywood movie stars. It boosted the morale of the American public to see photographs of its screen heroes in uniform. What the public was not told was that the Roosevelt administration generally assigned the stars – with a couple of exceptions – to soft jobs at nearby bases so that they could continue to go to the studios to make films. The story behind the photographs of Princess Elizabeth in her uniform also represented something of a gap between image and reality. To the British public, she had joined the ATS and was learning how to be a mechanic at the ATS depot at Camberley, working on a utility vehicle and a fifteen-hundredweight truck, jacked up, its chassis stripped to the bare bones. She was seen to be 'doing her bit', and that was important.

There was, of course, no mention in the media of the fact that the King and Queen had insisted upon, and Churchill's war cabinet had approved, conditions prior to her enlistment. Letters flew back and forth to Buckingham Palace covering every detail. One memorandum from the ATS confirmed that, yes, the Princess would learn to drive the heavy truck, and would get her hands dirty. By prior agreement with the Queen, Princess Elizabeth, who was an officer-cadet, was excused the requisite ten-week 'recruits' course' – in other words, boot camp – because according to the Deputy Director of the ATS, Mary Baxter Ellis, 'it would be rather a waste of time, as HRH has a brain already trained to learn.' Elizabeth was also spared the experience of sharing a sleeping hut with a cross-section of Britain's younger womanhood. Instead, the Princess drove home under escort to Windsor every night, and slept in her own bed. She did not have to eat powdered scrambled egg slopped from a bucket but had her meals in the officers' mess. (For the Princess there was always a small jug of condensed milk

– a treat nobody else got.) And when she enlisted her hair was not checked for lice.

She eventually reported for duty at No. 1 Mechanical Transport Training, Camberley, a month short of her nineteenth birthday on 23 March 1945, after a bout of mumps, and became 230873 Windsor, Elizabeth Alexandra Mary. Taking the driving and maintenance course with her were eleven specially picked girls of the 'right sort', all sergeants and corporals who were already instructors but who had to pretend that – like the Princess – they were hearing it all for the first time. The deception was carried further. The 'students' were instructed to ask questions. Years later, Pat Hayes, one of the eleven who had been a sergeant, recalled, 'You felt a bit silly asking about [spark] plugs when you had been telling students these things for a couple of years.' Nevertheless, the eleven girls followed orders.

Subsequent accounts of the experience by some of her colleagues have always been friendly and good-natured. Yet Elizabeth emerges as polite but distant; not stand-offish but awkward in the unfamiliar company. They were in their early twenties, and therefore a few years older, but if anything the age gap seemed reversed. 'Would you like some coffee, Ma'am?' – 'How kind.' During coffee break they would ask each other about weekend plans. Elizabeth would say things like, 'Oh, King Olaf is coming to stay [at Windsor] and it's going to be boring because he wants to watch a football match.' She queued dutifully with the rest for candy ration coupons and was always delighted with her weekly two-ounce chocolate bar – hardly enough to assuage her lifelong sweet tooth. She worked diligently at her course and talked about it constantly at Windsor Castle. 'We've had sparking plugs throughout dinner every night this week,' the Queen told senior ATS officers on 9 April when the royal family descended on Camberley to watch the Princess in dungarees up to her elbows in engine grease. The King seemed amused. 'What are you doing, or don't you know?' he asked her. To the girls on Elizabeth's course, Princess Margaret looked bored. But then, they had privately decided that Margaret was a 'jealous, tiresome little girl, always needling her older sister.'

On 16 April 1945, Elizabeth finished the course as Second Subaltern Windsor and said goodbye to her fellow students. Years later she would meet Pat Hayes again and enquire wistfully, 'Do you ever see any of the others?' By 8 May the Princess's military career vanished in the general explosion of public joy and relief at the end of the war in Europe. A huge crowd assembled outside Buckingham Palace. Throughout the day, in response to continuous cheering, the royal family appeared on the balcony almost every hour – sometimes the King and Queen alone, sometimes together with the princesses – the whole family – and once with Winston Churchill who was greeted by the crowd with the singing of 'For He's a Jolly Good Fellow'. In the evening, the Queen put on her tiara, which she had not worn in public since the outbreak of the war. The princesses pleaded with the King and Queen to let them go out into the street. The Queen was dubious, but the King agreed on condition that the princesses avoided Piccadilly Circus, epicentre of London's euphoria.

They ventured out in a large group including Crawfie, their French teacher Antoinette de Ballaigue (who was actually Belgian), Peter Townsend and several other officers. They behaved like two birds let out of a cage, running along the Mall in the almost forgotten luxury of streetlights and floodlit buildings with Crawfie and the rest puffing to catch up. 'We cheered the King and Queen on the balcony and then walked miles through the streets,' Princess Elizabeth would recall forty years later. She wore her ATS uniform, and because she was 'terrified of being recognized, I pulled my uniform cap well down over my eyes.' But an officer in the group said he would not walk with her if she persisted in being improperly dressed. The one time they were conscious of having been recognized was when a Dutch sailor linked arms with the end of their line. Glancing towards the centre, where the princesses had carefully been placed, he recognized first one and then the other and backed away in amazement. 'I remember lines of unknown people linking arms and walking down Whitehall,' Elizabeth remembered, 'and all of us were swept along by tides of happiness and relief.'

To her surprise she saw a cousin, who had been a prisoner of war for four years, walking with his family. After crossing Green Park the princesses and their group stood outside Buckingham Palace chanting 'We want the King' along with the crowd, and cheering when their parents came out on to the balcony. 'But we cheated slightly as we had sent a message inside the house that we were waiting outside.' They got back into the Palace by a garden gate to find the Queen anxiously waiting for them. 'I think,' the Princess remembered, 'it was one of the most memorable nights of my life.'

It was another memory stored to tell Philip when they met on his next leave. But they were soon to have more serious things to discuss. A quarter of a century later, Prince Philip himself hinted to his biographer Basil Boothroyd that he proposed to Elizabeth in 1946: 'I suppose I began to think about it seriously . . . when I got back in forty-six and went to Balmoral. It was probably then that . . . we began to think about it seriously, and even talk about it . . . ' Mountbatten and the Greek royals continued to meddle, especially the former who, despite his earlier advice about 'letting [the marriage] happen without parents' interference,' kept up such a flow of advice on how to conduct the romance that Philip pleaded for a pause in the bombardment. 'Please, I beg of you, not too much advice in an affair of the heart, or I shall be forced to do the wooing by proxy.'

Besides the advice, Mountbatten also sent Philip books to broaden his political education. He sent him Bernard Shaw's *Intelligent Woman's Guide to Socialism and Capitalism*. Philip found it long on opinion and theory, short on solid information. 'Don't forget you are attempting to educate me politically for a certain job, and a little knowledge is a dangerous thing, if not worse than none at all,' Philip wrote to his uncle in 1945. 'There is still another aspect and that is that for this particular job it is not only necessary to know reasonably intimately the two opposing creeds but every other credo that may be attempted in the future.'

Prince Philip's remarks to Mountbatten suggest that he had a clear expectation of what his 'job' as husband of the Queen of England would be – an expectation that ultimately seems to have proved higher than was the case. There is also a note of confidence that the 'job' would be his. Yet the King and Queen still needed to be fully persuaded that Philip was the right choice. The royal family was scanning the field of available royal bachelors for possible alternatives. Passing through Cairo after visiting London, Lord Linlithgow, the Viceroy of India, told the British ambassador that there was talk of 'possible consorts from the royal houses of either Norway or Sweden,' but Prince Charles of Belgium, younger brother of King Leopold, was also being mentioned.

Though he was growing to like Philip, the King found it hard to accept that Elizabeth had fallen in love with the first man she met. As Queen Mary explained to Lady Airlie, 'They have been in love for the last eighteen months . . . but the King and Queen felt that she is too young to be engaged yet. They want her to see more of the world before committing herself, and to meet more men. After all, she's only nineteen, and one is very impressionable at that age.' When Lady Airlie pointed out that she herself had fallen in love at nineteen and it had lasted for ever, Queen Mary replied, 'Yes it does happen sometimes and Elizabeth seems to be that kind of girl. She would always know her own mind. There's something very steadfast and determined in her – like her father.'

Elizabeth had long since committed herself. By temperament she was unaggressive, unselfish, and – as Lady Airlie observed – 'always ready to give way in any of the small issues that arise in every home,' especially, no doubt, when it came to her spoiled, high-spirited younger sister. But she was not submissive: there was a hard core of determination, even toughness, when it came to fighting for what she really wanted. And what she wanted was to marry Prince Philip. She now had her own separate 'nucleus' within the royal household, with two ladies-in-waiting, her own footman and housemaid, and her own suite of rooms, and was referred to in Palace circles by a new set of initials. The Palace has always loved to use initials, so Elizabeth was HRH, while her sister was (and always remained) PM. Elizabeth had also gone public, with her programme of social and official engagements, which was widening her experience, but also bringing home to her the drawbacks of her sheltered upbringing and narrow-based education.

Elizabeth had the intelligence to be fully aware of the problem. An earlier biography quotes her as confiding to a friend, 'Believe it or not, I lie in my bath before dinner and think, Oh, who am I going to sit by and what are they going to talk about? I'm absolutely terrified of sitting next to people in case they talk about things I have never heard of.' She came alive if they talked about horses, dogs, stalking, history, her relations, or the Guards. The challenge – and to some extent, perhaps, the shock – of this sudden exposure to the broad canvas of human activity made her seem more serious than she actually was, and even boring – which she wasn't at all. Her clothes – chosen by her mother – emphasized the staid side of her character when a touch of liveliness would have been more helpful. The total effect was to give the impression that Princess Elizabeth had jumped from childhood to mature womanhood without going through the intervening stage of adolescence, an impression heightened by her virtual disappearance from public view for the duration of the war. In those difficult early days of her 'public' career she needed the support and encouragement of a worldly, mercurial personality who could show her the light side of life. She needed Philip.

The object of her interest was now serving in Australia, where stories of his romance with Princess Elizabeth had made him a reluctant celebrity. In Australia he teamed up with Lieutenant Michael Parker, a former shipmate who was later to become his private secretary. Parker, an Australian, was 'adept at organizing parties', and there were stories about 'the men's torrid associations and the various heiresses . . . who were out to seduce Philip.' As his cousin Queen Alexandra of Yugoslavia commented, 'Women flung themselves aggressively at Philip.' Had he had a more self-effacing personality he might have escaped gossip. As neither was the case, he was an easy target for stories some of which, inevitably, reached London.

When Philip was in London his visits to Buckingham Palace had become a matter of course. According to Marion Crawford, he would have dinner in the nursery with Elizabeth and Margaret, and then they would expend their youthful energy playing games in the corridors. They would play ball – and a good many electric lights suffered. Occasionally, Crawfie would draw Margaret away on some pretext so that Lilibet and Philip could be alone. 'I felt that the constant presence of the little sister, who . . . liked to have a good bit of attention herself, was not helping on the romance much,' Crawfie recalled.

In the autumn of 1946, Philip spent a month at Balmoral with the family and their other houseguests. The young couple went out with the guns and picnicked together, but – except for the occasional drive or walk in the grounds – they were seldom alone. The royal social programme at Balmoral provided very little private time for either of them. A question hung over Philip's continued presence. Protocol required that the Princess should be the one to propose. However, as he has hinted himself, it was about this time that he made his feelings known to the Princess. The next hurdle was to gain her parents' approval. When Philip saw the King in his study and asked for permission to talk to Princess Elizabeth about marriage, King George advised him to wait, pointing out that Lilibet had just turned twenty. But the couple had already expressed their feelings for each other, and neither Lilibet nor Philip were inclined to wait. So Philip returned to the King's study for a second meeting. According to Queen Alexandra, King George insisted 'there were still too many difficulties.'

The King was not enthusiastic about an engagement. For him, it represented the end of what one British general, seeing them together, once described as a 'thoroughly close knit and happy family all wrapped up in each other.' Some of his advisers, among them Tommy Lascelles, did not conceal their opposition. In a conversation with Crawfie, Princess Margaret mentioned one of Philip's perceived drawbacks. 'Crawfie, do you like Philip?' she asked one day. 'Very much,' replied the governess, who had changed her initial view of Elizabeth's hero. Margaret pointed out, 'But he's not English. Would it make a difference?'

Margaret was voicing a Palace concern over public reaction to the heir to the throne marrying a foreigner – and one with troops of German relations. Aside from the German/Danish origins of the Greek royal family, Philip's four older sisters had all married wealthy Germans in the early 1930s. One sister, Cecile, had been killed in a plane crash with her husband and children prior to the war. But of the surviving three, Margarita, the oldest, was married to Gottfried, Prince Hohenlohe-Langenburg, an officer in the German army; Sophie's husband, Prince Christopher of Hesse, had been a dedicated Nazi who worked for the Gestapo and a Luftwaffe pilot who was shot down over Italy; and Theodora was the wife of the Margrave of Baden. Crawfie argued that Philip had lived in England all his life – 'He's as English as you or I, really.' Margaret pondered this information. Then she said, 'Poor Lil. Nothing of your own. Not even your love affair!'

Faced with Elizabeth's desire to marry Philip, Crawfie said, 'Neither the King nor the Queen could make up their minds what was best for their very dear daughter, and so postponed decision. They wanted the best for her, and it is never easy for parents . . . to decide what that best is.' Besides, the timing of this unsettling news could not have been worse, for it threatened to disrupt the royal family's planned two-month tour of South Africa early the following year. At first, the King, with the Queen's backing, would not hear of an engagement until after the family returned in April. The tour was the most ambitious ever undertaken by Britain's royals. It was long, politically and racially complex, and covered a vast area. The King needed his daughter with him, and he needed her undivided attention.

But Elizabeth stood her ground. She wanted the security of an engagement, and – according to one reliable diplomatic report at the time – threatened to put love before duty if her father continued to withhold his approval. In a dispatch to the Secretary of State – written when the engagement was eventually announced – the United States embassy in London reported that 'Some six months ago, it was learned that Princess Elizabeth had determined to marry [Prince Philip] and declared that if objections were raised she would not hesitate to follow the example of her uncle, King

Edward VIII, and abdicate. She has a firm character.' Presumably, what the American report meant to convey was that Elizabeth warned her father she would renounce her claim to the throne rather than give up the man she loved. It seems out of character for Elizabeth, with her strong sense of duty, to have contemplated marrying against her father's will, and still less to have issued such an ultimatum – except perhaps in the heat of a family argument. But the American envoy to London, Lewis Douglas, was on friendly terms with the royal family and regarded as very well informed. His daughter Sharman was to remain a close friend of the princesses, especially Princess Margaret. At the very least, US Embassy Dispatch number 1649 reflects Princess Elizabeth's determination, and the tension within the family over the issue of her love for Philip of Greece.

In the end, according to Elizabeth of Yugoslavia, 'the idea of an engagement was tacitly accepted', but it would not be announced until the royal family's return from South Africa. At the same time, Prince Philip's naturalization received approval, but there was a question of what he would call himself. As a British citizen he was expected to renounce his Greek title and any claim to the Greek throne, a step which effectively rendered him nameless. His Uncle Dickie, who was in the forefront of the discussions, pressed the King to agree that Philip would be granted the title of His Royal Highness, and that he would be called HRH Prince Philip of Great Britain. The King was willing to agree to grant his daughter's future husband the right and privilege of the title HRH, once the wedding was due to take place, but drew the line at Prince Philip of Great Britain. Philip himself cut into the three-way wrangle between the King, the Prime Minister and Mountbatten with the announcement that he would be known as plain Lieutenant Philip —— RN. The question was Philip what? Part of the problem was that the Greek royal family had no family name other than their original Danish one of Schleswig-Holstein-Sonderburg-Glucksburg, which had sprung from the Oldenburg family. Hence the suggestion was made that he should take the name of Oldcastle, the English rendition of Oldenburg. Nobody was happy with Philip Oldcastle, and in the end the Home Secretary, James Chuter Ede, resolved the dilemma by suggesting that Philip should take the name of his mother – hence Philip Mountbatten.

Elizabeth had to be content with the family compromise, even if she sometimes found it hard to stick to her commitment to keep the engagement secret, and would drop broad hints. Two days before the royal family's departure, Queen Mary's household presented the Princess with her twenty-first birthday gift of a silver inkstand. The Countess of Airlie led the delegation, one from each grade of staff – the head housemaid, the head footman, the head porter and the head kitchenmaid. The Princess told the group it was going to be sad to be away from England on her birthday. Then, cheering up, she said, 'But when I come back we shall have a celebration – perhaps two celebrations.' Lady Airlie guessed that the second would be her engagement. This prospect had helped Elizabeth to rationalize the coming weeks of separation, but she did not look forward to the experience. 'It is absolutely staggering how much they expect us to do and go on doing for so long at a stretch,' was her comment on the daunting programme. 'Well, I hope we shall survive, that's all.'

It was indeed a formidable itinerary, put together with American and Canadian help. Having had no previous experience with royal visits, the South African government realized their ignorance when it came to protocol, precedence, and the type of functions suitable for such occasions, and in 1946 turned for help to the United States. What Pretoria wanted was anything they could glean on the 1939 royal visit to America and Canada. '[The South Africans] themselves,' the American ambassador in South Africa reported to Washington, 'do not wish to ask the Canadians advice in this matter . . . I do not see why, but it may be easier on their pride to ask our advice.' There was some irony in this because both the King and Queen saw the tour as a landmark in the postwar evolution of a strong, democratized British Commonwealth, with, as one of its aims, the capacity to challenge growing United States influence in the world.

The royal family sailed from Britain on 1 February 1947, on board the battleship HMS *Vanguard*, the Royal Navy's most modern ship, launched by Princess Elizabeth in 1944. They left a country in the grip of the century's worst winter exacerbated by a severe fuel shortage. There was snow on the ground at Portsmouth. Storms and rough seas marred the first half of their two-week passage. But once the *Vanguard* entered calmer waters, everyone was able to relax, and bone up on South African history and the country's increasingly complex political situation. Writing to her former governess from the *Vanguard*, Elizabeth commented on the handsome officers – 'There are one or two real smashers' – and voiced her guilt at having a good time while Britain suffered. 'Sometimes we feel (I say we but I really mean I) rather guilty to be right away from it all and . . . enjoying ourselves so much.' Elizabeth told Peter Townsend that the family was apprehensive about the strong republican feeling among the nationalist Afrikaners, political opponents of Field Marshal Jan Smuts, the pro-British prime minister. The nationalists were expected to give the royal visitors a cool reception, and perhaps even boycott their tour altogether.

The *Vanguard* sailed into Table Bay on 17 February, and on 21 February the royal family left Cape Town in a new gold and ivory train a third of a mile long, on which they spent thirty-five nights, crossing four provinces of the Union of South Africa itself, the High Commission Territories (Basutoland, Swaziland and Bechuanaland) and Southern Rhodesia. It was called the *White Train* and as it sped across 'the great empty spaces of the *veldt*' groups of people were often seen beside dusty horses on which they had ridden for miles to see it. Each member of the royal family had their own bedroom and bath. The King had a study and the family shared a dining room which doubled as a cinema.

The American embassy, which kept a discreet watch on the visitors, reported later that only in Durban could the welcome be called tumultuous, 'in keeping with that city's reputation as one of the last citadels of Imperialist feeling of the late Nineteenth Century variety.' Elsewhere, English-speaking crowds were 'stirringly cordial', and the Afrikaans population 'friendly but restrained'. The Afrikaans press was 'coldly restrained', with some leading papers hardly mentioning the tour at all.

The black population also welcomed the royal family. The blacks 'noted that the royals represented something even more powerful than the Union Government, as symbolized by Smuts,' the American embassy told Washington in its classified report on the tour. 'They took in the obsequious deference to the royal family by Smuts and other officials. They noted that the King and Queen went out of their way to go over to groups of blacks in the segregated crowd and speak to them. The "native telegraph" worked wonderfully well. Stories of the good impression made by the King and Queen on the Basuto nation reached Zululand almost in a flash, with the result that the Zulu nation was in a mood to welcome the Royal Couple.'

The combined pressure of the action-packed programme and the intense heat tested the royal family's endurance, especially that of King George who, as well as his other problems, suffered from crowd claustrophobia. Pushed beyond endurance, he would occasionally explode. Touring the mining towns of the Rand on an extremely hot day, the King and Queen's open Daimler was choked by hundreds of thousands of black miners and their families. The King became increasingly edgy and began to fire instructions at the driver, unsettling him in already difficult conditions. The Queen tried unsuccessfully to soothe her husband, and the atmosphere in the car was so tense that Peter Townsend – who sat beside the driver – turned round and shouted at the King, 'For Heaven's sake shut up or there's going to be an accident.' The princesses did their share in stopping these embarrassing scenes. At a state dinner in Pretoria, which was directly broadcast to Britain, the radio microphone had been left on after Smuts had spoken, in anticipation of King George's speech. When the King did not get up to speak, Smuts said, 'You are to follow me now, Sir.' The King replied, 'I'll speak when I've had my coffee and the waiters have left the room.' But Smuts told him, 'They're waiting for you now in England, Sir.' The King said firmly, 'Well, let them wait. I have said I will speak when the waiters have left the room.' Princess Elizabeth, realizing that the microphone was open, asked quietly, 'Can't we be heard?' So the King, heeding the warning, delivered his speech. When he sat down again, the microphone was still on. 'Well,' he said, 'I suppose *now* I may have my coffee.'

The two princesses trailed behind their parents and often looked as bored as they felt. Distractions were rare, but there was one the princesses seldom missed. At most stops, horses were waiting for those who felt like riding in the early morning before breakfast, and the princesses came to look forward to speeding along the sands or the *veldt*. The family were also capable of privately finding an amusing side to the seemingly endless succession of speeches, visits and ceremonial. Fortunately, they had also developed a knack for controlling their laughter in public and could remain outwardly straight-faced but at the same time be convulsed inside. There was one occasion on the tour when the royal family sat on a vast open dais overshadowed by trees. As George VI spoke, a slight breeze dislodged large berries from the trees, which bounced off the King's flat navy hat and on to the ground. According to Townsend, the Queen never once lost her customary encouraging smile at her husband, but he could hear her gurgling quietly with suppressed laughter, and Princess Elizabeth began to scowl, her habitual expression when she does not want to laugh, or to show emotion in public.

On 20 April, the royal family returned to Cape Town, and the following day Princess Elizabeth made a twenty-first birthday broadcast in which she publicly dedicated herself to the service of the British Commonwealth of Nations and asked the peoples of the Commonwealth for their help in carrying out her pledge. The speech was written on the trip by Dermot Morrah, a London journalist covering the tour, and altered by the King. 'All my whole life, whether it be long or short, shall be devoted to your service and the service of the great Imperial Commonwealth to which we all belong,' the Princess declared. 'But I shall not have the strength to carry out this resolution unless you join in it with me, as I now ask you to do.'

It was a clever broadcast, in fact a landmark in the evolution of the Crown's relationship with the emerging British Commonwealth. It was apparent the King had recognized the progressive decentralization of authority – in other words, the decline in London's control – and the importance of adapting the monarchy to the changes. In the old Empire, the monarch was at the apex of the British imperial power structure: in the new Commonwealth, the future monarch is at the service of all people. The Crown was establishing direct links with individual nations – not as an English institution, but as a Commonwealth one. In this context, the Princess's phrase 'Imperial Commonwealth' was almost a contradiction in terms. The writers of the speech were trying to convey the impression that the old Empire lived on in the new. It didn't. The war had put paid to it.

Elizabeth was deeply in love and the longing she felt to be near Philip had made her unusually moody throughout the trip. She wrote to him daily, the letters speeding to London by diplomatic pouch. Philip's eagerly awaited replies reached her less regularly because the mail had to catch up with the speeding *White Train*, and the delays caused her great anxiety. But as the end of the tour came in sight, her mood began to lighten. Her birthday was literally a sparkling day. At a reception in her honour that evening, Smuts presented her with South Africa's birthday gift in a silver box. When she opened it, twenty-one superb diamonds of different sizes up to ten carats glittered in the light. On her return to London she had the stones made into a long necklace, with a six-carat blue diamond given to her by the South African mining corporation De Beers as the centre stone. She called the necklace her 'best diamonds'. Her gift from the King and Queen was a pair of ivy-leaf diamond brooches with a round brilliant in the centre. The Grenadier Guards sent her the regimental badge set in diamonds. And from Philip she received a heavy parcel which contained a small jewelled Bible.

'Today,' said the King as the royal family left for home on 24 April, 'the curtain is being rung down on a visit that is almost unique in the history of the British Commonwealth but which I hope will be less unusual in the future.' The tour was setting a pattern of royal tours, so that the Crown could be a living reality to the people of the great Commonwealth family.

On 9 June, a brief statement from Buckingham Palace finally broke the news of Princess Elizabeth's engagement to Lieutenant Philip Mountbatten RN. 'They both came to see me after luncheon,' wrote Queen Mary, 'looking radiant'. Seeing Elizabeth, the Countess of Airlie was reminded of Queen Victoria. This was meant as the highest compliment. 'Although the Queen had been old, plain and fat when I had seen her and this girl was young, pretty and slim she had the same air of majesty,' declared Lady Airlie. The King created Philip Duke of Edinburgh – one of the family titles: the last holder had been Queen Victoria's son Alfred – and at a lunch given in the couple's honour by the Duchess of Kent following the announcement, Elizabeth told guests she insisted on using the same title as her husband, until she succeeded to the throne. However, Princess Elizabeth was not referred to as Duchess of Edinburgh.

The couple were at last able to appear in public together, and London was eager to fête them. In October they dined with the American ambassador, Lewis Douglas, and afterwards played 'The Game', with Philip leading one team and his fiancée, the other. Philip gave Elizabeth 'The Rape of Lucrece' to mime for her team, but she got out of it by acting out an ape and signalling a rhyming word. While 'The Game' was in full swing, Danny Kaye arrived. 'To say the least he livened things up,' an American guest at the dinner said. 'The next thing we knew we were playing Pass the Orange, and I was necking with Princess Margaret, who was also invited.' At the end of the evening, the ambassador produced the guest book to sign. The Princess signed 'Elizabeth' with a flourish, her fiancé wrote 'Philip' and her sister wrote 'Margaret'. The book was passed to Danny Kaye, who, according to the American guest, 'with an elaborate comical gesture signed 'Danny' in flowing letters. The gesture was greeted with an icy silence.' On her finger, the Princess now wore a solitaire diamond engagement ring with five smaller stones set in each shoulder. The diamonds had come from a tiara given to Princess Andrew by her husband, Philip's father, and broken up to provide Elizabeth's impoverished fiancé, whose possessions fitted into one suitcase, with the engagement ring and a diamond bracelet that was to be his wedding gift to his bride.

Throughout the summer there had, of course, been preparations for the wedding. The King was advised against too much lavish display. Nearly three years after the end of the war, the British still lived a life of hardship and austerity more typical of a vanquished nation than of a victorious one. Rationing was still in force. There was a shortage of everything, including food, clothing and petrol. London still bore the scars of the conflict – the shells of burnt-out buildings, craters gouged in the ground where handsome houses had once stood. The Palace advisers feared that an expensive wedding would create a public backlash. To the chagrin of the Court – and the annoyance of the royal family – Lord Mountbatten took an active interest in the arrangements. He claimed credit for the engagement, and he was not going to be left on the periphery. In the end, an embarrassed nephew hinted gently to his uncle that he should not interfere. Philip warned him of the sensitiveness of the situation. 'I am not being rude, but it is apparent that you like the idea of being the General Manager of this little show,' he wrote, 'and I am rather afraid that she might not take to the idea as docilely as I do. It is true that I know what is good for me, but don't forget that she has not had you as Uncle *loco parentis*, counsellor and friend as long as I have.'

On 11 November, the King invested his daughter with the Order of the Garter, the country's highest order of knighthood – eight days prior to conferring it on her husband-to-be, 'so that she will be senior to Philip,' as he told Queen Mary. And on 18 November, a reception was held at St James's Palace to view the wedding presents, which included a tiara consisting of a wreath of diamond roses, with a matching necklace, from the Nizam of Hyderabad, and a tray cloth woven by himself from Mahatma Gandhi. Queen Mary's gifts to her favourite granddaughter included a large diamond brooch which had been Gangan Victoria's wedding gift to her, a diamond tiara, a ruby and diamond bracelet and a pair of diamond and pearl earrings. Another diamond tiara came from Elizabeth's future mother-in-law. The King gave her a sapphire and diamond necklace and a pair of shotguns made by Purdey, the world's leading quality gunsmiths; and the Queen a two-strand pearl necklace. Hundreds of tons of canned food of every variety were sent by British communities abroad. The food was turned into thousands of food parcels and distributed to needy widows and pensioners.

Another reception was held at Buckingham Palace, which after years of austerity seemed to one guest 'like a scene out of a fairy tale'. Recalled Lady Airlie, 'Most of us were sadly shabby – anyone fortunate enough to have a new dress drew all eyes – but all the famous diamonds came out again, even though most of them had not been cleaned since 1939.'

Princess Elizabeth, however, did have a new dress. Her wedding gown was made by Norman Hartnell of white satin embroidered with ten thousand small American pearls. The grey morning of 20 November 1947 began with Bobo MacDonald's arrival with the Princess's tea. Elizabeth looked out of her window at the gathering crowds just as she had done before her parents' coronation, and then went to see her mother and father. The streets had few decorations, and no public holiday had been declared. Yet as she drove to Westminster Abbey in the Irish state coach with her father, cheering crowds filled the pavements. The cross-section of guests in the Abbey included Noël Coward and Beatrice Lillie. But the biggest applause was for Winston Churchill, ousted as Prime Minister by the Labour Party in 1945. The whole congregation rose to honour him, and the ovation he received outside was second only to that accorded to the bride and the King.

In the front pews and around the altar was gathered a concourse of royalty regnant and exiled. The royal family is generous with its relatives on the grand occasions. When Elizabeth and Philip were married all the travelling, transport and hotel accommodation were paid by the King. The passengers on the Golden Arrow boat train from Paris on 18 November read like the *Almanach de Gotha*. Freddie and Uncle Palo (Queen Frederika and King Paul of Greece), Aunt Sitta and Aunt Tim (the Queen of Rumania and the Duchess of Aosta), and Aunt Ena of Spain. Also present were the King and Queen of Denmark, the King of Norway, Princess Juliana and Prince Bernhard. In the Abbey, Princess Andrew sat with the royal family. She had bowed to strong pressure from Buckingham Palace to abandon the nun's habit she always wore in favour of a floor-length grey dress and matching hat. Also present, but not on display, were Philip's three surviving sisters. The royal family had not invited any German relations, but an exception was made in their case at Philip's insistence. The sisters were there unofficially. Their presence was not announced by the Palace, and they had places among the guests, not the family. Notable absences included the Duke and Duchess of Windsor. Later on, the Windsors would take for granted their exclusion from family functions, but this was the first significant royal event since the coronation of George VI and the fact that they were not present excited press comment. The Duke was asked not to say that they had not been invited. 'I think the answer to the question "were you invited to the wedding" should be the plain truth "no" and then refuse to comment, don't you?' Wallis wrote to her aunt. ' . . . the Duke has been told he should avoid answering! Why should we go on protecting their rude attitude after ten and a half years?'

At the altar the King took Elizabeth's hand and placed it in Philip's. As he left his daughter's side to join the Queen, he stooped to help the pages, Michael of Kent and Richard of Gloucester, to arrange the train. In the service, Elizabeth had insisted on including the promise to obey her husband as well as love and honour him. Then, as the couple left the Abbey, with Philip leading Elizabeth by her left hand, they drew level with the King and Queen and Queen Mary. Elizabeth gently turned, and sank into a deep curtsy, the lovely satin folds of her dress billowing and spreading around her. When the couple appeared on the balcony of Buckingham Palace the crowd sang the popular song: 'Every Young Girl Loves a Sailor'.

By royal standards, the wedding breakfast was a relatively simple meal. But the wedding cake, with its little temple of love and garlanded pillars, was a small masterpiece, and the visiting royals were dazzled by the glittering Buckingham Palace gold plate. On the centre table was a link with the past. The sprigs of heather and myrtle, forming part of the table decorations, had been grown from the wedding bouquet of Queen Victoria. There was a sudden hush and the King stood up, champagne glass in hand. Instead of making a speech, he held up his glass, looked at Elizabeth, and said, 'The bride.' Queen Alexandra of Yugoslavia – the Cousin Sandra whom the young princesses had welcomed at Windsor – observed, 'I thought as we resumed our seats that he looked very wistful.'

Despite a light rain, the couple left for Waterloo Station to board the royal train in an open landau drawn by two grey horses. Warmed by four hot-water bottles and with her favourite corgi, Susan, on Elizabeth's knees, bride and groom set off across the Palace courtyard with the King and the wedding guests running behind throwing rose-petals. Close to the Palace gates, King George stopped and stood watching his daughter disappear into the gathering dusk. The couple spent the first part of their honeymoon at Broadlands, the Mountbattens' magnificent Elizabethan manor in Hampshire. Her father's sense of loss was evident in a letter he wrote to his newly married daughter: 'When I handed your hand to the Archbishop I felt that I had lost something very precious. You were so calm and composed during the Service & said your words with such conviction that I knew it was all right . . . Our family, us four, the "royal family" must remain together with additions of course at suitable moments!! I have watched you grow up all these years with pride under the skilful direction of Mummy, who as you know is the most marvellous person in the world in my eyes, & I can, I know, always count on you, & now Philip, to help us in our work.' Elizabeth, for her part, had written to the Queen in conciliatory tones – a further hint of the earlier family tensions. She now realized, she said, that the long wait before her engagement, and the further delay until the wedding had been for the best.

The couple moved into Clarence House, a few hundred yards from Buckingham Palace. Three months later, Chips Channon saw them at a fancy dress dance given in their honour by the Duchess of Kent. Elizabeth wore black lace with a large comb and mantilla and danced every dance until three in the morning despite unconfirmed reports of her pregnancy. Philip wore a policeman's hat and carried handcuffs, and 'although as always extremely handsome and pleasing, [he] looked worn out,' Channon noted. 'He leapt about and jumped in the air as he greeted everyone.' The rumours that she was pregnant were true, which made a four-day official visit to France in April 1948 something of an ordeal. She went through the exhausting schedule, surrounded by enthusiastic crowds, but often feeling extremely ill.

Another concern was the King's health. He would allow no word of his condition to be revealed to the Princess, but it was clear for her to see that he was ill. Weak and exhausted, he was suffering from an obstruction to the circulation through the arteries of the legs. An operation in the spring of 1949 had rectified the condition but he was recovering very slowly.

On 14 November 1948, Prince Charles Philip Arthur George was born at Buckingham Palace six days before his parents' first wedding anniversary. 'Don't you think he is quite adorable?' wrote the Princess to Crawfie. 'I still can't believe he is really mine, but perhaps that happens to new parents.'

VI

The Principal Position

In March 1949, George VI successfully underwent surgery to clear the obstruction in his right leg. A lumbar sympathectomy was performed at Buckingham Palace, where a room was converted into an operating theatre for the purpose. As the King slowly recovered and things returned to normal in the royal family, the Duke of Edinburgh raised the question of resuming his career in the Royal Navy. King George had given permission for him to be kept on the Active List so as not to lose seniority, but he still needed the King's consent to return to active duty. Elizabeth backed Philip – but appears to have made it quite plain that if the posting was overseas, she was going too.

The King and Queen were sympathetic. The Senior Service had a special place in King George's esteem; and Philip's stock in the family had been done no harm by his fathering a son. Elizabeth's determination to follow her husband, however, posed an awkward problem. There was the usual family discussion. The King had reservations, and Lascelles had even more. Except for her honeymoon and her parent's two pre-war foreign trips, the Princess had never been separated from her family for more than an occasional few days. And as Lascelles pointed out, before the Princess could join her husband abroad the Palace would have to look into whether the Cabinet needed to waive a standing ban forbidding the heir to the throne from making long-distance flights.

Meanwhile, Lieutenant Philip Mountbatten, Duke of Edinburgh, was duly gazetted First Lieutenant in the destroyer HMS *Chequers*, leading ship in the First Destroyer Squadron of the Mediterranean Fleet based at Malta. The Vice-Admiral commanding the squadron, and second-in-command of the fleet was Lord Louis Mountbatten. The knowledge that Uncle Dickie and Aunt Edwina would be on hand naturally reassured the King and Queen. The Mountbattens eased matters further by offering to accommodate the young royal couple at Villa Guardamangia, their home in Malta. But even without the Mountbattens, the outcome was never in very much doubt. Typically, the Princess stuck to her guns: a long separation from her husband was simply out of the question.

Her insistence made eminent sense, of course. At the time, thousands of British officers were stationed in Malta, either afloat in His Majesty's ships of the Mediterranean Fleet, or ashore in the Army and Royal Air Force. Inevitably, the large number of eligible bachelors among the officers was a great lure, and more-or-less single women of more-or-less marriageable age arrived from Britain by the planeload to stay with relatives. They were known collectively in the Service as 'The Fishing Fleet' and added greatly to the conviviality of the posting. It was a situation calculated to make a certain type of young married woman nervous and the Princess had already shown herself to be that type of young married woman.

Philip arrived on the island to report for duty on 14 October, his wife joined him on their second wedding anniversary a month later. From November 1949 to April 1951 the Princess divided her time between London and Malta. Like some migratory bird she flew to her Mediterranean sanctuary as winter set in, returning to England in good time for the summer stream of royal 'custom and ceremony' – the presentations, the King's Birthday Parade, Ascot, etc. Prince Charles remained at Clarence House in the care of his nanny, Helen Lightbody, supervised by his vigilant and doting grandparents. Even the birth of a daughter in August 1950 failed to interfere with her seasonal escape – without the new baby. 'Whatever we did, it was together,' Prince Philip was to say later of their early years of marriage. 'I suppose I naturally filled the principal position.'

The crew of *Chequers* were initially very wary of their new First Lieutenant. The fact that he was married to the future Queen of England was reason enough. But his relationship with the Flag Officer commanding the squadron stirred a more immediate natural unease. Slowly, his evident professional skill, forthright manner, and obvious annoyance whenever he thought he was receiving special treatment earned him the ship's respect. He was well liked by his fellow officers, five of whom went on to become admirals: serving with him did them no harm.

Princess Elizabeth can hardly be said to have slipped unobtrusively into Malta. With Philip at Luqa Airport to welcome her was a phalanx of colonial and local officials including the governor of the island, the prime minister, a representative of the Roman Catholic Archbishop, the service chiefs, Lord Mountbatten, his wife, Edwina, and their younger daughter, Pamela. The formalities over, the Princess drove to the cool, stone hilltop villa she was to regard as her second home for the next two years, with its shining floors of patterned tiles, its high arched ceilings, and its view of navy shipping in the harbour creek below, and, overnight, her life changed. It was as if by entering Villa Guardamangia she had made the official world of ceremonial disappear; and personal freedom, which had always been a rationed commodity overshadowed by the demands and formalities of her position, was suddenly available in abundance. The freedom to drive alone in her husband's small yellow roadster, to go to the hairdresser, spend lazy afternoons on boat picnics in one of the island's many secluded rocky inlets, the freedom to do her own shopping in Valletta, paying personally for her purchases with money supplied by Philip. None of her royal aunts had ever held a wallet. That was what a lady-in-waiting was for.

Another woman might have found the heady change hard to cope with, but Elizabeth – canny and level-headed as ever – recognized the fiction at its heart, and her built-in self-control never failed her. The fiction – in which the tiny island cheerfully cooperated – was that she was just the wife of a British naval officer on the station. It was not that people failed to recognize her. There was no anonymity on a ninety-square-mile island. But people kept a discreet distance . . . while at the same time watching closely out of the corner of their eyes. There was the occasional visit to school or hospital, but the relaxed atmosphere of these engagements only emphasized the distance from Court life in London.

The Mountbattens knew Malta well, and they knew how to enjoy themselves. Lord Mountbatten made it his business to see that the Princess and Philip got the best out of the social life of what was still a garrison island. In the afternoon, there was swimming, or the races, or polo, which was Mountbatten's passion and was rapidly becoming his nephew's. Philip had taken it up in Malta with characteristic zest, and showed an aptitude for it. At night, to the couple's delight, there were dances galore – on ships, in romantic seventeenth-century forts and palaces at Valletta, the city built by the Knights of St John, at the private homes of Maltese society. After dancing with the Princess at a ball Lord Mountbatten wrote in his diary: 'She dances quite divinely, and always wants to Samba when we dance together.' He could not resist adding that she had made 'some very nice remarks about my dancing.'

But without question the focal point of the Princess's life in Malta was Philip, and his world. As the wife of HMS *Chequers*'s First Lieutenant she was a key member of an extended family consisting of the ship's company and their dependants – for many were living in Malta for the duration of the posting. She mixed easily with the other wives, and was a member of the ship's welfare committee.

Philip's polo playing created a common interest in horses, and whenever he took to the field, whether in club chukkas (practice games) or in a regular game, the Princess was sure to be an intent spectator, sitting in the tiny grandstand of the Marsa Polo Club. But most precious, certainly, was the luxury of time spent alone together out on the town – or dining on the moonlit terrace of Villa Guardamangia, with the phosphorescent glint of the Mediterranean below.

Out on the town usually meant dinner and dancing in the restaurant of the Phoenicia Hotel, a colonial-style establishment built against an escarpment of the outer walls of Valletta. It had acres of marble flooring, servants in starched white mess jackets, giant rotary fans suspended from the ceiling, and an unmemorable Anglo-Italian cuisine. But young officers went there to dance to the music of Jimmy Dowling, a roguish, beery-voiced Maltese bandleader. At the sight of the royal couple Dowling would play one of Philip's frequent requests, among them 'Take the "A" Train' and 'People Will Say We're in Love' – the latter from the musical *Oklahoma!* Twenty years later, on one of Elizabeth's periodic return visits to the island as Queen, Dowling waited until she took the floor with Prince Philip and then launched into a medley of their old favourites. And Philip, dancing past the bandleader, told him simply, 'You remembered'.

Then on 28 December, Princess Elizabeth stood with other young wives on a rocky foreshore overlooking Malta's Grand Harbour watching HMS *Chequers* sail out on a Red Sea patrol with the rest of the fleet. A camera hanging around her neck and a cine-camera in her hands, she alternately took still and cine shots of her husband's departing ship. As the assembled squadrons faded into the distant greyness of an overcast day, Elizabeth walked slowly away. That same afternoon, she was due to fly home to a country in the grip of strikes, shortages, deprivation, cold weather; and to a reunion with Charles, who had tonsillitis. Six weeks later, she learned that she was pregnant and expecting a second child in the summer.

To her parents, the news of her fresh pregnancy was a bright spot in the general gloom. The Queen in particular tended to be more openly pessimistic about conditions in the United Kingdom. She 'talked as though everybody was in a very bad way nowadays, not happy, poor, dispirited, etc.,' Hugh Gaitskell, the Chancellor of the Exchequer, complained in his diary after spending the night at Windsor. 'She did not say this in anger but implied that it could not be helped and that she hoped it would come to an end some day.' The Queen's pessimism may have been accentuated by her dislike of the Labour government, but neither was it unfounded. The postwar slump was at its depth; a damaging dock strike was badly undermining British exports, and the pound had been devalued against the dollar by almost 30 per cent. Clement Attlee's government, barely clinging to power after returning for a second time in February 1950 with a six-seat majority, seemed hardly likely to survive the winter.

Attlee was still in office in April (in fact, he carried on until October 1951) when Elizabeth returned to her fairy-tale existence in Malta just in time to watch HMS *Chequers* lead the First Destroyer Flotilla into the Grand Harbour at the end of the fleet's spring cruise, and she was reunited with Philip that afternoon at Villa Guardamangia. Just in time, too, for her twenty-fourth birthday, which began with the only anonymous telephone call she is ever known to have received. When she answered, she heard a lusty choral rendering of 'Happy Birthday to You' accompanied by a band. Her maid, who was in the room, later reported to Mountbatten that 'Lilibet first went white, then quite red, and ended up with tears in her eyes.' She kept telling her callers, 'Oh, thank you, thank you! That was sweet but, who are you?' The response was a second verse, harmonized, followed by the bagpipes. The choir, it turned out later, consisted of a group of young officers from Mountbatten's flagship, HMS *Liverpool*, backed by the ship's band. The birthday also occasioned a photo session at the villa with a photographer from the *Times of Malta*. Elizabeth and Philip posed in the garden, and then Elizabeth sat on a wooden bench on their terrace, while her uniformed husband stood behind her. When, after more pictures standing together by the fireplace in the drawing room, the session was still not over, Prince Philip began to lose his patience and – typically – showed it. Elizabeth was amused. 'You'll have to face this from now on,' she told him gently. 'Better to smile than scowl. The picture will be taken just the same.' The Princess was to spend a lifetime urging patience on her quick-tempered husband, but it was a royal skill he never quite mastered – which has perhaps always been part of his appeal.

Two years of marriage to the heir to the throne of England had not dimmed his natural capacity for mischief, which occasionally landed him in hot water, and sometimes his wife with him. On one particular Saturday, Princess Elizabeth had gone on board HMS *Liverpool* to watch scheduled naval landing exercises. It was a complex operation, involving several ships of the fleet under the overall command of Mountbatten. But as Royal Marines in full combat gear hit the beach they were amazed to see a group of riders clad in cardboard 'armour' charging towards them across the sand. The 'cavalry' consisted of men and women from the Marsa Polo Club putting up an unscheduled defence of the beach against the invaders, and their leader was Lieutenant Philip Mountbatten, Duke of Edinburgh. The Princess immediately came ashore in one of *Liverpool*'s rowboats to meet the quixotic knights.

Unfortunately for all concerned, a photograph of this escapade found its way into a London newspaper, showing Philip on his horse and Elizabeth – visibly pregnant – edging cautiously down a shaky plank to reach the beach. The Commander-in-Chief, Mediterranean, received a sharp message from the King asking him to explain what a serving naval officer was doing on horseback in the middle of a fleet exercise, and why the King's daughter had been allowed to risk her pregnancy by going ashore in that dangerous manner. It was an unwonted embarrassment for the Commander-in-Chief, Admiral Sir Arthur Power, who had not been connected with the exercise and would have found it hard to deliver an appropriate rebuke to his well-connected second-in-command. In his frustration the Admiral turned on the media and banned all photo coverage of future navy events.

By 25 June, when North Korean forces crossed the 38th Parallel and the Korean War began, the Princess was back in London, and on 15 August gave birth to a baby girl at Clarence House. The Duke of Edinburgh flew to London for the christening of Princess Anne Elizabeth Alice Louise. This time there was no George V to oppose the name Anne. Elizabeth and Alice were tributes to both the parents' mothers; and Louise was the name of the Queen of Sweden, their common relative. The Princess nursed the new baby for three months. Then she hired an assistant to Nurse Lightbody, Mabel Anderson, and promptly returned to Malta for what was to be her longest stay: November to the middle of February.

In the interim Prince Philip had passed the qualifying examination for commander and had fulfilled the dream of every naval officer – to command a King's ship. Princess Elizabeth was now the wife of Lieutenant Commander Mountbatten of the frigate HMS *Magpie* and her role in the extended family had grown correspondingly. An important function was taking an interest in the welfare of the ship company's families. It brought her for perhaps the first time into regular contact with a social cross section of the British people. She took to wearing cheery cotton dresses by Horrocks Ltd and thoroughly looked the part of the junior captain's wife. She met naval ratings' wives at tea at Villa Guardamangia, and officers' wives of the frigate flotilla some days later. As Christmas approached, she presided over the ceremonial stirring of the ship's traditional plum pudding, and helped organize the children's Christmas party. Her own children spent Christmas with their grandparents. 'He is too sweet stomping around the room & we shall love having him at Sandringham,' her father wrote of Prince Charles, aged two. 'He is the fifth generation to live there & I hope will get to love the place.'

Early in 1951, Princess Margaret went to stay with her sister at Villa Guardamangia. Elizabeth arranged parties in her honour, found eligible partners for her, and generally behaved as if Princess Margaret were 'The Fishing Fleet's' most distinguished member. But one motive behind the trip appeared to be that her mother had observed a growing friendship between her younger daughter and Group Captain Peter Townsend, the King's favourite equerry, and suggested a change of scene. Townsend the temporary aide had long since become a permanent member of the household. When Princess Margaret had begun to talk about him during the South African tour four years earlier nobody had been listening. Elizabeth's thoughts were only on the absent Philip, and the minds of the King and Queen were focused on the difficulties of the long and complex tour. So what was to escalate into a serious royal crisis may have started off as one of Margaret's devices to attract attention. But the friendship had deepened, and by 1951 loomed as an awkward situation.

While Margaret was in Malta, Townsend was divorcing his estranged wife, Rosemary, and successfully obtaining custody of his two sons. No doubt the timing was coincidental. For if Townsend the thirty-three-year-old married man was out of the question as a suitor for Margaret, then approaching twenty-one, Townsend the thirty-three-year-old divorcé was even more so. The problem did not prevent the visiting Princess from cutting a swath through the island's bachelor population, but no one man seemed special. And when she returned to London, there was Townsend waiting to greet her at the airport. Princess Elizabeth seemed vaguely disappointed with the outcome of her sister's trip. Shortly after Margaret's departure, she was asked if Her Royal Highness enjoyed her stay. 'I haven't the faintest idea,' came the reply. 'She hasn't written to me yet, or thanked me.'

Other clouds on the family horizon concerned Elizabeth herself. When she had been away for two and half months, the British press was beginning to raise questions about her long absences. It hardly amounted to a clamour of protest, but it was the first time Princess Elizabeth had been openly criticized. One comment was that she was spending too much time away from her children. Before the war it had been the usual practice among wealthy families to leave children primarily in the care of nannies and nursery maids. But in the 1950s the situation was radically different. Domestic staffs had shrunk in all but the wealthiest households, and nannies were a luxury few people could afford. Besides, the emphasis in postwar Britain was on rebuilding family ties and giving children the affection and attention they lacked in the years of conflict. So Elizabeth's lengthy separations from Charles and Anne seemed somewhat out of keeping with the times. The separation also appeared to be in sharp contrast to the close-knit family atmosphere of her own childhood. The King and Queen had been extremely reluctant to be parted from nine-month-old Lilibet when they went to Australia and New Zealand, and thereafter – except for the 1939 North American visit – were rarely separated from the princesses. Given the length of Princess Elizabeth's visits to Malta and her relaxed life on the island, one wonders why her children did not go too. As it was, her absences suggested a surprising degree of detachment from them, and probably contributed to the alienation evident in her relationship with both Charles and Anne in later years. Some thirty years later Charles's wife was to insist on taking her six-month-old son William with her on a lengthy tour of Australia. Another criticism was that Elizabeth was not shouldering her share of royal obligations. She had, it was true, undertaken several public engagements in Malta, but such excursions as touring the Church of Saint Paul Shipwrecked in the island's capital on the eve of the saint's feast day to admire the silver plate and decorations were hardly up to the normal royal workload.

It was at this time that the Palace announced she would go to Athens to visit the Greek king and queen. As the senior member of the reigning houses of Europe, George VI saw it as his duty to help his fellow kings – most of whom were relatives anyway – as much as he could. When the war ended, he had pressed for the restoration of the Greek and other Balkan monarchies, often against the advice of the Foreign Office, which tended to regard sovereigns as an irrelevant nuisance. By 1951 the royal houses of Yugoslavia and Rumania had been washed away by the Soviet tide in Eastern Europe, but with American and British help King George II and Queen Frederika were firmly established in Greece and Princess Elizabeth's visit, though unofficial, was intended as a gesture of solidarity and friendship.

The Princess sailed for Greece on board the dispatch vessel HMS *Surprise* with an escort which included her husband's ship HMS *Magpie*. During the journey, the couple amused themselves exchanging flag signals, usually in the form of biblical references – an old navy signalling trick because it eliminated the necessity to spell out the whole sentence. On one occasion, Elizabeth signalled, 'Isaiah 33.23', which is 'Thy tacklings are loosed'. To which *Magpie*, after a while, replied, 'I Samuel 15:14': 'What meaneth then this bleating of sheep?' Quoting biblical references became from then on an inside joke to which Prince Philip resorted when he felt his wife needed to smile.

Returning home from Malta in February the Princess was able to see that the stock of public knowledge about her childhood had been considerably enlarged because Crawfie had gone public. Marion Crawford had married Major George Buthlay, a Scottish bank manager, three months before Lilibet's own marriage, and she and her new husband had been among the guests at Lilibet's wedding at Westminster Abbey, where they sat next to the Duke and Duchess of Norfolk. As a trusted royal servant Crawfie received a pension, and was granted a grace-and-favour cottage in Windsor.

But still she nursed a deep disappointment: her wish for royal recognition in the form of a decoration from the King and Queen had never been fulfilled. She had set her heart on being made a

Dame Commander of the Victorian Order (DCVO). When this honour did not come her way, she agreed to write an account of her seventeen years as royal governess. Her best-selling book *The Little Princesses*, published in time for Christmas 1950, was a rather idealized intimate portrait of the two princesses as they were growing up under her care. The emphasis is naturally on the future Queen, and the former governess had clearly selected her facts with tact. In the royal family's eyes, however, she broke faith, and the once loved and trusted Crawfie, described by a friend of the royal family as 'The Queen's closest associate', became a non-person.

Buckingham Palace's official reaction to Crawfie's book was a frosty silence, but word of the royal family's deep displeasure soon got around and it became taboo even to mention her in the presence of the King, the Queen, or the two princesses – and especially the Queen. She was immediately ordered to vacate her grace-and-favour house, and accidental references to her were met with the famous Windsor blank stare. The family's handling of Crawfie showed them at their most unforgiving. For a while she wrote a column for a women's magazine, until a description of Elizabeth at the Trooping the Colour, written in advance of the event, ended her writing career. The ceremony was cancelled because of a rail strike – but too late for the magazine to kill the story. Retiring to Aberdeen in 1956, Crawfie took what amounted to a vow of silence about her royal experiences, but it was too late. The ostracism was total and would last for the rest of her life. Following her death thirty-six years later in 1988, not one member of the royal family attended the funeral or even sent a wreath. But Crawfie's book had come as a shock to the royal family. It was the first insider's account of life at Buckingham Palace and it exposed their vulnerability to growing popular media interest. To discourage further revelations, conditions of royal service were immediately tightened. Eventually, members of the royal household were brought under a section of the Official Secrets Act, making it a crime to pass on information about their work.

In March 1951, Princess Elizabeth returned briefly to Malta and her role of naval wife. There was an official visit to the tiny sister island of Gozo, with Prince Philip at the wheel of their open car. He made a bet with reporters following in other cars that they would not be able to keep up with him. After that, the tour became a series of hair-raising chases through narrow streets. Gozitans lining the streets were puzzled, but applauded warmly as the royal visitors flashed past, Elizabeth clinging, white-knuckled, to the side with one hand and waving sedately with the other. Philip lost the bet. Seven days later, on 11 April, they both flew to London via Rome, where they stopped briefly and had an audience with Pope Pius XII. On the tarmac at Luqa Airport, the Princess discussed her forthcoming summer visit with George Micallef, the butler at Villa Guardamangia. But the shadows were lengthening over her father's life and her fairy-tale existence was fading away. When she next returned to the sunny Mediterranean island it would be as Queen.

Elizabeth found her father looking ill and troubled by a hacking cough which he seemed unable to shake off. In the late summer of 1951, he had tomography tests on his left lung in London; and after seeing the results the doctors recommended a bronchoscopy, the removal of a portion of tissue for histological examination. The bronchoscopy carried out on 15 September by Mr Clement Price Thomas, a leading chest surgeon, confirmed that the King was suffering from cancer. The King was told that an operation was needed to remove a blockage from one of the bronchial tubes, and may never have learned the truth. Winston Churchill was told by Lascelles – 'The King has a growth in his lung,' he informed his own physician, Lord Moran. 'It means an operation – on Monday. The King did not know that Lascelles was writing to me. Poor fellow, he does not know what it means.'

Surgery to remove the King's left lung took place on Sunday, 23 September, at Buckingham Palace. There were complications: certain nerves of the larynx had to be sacrificed, which involved the risk that he might not be able to speak above a whisper. The Queen, her daughters, and the Duke of Edinburgh went to Lambeth Palace for a private service for the King's recovery held by the Archbishop of Canterbury. But doctors were sceptical about his chances. Harold Nicolson noted in his diary that William Harris, editor of the *Spectator*, had asked him to prepare an obituary of the King after meeting Lord Moran, who 'had shaken his head gravely.' And Sir Harold Graham Hodgson, the former royal radiologist, predicted to a friend: 'The King is not likely to live more than eighteen months. The end will probably come suddenly. The operation was six months too late.'

The King, who presumed the surgery had cured him, was willing himself to recover. Lascelles, however, feared the worst. On 7 October, Princess Elizabeth and the Duke of Edinburgh left on a tour of Canada and a side trip to Washington. They were to have sailed in the liner *Empress of France* direct to Quebec where the tour was to start. Because of the King's operation, however, their departure was delayed and they made the journey by air in an Argonaut Transporter of the King's Flight, the *Atlanta*. Among the Princess's papers was a sealed envelope containing the draft Declaration of her accession to the throne, a message to both Houses of Parliament, and all the documents necessary in the event of her father's death. In the week of her departure, it was announced that early in 1952, Princess Elizabeth would further undertake the scheduled royal tour of East Africa, Australia and New Zealand in her father's place. She had also been present on 1 October at a bizarre meeting of the Council of State to dissolve Parliament so that new general elections could be held, the former being something which only the sovereign can do. The councillors, including the Queen and Princess Elizabeth, clustered around the door between the Council Chamber and the King's bedroom. The Act of Dissolution was read out and then they listened as the King from his bed croaked the word 'Approve', with great difficulty, according to the formula. Alan Lascelles took in the documents which, with equal difficulty, the King signed. The Princess was under no illusion about the severity of her father's condition.

As an introduction to solo touring, the Canadian trip was a plunge into the deep end. Elizabeth and Philip crossed North America twice in thirty-five days, travelling nearly 10,000 miles in Canada, plus a three-day stay in the United States capital as a gesture of friendship and support to President Harry Truman in the Korean War. They visited every Canadian province, including Newfoundland, which had joined the Dominion in 1949 following a referendum. On both sides, it was a voyage of discovery: the Canadians meeting for the first time the young woman who would one day be their Queen; and the Princess getting a sense, as she had done in South Africa, of the vast scope of her inheritance.

Monitoring her progress, the American embassy in Ottawa was in no doubt that the Princess had scored a personal triumph. Yet, although the young royals were warmly welcomed wherever they went – the embassy reported to Washington – the tour had failed in its important secondary purpose, namely, to 'counteract the closeness which has developed between the US and Canada in the past decades.' The Princess's frequent reminders, in her speeches, that British threads were woven more than a century deep in the fabric of Canadian life, were seen as warnings against Canada's galloping Americanization. But the embassy maintained that 'Canada's growing self-consciousness and confidence in its destiny have not been altered in the slightest' [as a result of the Princess's visit].

No doubt, the American view was a biased one, but it was the reverse side of the King and Queen's expressed concern over what they saw as growing United States influence in the Empire. Canada's Governor-General, Lord Alexander of Tunis, gave an ironic twist to the worries about American influence by organizing a square dance in the Princess's honour at the official residence, Rideau Hall. Since Elizabeth and Philip had never do-si-do'd in their lives, the Governor-General spent the afternoon before the dance giving them a crash course. Prince Philip sent into town for a checked shirt, and the Princess dispatched Bobo MacDonald for a very full skirt.

There was nothing so folksy as square dancing in Washington, where the Princess and her husband arrived on 31 October to be greeted at Andrews Air Base by a huge official welcoming committee headed by President Harry Truman, his wife, Bess, and their daughter, Margaret. The motorcade to Blair House, the official American guest house where they were staying, followed a roundabout route so that they could take in such familiar sights as the Lincoln Memorial and Capitol Hill. Crowds lined the streets, the White House having instructed heads of government departments to 'excuse from work those employees in Washington whose services can be spared' to line the route to welcome the royal visitors.

Seeing the royal party's youth – the dashing officers in chocolate-soldier uniforms, the lovely Margaret Elphinstone, the Princess's lady-in-waiting who seemed hardly out of her teens – members of Truman's staff were at first dubious. However, it was soon plain to the Americans that they were dealing with professionals. The crowded programme seemed to be one long succession of motorcades and changes, but the Princess handled the whole thing with the skill of a quick-change artist. On the first night of her stay, she returned from her afternoon engagements with less than an hour in which to change into her evening dress, tiara and Garter sash for the President's dinner and reception in her honour. As she rushed downstairs to dinner from her bedroom with Prince Philip she was muttering in an exasperated voice, 'Bobo tells me my dress is too long!'

She lived up to American expectations of what a princess should be like. She was pretty, delicate and charming if perhaps a little too quiet. But as the Trumans discovered, the sweetness could be deceptive. Faced with a clamour from all sides to meet the visitors, Bess Truman decided to invite three senior Washington couples to the President's private White House luncheon for the Princess. When the royal party was told of this, word came from the Princess that she wanted her lunch with the Trumans to be strictly a family affair and the three couples had to be disinvited. The object of real curiosity was her handsome, outgoing husband. Washingtonians quickly noted that he walked a couple of paces behind her at all times, even when they were out of the public eye, and wondered how an American male would cope with such a state of affairs.

The homey Trumans and their staff were equally intrigued by the royal sleeping arrangements. When Major Sir Martin Charteris (as he then was) came to Washington in advance of the visit he had somewhat surprised the White House by requesting separate bedrooms for Elizabeth and Philip. Bess Truman moved her own king-size four-poster into Blair House for Elizabeth, and prepared an adjoining bedroom for Philip. The Princess's bed had a blue damask canopy, linen sheets, and flowered shams and ruffles. All the air-conditioning units were removed at the visitors' request. When Bobo MacDonald inspected the Princess's room, she exclaimed, 'Why, it's just like her bedroom at [Windsor] Castle!'

In his forthright way, President Truman wrote to the King expressing his pleasure at the visit. The Princess and her 'personable husband', he said, 'went to the hearts of the citizens of the United States . . . As one father to another, we can be very proud of our daughters. You have the better of me – because you have two!' The King was indeed proud of his daughter's success, and to mark it he made her and her personable husband Privy Councillors. The couple arrived home in mid-November – just too late for Charles's third birthday, which he spent with his grandparents at Sandringham. Elizabeth and Philip took up residence at Clarence House, where so little time out of their four years of marriage had been spent. Elizabeth was also able to devote more time to being with her children, even though it was nowhere near the extent her mother had found time for. She played with Anne and Charles for half an hour after breakfast, and again after tea. Whenever possible she also supervised their baths and put them to bed herself.

Her days were often full of official engagements, for she was taking on a considerable number of her father's. But the King was making a remarkable recovery and by early December was well enough to resume the responsibilities which, during his illness, had been transferred to the Council of State headed by his wife.

The training he was giving Elizabeth did not extend to sharing official documents with her. On the contrary, he was cautious about giving her access to state papers – as she, in her turn, was to be sparing with access for her eldest son, the Prince of Wales.

She was not allowed to see the cabinet papers which arrived daily at Buckingham Palace in the red dispatch boxes: they were for the King's eyes only. When Sir John (Jock) Colville, her newly appointed secretary, proposed to Tommy Lascelles that she should at least be allowed to get the Foreign Office telegrams as part of her preparation, Lascelles was not enthusiastic nor was the King himself – and neither, for that matter, was the Foreign Office. To the Princess's annoyance, it took several months before the King reluctantly agreed. The reluctance had less to do with the Princess herself and more with Lascelles's sepulchral discretion and iron resistance to any relaxation of the rules, and also with memories of the immediate past. King Edward VIII's nonchalant attitude towards the dispatch boxes had shocked his staff. There were stories of papers left lying about at Fort Belvedere, and being returned marked with the wet rings of cocktail glasses. The experience had made the Palace more protective than ever of state papers sent in the boxes which have to be returned to their respective departments in good time and in good order.

Elizabeth studied the papers she was given more out of a sense of obligation than any feeling of real involvement. She was not a political animal: and, according to Colville, 'she wasn't interested in foreign affairs. She was young, just married . . . She wasn't interested until she was personally involved.' Still, she accepted the routine as a prelude to the time when, as Queen, 'doing the boxes' would become a large part of her daily life.

VII

A Death in the Family

'It is not always easy to feel confident that 1952 will bring happiness to the world,' King George VI wrote to Dwight D. Eisenhower – then the North Atlantic Treaty Organization's first Supreme Commander in Europe – on 7 January. And there did seem little room for optimism. The Cold War was the reality that dominated world politics. British and American troops (not to mention other western nationalities) were dying in the snow in Korea. At home, full economic recovery remained elusive. The previous October, the Conservative Party had succeeded in defeating Labour, and at seventy-eight Winston Churchill was once more Prime Minister. Initially, the King was delighted at Churchill's return to office, but his pleasure was soon overshadowed by concern over signs of the Prime Minister's advancing age. At their weekly meetings, the old Churchill magic waxed and waned. There were awkward lapses of memory and occasional speech problems which made understanding him difficult, and by January the King was contemplating raising the subject of making way for a younger man.

The uncertainty over the King's own health was by no means over. True, he seemed to be edging towards recovery, but slowly. Lascelles, writing to Eisenhower two weeks after the King, told him, 'His Majesty seems to be going on very well and we all hope that his cruise in the early spring will set him up again completely.' But it was a reassurance Lascelles did not feel. On the same day, he dispatched a telegram to Churchill, who was in Washington, worrying over the King's slow progress. The family and the Court's inner circle hoped for the best but were steeled for the worst. They knew that a coronary thrombosis could come at any time. Lascelles established a code word to be used to communicate the King's death. It was 'Hyde Park Corner'.

As Lascelles told Eisenhower, the King planned a March convalescent cruise to South Africa. Dr Daniel Malan, the nationalist leader who had boycotted the royal tour five years earlier, but had met the King privately at the monarch's request, was now Prime Minister of the Union following the death of Jan Smuts, and he had offered the King the use of his official country residence. Early in January, the King had sent Peter Townsend to look it over and to begin preliminary arrangements for the trip. Townsend returned to find the King at Sandringham shooting. But on 30 January, the King and Queen, Princess Elizabeth and Philip, and Princess Margaret (with Peter Townsend also in the party) went to see *South Pacific* at the Drury Lane Theatre in London, a farewell outing on the eve of Elizabeth and Philip's departure for Kenya, the first stop on their five-month trip to New Zealand and Australia.

The following morning, Prince Charles waved from the pavement outside Clarence House as his mother and father drove away, and Elizabeth waved back until the car was out of sight. Perhaps because it was a tour they were undertaking in his place and he wanted to show his appreciation, the King – unusually – went to Heathrow Airport to see them off. He said his goodbyes on board the plane which bore the apt radio code name 'How King'. He told Bobo: 'Look after the Princess for me, Bobo. I hope the tour is not going to be too tiring for you.' Coming back down the steps, he faltered and stumbled slightly. To the Colonial Secretary, Oliver Lyttelton, who was 'in attendance' at the airport, the King 'seemed much altered and strained, and I had the feeling of doom.' The King went up on to the roof of the building to wave goodbye. 'The high wind blew his hair into disorder,' Lyttelton (later Lord Chandos) recalled. 'I felt with deep foreboding that this would be the last time he was to see his daughter, and that he thought so himself.' Returning to London with Churchill, Lyttelton repeated this view to the Prime Minister, who 'was very angry and told me that I was completely wrong: a not unusual reaction from people who do not want to believe bad news.' Chips Channon thought the King looked 'cross, almost mad-looking, waving farewell to the Edinburghs . . . He is reported to be going out duck shooting next week. Suicidal.'

The airport leave-taking was indeed the last time Elizabeth saw her father alive. On 1 February, he returned to Sandringham in the royal train. On 5 February, he had a successful day shooting hares on the Sandringham estate with about twenty other guns. It was 'Keeper's Day', the end of the season, and the King shot nine hares. Among the guns were the King's friend Lord Fermoy, and Sir Charles Fellowes, manager of the Sandringham estate. (Lord Fermoy was the maternal grandfather of the as yet unborn Lady Diana Spencer, and Sir Charles the father of Robert, future husband of Diana's oldest sister Jane, and a future Private Secretary to Queen Elizabeth II. A glimpse of the interlocking relationships inside the magic circle.) Several of the party dined with the King and Queen, and Princess Margaret, and the King had gone to bed about 10.30 p.m. In the morning, his valet James Macdonald came to wake him at 7.30 with his usual tea, but found him dead. The threatened coronary thrombosis had ended his life in his sleep in the early hours of the morning of 6 February. He was fifty-six.

Lascelles telephoned Sir Edward Ford, the Assistant Secretary, and said, 'Hyde Park Corner last night. Go and tell the Prime Minister and Queen Mary.' Ford found Churchill in bed working on a foreign policy speech he was to deliver that afternoon in the House of Commons. 'I've got bad news, Prime Minister, the King died last night,' Ford told him. 'I know nothing else.' Churchill was stunned. 'Bad news? The worst.' Shortly afterwards, Jock Colville, who had shifted from being Elizabeth's Private Secretary to being Churchill's once again, arrived to find Churchill sitting alone in tears. Colville tried to cheer him up by saying how well he would get on with the new Queen, 'but all he could say was that he did not know her and that she was only a child.'

The official news of the King's death was held up for three hours while the Palace attempted to contact Princess Elizabeth in Kenya, where the Princess and her party had returned from Treetops to Sagana Lodge. Martin Charteris, the Princess's Private Secretary, was the first to receive it – not from Buckingham Palace but from a reporter, while he was having lunch at the Outspan Hotel across the valley from the Lodge. Called urgently to the telephone, he found the reporter in the phone booth, who told him of the unconfirmed Reuters newsflash. Charteris contacted Prince Philip's equerry, Lieutenant Commander Michael Parker, at the lodge. 'Mike, our employer's father is dead. I suggest you do not tell the lady at least until the news is confirmed.' But shortly afterwards, at 10.45 a.m. London time – 1.45 in the afternoon in Kenya – the news was officially announced in London, and this information was relayed to Charteris. There followed a half hour when those closest to the Princess knew that she had become Queen while the Princess herself, unaware, was relaxed and in sparkling spirits. Then Philip took her aside and told her the news. Since the King had died in the early hours of the morning the new sovereign learned of her accession with a delay of at least eight hours.

When Elizabeth appeared before her household, a small group now relieved of a dreadful confidence, she seemed – as Charteris recalled later – 'very composed, absolute master of her fate.' But it was Charteris and not the new Queen who talked to the reporters who had quickly converged on the banks of the Sagana River. This was the day Elizabeth and Philip were to have sailed from Mombasa for Ceylon on the next stage of the royal tour. Instead, by 5.45 in the afternoon they were speeding in a convoy of cars to the nearest airport, Nanyuki, where a Royal Air Force Dakota had been commandeered to fly them the five hundred miles to Entebbe, in Uganda, for the return journey to London. At the small local airport, waiting photographers were persuaded not to take pictures of the Queen who was wearing a beige and white dress instead of mourning. Her black clothes were in Mombasa and had to be flown to join her plane. As the Dakota sped bumpily over the bush, so low that they could see fires burning in the bush, Charteris briefed her about what to expect when she arrived home. Prince Philip's valet, John Dean, noted that the Queen left her seat once or twice 'and when she returned she looked as if she might have been crying.'

At Mombasa, the royal plane that had brought the couple to Africa five days earlier was waiting. Their departure was delayed three hours by a tropical electric storm, but once they were in the air the flight to London was free of any further trouble. When the plane was flying over the Alps, the Queen sat in the co-pilot's seat for twenty minutes filming the snow-covered mountains with her cine-camera.

Touching down at Heathrow on the afternoon of 7 February, the Queen looked out of the window. In the gathering dusk, the sky was grey. The Sagana River had been a dream, and waiting on the tarmac was reality – a frieze of sombre officials and politicians headed by Churchill, Attlee, now leader of the Opposition, and Anthony Eden, the Foreign Secretary, and beyond them the massive black Daimlers and Rolls-Royces that had come to fetch her. 'Oh, they've sent those hearses,' she said. It was a word she and Margaret had always used for the royal cars, but at that moment it had a macabre ring to it. The aircraft door opened and her uncle the Duke of Gloucester entered followed by Tommy Lascelles, more grim-faced than ever. The Queen was ready: black coat, hat and shoes, black handbag hanging from her left arm, leaving the right free for shaking hands. But underneath she wore a light green dress because no black dress had been sent from Mombasa. 'Shall I go down alone?' she asked Lascelles. This has always been mistaken for hesitancy on the Queen's part, but it was more a mode of expression than a question, and her collaborators would soon become accustomed to such questions which tolerated no negative answer.

So she came down the steps alone, as she had intended to do all along, smiling slightly at the reception committee. 'The sight of that young figure in black,' Eden wrote later, 'coming through the door of the aircraft, standing there poised for a second before descending . . . is a poignant memory.' Churchill bowed low from the waist and clasped her hand, too moved to speak. In the car on the way to the airport he had begun dictating his Commons speech on the death of the King to a secretary and had burst into tears.

A single motorcycle policeman preceded her 'hearse' as it sped to London. Some pedestrians along the way noticed the small motorcade and waved. The Queen waved back. Her subjects! The streetlights were coming on when the royal car swung into the grounds of Clarence House. The double doors were thrown open, and the sovereign's Royal Standard broke over the house for the first time. Inside waited Queen Mary, wearing deep mourning. The old lady, who was eighty-five, insisted on the ancient form of homage to her granddaughter. 'Her old Granny and subject must be the first to kiss her hand,' Queen Mary said. Then she looked at the Queen's dress and added, 'Lilibet, your skirts are much too short for mourning.' That night, Mountbatten wrote in his diary, 'Poor, sweet Lilibet – now our Queen.' Fifteen years earlier, Princess Margaret had said much the same thing.

On the other side of the Atlantic, the Queen's other surviving uncle sailed for England aboard the *Queen Mary*. 'The voyage upon which I am embarking . . . tonight is indeed sad,' declared the Duke of Windsor as he left New York to be present at his brother's funeral, 'and it is all the sadder because I am undertaking it alone.' Even before his niece's return from Kenya, Buckingham Palace had made it plain to the Duke that there was no question of Wallis accompanying him to his brother's funeral. Neither Queen Mary nor the Queen Mother were prepared to tolerate her presence. But if the Duchess was not there in person, she was there in correspondence. She kept up a stream of letters giving him courage to face his family after almost fifteen years of estrangement, bolstering his hopes of a reconciliation, and urging him to try to persuade Shirley Temple (their nickname for the young Queen) not simply to continue his allowance, but to increase it. 'I hope you can make some headway with Cookie [the Queen Mother], and Mrs Temple,' she wrote in one letter. In another she advised him to see 'the Queen and Philip casually just so they will know what you are like etc. You should also talk to your mother.' This was, she told him, 'a golden opportunity'.

Elizabeth did not go to Sandringham to see her mother and view her father's body that night. The ceremonial connected with the Accession required her presence in London. On the morning of 8 February she presided over her first meeting of the Privy Council. It is at regular sittings of the council made up of leading politicians, officials and members of the House of Lords that the Queen formally approves and signs new legislation and official appointments. About a dozen privy councillors – mostly government ministers – regularly attend the meetings, but on this occasion, according to Oliver Lyttelton, who was present, 'There must have been nearly two hundred ... The door opened, and the Queen in black came in. Suddenly the members of the Privy Council looked immeasurably old and gnarled and grey.' While the assembled councillors remained standing, as they always do throughout Privy Council meetings, the Queen read out her Declaration of Sovereignty. The need to mention her father twice was a strain, but she got through it without faltering. As soon as she finished, the Duke took her by the hand and slowly led her out of the room.

Only then did she go to Sandringham to see her mother and sister, both devastated by the King's death, and to view her father's body lying in its open coffin in the local church in which he had so often worshipped. But the time for private grief was short. Three days later, the ceremonial of the King's funeral began with the five days lying-in-state. Royal relations were arriving in London – King Paul of Greece, Princess Margarethe of Bourbon-Parma, some of Prince Philip's German kinsfolk, invited officially for the first time since the war, and Prince Paul of Yugoslavia, who was living in exile in Italy. The usual meticulous arrangements; the usual hospitality – Claridges, huge cars. Foreign diplomats received a flow of instructions printed on black-bordered paper from the Duke of Norfolk, who as hereditary Earl Marshal of

England was responsible for the organization of royal occasions. They were told where to be, how to get there, and what to wear. If Court dress was worn, it had to be with black breeches instead of white, with black buckles at the knee, and rosettes, not buckles, on court shoes.

On 11 February, Winston Churchill stood up in the Commons to deliver his tribute to George VI. For half an hour the chamber was bathed in sonorous Churchillian language. When he came to speak of the new Queen, he said, 'A fair and youthful Princess, wife and mother, is the heir to all our traditions and glories never greater than in her father's days, and to all the perplexities and dangers never greater in peacetime than now . . . She comes to the throne at a time when a tormented mankind stands uncertainly between world catastrophe and a golden age.' At three-forty, the Members of Parliament and the Lords trooped in pairs into the empty vastness of Westminster Hall, adjoining the Commons. There they waited in the cold until there was a knock on the big door, which was slowly opened. Solemnly, sedately, the heralds and heraldic kings in their finely worked red, blue and gold tabards entered led by the Earl Marshal, and the Lord Great Chamberlain of England, Lord Cholmondeley. Then came the King's coffin on the shoulders of eight grey-coated Grenadier Guardsmen. Behind the coffin as it was carried to the catafalque where it would lie in state walked the three Queens, veiled and in black. In the centre was the young Queen, wearing flesh-coloured stockings. On her right was her mother. On her left was Queen Mary, looking very fragile and carrying a black umbrella. Behind them walked Philip, looking 'as if he felt that anything might happen to any of them at any time,' wrote Selwyn Lloyd, a senior Tory parliamentarian. 'However, they all played their parts with great dignity and composure.'

Chips Channon's dismissive assessment of the dead King as 'uninteresting and unintellectual, but doubtless well-meaning,' as a man with 'no wit, no learning, no humour, except of a rather schoolboy kind,' and a nervous, insecure monarch 'entirely dependent on the Queen whom he worshipped,' reflected the view of sophisticated London society. It was not entirely untrue, either, but it missed the point. George VI had been totally unprepared for kingship, and there were many ways in which he was unsuited to the demands it made on him. Yet he found the necessary reserves of courage and energy to meet the challenge. Ordinary Britons knew little, if anything, about his gnashes and insecurities. What they remembered were his morale-boosting tours of bombed areas, his forthright manner, and his sound, practical good sense, and when he died there was genuine sorrow. He had taken over a monarchy weakened by crisis and uncertainty and bequeathed to his heir a monarchy enjoying bedrock popular support.

After lying in state the body was taken by train to Windsor and buried in St George's Chapel, the royal family's main place of worship. In a church filled with distinguished mourners, only Winston Churchill and Dwight Eisenhower 'attracted general notice', as *The Times* put it. The Prime Minister endeared himself to the royal family by sending a wreath with a card bearing simply the words 'For Valour'. The exiled Queen Alexandra of Yugoslavia, observing the girl she had seen walking in Windsor Great Park holding hands with the man who was to become her husband, noticed 'that her veil glistened with tears.' King Peter, lunching with Elizabeth and Philip a couple of days later, was shocked and surprised to see how thin she had become. He found her very subdued and quiet, but exceedingly composed. According to his wife, Alexandra, 'Peter had the feeling that she was summoning up too much composure, and that if only she could have broken down a little it would have been easier for her.' As he left, the Yugoslav monarch, deposed by Josip Broz Tito's Communists, suddenly told Elizabeth, 'I know what it's like.' She smiled briefly and said, 'Yes Peter, I know you do. Thank you, it helps.'

Meanwhile, behind the scenes at the funeral, members of the family intrigued and squabbled royally. The Duke of Windsor went to lunch at Clarence House, where Elizabeth and Philip were still living, the Queen having asked Chips Channon to entertain the other visiting royals so that she and her husband could see her uncle alone. In anticipation of this meeting, the Queen Mother had briefed her daughter on the state of affairs between the King and his brother. 'Clarence House was informal and friendly,' Uncle David wrote later. 'Brave New World. [Elizabeth and Philip] full of confidence & seem to take the job in their stride.' It was a surface friendliness, and the Duke knew it. There seemed little likelihood of a change in the royal family's ostracism of the Windsors. If anything, Elizabeth's attitude was more hostile because of the prevailing view in the family that the strain of being King had hastened George VI's death. Almost as soon as he set foot in England, the Duke had been told that the allowance of about £10,000 settled on him at the time of his abdication was to be discontinued: it was considered a personal concession by the King, who was now dead. The Duke's lawyer argued in vain that the money was a pension for life granted to the Duke by his brother in return for renouncing ownership of the royal residences and other inheritances. 'It's hell to be even that much dependent on these ice-veined bitches,' the Duke told Wallis from London. 'I'm afraid they've got the fine excuse of national economy if they want to use it.' They did.

Three days after George VI was buried in his final resting place Queen Mary summoned Jock Colville (his mother was one of her ladies-in-waiting). The old Queen had been greatly agitated by Prince Ernst August of Hanover who had come back from Broadlands, the Mountbatten home, quoting Dickie Mountbatten's boast that the House of Mountbatten now reigned. The story had given her a sleepless night. Her husband, she protested, had founded the House of Windsor *in aeternum*, and no Battenberg marriage could change that. In reality, of course, King George V had picked the name of Windsor more or less out of the hat at the outbreak of the First World War, when Saxe-Coburg-Gotha seemed inappropriate for an English royal house at war with Germany. But Colville obediently reported the Queen's complaint to Churchill, who 'went through the roof,' as Colville remembered later.

In fact, the Prime Minister had received a strongly worded memorandum from Philip making the not unreasonable point that he wanted his children to bear his name, and suggesting the House of Edinburgh as an alternative. Churchill was personally against any change in the name of the reigning house. Churchill was a sentimental monarchist: he saw himself as Lord Melbourne and Elizabeth as the young Victoria. Gazing at a new photograph of the young Elizabeth, smiling and radiant, he murmured, 'Lovely, inspiring. All the film people in the world, if they scoured the globe, could not have found anyone so suited to the part.' But his sentimentality about Elizabeth did not extend to Philip: Melbourne's young Victoria had been unmarried so there was no consort to content with. When the Prime Minister brought the issue up with the Queen she clearly did not relish the prospect of being caught in the cross-fire between her husband and her revered grandmother.

Perhaps unfortunately for the Queen's husband his Uncle Dickie chose the same moment to suggest (or persuade a prominent English genealogist to suggest) that the Queen, being married to a Mountbatten, must be the first sovereign not of the House of Windsor but of Mountbatten. From Philip's viewpoint, the interference could not have been worse timed because it made his request look like a coordinated campaign by nephew and uncle, and hardened Churchill's opposition and that of the Court. The Prime Minister, encouraged by senior members of the household, saw Mountbatten as the grey eminence behind Philip and, without consulting the Cabinet, ruled out any change of name. His argument to the Queen was first, that Mountbatten was not Philip's real name, but one he had taken because he was short of a surname, and second, the name Mountbatten was nothing but the Anglicization of Battenberg and public opinion would not accept a switch to a German name. Mountbatten's own explanation for the refusal was that the Tories had never forgotten that as Viceroy of India appointed by a Labour government he had negotiated Indian independence. But Churchill had given the Queen the out she needed, and the consequent rebuff to her husband came in the form of a royal statement confirming the House of Windsor as the royal house and declaring that her descendants would bear that name. The matter was thus buried, at least until Queen Mary's death.

Inevitably, Philip's situation prompted comparisons with that of Queen Victoria's husband, Prince Albert, who had not only given the family his name, but had acted as the Queen's Private Secretary and was frequently present when the Queen met her ministers. Would Elizabeth follow her great-great-grandmother's precedent and also appoint Prince Philip her Prince Consort?

At the time of the wedding the word in European royal circles was that an understanding existed between King George VI and King George of Greece that once Elizabeth became Queen, Philip would enjoy a position roughly similar to that of Prince Albert. This would help explain the young bridegroom-to-be's sudden interest in researching the life of his great-great-grandfather. Philip regarded the royal household as entrenched and old-fashioned, and perceived a need for change. Given his assertive nature, he would not have been coy about seeing himself as the instrument of that change. Yet if Philip did identify with Prince Albert, Elizabeth II made no move to follow Queen Victoria's example in giving her husband a publicly acknowledged role as her adviser. Over the years, Philip was to exert considerable influence on his wife – but behind the scenes. Officially, he was on the margin. When the Queen opened Parliament for the first time in November 1952, she walked into the House of Lords with the Imperial Crown on her head and her left hand in her husband's. In the chamber, she took her place on the throne. Philip sat on the consort's chair beside her and film of the opening shows him looking briefly upward. It was the same chair Queen Elizabeth the Queen Mother had occupied on similar occasions with one significant difference: the canopy that used to jut out over it had been removed.

It has been pointed out that the different historical context made it impossible for Queen Elizabeth to replicate Prince Albert's role for her husband. This is in part a polite way of saying that there would have been public opposition to such a step because of Prince Philip's many German connections. It is, however, surprising that a formula could not be found somewhere in between Prince Albert's pre-eminent position as his wife's most influential adviser and Philip's life in Elizabeth's shadow. One important difference between the two queens was the fact that when Victoria wed her adored Albert she had been queen for three years and knew her own mind. Elizabeth, for all her preparation, was too inexperienced in those tentative early days of her reign to involve Philip in a similar way without the backing of her advisers, and they were not anxious to further the idea of a second Prince Consort. In the four years of marriage before Elizabeth became Queen, her husband's determination to pursue his naval career, and his attempts to break away from the strictures of Court life, had not endeared him to the royal household.

Philip's reputation as a hell-raiser received a boost following one night at London's Milroy Club in 1949 (while Elizabeth was at Balmoral) when he danced for hours with Pat Kirkwood, a popular British film actress and singer, who was out with her friend, the photographer Baron Nahum, also a friend of Philip's. They danced any tune the band played – fox-trots, rumbas, sambas. Realizing that they were attracting considerable attention – as she later re-called – she asked him, 'Don't you think we ought to sit down?' But, she said, '[Philip] didn't want to. Then he started impersonating the expression of the people coming in. What I didn't know was that they were from the Court.' After the club closed, the group had scrambled eggs at Baron's flat. Inevitably, word of Philip's night out reached the King, who sent for his son-in-law and told him such high jinks in public had to stop. Unjustifiably, Pat Kirkwood told Unity Hall for her biography of Prince Philip, 'it went round that I was Prince Philip's mistress.' Especially some weeks later after she had appeared in a variety performance by television stars for the Queen. As the singer waited in the presentation line, Philip stood in front of her and, with Elizabeth a few feet away, said, 'I did enjoy myself that evening.' She replied, 'Oh, good.' Of course, she commented, 'It was just what everyone was waiting to hear.'

Pat Kirkwood protested that their meeting amounted to nothing more than 'a night of innocent fun'. But it helped to establish Prince Philip as a man who shared his Uncle Dickie's attraction for good-looking women. After that, it was hardly surprising that stories about Philip were grist for the gossip mill. From the royal household's viewpoint, one of his more questionable activities was his membership of the Thursday Club, a raffish group of actors, artists, and politicians who met weekly for lunch at Wheeler's, a fish restaurant in Soho.

Lunch went on for hours while jokes were told and bawdy songs sung. Each month a Cunt of the Month was chosen. The member who had told the worst joke or made the biggest fool of himself received the award. The actors among the Thursday Club stalwarts included James Robertson Justice, Peter Ustinov and Michael Trubshawe. Among the politicians was the brilliant Tory journalist and parliamentarian Iain Macleod. Others were the artist Feliks Topolski; the much-married American harmonica player Larry Adler; Philip's cousin, the Marquis of Milford Haven; and Baron Nahum, the son of a Jewish immigrant from Tripoli who had grown up in a middle-class home in Manchester and was then much in vogue as a portrait photographer. The gatherings were boisterous, somewhat drunken, strictly stag, but basically harmless. Some members of the Thursday Club, however, had a lurid reputation. One artist – Vasco Lazzolo – was known to have a liking for young girls and prostitutes. And Baron himself has been described as no model of propriety. He hosted dinner parties at which anything went between the sexes and girls appeared clad only in Masonic aprons. However, there is no indication that Prince Philip was ever present at Baron's gatherings.

To senior courtiers the young Queen was a known quantity: what's more, she had so far shown reassuringly little inclination to be an innovator. Following the lessons of the Abdication, orthodoxy was the order of the day where she was concerned. Philip's proposed changes could hardly be called radical either – cross-referenced card-index files of people met and entertained, regular lunches with leading businessmen, sportsmen, actors and other prominent Britons to broaden the Queen's range of contacts, doing away with the footmen's white wigs – but they were enough to antagonize the Palace old guard. Tommy Lascelles,

112

who had endured the disastrous (at least as he saw it) experience of King Edward VIII's 'modern' ideas, referred disparagingly to the Queen's husband as 'a German princeling'. Lascelles didn't like change, and even less did he like Germans.

In later years, when Elizabeth had gained in self-assurance and could have altered Philip's position, she had possibly become too accustomed to solo flight to want a co-pilot; and perhaps – as some said – the vicissitudes of their early life together were to dampen any enthusiasm that she might have had to give her husband wider official responsibilities.

So Philip learned early on that he was a background figure in the monarchy. He would not see the contents of the boxes, or sit at his wife's side when she met with her ministers, or advise on policy. The conventional wisdom has always been that the Queen balanced this by deferring to him in family matters. His had been the final say on problems relating to the children. For example, Charles would follow in his father's footsteps and go to Cheam School and then on to Gordonstoun rather than one of the better-known schools such as Eton or Harrow. The extent of this deference to her husband when it came to the children was evident at a dinner for the royal couple at the Mountbattens during Charles's first year at Cheam. One of the guests recalled: 'The Queen had apparently just been to see Charles at school without the Duke [of Edinburgh] and was giving her husband an account of how Charles was doing. She kept referring to Charles as "your son," as though Charles were solely Philip's achievement.'

But with his independence, strong personality and intelligence, Philip found it hard to adjust to the double setback over his name and his role, and it was about this time that he was quoted as complaining, 'I'm just an amoeba, a bloody amoeba!' His socializing with his own set was his way of preserving his identity. In this group of assorted non-conformists he did not need to hide his predicament. On one occasion – Larry Adler recalled – Philip brought Prince Bernhard of the Netherlands to a Thursday Club lunch as his guest. When the Dutch queen's consort was leaving, Philip 'knelt down on the floor, made a lavish bow and said [to him], "Give my regards to her Imperial Majesty," ' an ironic reference to Queen Juliana. It was an inside joke between the two men about Juliana's domineering manner. But there must have been occasions when the same irony could have been directed at Philip himself.

One can only speculate in what respect the reign of Queen

113

Elizabeth would have been different had fuller and more specific use been made of his energy and talents. He was known to favour increasing as much as possible direct contact between the monarch and people from all walks of life, a less traditionalist Court released from the grip of its conservative functionaries, and a streamlined, more efficient royal household. In short, an innovative monarchy. It is difficult to imagine that he would have toned down his often very outspoken and highly opinionated speeches, but as Prince Consort his pronouncements would have carried more weight. Buckingham Palace would have been in the lead in campaigning for British scientific and technological advancement, one of his early interests. The Queen's eyes almost glaze over when technology is discussed. The improvement of British management standards and the advancement of Britain's all-important export trade would have been two other Palace priorities. Politically, he became progressively more conservative as he grew older, sympathizing with the white South Africans while his wife was more inclined to see the black African point of view, and seeing the Commonwealth as a diminishing investment for the royal family. It would have been a monarchy less cautious in its actions and more prone to eruptions and errors of judgement. But certainly livelier and probably more interesting.

Meanwhile, his wife was having adjustment problems of her own. Unlike her father, she had been marinated in the business of the monarchy from the age of eleven. Yet though the task held few surprises, there was a world of difference between looking over King George's shoulder and herself occupying his desk in the second-floor study at Buckingham Palace, and the sheer scale of the task would sometimes reduce her to tears. The paperwork was voluminous. There were cabinet minutes to be studied, reports and memoranda sent in by the various ministries to be read, and 'homework' to be done on the following day's visitors. Her office day began at eight-thirty in the morning with the arrival of a large basket marked 'The Queen' full of the day's mail, and her work load was not reduced by her insistence on writing several replies in her own hand. There were official appointments that needed royal approval, and choices to be made for the gallimaufry of posts in the royal domain – posts ranging from the important to the arcane, from the Master of Trinity College, Cambridge, to the Keeper of the Swans, all swans in England being the property of the Crown.

But papers she could handle. She also had a fine sense of the dignity of ancient ceremonials, even when they were slightly ridiculous, such as approving the nomination of local officials by pricking his or her name on a list with a bodkin – an oversize pin. The real trauma of her changed status was the old bugbear of dealing with people, but on a magnified scale. Her sheltered life had not prepared her to cope easily with the sudden widening of her personal contacts. At the beginning of her reign, it sometimes must have seemed as though her schedule required her to meet the entire British nation. On one day the Anglican bishops, led by the Archbishop of Canterbury, came to pay homage. Then it was the country's judges en masse, and the military, and the leading dons of Oxford and Cambridge, and the top businessmen. Every British ambassador has an audience with the Queen – which is termed 'kissing hands' – before taking up his appointment, as well as often being received again when he returns home. Every foreign envoy to the Court of St James presents his credentials, and calls to take his leave on his departure. For a diffident and intensely private woman of not yet twenty-six it was an awesome undertaking. Her mother, a consummate actress in the social sense, somehow seemed always to know what to do and say. The new Queen, like her father, was often a prey to boredom and had not learned to conceal it.

Because Elizabeth lacked her mother's gift for putting people at their ease, they were often awkward in her presence. Royal protocol dictates that one does not speak to the monarch until she has spoken first, which often led to painful silences. One woman who dreaded being 'commanded' to a Balmoral house party was the wife of the Queen's Comptroller of the Household, Lieutenant General Sir Frederick 'Boy' Browning. Shy and retiring herself, Lady Browning sat endlessly with the Queen while the latter, apparently deeply withdrawn into some world of her own, stared out of the window drumming her fingers on the table. As she beat her soft tattoo on the highly polished surface, she seemed to Lady Browning bored, miserable and rather hopeless, like an animal caught in a trap.

Lady Browning had another life as the novelist Daphne du Maurier. Yet the Queen never showed more than a polite interest in hearing about the writer's work. It was different with the Queen Mother, however. Visiting Balmoral from Birkhall, which she now occupied, she pounced on Daphne du Maurier, interrogating her eagerly about the book she was writing.

Ironically, it was only when the Queen Mother appeared that Balmoral brightened up, even though for her, too, this was a time of painful changes. 'It is difficult to grasp that he has left us,' she wrote to Eisenhower concerning her dead husband, 'he was so much better, and so full of ideas & plans for the future. One cannot imagine life without him, but I suppose one must carry on as he would wish.' And carry on she did. She was going through the very real depression of widowhood, but she still managed to bubble with vitality. In reality, George VI's widow had grown closer to Margaret than to her eldest daughter who had ways of occasionally reminding her mother that she, Elizabeth, was of royal blood and her mother was not. And if the older Elizabeth sometimes found her daughter a trifle stuffy, the daughter in turn sometimes thought her mother's high spirits misplaced in a queen. Moreover, they had in a way competed for the King's love. Yet the Queen Mother rallied to her more subdued daughter in her difficult first year as monarch, giving her encouragement and support when it was most needed. To the younger Elizabeth, her mother's advice was a useful counterweight to that of her Court, just as it had been to George VI. The Queen telephoned her mother almost daily, and the calls were to become a family ritual.

To add to the Queen's problems her Prime Minister was proving more hindrance than help in her first year in office. Nine days after his first weekly audience (for which he insisted on returning to the old tradition of wearing a top hat and morning suit) Winston Churchill suffered a small arterial spasm, a mini-stroke, while talking on the telephone. Lord Moran, his physician, feared it might be a warning of worse to follow if the pressure of work was not reduced. A gradual deterioration had been at work for some time and Churchill's performance had been inconsistent even when King George was alive. He could be sharp, but in the Cabinet he would sometimes ramble: he once talked for two and a half hours about Egypt without once coming to the point. There were other lapses. A few weeks after Elizabeth's accession Churchill gave a dinner at 10 Downing Street for a visiting senior American admiral. When the Prime Minister rose to make the royal toast he said, 'Gentlemen, the King.' There was a slight, awkward pause and then the assembled company, consisting of British and American officers replied, 'The Queen.' Realizing his mistake Churchill became very flustered. His embarrassment was all the greater because Prince Philip was one of the guests. Presently, Churchill was overheard to say to Philip, 'What can I say? The Queen will never forgive me.' But Philip replied gently, 'She will think nothing of it, even if I tell her.' His stroke strengthened the hand of those Tories who felt the time had come for him to step down. So on 22 February, two of Churchill's closest associates, Colville and Lord Moran, went secretly to see Tommy Lascelles. They had the backing of the senior Tory grandee Lord Salisbury, a close political friend of the royal family and widely known in social circles by the nickname Bobbety, and their aim was to explore the possibilities of enlisting the Queen's help. An essential element of their plan was her consent to raise Churchill to the peerage so that he would sit in the House of Lords and still remain nominally Prime Minister. But Anthony Eden would be in virtual charge of the day-to-day running of the Government.

The Palace was equally concerned about Churchill's lapses. At a moment when the young Queen needed to be guided she was having to cope with a Prime Minister in the fading years of his illustrious life. With no written Constitution nor a defined role the sovereign's scope of action had been narrowed down over the centuries by trial and error, and what she could do was enshrined by Walter Bagehot in the formula: 'The right to be consulted, the right to encourage, the right to warn. And a King of great sagacity would want no others.' The sovereign can, in addition, intervene in the choice of Prime Minister to resolve a political deadlock, and can also start and end wars.

Of course, the extent of the monarch's influence in Whitehall and in the wider society is another story. But Bagehot's book *The English Constitution*, published in 1867, had defined the limits of the modern sovereign's political power and was the royal family's bible. The practical application of Bagehot's formula is the Prime Minister's weekly evening audience with the sovereign. The meeting is private, with no-one else present and no formal record kept of these talks. If the Prime Minister was incapacitated, this line of communication was broken. Lascelles told Colville and Moran, 'It is true that sometimes the Prime Minister is all on the spot, and then I say to myself, *Why am I worrying?* But at other times he doesn't seem able to see the point of a discussion.' But Lascelles felt Churchill's sentimental attachment to his young sovereign did not extend to accepting her suggestion to step out of the political limelight. 'If she did her part,' he said, '[Churchill] would say charmingly, *It's very good of you, Ma'am, to think of it* – and then he would very politely brush it aside. The King might have done it, but he's gone.'

So the Queen's help was not enlisted in pushing Churchill gently upstairs – at least not yet. There was an element of surprise in their regular audiences in that she never knew whether the Prime

Minister would be 'all on the spot', as Tommy Lascelles put it, or all off it. At one audience when he had his wits about him Churchill won the Queen's support in arranging an amnesty for Second World War deserters who had been on the run for eight years. The forces' senior officers had strongly opposed the amnesty, arguing that it was an insult to the servicemen who had fought and died in the war, but by winning the Queen to his side Churchill effectively silenced their protests. There were times, however, when the Prime Minister was clearly so poorly prepared that it was better to talk about horse racing, their common passion, than government business.

The Queen had inherited twenty mares from her father, and racing was to be her escape from the pressures of her position. In the 1940s she used to pick the brains of her father's trainer on the highly intricate subject of Throughbred bloodlines, stable management and breeding, and she was something of an expert. She had Royal Studs at Sandringham, Wolferton and Hampton Court with home-bred horses trained by Captain Cecil Boyd-Rochfort, and in addition leased horses from the National Stud. After the Court came out of its three-month mourning period, her first winner in the Queen's dazzling colours (purple, scarlet sleeves, gold tassel, black velvet cap with gold tassel) was Stream of Light, who won the Lancashire Oaks race. But her hopes rested on Aureole, bred by her father. The colt had made a promising start to the season. But in the Derby Aureole came up against Pinza, ridden by the famous jockey Gordon Richards, and finished a disappointing second.

Whatever Churchill's condition, the Queen used a gentle touch. When his friend the newspaper publisher Lord Beaverbrook arranged for him to stay at his villa on the French Riviera in August 1952 and Churchill sought her permission to leave the country, she wrote encouragingly, 'To be lent a villa sounds the perfect way to spend a peaceful few days.' Early the following year, she offered to make him a Knight of the Garter, reviving an offer made by her father at the end of the war. George VI had been disappointed when Churchill had declined, but Churchill had little interest in titles – medals and decorations, yes, but not titles. Could he, he asked in response to the Queen's offer, accept the Garter but remain Mr Churchill? The Queen was not about to make such a concession, not even for Churchill. Still the Prime Minister felt that he could not refuse her and the country's most famous commoner became, in coronation year, Sir Winston Churchill.

VIII

New Elizabethans

'People are prattling of the Coronation,' Chips Channon noted in his diary. Conversation, he said, had taken on a Gilbert and Sullivan quality. At a luncheon of noble ladies, 'Winnie Portarlington announced that she has harness but no coach; Circe Londonderry has a coach but no horses; Mollie Buccleuch has no postillions but five tiaras. People are obsessed by their coronation prerogatives.' Coronationitis was running rampant because the Conservative government decided to go the whole hog with the pageantry of the occasion. The crowning of the young Elizabeth was planned as a momentous event designed to lift the population out of the doldrums of the postwar era – to jump-start Britain and set it on the road to a new prosperity. There was much talk of a new Elizabethan Age to rival the artistic and commercial dynamism of the earlier one, and a British expedition to climb Mount Everest acquired a new symbolism.

The war had caused large-scale gaps in the accoutrements of royal panoply. Dukes, earls, lords and ladies who were 'Abbey Happy', that is, certain to attend the coronation ceremony in Westminster Abbey, unearthed their coronets and purple and ermine robes from the family vaults and banks. Those without robes borrowed them from friends and relatives, or scrambled to rent them from Moss Bros. – or as a last resort had them made at considerable cost. The Household Cavalry, which was to provide the mounted escort for the coronation coach, brought their breastplates and plumed helmets out of mothballs, but faced an acute shortage of horses. However, the day was saved by Queen Wilhelmina of the Netherlands, who presented them with a

119

number of mounts as a token of her gratitude for the royal family's wartime help. There was also a dearth of horse-drawn carriages in which not only royal relations but also Commonwealth prime ministers were supposed to ride in the coronation procession. The problem was resolved by renting several from the film company of the producer Alexander Korda. They were the very same ones Korda had snapped up for a song from Buckingham Palace at the outbreak of the war when the Royal Mews did not have the staff to take care of them. Korda simply let the original owners borrow them back – at a price.

The man responsible for organizing the Coronation was a chubby, red-faced, energetic man known in royal circles as Bernard Norfolk, in other words Bernard, Duke of Norfolk, the Earl Marshal of England. His finest hour was the coronation, and his preparations began a full twelve months before the 2 June ceremony. A Coronation Commission of senior officials and distinguished figures was set up as an umbrella organization with the Duke of Edinburgh as chairman, representing the Queen. The members included the Archbishop of Canterbury and the heads of several government departments involved in the arrangements. There were no women members, a curious omission considering that a woman was about to be crowned. The High Commissioners to London of Australia, New Zealand, South Africa, Canada, India, Pakistan and Ceylon (now Sri Lanka) were appointed Commission members as a royal gesture to the British Commonwealth.

The Queen's accession provided Commonwealth countries with an opportunity to show their independence from London by adopting different official titles for the new sovereign. In the United Kingdom she was officially known as: Elizabeth the Second, by the Grace of God of the United Kingdom of Great Britain and Northern Ireland and of Her Other Realms and Territories Queen, Head of the Commonwealth, Defender of the Faith. Individual Commonwealth countries, however, wanted the right to concoct mouthfuls of their own. After weeks of discussion a breakthrough was achieved in December 1952 at the Commonwealth Economic Conference in London whereby individual member countries acquired the right for the first time to compose their own designations for the Queen. Thus in Canada, she was to be formally known as Elizabeth by the Grace of God of Canada, and Her Other Realms and Territories Queen, Head of the Commonwealth, Defender of the Faith. But she was also termed respectively Queen of Australia, of New Zealand, of South

120

Africa, and of Ceylon. The last did not name her Defender of the Faith, since she was the defender of neither the Islamic faith nor of Hinduism. Pakistan could not live with the notion of a woman at its head, while India felt the title of Queen did not jibe with the country's republican status.

Commonwealth governments regarded this change to a flexible format as a major triumph, and the British government was clever enough not to disabuse them in this view. In the decade of decolonization that followed, Elizabeth was to be named Queen of several more newly independent former colonies which became members of the British Commonwealth, and the new form raised the intriguing theoretical possibility that if Elizabeth ever stopped being Queen of the United Kingdom, she would still be monarch of at least a dozen other countries across the globe.

The presence of the Commonwealth representatives on the Coronation Commission reflected this new plurality, but their membership was more show than substance. A senior Commonwealth official confided to an American diplomat that the High Commissioners were perfectly aware of this state of affairs but went along with it because the prime ministers of their respective countries were afraid that if they were asked to play a bigger part in the Coronation, they might also be asked to help pay for it. As the London American embassy reported to Washington, 'One official of a Commonwealth country told a US colleague that the coronation rehearsals were "frightfully embarrassing" because of the court officials' obvious pain in trying to fit all of the High Commissioners into a ritual designed for the crowning of a monarch of a few small Saxon tribes.' There had been calls in the press for the ceremony to be modified to give them specific roles. One correspondent proposed in a letter to *The Times* that Australia's prime minister should hold the Sword of State. But Commonwealth prime ministers were happy to ride in an honoured place in the procession without any further involvement in the four-hour Abbey service.

The ancient rite is spelled out in a small book written about 1307 by an abbot of Westminster. Called *Liber Regalis* – the Royal Book – its opening sentences, translated from the Latin, are: 'This is the order according to which the King has to be crowned and anointed. First, there shall be prepared a stage, raised between the High Altar and the Choir . . . ' It is a ceremonial in which only the higher clergy and the nobility participate, carrying the symbols of state and paying homage to the newly crowned sovereign. The idea of making the members of the House of Commons – as representatives of the British people – more visible in the service was raised in the Coronation Commission. One proposal was that a representative group of MPs should follow the peers in doing homage to the newly crowned Sovereign. Another was that the Speaker of the House should be designated. But the Commission turned down both ideas as too radical, and 'not in keeping with the spirit of the coronation ceremony.'

But for the Queen's intervention, the same unshakeably traditionalist approach would have torpedoed television coverage of the whole service. In July 1952, the Commission discussed the question of allowing BBC television cameras inside the Abbey and almost every member, starting with the Duke of Norfolk, expressed opposition. When Tommy Lascelles complained of 'the great and blinding light' the Queen would have to endure they assumed he was his mistress's voice. Quite right, chimed in the Archbishop of Canterbury, it would be 'unfair to expose the Queen ... to this searching method of photography, without the chance of correcting an error, for perhaps two hours on end.' The Archbishop and others – including Bobbety Salisbury – also had a more archaic concern. The idea that the coronation service would be shown on television screens in public houses offended their sensibilities. The audience would be drinking, and in some working-class pubs, wearing their cloth caps, which – they felt – would be disrespectful of the Queen. Based on the Commission's decision, Churchill announced in the Commons that television cameras would film the procession in the transept, the outer area of the Abbey, but the Queen's coronation would not be seen.

Elizabeth, however, liked television. Her father had owned one of the very first television sets in 1937. More important, she was well aware of the enormous public impact of the small screen, even if her advisers were not. Tommy Lascelles warned her of the danger of overexposure. But Lascelles had even been against instituting the King's Christmas radio broadcast for the same reason. The word from the Queen was that the Commission should reconsider its 'no-television' decision. There were discussions between the Duke of Norfolk, the Archbishop and the BBC about reducing the lighting requirements of television coverage, with Prince Philip also involved, and five months later, the Queen's husband finally told another meeting of the Commission that the service would be televised, on condition that there were no close-ups.

The Queen's involvement showed her close attention to the planning. Many of the arrangements originated with her. For example, Philip arrived at the Commission with a detailed route for the royal procession through the streets of London worked out by the Queen and himself, and documents on the coronation preparations in the government archives do not indicate that their proposals were subjected to close critical scrutiny. To cover areas of the city not included in the route, she proposed a series of later drives through certain London neighbourhoods. She also lengthened her coronation visit to Scotland so that her Scottish subjects would not feel they were getting short shrift. She practised wearing the crown and carrying the heavy orb and sceptre – so heavy that she had stands fixed for them inside the coach of state for her return journey from the Abbey. And she made sure the pile of the Abbey carpet was not so deep that the long robes worn by the participants would stick to it, as had happened in past coronations.

As 2 June drew closer, she appears to have become progressively more imbued with the solemnity of the ceremony. She tolerated no horseplay at the rehearsals. In the ivory and gold ballroom of Buckingham Palace under the six great chandeliers she and her six train-bearers practised moving with her long coronation train made from sheets sewn together. When Philip was flippant as he rehearsed the oath of allegiance, she scolded her husband in front of at least one eyewitness: 'Don't be silly. Come back here and do it again properly.' One of the Queen's secretaries, perhaps somewhat carried away by the sense of occasion, told an American embassy diplomat: 'She looks towards [the coronation] with a mixture of apprehension and keen anticipation, something like a bride who knows that this is to be her day and that until it has taken place her status and her dedication have not been formalized or completed.'

In other words, Elizabeth fully appreciated the importance of her investiture in confirming her position. By the end of her first year she veered between confidence and uncertainty. 'Extraordinary thing,' she told a friend soon after her accession, 'I no longer feel anxious or worried. I don't know what it is – but I have lost my timidity.' But in her moments of self-doubt – usually about dealing with people – she agonized over not living up to the Queen Mother's standards. 'If only I could do it as well as my mother does it,' she would say. The picture of her working style was already well established. She was a quick study, with a knack for coming to the heart of the matter in a long state document or a discussion. The inevitable American embassy dispatch stated: 'With all her gracious charm she is a steady-minded, hard-headed, competent administrator who as a member of her staff said "never puts out the wrong foot." ' In addition, she was as controlled and unflappable as her late father had been excitable, and it took an experienced eye to detect the small signs of royal displeasure – the drumming fingers, the slight tightening of the mouth.

The hardheadedness was evident in the Court's refusal to invite her Uncle David to her coronation. Based on his friendly lunch at Clarence House, the Duke retained a lingering hope that the new Queen might use the occasion of the Coronation to bury the past. What greater symbol could there have been of family reconciliation than his presence in Westminster Abbey together with that of the Duchess? But he had not realized the depth of Elizabeth's personal disapproval of his abdication and of the Duchess – to say nothing of her sympathy for her bereaved mother.

In October 1952, the Earl Marshal had told journalists that as a royal duke the Queen's uncle was entitled to be present, but his wife was not. But he 'did not believe the Duke would come.' When no invitation came, the Duke instructed his solicitor to take up the matter with Tommy Lascelles. The tone of the Secretary's reply betrays a certain vindictive relish. The presence of the Duke and Wallis in the Abbey would be 'condemned . . . as a shocking breach of taste.' It would strike 'a distressing and discordant note' if the Duke 'who, however good his reasons, did not feel able to undertake its obligations himself,' attended the coronation service. The solicitor, George Allen, pressed the point. Surely attitudes can change in seventeen years? Lascelles's reply seemed to define the royal family's attitude towards the Windsors: some things, he wrote, could never be forgotten or forgiven.

It is inconceivable that Lascelles, whatever his personal feelings about the Duke, would have taken it upon himself to make such a pronouncement without the Queen being aware of it, and even less so that he would have agreed to the Duke's subsequent request that no other ex-king should attend the ceremony if he was not invited (by tradition, reigning kings and queens are not asked to the Abbey). The Palace refused to make an announcement, and the Duke had to explain that the coronation would not be attended 'by the sovereign or ex-sovereign of any state.'

Those who were 'Abbey Happy' received the usual elaborate instructions, including what to wear. For example, the required head covering for women was a tiara or a veil. Hats were not permitted. The veil could be in any colour except black and 'should be attached by a comb, jewelled pins, flowers or ribbon bows, but not with feathers.' The Queen herself was to wear a coronation dress designed for her by Norman Hartnell. But as part of her homework before commissioning the dress Elizabeth had gone with Queen Mary to Kensington Palace where the robes worn by Queen Victoria at her coronation were kept, and tried on Victoria's dress, a simple, wasp-waisted, floor-length gown in white satin. It was, as Crawfie recalled, 'far too short', for though Elizabeth was not tall, her great-great-grandmother was diminutive. But the inspection helped her to form a mental picture of the dress she wanted for her own coronation: a traditional gown in white satin. The velvet robe of royal purple worn over the dress by Queen Victoria could not be found, so Elizabeth tried on her father's, which must, no doubt, have brought back memories of an eleven-year-old girl wearing a coronet, sitting beside her grandmother at Westminster Abbey.

Hartnell submitted eight sketches including a virtual copy of Queen Victoria's gown, a crinoline dress with a train of silver tissue and with the rose of England richly embroidered on the skirt in diamonds and crystals, and a roomier, more modern A-line dress. The Queen kept the sketches, consulted her mother and sister, and in subsequent discussions with Hartnell a ninth and final design emerged combining the line of the Victorian dress and the heavy embroidery of the crinoline dress. But besides the English rose, the Queen asked for the emblems of Scotland, Wales, Ireland and the Commonwealth countries to be embroidered on the full skirt. In preparation for the big day the Queen also went on a diet to shed about two inches from her waist. She did not share her mother's pronounced tendency towards plumpness, but the sudden increase in the number of hours spent at her desk as a result of becoming Queen had forced her to shorten her daily walk with the corgis in the grounds of Buckingham Palace and to be present at more formal meals.

In the midst of the whirl of preparation, Queen Mary's health declined rapidly and Elizabeth was advised that her grandmother was nearing the end of her life. The Duke of Windsor was called to London, and on 14 March he wrote to Wallis that 'Mama is very sick indeed and it's just a question of how long she will last.' The doctors 'paint a very black picture indeed . . . ' When he went to see her with his sister, Mary, the Princess Royal, he said, 'While she notices if you are one minute late and talks coherently she repeats herself a lot and has one or two theme songs upon which she harps all the time.' The Duke was present at Marlborough House on 24 March, when the Queen died at the age of eighty-five. She left the bulk of her possessions – jewels, silver, antiques, wealth – to Elizabeth, her favourite granddaughter. And one of her last requests was that if her death occurred before June, Court mourning should not interfere with the date or splendours of the coronation. Once again, barely a year after her father's death, the Queen returned to the vastness of Westminster Hall as the body of Queen Mary lay in state beneath the great vaulted ceiling. Four days later, the old Queen was buried at St George's Chapel, Windsor. And as the choir sang 'Abide With Me', Queen Mary's favourite hymn, Elizabeth stood alone in front of the bier. Then, head bowed, she watched the coffin being carried into the vault. The grandmother who from an early age had taught her so much about the rudiments of her office had not lived to see her reach the apotheosis of kingship.

In the midst of last-minute arrangements the Queen stepped in to resolve a crisis involving one of her favourite places: Malta. In May, Prime Minister George Borg Olivier announced that he was boycotting the coronation, having learned he would not be driving in the procession with the heads of government of the self-governing Commonwealth countries, but with representatives of the colonies, that is, countries still under direct British control. The Commonwealth prime ministers, as we have seen, were scheduled to ride in carriages. The colonial officials were assigned cars – and a less prominent position in the procession.

Borg Olivier regarded this as a snub, since the prime ministers respectively of Northern Ireland and Southern Rhodesia had been included among the coach riders, and the two countries were generally regarded as having forms of government similar to that of Malta. If he could not ride with the Commonwealth prime ministers as well, Borg Olivier informed London, his island would not be represented at the coronation and Malta's coronation celebrations would be cancelled altogether. To some extent Borg Olivier had been manoeuvred into delivering an ultimatum by the local left-wing opposition, but the point was a touchy one with the Maltese. At the time, Britain and Malta were in the middle of complex negotiations over the island's political status, and the Prime Minister's inclusion among the colonial representatives was interpreted as a step backwards in Malta's status.

The Colonial Secretary, Oliver Lyttelton, was prepared to resist

126

Maltese government pressure. But he had reckoned without the Queen's intervention. The Honourable Mabel Strickland, the island's formidable newspaper publisher who was a friend of the Queen, flew to London and approached Elizabeth directly on Borg Olivier's behalf. The Queen was not about to allow such a discordant note to mar her coronation – and especially one involving the island where she had spent perhaps the happiest two years of her adult life. The Queen asked Churchill to make the necessary change in the arrangements for George Borg Olivier. Lyttelton was, in effect, overruled. There was a postscript to the crisis: a carriage was found for Borg Olivier and his wife to ride in in the procession, but the equerry in charge had no more horses. The horses in the procession had been trained for months to accustom them to the cheering and the crowds. Some of the more excitable ones had even been successfully calmed by a non-veterinarian neurologist. So the acquisition of fresh horses at this late date was out of the question. The equerry was keeping two in reserve in case any of those in use went lame. He would only throw in his reserve if he received instructions directly from the Queen herself. The Queen released the horses and Borg Olivier had his carriage in the coronation procession.

In late May a round of social events resurrecting a forgotten splendour was added to the Queen's schedule. So besides resolving coronation disputes, rehearsing and re-rehearsing the coronation service with the Dean of Westminster who by tradition had the privilege of instructing the sovereign in its complex choreography, going to Norman Hartnell's atelier for last-minute fittings of her robes, to say nothing of coping with the regular flow of dispatch boxes, the Queen was also present at a series of balls and receptions. On 29 May, she attended the Household Brigade Ball at Hampton Court, one of the high points of the coronation social calendar. The Palace was floodlit and the fountains surrounded with massed flowers. It was literally a glittering evening because, as Jock Colville noted in his diary, 'Almost every woman wore a tiara and a dress worthy of the occasion . . . a world that vanished in 1939 lived again for the night.'

On 2 June the atrocious weather throughout Britain could not dampen national enthusiasm. A nation still experiencing postwar rationing and shortages staged celebrations in every city and town. In London, the route of the coronation procession decorated with huge cutout crowns, lions and unicorns was jammed with people. The paid seats in the enclosures at various junctures along the route could have been sold several times over – and indeed some were. At eleven in the morning, under a steady drizzle, the Queen's procession left Buckingham Palace for Westminster Abbey. As she stepped into the huge gilded coach in all her finery with her husband by her side the Queen was calm, even a little distracted, as if her thoughts were far away. 'Is all well, Ma'am?' asked one of her ladies-in-waiting. 'Oh yes,' the Queen replied. 'The Captain has just rung to say that Aureole went really well.' Aureole's morning training was supervised by the Queen's horse trainer, Captain Boyd-Rochfort.

In the Abbey, the coronation area was covered with a gold carpet. The magnificent Abbey plate gleamed on the high altar and facing the altar was the ancient oak coronation chair, with, on its shelf under the seat, the blackened Stone of Scone, the stone of destiny, on which King Edward the Confessor was traditionally believed to have sat at his coronation. Beyond that was the raised platform with the scarlet-covered throne. The newly crowned Queen would be seated on it to receive the homage of the peers of the realm. Tiers of extra seats had been constructed so that a record number of people could be squeezed into the Abbey. Behind the scenes the Abbey had also been well supplied with prefabricated cubicles, and the way to them was discreetly signposted.

Jewels and uniforms were the order of the day. Every man who had ever worn a uniform resurrected it for the occasion. Every woman who had them was festooned with as many diamonds as her head, neck, bosom and hands could carry. Noël Coward – watching the event on television – thought Winston Churchill looked 'both disagreeable and silly' in admiral's ceremonial uniform as the Warden of the Cinque Ports, the ancient ceremonial post of administrator of the five principal southern seaports of England. In fact, the Prime Minister was in a state of near total exhaustion and had to be carefully shepherded by his wife, Clementine. The strain of the coronation on top of his regular work had taken its toll, and less than three weeks later he was to suffer a massive stroke. The emphasis on uniforms was so infectious that the composer William Walton, who had written the *Te Deum* for the service, decided to wear his academic gown of Doctor of Music from Oxford University. Inside the flat, round velvet hat on his head were a number of miniature whiskey bottles to sustain him through the long ceremony. The United States official party at the Abbey was led by General George C. Marshall and the New York publisher

Fleur Cowles. And among the numerous American journalists reporting from various vantage points along the route was an aspiring photojournalist who less than a decade later would herself be lunching and dining with the Queen. Jacqueline Bouvier was covering the coronation for a Washington newspaper, but she was to remember it for another reason. While she was in London, Senator Jack Kennedy proposed by telegram.

The Queen entered the Abbey at the end of a long procession – so long that she retired to a small room in the Abbey to wait while the head of it moved down the nave. When she appeared, she was preceded by the Earl Marshal of England, walking backwards to face the monarch, and two lords carrying the royal symbols of office, the Sword of State, the Cap of Maintenance. Her train was borne by six young women from leading English families, including Lady Margaret Spencer-Churchill, the Duke of Marlborough's daughter. Behind them walked the Mistress of the Robes – the Queen's chief lady-in-waiting – the American-born Duchess of Rutland and the rest of her personal entourage. In the royal family's balcony overlooking the coronation area a little head peered over the balustrade beside the Queen Mother. It was four-year-old Prince Charles, brought in by a side door to watch his mother crowned. Members of the House of Lords were segregated, the peers in one place, peeresses in another. In their hands they held their own coronets, which they would put on at the moment of the Queen's coronation. In the first stage, the Queen was acclaimed by the people and in a clear, composed voice pronounced the oath, promising to govern well according to the Constitution. In the second, the sovereign was anointed with Holy Oil, and received the Insignia of her royal office, including the orb and sceptre. Then came the climax of the service in which the Archbishop of Canterbury held the crown of St Edward high above her head and placed it on her head. In the third and final stage, Elizabeth II ascended the throne and received the homage of the peers.

To the photographer Cecil Beaton, the peeresses were like a bed of auricula-eyed sweet william in their red velvet and white, liberally sprinkled with diamonds. Lady Haddington and the Duchess of Buccleuch wore huge diamond 'fenders', but Beaton felt that the Duchess of Devonshire, Nancy Mitford's sister, was the most beautiful of all. The robes she wore were the eighteenth-century robes of Georgiana, Duchess of Devonshire, and her hair was dressed wide to contain the huge coronet, shaped like a cake.

The service, conducted by the Archbishop of Canterbury, Geoffrey Fisher, assisted by the senior Anglican clergy, seemed to some an overdose of medievalism for a modern monarchy. But medieval or not, it was full of great moments evoking nothing but awe and admiration. The English gift for organizing ceremonial – what Noël Coward called 'The English State Ballet' – was at its best. Jock Colville was sitting directly in front of 'the massed peeresses whose robes and jewels sparkled with unique magnificence and whose movement as, with white gloved hands, they put their coronets on was aptly compared to the corps de ballet in *Lac des Cygnes*.' When the Queen was led through the choir screen to be presented to the people Archbishop Fisher declared, 'Sirs, I here present unto you Queen Elizabeth your undoubted Queen...' and this was followed by the shouted acclamations in Latin from the Westminster choristers: '*Vivat Regina Elizabetha! Vivat! Vivat! Vivat!*' To William Walton's wife, Susana, 'The crown looked far too heavy for such a slender person, and I began to wonder if she could carry it on her head.' But carry it she did, sitting erect on the throne as Philip led the homage of the peers. He knelt at his wife's feet and recited the formula that has changed little over the centuries, 'I, Philip, Duke of Edinburgh, do become your liegeman of life and limb and of earthly worship; and faith and truth I will bear unto you, to live and die, against all manner of folks.' The sovereign's consort has no established role in the coronation service, but at Elizabeth's discreet hint that she would like her husband to be given what the minutes of the Coronation Commission termed 'a special position' and not leave him sitting with the other royal dukes, the Archbishop of Canterbury and Bernard Norfolk had worked Philip into part of the service. Thus, following the homage, he knelt alongside the Queen to receive the blessing, and took Communion with her. It was another poignant moment in the ceremony.

Then came the triumphal return to Buckingham Palace, moving through the streets at a walking pace in relentless rain, past cheering crowds. Beaton, who had left for the Palace before the end of the service in order to set up his camera, first realized that she was back from the Abbey when he heard piping girlish voices at the end of the Picture Gallery – the high voices of the Queen and Princess Margaret above the others as they chatted. 'Oh, hullo! Did you watch it?' the Queen asked Prince Charles. 'When did you get home?' It may seem strange to hear Buckingham Palace referred to as home, but to the Queen that is what it had been for nearly sixteen years. The Queen had tired eyes and her hands were white with cold as she posed for pictures still wearing the Imperial Crown against a painted backdrop of Westminster Abbey. 'The Duke of Edinburgh stood by making wry jokes, his lips pursed in a smile that put the fear of God into me,' Beaton said later. 'Yes,' she admitted, 'the crown does get heavy.' Then Charles and Anne were running around the Queen Mother's purple train and Margaret, says Beaton, was all pink-and-white makeup and 'a sex twinkle of understanding in her regard.'

It was getting dark when the Queen appeared on the Palace balcony more than seven hours after she had set out for Westminster Abbey. Throughout the long, arduous day her coolness had not deserted her for one minute. After the ceremony, as she prepared to move to the choir screen the lining of her purple robe had stuck on the carpet pile. 'Start me off,' she whispered to the Archbishop of Canterbury, who lifted her robe clear of the carpet and she was on the move. As for the much discussed television coverage, the BBC's seven-and-a-half-hour coronation day coverage proved to be a landmark in television broadcasting history. A record 20.4 million British viewers watched on 2.7 million black-and-white sets. Twenty-eight years later, on 29 July 1981, 39 million viewers in Britain, plus an estimated 800 million others in fifty countries around the world, saw the wedding of Prince Charles and Lady Diana Spencer – in colour.

To add glory to an already glorious day it was announced that the British Everest expedition had reached the summit. Years later, however, it would be revealed that Edmund Hillary and the Tibetan Sherpa Tensing had actually made it to the top on 29 May, but the British government had delayed the release of the news until 2 June in order to tie in the achievement with the coronation. It was the kind of enterprising venture which Churchill felt captured the spirit of the new reign – the man of action far from home conquering new frontiers for England just as other men of action had built an empire when another queen was on the throne a century ago, and still others had fought and vanquished an old enemy in the name of an earlier Elizabeth.

The cultural side was represented by the royal gala performance on 8 June of a new opera by Benjamin Britten, *Gloriana*, at Covent Garden Opera House. The auditorium was covered in flowers – garlands running from chandelier to chandelier, coming together in a central tent of white blossoms and green laurel leaves. As for

Gloriana itself, even the Queen's cousin, the Earl of Harewood, who had been involved in its staging, called the performance 'one of the great disasters of operatic history.' Harewood, a close friend of Britten, blamed its failure on the fact that the audience of courtiers, high government officials and diplomats did not take kindly to 'the passionate, tender drama'. As the tender drama in Britten's opera was Queen Elizabeth I's affair with the Earl of Essex, many of those present thought it an unsuitable choice for the occasion. For one thing, Elizabeth I may have been single, but Essex was married and the musical version of their romance must have seemed an undainty dish to set before the newly crowned Queen. Besides, Colville's complaint that 'the music was above our heads' was shared by many of those present, including almost every occupant of the royal box with the almost certain exception of Princess Marina, the Duchess of Kent.

Subsequent performances of *Gloriana* showed that it was not without musical merit, and its failure at the royal gala was an early indication that, whatever her other good qualities, Elizabeth was not likely to preside over a flowering of the arts. Early biographers pointed out that the Queen was not an opera buff. Her musical preference included musicals and Boston Pops classical favourites. Dinner guests at Windsor Castle got the Guards string band playing Franz Lehar and Ivor Novello, rather than a classical string quartet. At smaller private parties Noël Coward was a favourite performer, sometimes with Princess Margaret as his accompanist. 'Middlebrow' was not a term the Queen would quarrel with to describe her cultural taste. At Balmoral and Sandringham she read Agatha Christie mysteries, Dick Francis thrillers, and biographies of her royal ancestors. Seats were (and still are) reserved for the royal family every night at every London theatre, but the Queen and her husband did not go to the fine Coronation Year Shakespeare season at the Old Vic (*Measure for Measure*, *Henry VIII*, *Love's Labour's Lost*), but to the lighter comedies.

Elizabeth had been surrounded from birth by dogs and horses rather than intellectual pursuits. Her expert knowledge of horses was the result of a lifetime involvement, careful study, and what her father's trainer Fred Darling called 'a natural eye for a horse'. It was quite consistent with this deep and abiding interest that she should talk to her trainer on the morning of her coronation: almost inconceivable that she would have talked to her poet, the poet laureate John Masefield, or to Sir Arnold Bax, the Master of the

132

Queen's Musick. The Queen fulfilled her commitments towards the arts, but often more out of duty than personal involvement.

Once, Sir Michael Adeane, the Deputy Secretary who was to succeed Tommy Lascelles, approached Harold Nicolson to recommend the name of a writer worthy to be awarded the Order of Merit, an honour 'in the Queen's gift' (that is, personally bestowed by the Queen and not on the recommendation of the government) and usually given to a certain number of prominent scientists, artists and literary figures, theoretically, her personal intellectual élite. Nicolson felt that there was no-one worthy and it would be better to give it a miss. Oh no, Adeane replied, otherwise the Palace would be criticized for neglecting literature: what about Edith Sitwell? Doesn't have the stature, Nicolson replied (and then felt guilty about it). Avoiding criticism was what mattered.

Contrast that with the Queen's decision to switch jockeys for Aureole, made about the same time. In her coronation year, her racing manager Charles Moore and Captain Boyd-Rochfort disagreed over whether or not to change Aureole's jockey. To her disappointment, the temperamental chestnut colt had failed to win the Epsom Derby four days after the Westminster Abbey ceremony. Moore proposed switching jockeys from the dedicated Henry Carr to Eph Smith, who – the Queen's racing manager felt – was more congenial to Aureole. Boyd Rochfort was opposed to the change. The Queen admired Carr but turning Aureole into a winner mattered more. She picked the jockey for whom Aureole went most happily. Jockeys the Queen chose personally: finding a writer for one of the most distinguished royal honours – that could be delegated.

The royal couple's three-day trip to Ulster on 1 July gave the Queen her first taste of the ever-present threat of violence that lurks behind her public appearances. The night they arrived, there was an explosion on the Belfast–Dublin railway line near the border between Ulster and the Irish Republic, some twenty miles from the stretch of track which the royal train was scheduled to use the following day. At the end of July the Queen visited Scotland, where she took part in a special service of dedication in St Giles' Cathedral in Edinburgh. The service – her idea – was a gesture to Scottish nationalist sensibilities. Almost exactly a year earlier in Edinburgh, she noticed that a prize cup she was presenting to a member of the Royal Company of Archers, her personal bodyguard in Scotland, was engraved 'presented by Her Majesty, Queen Elizabeth.' The Queen observed pointedly that she was Elizabeth II and shouldn't that be corrected? So back to the jewellers went the cup, even though many resentful Scots felt that no correction was needed. Elizabeth I had been Queen of England, but not of Scotland.

By the autumn, the euphoria of the coronation had given way to the pressure of two major crises, one domestic, the other political. The political crisis centred on Winston Churchill's declining health and the choice of a successor as Prime Minister. The domestic crisis involved Princess Margaret and Group Captain Peter Townsend, Master of the Queen Mother's Household. In the midst of the coronation preparations, Princess Margaret had confirmed to the Queen that she was in love with Peter Townsend, and he with her. Once again, love threatened to shake the foundations of the monarchy.

IX

Margaret in Love

Emerging from Westminster Abbey following the coronation, Princess Margaret was spotted flicking a spot of fluff from the lapel of Peter Townsend's uniform. This intimate gesture did not escape the gimlet eyes of Fleet Street reporters, adding a dollop of substance – however small – to the rumours they already knew but were not printing. Gossip about Princess Margaret and Townsend surfaced in London shortly after King George's death. The stories were picked up by the press across the Channel and in the United States. But so far the British press had practised restraint so as not to undermine the coronation atmosphere. In May 1953, Margaret had approached the Queen with news that she and Townsend were in love. It is hard to believe that their growing fondness for each other had escaped Elizabeth's notice. Townsend had fallen under the spell of Margaret's sparkling personality in the spring of 1951. Nearly two years later, in February 1953, the couple were alone at Windsor Castle and – as he put it – 'we talked in the Red Drawing Room for hours – about ourselves'. Out of this conversation came 'the mutual discovery of how much we meant to one another.' Townsend 'told her, very quietly' how he felt about her. 'That is exactly how I feel too,' was her reply.

According to Townsend's subsequent account, when Margaret discussed the situation with her mother, the Queen Mother was sympathetic, but from the start ruled out marriage. Margaret's sister, on the other hand, was both pleased and concerned, says Lady Longford, who, for her biography of the Queen, interviewed the Princess on her relationship with Townsend. Pleased that Margaret had settled on a man who was well liked within the family, and was acceptable in almost all respects. Concerned because the main reason why he was unacceptable was that two years earlier he had obtained a divorce after a long period of estrangement from his wife, Rosemary. As the injured party, he was granted custody of his two sons, but the Queen immediately foresaw problems.

Divorce set off alarm bells in the royal family because of the Abdication. Moreover, at the time the Church of England's stricture against divorced people re-marrying was more strenuously applied, and it was simply unthinkable for the Queen, as head of the Church of England, to have given her consent. That consent was not merely an older sister's prerogative. Under the Royal Marriages Act of 1772, Princess Margaret, as third in line to the throne, required the Queen's permission to marry until she was twenty-five. Thereafter she was free to make her own choice without the Queen's consent or the approval of Parliament – but at a price. She would have to renounce her claim to the throne, and give up her annual allowance from the Civil List. In effect, this meant a two-year wait. Margaret was twenty-three, Townsend two years away from his fortieth birthday.

Those who knew Margaret during this period say that the Queen's acceptance of Townsend included a generous helping of relief that her sister's choice of future husband was not worse. Elizabeth had picked a young man from outside the magic circle and then stood her ground against her parents' opposition. Margaret, typically, wanted to go one better by seeking to marry a commoner. If it worked for Lilibet, why shouldn't it work for me? was her approach. Moreover, Margaret's interest in Townsend had all the marks of a young woman looking for security and reassurance in a father figure. But Townsend was not only considerably older than the eligible, titled Guards officers in her own group of friends. With few exceptions, he was better-looking, and – with hardly any exceptions at all – more intelligent, even erudite.

As the King's equerry, he had always been on hand with help and support. On the South African tour, when Elizabeth was cocooned in her own thoughts and dreams about her young Greek god, Margaret looked for more congenial company and found it in Peter Townsend, and their shared early morning rides and jokes helped to relieve the pressure of a heavy schedule. Back in England, Townsend was often pressed into service as an escort who could handle the spirited Princess and limit her scope for mischief.

136

But soon the teasing friendship had blossomed into something very different. In 1948, Townsend accompanied Elizabeth and Margaret to the Hague for the investiture of Queen Juliana of the Netherlands, and several of those present, noting her radiance when the couple danced together, drew the obvious conclusion. 'Without realizing it,' Townsend says, 'I was being carried a little further from home, a little nearer to the Princess.' After the King's death Townsend became more important to her as the link with her father, whose loss had affected her deeply.

At a family council at which Townsend was not present, the Queen Mother repeated her opposition to the match. Philip felt no particular affinity for the older Englishman, with whom he occasionally played strenuous games of squash (both were, predictably, aggressive players), but his view was that Margaret should be free to marry him if she renounced her claim to the throne. The Queen remained undecided. She invited Margaret and Townsend to spend an evening with her and Philip. Even after a decade in the royal household, Townsend could count on the fingers of one hand the evenings he had spent alone with the royal family at Buckingham Palace. But Philip relieved the initial awkwardness by telling jokes, and the Queen was 'movingly simple and sympathetic' towards her sister and charming towards the commoner Margaret wanted to marry. Nonetheless the Queen still found their romance 'a disturbing fact', and her quiet advice was to allow time to find a solution. 'Under the circumstances, it isn't unreasonable for me to ask you to wait a year,' she told them. And if the Queen was of two minds about the marriage, there were people quite determined to make it up for her.

While Margaret confided in the Queen and in the Queen Mother, Peter Townsend himself broke the news to Tommy Lascelles with a soldier's directness: Princess Margaret and he were in love. Enraged at the news, Lascelles's first reaction was, 'You must either be mad or bad.' But the Queen had already discussed the romance with him, and had not had the heart to tell Margaret and Townsend what his advice had been. As Lascelles saw it, the Queen had but one option: forbid the match outright. She could not afford a scandal so close to the coronation. He himself was in favour of seeking the advice of the Cabinet, doubtless because he had a very good idea what that advice would be. He also felt the Queen should consent to Townsend's immediate removal from Clarence House and the royal household. This would be done discreetly by assigning Townsend to an overseas embassy as air attaché. The

Queen refused to separate the couple. Remarkably, Margaret and Townsend remained under the same roof at Clarence House – at least until after the coronation.

Lascelles then set to work ensuring the Cabinet's response was the right one. In his published diary the late Jock Colville noted that on 12 June Lascelles drove to Chartwell, Churchill's country home, to brief the Prime Minister on the crisis in the royal family. Years later, Colville told a somewhat different story possibly forgetting – or wishing to correct – his earlier version. According to Colville's later, fuller, account, Tommy Lascelles broke the news to him first. The Queen's Secretary sent for him and recounted the whole story, stressing the need to end the affair before the Princess reached the stage when she could marry without the Queen's consent. 'The Queen Mother wept when I talked to her,' Lascelles told Colville. 'I have never seen her shed tears before.' Colville then went to Chequers, the Prime Minister's official country home, and delivered Lascelles's message to Churchill. The romance appealed to Churchill's sentimental nature. 'What a delightful match!' the old man exclaimed. 'A lovely young royal lady married to a gallant young airman, safe from the perils and horrors of war!'

Colville tried to convey to the Prime Minister that he was not thinking along the desired lines. 'But Winston, that isn't at all what Tommy was trying to say,' Colville protested. Somewhat mollified (according to Colville's account), Churchill called a cabinet meeting, which decided without a single dissenting voice that the Prime Minister must advise the Queen against a royal marriage. The outcome was hardly a surprise to the Queen's Private Secretary. Prior to the meeting, Lascelles had personally buttonholed more than one senior cabinet minister to whom he pointed out that it would be in the best interests of the Queen and the royal family if the Cabinet nipped the romance in the bud and saved the Princess from marrying a social climber. Lascelles had an ally in Bobbety Salisbury, a senior member of Churchill's cabinet and a strong opponent of the marriage.

Churchill duly informed the Queen of the Cabinet's decision and, from an official point of view, the issue was effectively shelved until August 1955, Princess Margaret's twenty-fifth birthday. But the press, which was now giving full coverage to the romance, had no intention of dropping the subject. Wherever the Princess or Townsend went an army of photographers and reporters was sure to follow. Any thought of a normal existence was now out of the question for either of them. So Lascelles got his way and the Queen agreed to a foreign posting for Townsend. Given a choice of serving as air attaché in Singapore, Johannesburg or Brussels, he chose the latter, which at least had the advantage of being reasonably close to his two small sons – and to Margaret. When the Queen Mother and Princess Margaret left London on 29 June for a tour of Rhodesia, their Master of the Household did not accompany them. He said goodbye to the Princess at Clarence House. 'The princess was very calm, for we felt certain of each other,' Townsend was to recall long after it was all over. With his departure for his new post scheduled for after Margaret's return, they had anticipated a final leave-taking before their final separation.

The day after Margaret's departure Townsend acted as equerry to the Queen and the Duke of Edinburgh on their one-day visit to Belfast, and the photographers concentrated more on him than on Elizabeth and Philip. When the royal party returned to Heathrow Airport, the Queen stood for some minutes on the tarmac talking to the handsome air force aide who at the time seemed likely to become her brother-in-law. The separation would help to take the pressure off the couple, she told him. Then, in front of the assembled welcoming dignitaries, she shook his hand and wished him good luck in his new appointment. At Buckingham Palace, however, Tommy Lascelles was waiting to launch another torpedo against the ill-starred couple. He told Townsend his departure had been brought forward to 15 July, two days before Princess Margaret's return. Townsend cabled the news to Margaret in Umtali, Rhodesia, and 'it came as an unpleasant shock.'

As Townsend said goodbye to his sons at their boarding school and flew to Brussels, press surveys showed widespread sympathy for the separated couple. Perhaps Churchill's instinctive reaction had been the right one. At the same time, published statistics showed that the number of divorces in Britain in 1952 had been the highest in history. 'A welter of pseudo-religious claptrap is now swirling around the feet of the poor princess and the unfortunate young man,' wrote Noël Coward in his diary. He was too much of a traditionalist in this respect to approve of the match. But he felt Townsend should have been discreetly transferred out of the country before the affair had become serious and not afterwards. 'One can only assume that the "advisers" at Buckingham Palace . . . are a poor lot.'

With Townsend at least temporarily out of the picture the Queen and the royal family had bought time to resolve the problem. But one crisis was swiftly followed by another. Winston

Churchill had a massive stroke, which impaired his speech and paralysed his left arm. So grave was his condition, the Queen was warned that she faced the immediate prospect of having to choose another Prime Minister. But who? The obvious successor was Foreign Secretary Anthony Eden, who was also Deputy Prime Minister. But Eden, also in declining health, was in America having a serious abdominal operation.

It has always been said of Queen Elizabeth that staying out of politics was second nature to her. She has made sparing use of her royal prerogative. Even so, each of the handful of major initiatives she has been called upon to take in this area has proved controversial. The reason is that when it comes to the sovereign and politics, much is left open to interpretation. Churchill's illness very nearly led to her first use of the royal prerogative's central component, the right to choose the Prime Minister. Churchill quickly forestalled this by writing to tell her he was 'not without hope' that he might recover sufficiently to stay on at least until the autumn, when he thought Eden would be able to take over. But that situation, like the Townsend crisis, was merely postponed.

In theory, the Queen is free to ask whoever she likes to form a government, but the fact is that this freedom is hemmed in by political realities. In the case of a party winning a landslide election victory, the Queen has a clear obligation to give the mandate to its acknowledged leader. It is the borderline situations, such as a hung parliament, when no party in the House of Commons can muster a decisive majority, that offer her considerable latitude. In such cases it is up to the Queen to decide who to ask to form a government. Common sense and usage dictate that she should consult politicians and experts, but such consultation is not mandatory. In the case of a party dispute over succession following the resignation of a Prime Minister the Queen could also play a decisive role, especially in the first decade of her reign. By the second decade, following one or two unseemly squabbles, the political parties had introduced clear-cut guidelines for deciding the succession to avoid the embarrassment of having the Queen exercise the royal prerogative to decide for them.

By 11 September 1954 Churchill had recovered sufficiently to accompany the Queen to the Doncaster races to watch Aureole run in the St Leger race from the royal enclosure. The Queen was cheered when she appeared on the balcony of the royal box, Churchill told his doctor four days later. 'I kept back, but when she came out and said to me "They want you", I went into the box, and when I

140

appeared I got as much cheering as she did.' When Aureole – the favourite in the St Leger – continued his run of defeats Churchill shared the Queen's disappointment. From not knowing her, as Colville observed, Churchill was now 'madly in love' with her. This attachment was one way in which he rationalized remaining in office after his stroke, while a frustrated Anthony Eden waited in the wings. The young Queen, Churchill felt, needed him. He could hardly burden her with a change of Prime Minister so soon before she left on her seven-month Commonwealth tour in November. Besides, he had unfinished business with Eisenhower. In early December he planned to meet the American President in Bermuda hoping to persuade him to agree to a summit with the Soviet leadership. To Churchill, Washington's hard-line approach merely exacerbated the Cold War and made the world a more dangerous place. When Eisenhower won the 1952 election, Churchill had gloomily told the Queen that his presence in the White House increased the probability of war.

From Churchill's point of view the Bermuda Conference was a bitter disappointment. He failed in his main purpose of breaking down Eisenhower's resistance to talking directly to the Russians, largely because of the inflexible position of the American Secretary of State, John Foster Dulles. Yet on 16 December the Queen, on her Commonwealth tour, wrote to the Prime Minister, 'We have followed with interest the news of the Bermuda Conference and all it implies for the good of the world. I hope you are satisfied with the way it went and I trust you did not find it too strenuous.' Either the Queen did not know or did not comprehend what went on at the conference, or she had not grasped – or had not been told – what it was Churchill had been hoping to accomplish. We are a long way from the experienced, knowledgeable monarch of later years. In his reply, Churchill did not mention the conference, perhaps out of tact. Instead, he praised, 'the amazing exertions of Yr Majesty and the Duke . . . for the sake of our world-wide but hard-pressed [Commonwealth].'

The Queen's amazing exertions had by then taken her as far as Fiji, but her first royal tour of the Commonwealth still had another six months to go. She and Philip had left London on the morning of 23 November. The previous night the Queen Mother had given a farewell dinner in their honour at which Noël Coward sang his songs and Peter Ustinov did imitations. 'Brilliant but too long' was Coward's verdict on Ustinov, but the Queen was greatly amused and didn't leave the party until three in the morning. The tour was both a link with the past and a model for the future. It was originally planned for George VI, but was begun in January 1952 by Elizabeth and Philip following the King's illness. In the afterglow of the coronation it acquired a new significance. The Queen of the Commonwealth was visiting many of the lands and peoples which claimed her as their own. George VI's prediction in South Africa of a monarchy on the move was being put into effect by his daughter. In the age of the Moscow –Washington confrontation, the emerging Commonwealth was Britain's sole hope of extending its influence beyond its shores. The war had ended Britain's position as a world power and the days of the Big Three, who had seemed so dominant seven years earlier, were over.

The tour was a blockbuster in scope, duration and distance covered, and its strenuous programme set the pattern for future Commonwealth trips. After a brief refuelling stop in Gander, the Queen spent a day in Bermuda, two days in Jamaica, one in Panama, two in Fiji, one in Tonga, thirty-nine days in New Zealand, fifty-seven in Australia, a day in Aden, two days in Uganda, one day in Libya, four days in Malta, and the last day in Gibraltar before sailing to Britain. The Queen made 102 speeches and listened to 276, shook hands with more than 13,000 people, and stood through the national anthem 508 times.

The tour even established a pattern of security scares. In Port Royal, the old capital of Jamaica, thirty-year-old Warren Kidd leapt over the ropes, threw his cream-coloured jacket at the Queen's feet, and prostrated himself. The police immediately seized Kidd and someone else picked up the jacket. If Kidd's intention had been more deadly than re-enacting Sir Walter Raleigh's chivalrous gesture to the first Elizabeth, there was little to prevent him from succeeding. But the Queen herself took the sudden disturbance in her stride, pretending not to see. 'I love the Queen, I just wanted her to walk on my coat,' Kidd protested as he was carried off to a psychiatric hospital, from which he was released after her departure. In Uganda, her trip to Kampala was cancelled because of Mau Mau death threats, and even in Entebbe most of the celebrations were held in the well-guarded Government House.

The tour also brought out her extraordinary capacity to witness the phantasmagoric, the bizarre, the exotic, the humorous with the Windsor poker face. In Uganda, an obliging official translated the words chanted by Acholi tribesmen and their women: 'The daughter of the chief is ringing her ankle bells. She is our

142

queen today. As a seabird she has come to us.' How interesting, deadpanned the Queen. In Whyalla, South Australia, fifty Aborigine tribesmen, their hair and beards ritually matted with kangaroo blood, did more than ring their ankle bells when she became the first woman to learn the secret behind the primitive tribal dance, the corroboree. Fascinating, remarked Elizabeth II.

On their overnight stopover in Tonga to return the visit of Queen Salote Tupou to London for the Coronation, Elizabeth and Philip got an insight into how the Fijian queen had reached her formidable physical proportions. The banquet in their honour included 3,000 lobsters, 4,200 suckling pigs, 2,100 chickens, and breadfruit pudding. There were, maybe, three hundred guests. The Queen picked delicately at this gargantuan feast, including the lobster even though she does not eat shellfish outside her own home because of the high risk of illness, but thereafter decreed that staffers advancing her future trips were to take better care to protect her from further assaults on her digestive system. The meal was followed by a sleepless night in the royal guest palace, where crickets and chattering Tongan guards kept her awake and a dawn serenade of nose-flutes woke her when she finally did get to sleep.

The Queen and Philip spent Christmas in Christchurch, New Zealand. In her Christmas message, the Queen spoke of the Commonwealth as an 'equal partnership of nations and races' to which, she said, 'I shall give myself, heart and soul, every day of my life.' It was a commitment that was to dominate her life. She spent the last day of 1953 quietly with her husband at a sheep farm fifteen miles north of Christchurch: the end of a year shaken by successive tidal waves of tension and emotional strain – the death of Queen Mary, the Coronation, Princess Margaret's romance with Peter Townsend, the political fall-out from Winston Churchill's near-fatal stroke. The Margaret–Townsend affair and the choice of a new Prime Minister still loomed ominously as unfinished business when she returned home in May, but her coronation had given her new confidence, a new sense of control over her own destiny, a renewed will to confront the problems ahead.

On 2 May, the Queen and her husband were reunited with their children in Tobruk harbour on board the newly completed royal yacht *Britannia* on which all four were to sail on the last stages of their tour. The Queen had sent instructions to the ship that the reunion with Charles and Anne was to take place in the saloon after her formal welcome on board by the ship's captain and officers. But as soon as she and Philip stepped on board, Charles came rushing across the quarter deck followed by his sister. The Queen patted him lightly on the head, said, 'Not you, dear,' and went on down the receiving line of officials.

The children had sailed to the Libyan port from Malta after spending a carefree week with the Mountbattens, and their stay on the island had offered an insight into Elizabeth's attempts at long-distance motherhood. In March, Boy Browning, as Comptroller of the Queen's Household, had written to Mountbatten (incidentally, his wartime commander in Asia) asking for 'a programme of excursions' for Charles and Anne 'to be submitted for the Queen's approval.' Offended by this bureaucratic approach, Mountbatten (now commander-in-chief of the Mediterranean fleet) had replied sharply that his wife would organize trips to the beach and other activities 'as desirable each day.' Mountbatten accompanied the royal children on these outings himself, watching over them as they waded in the sea and scampered over the rocks, and it was the beginning of a relationship which was to become progressively more important to both Charles and his great-uncle. So, in time, the same closeness that had existed between Mountbatten and Philip also grew with Philip's eldest son.

From Tobruk, *Britannia* sailed back to Malta on 3 May. Two hundred miles east of the island, the Mediterranean fleet met the royal yacht at sea with a spectacular manoeuvre. Led by Mountbatten in his flagship HMS *Glasgow* the ships of the fleet approached the yacht in two columns on an opposite course at twenty-five knots, twice the speed of *Britannia*. Then the two lines turned inwards and closed in on *Britannia* from astern, sweeping past so close that the spray from some of the ships splashed the royal yacht's decks. 'The exercise was perfectly safe provided that no mistake was made,' according to Mountbatten's official biographer. 'But a tiny deviation could have caused a disastrous accident.' Mountbatten was then transferred by jackstay to the yacht and landed in Valletta with the Queen's party.

One purpose of the exercise had been to outmanoeuvre Malta's governor, Sir Gerald Creasy, with whom Mountbatten had earlier had a clash of wills over precedence. As a member of the royal family as well as commander-in-chief, Mountbatten claimed the right to be the first to greet the Queen. Creasy, an official of high standing in the British Colonial Service, maintained that he – Creasy – was the Queen's representative on the island and therefore had seniority. As governor, he had the decisive word in the argument. But here was Mountbatten arriving with the Queen, while Sir Gerald kicked his heels on the quay at the head of the welcoming committee. A royal tour brings on an epidemic of behind-the-scenes arguments over protocol, but this was one the Queen got to hear about. Creasy pointedly expressed his regret that the Queen's governor had not been the first person to welcome her to the island. The Queen turned to Mountbatten and said, 'Sir Gerald is right, Uncle Dickie.'

On 14 May, in a repetition of her father's return from his American tour, she sailed up the Thames to London in a navy destroyer. Churchill was invited on board and was greeted by the Queen wearing khaki trousers under her coat. 'I could not detect the slightest evidence of strain,' he later told his physician admiringly. After dinner, the film *Maggie* was shown in the ship's cinema, which was so cold the Prime Minister clutched a cushion to his chest for warmth. The following day in the House of Commons he eulogized the tour in his own inimitable style: 'All over the globe there has been a sense of friendly feeling and generous admiration. Even envy wore a friendly smile.'

The tour was a royal progress in the old sense of a sovereign's journey through her lands, and there is no doubt that in Fiji, in Tonga, even in Sydney, like the monarchs of other times in other kingdoms, her presence brought a certain magic – the magic of incarnation. As Mountbatten's daughter Pamela, one of the ladies-in-waiting on the tour, put it, 'People were so fascinated to see what they might have thought of as a waxwork, actually moving and speaking.'

For Elizabeth herself it was a gallery of vivid memories, and a collection of closely observed situations with which to amuse her family and her circle of close friends, wickedly mimicking the people involved. It was also an exercise in total immersion, in which the concentrated public exposure highlighted both her strengths and her weakness. Her physical stamina was remarkable. In those early days whenever her aides advised against some event as too strenuous for her, she would say, 'Did my father do it? Then I will too,' and 'I'll be all right, I'm as strong as a horse.' Wherever she went, thanks to her growing ability to master complex briefs and to a retentive memory she was able to demonstrate that she had done her homework, which was flattering to her hosts.

With her youth and good looks, glamour and natural dignity, she was both monarch and superstar. Yet she was not yet comfortable in her public persona. Everywhere she went crowds of people waited to catch a glimpse of her, if only for a moment. Once in New Zealand, gazing from the window of the royal train at an expectant group at a railroad siding, she remarked, 'If I were Mummy, I would be out there and they would adore it.' The point is that Mummy adored it too. But Elizabeth had not inherited the Queen Mother's hammy streak, and got no adrenalin from contact with the public.

The Florentine artist Pietro Annigoni, who began work on what was to be perhaps the most famous portrait of the Queen shortly after her return, grumbled that, 'As a model [the Queen] does not facilitate my work. She doesn't "feel" the pose, and she doesn't appear to be concerned about it.' Harold Nicolson, receiving a knighthood from the Queen at a private investiture three months before the Coronation, admired her trim figure, her neat hair, beautiful complexion and charming voice, but thought she lacked the spontaneity of her mother, as she lacked her radiance. And Mountbatten's daughter recalled, '[The Queen] went through some awful ordeals. [She] would be in her box looking at the racecourse and the entire crowd . . . would have their backs to the course and would gaze at her with their racing-glasses. There is a strain after, say, the first twenty minutes.' Another strain was the permanent smile. 'You get a twitch,' explained Lady Pamela. 'So there is a moment when you have to relax your muscles, and of course that one moment when you are not smiling – it's the despair of some people who then think you are looking frightfully cross.'

But the greatest strain of all was speaking in public. In the grip of nerves the charming voice became close to a squeak. Within weeks of her accession a radio comedian had only to say 'My husband and I' in a high-pitched voice for everyone to know the comic was mimicking the Queen making a speech. Philip, who had an easy relaxed delivery himself, sympathized with his wife's nerves, but the couple had from the start agreed that he should not look at her when she was struggling through a public speech. On one occasion before one important address on the tour, when he thought the microphone was not yet switched on, he was heard to say encouragingly, 'Don't look so sad, Sausage.'

The Duke was a definite asset to Elizabeth. He was protective and supportive, and he kept up her spirits with his outrageous jokes and one-liners. Her eye for the absurd has been enhanced by Philip's own keen perception of the ridiculous. Private laughter, in fact, has been a valuable bond between them. Walking under a colourful fringed umbrella borne by a huge black bearer to protect her from the sun in Uganda the Queen muttered in an aside to her husband, 'I feel like an African queen.' Her husband muttered back, 'You *are* an African queen.' Whenever overzealous courtiers tried to overload her programme and the Queen did not have the will to refuse, Philip would have the decision reversed through a combination of naval forcefulness and charm, and it was to protect her interests that she had appointed him chairman of the Coronation Commission.

Their relationship seems to have progressed along the lines of public recognition by the Queen for not necessarily public actions by Philip. Shortly before their departure on the royal tour, Elizabeth amended the so-called Regency Act of 1937 so that if Prince Charles succeeded her before reaching the age of eighteen the Regent would be Philip and not Princess Margaret, as previously designated. The change made sense, as the Home Secretary, Sir David Maxwell-Fyfe, argued in the Commons, because 'a combination of Regency, guardianship and parental influence' would be 'in the same hand'. Moreover it was public acknowledgment that Philip was the decision maker in the family. But the reason for the timing of the change is one of those unanswered questions in the relationship. One theory was that the Queen had been wanting to alter the Regency Act in Philip's favour for some time and Margaret's romance with Peter Townsend together with the prospect – however remote – of her marriage had provided a justification without giving undue offence. Another was that the appointment had been intended as a conciliatory gesture for the rebuff Philip had received in his effort to change the name of the royal house.

The American embassy described Philip to Washington as a 'man of genuine leadership, energy and vitality, who would have in all probability risen to the top of the naval ladder had he remained free to follow his profession . . . In a sense and partly through the adroit manoeuvring of his uncle, Philip was almost as well trained for his role from an early age as was Elizabeth [for hers]' and he had a clear appreciation of 'what can be done from his present position.' What could not be done was to involve himself in matters political, but outside the hallowed ground of dispatch boxes and ministerial audiences, the field was wide open and he set about making his mark wherever he could. His first assault was on the creaking, archaic royal household, which was badly in need of overhaul. Changing the system was such a struggle that relatively standard innovations such as introducing dictaphones in his office, and an intercom system linking the various departments on the administrative floor of Buckingham Palace took on the stature of major achievements (the Queen and her husband have always had their offices side by side, with their respective staffs working together on the floor below).

Philip also had hopes of relaxing the rigid life that royalty still lived, and in some respects Elizabeth supported this view. To meet a wider variety of people, as we have seen, she began – at Philip's suggestion – to hold periodic Buckingham Palace lunches for leading businessmen, film stars, sports personalities, and other figures in British public life. Because she did not share her father's passion for Sandringham, she made Windsor her real home. As she used to tell friends, it was where she had been happiest as a child. Entertaining at Windsor was kept as informal as she could make it, and on weekends she could be seen in Windsor town driving her own car with Charles and Anne seated in the back.

But Philip's early notions of informality went somewhat further. A lot of it had to do with what later became known as macho, for he exuded masculine drive and self-confidence. Philip did not so much walk into a room, he exploded into it like a sudden gust of wind blows open a window on a blustery day. Having just learned to fly a helicopter, he had a helipad built in the grounds of Buckingham Palace and – against his wife's wishes – travelled by helicopter whenever he could. The Queen had enlisted Churchill's help in trying to persuade her husband not to fly helicopters but it had done no good. The Prime Minister would have been more emphatic had the Queen shown any interest in helicopter flying, but she needed no warning not to accompany her husband. In fact, it was not until twenty years later that she flew by helicopter for the first time. One foggy, wet morning in the autumn of 1954, the Queen was sitting for Annigoni. Precious little daylight came through the windows of the Yellow Drawing Room overlooking the Palace forecourt and the Mall that morning, and Annigoni grumbled as he daubed at the canvas. The Queen, posing in her dark blue Garter robe, remarked in French, their common language: 'The weather makes me happy, because when it's like this I know my husband won't be flying his helicopter.'

The contrast between the outgoing, energetic Duke and his quiet, introverted wife was so marked that gossip about Philip was inevitable. His royal status was both intriguing and seductive, and with his enemies in Court and establishment circles, stories about him continued to get around. For example, a lover of cricket

148

from his schooldays, he enjoyed both playing and socializing with leading English cricketers, some of whom had a reputation for mayhem and nightclubbing. Aside from the Thursday Club, there would be 'sightings' of Philip accompanied by the inseparable Mike Parker at this late-night cricketers' party, or with his photographer friend, Baron, at that nightspot. At the time of his wedding, there were reports – never published in Britain, but rife in the rest of Europe – resurrecting his earlier friendship with the hostess of a BBC television show, *Café Continental*.

A striking, vivacious brunette with a slight French accent, she was typecast for the role of Philip's rumoured former girlfriend, which she denied. In Britain, she was known by her stage name Hélène Cordet, but he had first known her as Hélène Foufounis, daughter of Greek royalists in Paris who were friends of his family. It was no secret that Philip and Hélène had been close friends since childhood. In 1938, while still a schoolboy, Philip gave Hélène away at her wedding in London to an Oxford undergraduate. But the Prince was also best man. He was later godfather of both her children from a second marriage, Max Philippe and Louise. Max Philippe was enrolled at Gordonstoun, Philip's old school. Shortly before Philip's marriage to Elizabeth, the French press reported that the Princess's husband-to-be had been seen in Paris in the company of a 'mystery blonde'. The blonde was no mystery: she was Hélène, then living in the French capital. She was not invited to the wedding, but her mother, Madame Anna Foufounis, was.

So much for the past. By one of those flukes of fate, Hélène Cordet's rise to fame in Britain coincided with Queen Elizabeth's accession. *Café Continental* was a popular show and its singer and presenter as much a household name in her own way as Prince Philip was in his. In London, they met from time to time as childhood friends with common interests, but it was hard to escape the gimlet eye of the press. One Sunday, she appeared at Windsor Great Park with her children at Philip's invitation to watch him play polo. Hélène and Philip chatted between chukkas, and then noticed the photographers taking pictures. 'We said goodbye to Philip and left early because of all this fuss,' she remembers in her memoirs, written several years later.

Inevitably, the Queen's husband's association with a glamorous French singer caused comment in London social circles, if not among the general public. In her autobiography, published in 1961, Hélène Cordet mentions Philip several times, and with a certain coyness. For example, she is watching a circus performance on television and 'quite incredibly,' she writes 'one of the spectators was Philip himself! For one moment I went back years and got quite hot under the collar.' At the same time, she is emphatic that speculative gossip about them was unfounded. Yet the friendship stood out.

X

The End of the Affair

On Churchill's eightieth birthday, 30 November 1954, the Queen sent him four silver wine coasters engraved with the ciphers of all the members of the royal family who had contributed towards the cost – the Queen herself, the Duke of Edinburgh, the Queen Mother, Princess Margaret, the Princess Royal, the Duchess of Kent, the Duke and Duchess of Gloucester, and Princess Alice of Athlone, Queen Mary's sister-in-law and the Queen's great-aunt. It was not one of Churchill's most remarkable birthday presents, but extravagant gift-giving was not a Windsor trait. When Richard Dimbleby, the BBC commentator whose marathon description brought the coronation alive to millions of Britons, became ill, the Queen sent him a get-well gift of two champagne splits (half bottles), but this was signal honour: signed photographs of themselves are the standard practice. On her tours abroad the Queen has been given race horses and diamonds. But her own gifts never varied. They were picture frames, wallets and, for the senior hosts, cuff links bearing the royal cipher.

But the Queen added a personal gift to Churchill – the remaining vacant period in Aureole's sireship. The colt was retired at the end of the 1954 season after nobly redeeming himself for the previous year's dismal performance. He won the Hardwicke Stakes at Royal Ascot. In addition, the Queen's colt Landau also won his race, giving the Queen her first double win at Royal Ascot. Aureole went on to a spectacular victory at Epsom Downs despite a disastrous start in an international field that included the French horse Vamos. As the horses approached the start Aureole unshipped his jockey and cantered riderless down the course. In

151

desperation, Eph Smith snatched up a tuft of grass and called the horse back. Miraculously Aureole returned for his jockey and went on to a sensational win, three-quarters of a length ahead of Vamos. The Queen almost ran to greet the horse. Thanks to his performance she was for the first time the season's top owner in terms of stake money.

Unlike Aureole, who settled down at the Queen's stud farm, producing the Derby winner St Paddy among other famous off-spring, Churchill was showing a distinct reluctance to quit the field despite his waning faculties. On 15 December, he arrived at Buckingham Palace for his evening audience totally exhausted. He had chaired a cabinet meeting that morning, and answered parliamentary questions in the House in the afternoon before returning to Downing Street to change into his top hat and morning coat to see the Queen. Colville records that 'more and more time was given to bezique and ever less to public business . . . it was becoming an effort [for Churchill] to sign a letter and a positive condescension to read Foreign Office telegrams.' Eighteen months earlier, Churchill's expressed intention to the Queen was that he would resign after the Tory Party Conference in October. But the conference came and went and Churchill clung to power.

On 8 March 1955, Churchill and Eden agreed privately that 5 April would be the resignation date. But almost immediately the Prime Minister seemed to regret this commitment. He spoke of Eden's 'hungry eyes' and developed what Colville calls 'a cold hatred' for his successor. A faint possibility that Eisenhower might be less opposed to a summit with the Russians, and a hint of interest in four-power talks from the new Soviet leader Marshal Nikolai Bulganin were enough to tempt him to postpone his departure one more time. A farewell dinner with the Queen had already been scheduled for 4 April, but at his audience of 29 March, Churchill asked her if she would mind if he put off his resignation. The Queen's reply was that she would not. The Tory leadership was by now restive and had let her know it. The argument used was that Churchill's incapacity effectively left the country leaderless. But there is no evidence that the Queen even as much as gave the old man a gentle prod. In her own way she was as fond of him as he was of her, partly because of his association with her father, and partly because she was fascinated by his sense of history and breadth of vision. In her valedictory letter to Churchill, the Queen was to say that none of his successors 'will ever, for me, be able to hold the place of my first Prime Minister, to whom both my husband and I owe so much and for whose wise guidance during the early years of my reign I shall always be so profoundly grateful.' A man with a firmer grasp of his job would have provided a more practical grounding, but that was to come from later prime ministers who would not be – as she was later to say of Churchill – 'always such fun'.

On 30 March, the Queen was posing for another portrait when Michael Adeane, her new Private Secretary, told her Churchill was quitting on schedule after all. She thoughtfully sent word that she 'understood the uncertainty' but 'recognized the wisdom' of going forward with his resignation. Elizabeth and Philip attended a dinner of senior cabinet ministers and grandees like the Norfolks, plus some close friends and members of the Prime Minister's personal staff. Strict precedence was observed in being presented to the Queen and, according to Colville, 'the Edens, whose official precedence was low, tried to jump the queue . . . and the Duchess of Westminster put her foot through Clarissa Eden's train. "That's torn it, in more than one sense," said Philip.' And on 5 April Churchill finally resigned – an event for which his cabinet colleagues had been plotting and waiting since his first stroke in 1952 had brought home his age and declining capacity.

At Churchill's last audience as prime minister the Queen was involved in an elaborate deception which was designed to flatter the departing statesman but nearly misfired. Unknown to Churchill there were hurried discussions between Colville and Adeane about whether or not the Queen should offer him a valedictory peerage. Colville thought Churchill would refuse to go to the House of Lords, but felt the only fitting offer would be that of a dukedom. Adeane replied that the Palace had stopped giving dukedoms, except to royal relations, but it did seem the appropriate offer to make – if Colville could confirm that Churchill would refuse it. So Colville asked Churchill what would happen if the Queen offered to make him a duke? Churchill's reply, according to Colville, was that 'nothing would induce him to accept it.' The nephew of a duke, born in one of the great ducal palaces in England, the Prime Minister told his secretary that he wanted to leave the world with the same name with which he had entered it.

This was relayed to the Queen, and what was already an emotional audience for Churchill became even more so when she surprised him with her remarkable offer. In his words, 'She believed that I wished to continue in the Commons but that otherwise she would offer me a dukedom.' He said he wished to remain in the Commons, 'while I felt physically fit, but that if I felt the work was too hard I would be very proud to consider her proposal.' This was not what the Queen had in mind, and she avoided a direct answer. But back at Downing Street after the audience, and still in tears, Churchill jolted Colville by confessing, 'For a moment I thought of accepting. But finally I remembered that I must die as I have always been – Winston Churchill . . . Do you know, it's an odd thing, but she seemed almost relieved.' So relieved was the Queen, in fact, that as soon as Churchill had taken his leave she telephoned Adeane to tell him that all had gone according to plan. The audience, in Churchill's own account, also offered a glimpse of how the royal prerogative worked in practice. Elizabeth asked him to name a successor. 'I said I preferred to leave it to her. She said the case was not a difficult one and that she would summon Sir Anthony Eden.'

The eternal heir apparent, Eden had at last made it to 10 Downing Street. He was troubled by health problems, but he was the Prime Minister. Meanwhile, a significant change had also taken place at Buckingham Palace. In October 1953, Tommy Lascelles retired, having reached the age of sixty. His departure was generally welcomed by the royal family, and the appointment of Adeane, the assistant secretary, to the post signalled a change in style. To his friends, Lascelles was a cultivated man with a weakness for making puns who really wanted to be a writer. His critics said he was reactionary, autocratic, and apt to pass off his own views as those of the Queen, as in the case of the argument over televising the coronation ceremony.

It is at least arguable that someone with a less narrowly rigid outlook would have served the Queen better in the crucial first years of her reign. Certainly, had he not been the Queen's adviser, the Margaret–Townsend affair would probably have ended less harshly, and perhaps even happily. His active opposition to the marriage earned Lascelles the Princess's enmity and she never spoke to him again. But from the Queen's viewpoint, Lascelles and Peter Townsend rather ironically had one thing in common. As valued aides of her father, they had earned their respective places in her own household: neither was re- movable, except *in extremis*. So the Queen waited until Lascelles retired to look around for a replacement. However, what kings (and queens) fail to do can be as significant as what they do. Tommy Lascelles was not made a peer on retirement. Considering

154

his years as a senior member of the royal household in the service of three monarchs, this omission was surprising – and perhaps pointed.

Michael Adeane was virtually raised in the royal household. He was the grandson of Lord Stamfordham, King George V's Private Secretary. His mother had been a lady-in-waiting to Queen Mary, and as a boy he himself had been a page to the Queen. In the early years of the war he was assigned to Washington as the British liaison with American Intelligence – an experience which probably helped him as the Queen's Secretary: he had a reputation for being very well informed. He was small, dedicated and unobtrusive, and was to manage the Queen's affairs with quiet efficiency for sixteen years.

On 1 July 1954, Adeane sent Brigadier Norman Gwatkin of the Lord Chancellor's office to the book department at Harrods where he was to wait by the cash desk. In due course, he saw Peter Townsend making his way towards him unnoticed through the crowd of shoppers. The Queen had agreed to Princess Margaret's request to see Townsend again after more than a year's separation, and – with Margaret's crucial twenty-fifth birthday less than two months away – he had flown to London from Brussels. The Harrods rendezvous was intended to throw off the scent any reporters who might be following Townsend. Gwatkin drove Townsend to Clarence House and a reunion with Margaret. 'Our joy at being together was indescribable,' Townsend wrote later. When he asked whether she thought a marriage was feasible, however, the Princess could only reply that the situation seemed frozen where it had been two years earlier. Still, she seemed confident that once the magic date of her twenty-fifth birthday was passed, royal permission to marry would be forthcoming.

Townsend was back in Brussels on Margaret's fateful twenty-fifth birthday, 21 August 1955, and the Princess herself was out of reach of reporters at Balmoral. But with her birthday, the situation entered a new phase. From Fleet Street, the *Daily Mirror* shouted, 'Come on Margaret! Please make up your mind!' However, Margaret still had no clear idea of the full implications of her decision and neither did anyone else. Her matrimonial plans had become the subject of intense debate – actually two debates, one in the press, and a more private, but more decisive, one in the inner recesses of the Church and the Establishment. Leading Anglican prelates slugged it out daily on the front pages of the Fleet Street papers. One day a cleric would argue that if Princess Margaret married a divorced man, she would not be married at all in the ecclesiastical sense, thus raising questions about the legitimacy of her children, but the next day another cleric would denounce this view as a narrow interpretation of the Church of England's moral teaching on divorce.

To the outside world the royal family seemed as united as ever, and in a sense this was true: their concern for Princess Margaret never faltered. But as the crisis dragged on with its daily bombardment of newspaper headlines the Princess began to face hardening attitudes against the marriage. According to William Clark, Eden's spokesman at 10 Downing Street, Princess Margaret was 'obviously lonely and distracted, with disagreements between herself, the Queen Mother, and the Queen burgeoning.' The Queen Mother remained gently but firmly against it, perceiving it as unwise in itself, potentially harmful to 'the firm', and impractical – and it must be said that it was not the future a doting mother dreams of for her twenty-five-year-old daughter. In addition, there was a growing tension between the two sisters. Margaret felt the Queen was not being sufficiently supportive. As the clamour grew louder, the situation began to give the Queen some feelings of angst. She also resented being forced into a crisis by her younger sister and one evening at Balmoral told her so in no uncertain terms. The resulting row was the worst confrontation between the two sisters since their teens.

With a few more years experience and confidence behind her, Elizabeth might have chosen a different approach to the problem. In the circumstances she placed the matter in the hands of Prime Minister Anthony Eden's Conservative government. 'Eden behaved very honourably in all this,' William Clark was to write thirty years later, 'stressing that Margaret must be allowed to do as she chose and must not be punished if she did decide for Townsend: she must be allowed to keep her royal wages, for instance.' At Adeane's (that is, the Queen's) request, Downing Street prepared the constitutional formula: Margaret would have to write to the Queen, renounce her succession rights, and ask permission to marry (even though she was now free from the royal veto). The Queen would then – incredibly – ask the governments of Britain and the Commonwealth (in other words, the governments of Canada, Australia, New Zealand, South Africa, India, Pakistan and Ceylon) to pass the necessary Act of Renunciation.

On 1 October, Eden went to Balmoral where the Queen told him that Princess Margaret formally sought Parliament's consent

156

to her marriage to Peter Townsend. The Prime Minister outlined the Princess's options and said he would start the process by calling a cabinet meeting. At Margaret's insistence, Townsend returned once more to London. He was warned by Buckingham Palace not to talk to the press and lodged with the Marquis of Abergavenny, a member of the royal household who was to be his 'minder', in Lowndes Square. As soon as he arrived Townsend saw Margaret in her sitting room at Clarence House and 'as we rediscovered one another, we realized that nothing has changed.'

No change in their feelings, but also no thinning out of the thicket of obstacles standing in the way of marriage. The looming constitutional problems were compounded by public relations ineptitude. The Palace never announced that Princess Margaret had in fact made up her mind to seek royal permission to marry, nor was there any detailed official explanation of the procedures involved. On 12 October, the Queen's Press Secretary, Commander Richard Colville (no relation to Jock Colville) issued a cryptic statement that only served to confuse the situation. 'No announcement concerning Princess Margaret's future is at present contemplated,' Colville said. Instead of dampening press speculation as it was supposed to do, Colville's statement increased it. Margaret and Townsend were now seeing each other daily, but not in public. When they dined with friends, each arrived and left separately. On 14 October, they arrived at Allanby Lodge, the Berkshire country home of John and Jean Lycett Wills, where they were to spend the weekend. Margaret's hostess was the Queen Mother's niece. Inevitably, the press converged on the house in force armed with telephoto lenses and local police with dogs were deployed to keep them away.

While senior Tories continued to warn the Queen that the marriage could do irreparable harm to the position of the Crown, one newspaper poll after another contradicted this view. General sympathy was with the Princess. She received overwhelming support from the public. Yet, curiously for a situation with political overtones, the public view appears to have had little impact on members of Eden's cabinet, who met on 18 October in an attempt to come to some conclusion about the Princess and the Group Captain. The ministers took a harder line than the Prime Minister. After the meeting, Eden told the Queen that his cabinet was against making it easy for the Princess and imposed harsh conditions. On Sunday 23 October, after attending church together at Windsor, the Queen spelled out for her sister the Cabinet's terms.

If Margaret married Townsend, besides divesting her of her royal rights and functions, the Cabinet also favoured terminating her annual allowance from the Civil List, leaving her without income (or, as Townsend put it, 'ruined'). The Cabinet argument was that the allowance from the Civil List envisioned carrying out certain engagements and other commitments which Margaret would no longer be in a position to fulfil. She would have to marry in a civil ceremony, which would have to take place outside Britain. Moreover – and this was perhaps the worst news of all – the couple would have to live out of the country 'at least for a time'.

At Clarence House, Townsend and Margaret went through some soul-searching over tea with the Queen Mother. The Cabinet had painted Margaret's altered status as Townsend's wife in the harshest terms, and the choice before her was now sharply defined. There is more than a slight hint of the dilemma which she now faced in Peter Townsend's observation that the 'Princess now had confirmation, for the first time, of the consequences of a marriage to me. If only she had known before the . . . drama might have been avoided.'

Reduced financial circumstances represented only part of the problem. The Queen could – assuming she wanted to – have gone a considerable way to resolving that aspect of the situation by granting her sister an allowance from her own personal resources. In addition to her annual allowance from the Civil List the Queen could count on a private income worth as much again from her estates at Sandringham and Windsor, and any help to Margaret would have to come out of the latter. She could also have solved any housing problem by providing one of her 'grace and favour' residences, or an apartment in Kensington Palace. But the Cabinet seemed bent on making Princess Margaret an outcast. The precedent of her uncle's abdication loomed over the whole affair, and there was more than a hint that she and Townsend should be prepared to face the possibility of having to live out of England permanently as Edward VIII had done.

On 20 October, Anthony Eden's cabinet met again to draft a Bill of Renunciation to be presented in Parliament, freeing Princess Margaret from the obligations of the Royal Marriages Act. However, Bobbety Salisbury objected that he could not reconcile the marriage with his High Church beliefs. If the Cabinet gave Margaret the green light he would resign from the Government rather than introduce the bill in the House of Lords which he would normally be expected to do as chief government minister in the upper house.

Salisbury's resignation threats were famous in political circles. As Harold Macmillan would say later, 'when he is worried, [Salisbury] always wants to resign (this is a Cecil tradition) . . . All through history the Cecils when any friend or colleague has been in real trouble, have stabbed him in the back – attributing the crime to qualms of conscience . . . ' But while Macmillan, who was related to Bobbety through marriage in three separate directions, had the political nerve to face up to what he called his kinsman's 'resigning moods', and indeed was to let him quit the Cabinet within two years of the Townsend affair, Eden was not in a position to take the political risk of a split in the Cabinet and perhaps in the party. Patrician, overbearing and ultra-conservative, Bobbety Salisbury was a figure of considerable political power, and he saw himself as enjoying the same position of influence with the Queen as his Cecil ancestors had with the earlier Elizabeth. Without voting on the issue, Eden's cabinet refused to give its approval.

Six days later, an editorial in *The Times*, written by the editor, Sir William Haley, drove home the point. The Queen's subjects, the paper declared, believed that the royal family reflected the ideal in the society, including family life. But if Princess Margaret married Townsend 'it is inevitable that this reflection will become distorted.' The Queen's family was also 'a symbol and guarantee of the unity of the British peoples.' However, as Townsend's wife Margaret would be 'a cause for division.' Furthermore, she would leave her sister 'lonely in her life of public service' in which she needs the support of those close to her. 'Happiness in the full sense is a spiritual state,' *The Times* went on, 'and its most precious element may be the sense of duty done.'

The Times served as the voice of the Establishment, and *The Times* was in effect saying that a private life incompatible with Princess Margaret's royal background and public persona was inadmissible. By then, however, Margaret and Townsend were beginning to feel that even if they won, it would be a bitter victory. When she and Townsend met at Clarence House they said in the same breath, 'It's not possible. It won't do.' She clung to him for a long time. Then Townsend produced an envelope from his pocket on which he had scribbled some notes and between them they drafted a statement – her first public comment since the start of the affair four years earlier. But she held up publication until after she had seen the Archbishop of Canterbury the following day and Peter Townsend had had time – after a highly emotional parting in which the weeping Princess had to be pulled away from him by

159

the Queen Mother - to get out of London and return to Brussels, where, on instructions from the Prime Minister, he was housed at the embassy for a few days by the ambassador, Christopher Soames, Churchill's son-in-law, to protect him from the press.

Margaret once told Lady Longford that when she went to see the Archbishop of Canterbury, Dr Fisher put on his glasses and went to a bookcase and began to bring out a book. 'Put it back,' said Princess Margaret. 'I have come to give you information, not to ask for it.' She told him about her decision and he sat down. A smile spread over his stern features. 'What a wonderful person the Holy Spirit is!' he said.

William Clark, who had followed the unfolding events from the less spiritual vantage point of Downing Street, had a different attribution. 'The drama,' he said, 'stands out as the event that for the last time simultaneously and automatically brought into play all the pieces on the traditional English chessboard – Crown, Prime Minister, Archbishop, *The Times*, Lord Salisbury.' He called it 'a poignant colophon to a dead era.'

Margaret's statement, released on 31 October 1955, said, 'I would like it to be known that I have decided not to marry Group-Captain Peter Townsend. I have been aware that, subject to my renouncing my rights of succession, it might have been possible for me to contract a civil marriage. But, mindful of the Church's teaching that Christian marriage is indissoluble, and conscious of my duty to the Commonwealth, I have resolved to put these considerations before any others . . . ' To the Palace, Townsend had become a non-person. The doors were closed to him, the lines of communication shut down. Townsend quit the air force, married a young Belgian woman, and moved to Paris to live as a voluntary but (at least in the years following the bust-up romance) inevitable exile. His version of the story, published two decades later, is told with discretion and hardly a detectable quiver in the stiffness of the upper lip. Remarkably, there is no bitterness, and there are no villains, and nearly forty years later the stoic mask does not slip, and Tommy Lascelles, Michael Adeane and the rest of the Palace crowd remain 'nice chaps'.

Two important factors conditioned the outcome. First, the Queen allowed the traditionalists – courtiers, Tory cabinet ministers, churchmen – to determine the course of events. It was as though the young Queen knew the Establishment was too strong to fight on the issue and therefore did not attempt it. But did she want to? Divorce was a subject that stirred her up.

Some time after her sister's romance she delivered an untypically forceful condemnation in an address to a British women's group: 'When we see around us the havoc that has been wrought – above all among children – by the break-up of homes, we can have no doubt that divorce and separation are responsible for some of the darkest evils in our society . . . the relation of a husband and wife is a permanent one.'

Second, Anthony Eden was hamstrung in dealing with the problem by the fact that he himself had, like Townsend, been the injured party in a divorce case and was remarried. Because he felt his situation disqualified him from taking a position either in favour of or against Margaret's marriage he took no active part in the controversy and simply passed on the Cabinet's decision to the Queen. The result was that the Queen was, in effect, deprived of the advice of her Prime Minister.

There is no doubt the affair tarnished the image of the monarchy, although not in the way envisaged by those who opposed the marriage. A national poll taken the week of the break-up showed that 59 per cent of the population was in favour of the marriage, and only 17 per cent opposed it. Of that 17 per cent, only half were against it because of Townsend's divorce. With the exception of *The Times*, the Fleet Street papers reported a groundswell of public sympathy for the Princess. 'The typing pool at Morgan's Crucible Works is simply seething,' one newspaper reported. 'They all think that she ought to have married him.' But the British public had seen something that had not been evident since the Abdication: they saw the human face of royalty. Margaret's affair had shown that behind the panoply the members of the royal family were (more or less) ordinary mortals with human feelings.

Margaret's restrained announcement gave no hint of her own intense bitterness at being forced to sacrifice her romance on the altar of the British Establishment. In her resentment, nobody was spared, least of all her sister. Striking where it hurt most, she began to tell Elizabeth existing gossip about Prince Philip. If she could not have a happy marriage, why should Lilibet? The Queen was furious and it was some time before their differences over the Townsend business were patched over. But because of their residual affection for each other, the relationship recovered. Once again Elizabeth was making allowances for her younger sister. Besides, as Princess Margaret has said, 'In our family we do not have rifts. A very occasional row but never a rift.'

The end of the affair left its mark on an already high-strung personality. If Margaret was rebellious before her romance with Townsend, she was outrageously so after it. She also emerged as something of a 'character'. She smoked cigarettes through a long holder. At parties, she stayed on and on. According to protocol, royal guests always arrive last and leave first. But there was an understanding among London hostesses that when PM was invited, other guests were allowed to slip quietly away until in the end the Princess was almost alone with her hosts.

Audiences, engagements, visits, investitures, followed each other so rapidly that there was little time for soul-searching about past dramas. In November 1955, the Queen was deeply involved in preparations for her three-week trip to Nigeria, the biggest and most populous colony and well on the way to independence. The purpose of the visit was to ensure that the emergent independent African nation joined the Commonwealth, and at the same time to try to reduce the danger of internal strife by bringing the squabbling Nigerian tribes closer together.

An important part of that preparation was the tour wardrobe designed by Norman Hartnell. Elizabeth has never shared the Windsor fixation with clothes and dressing up. Her Uncle David fancied himself as a trend-setter. Her father spent long hours with his tailor. Her grandfather George V's enormous wardrobe contained one hundred and forty suits, and six thousand pairs of socks and stockings. Both the Queen Mother and Margaret have always been very clothes-conscious. The Queen Mother orders her elaborate draped pastel-coloured outfits by the dozen. Princess Margaret was among the first women in England to wear the New Look lengths, the first postwar fashion extravagance introduced by Paris couturier Christian Dior. But though the young Queen did not go overboard, she could get excited about a dress and had a sensuous appreciation of silks and brocades. Her approach to clothes was – and is – professional. She chose her outfits knowing that what she wore must be in character, and that she must stand out for the crowds and the photographers.

At the time, Hartnell was jointly dressmaker to the Queen with another leading couturier, Hardy Amies. A London-based milliner from Denmark named Aage Tharup made most of her hats, the Bond Street firm of Rayne made all her shoes. As usual, Hartnell began by submitting sketches for the Queen's approval. His designs were, also as usual, based on a study of her itinerary, and conditioned by the wardrobe ground-rules, which were already set in stone. Hems were about one and a half inches below the knee; and though her figure was good, not for her the *décolletage* with which her daughter-in-law was to wow the public on her first evening appearance following her engagement to Prince Charles. Stylishly flamboyant designs were rejected in favour of clean, classic lines, and clothes had to be easy to get in and out of, because – as she frequently told designers – 'I often only have twenty minutes, at the most, in which to dress' – so no fussy rows of buttons, or elaborate fastenings. Hats had to be off the face to avoid awkward shadows and never so big that they caused problems as she stepped out of cars. A long train on a full-length dress was taboo in case an official put his foot through it. She wore bright colours to be noticeable – her favourites were lime green, pink, aquamarine, peacock blue and red. Sophisticated dark colours were avoided. The first, and by 1956 the only, time the Queen wore black other than at a funeral was when – as Princess Elizabeth – she had an audience with the Pope on her way home from Malta in 1950. Only Roman Catholic queens and princesses wear white at papal audiences: their Protestant counterparts wear black.

The bright colours of her clothes would be complemented by light makeup: pale powdered face and bright red lipstick. Other colours may suit her creamy, supple complexion more than the hard red she always wears in public, but its use is deliberate – red lipstick best shows off her smile. She never wears red nail polish: just natural varnish.

Once the designs were approved and the clothes made up there were fittings on what couturiers call 'Palace days' – Tuesdays at two-thirty in the afternoon. Hartnell arrived, followed in solemn procession by Miss Whistler the vendeuse, Mrs Price his secretary, Mara the house model, whose size twelve measurements and five feet four inches height matched the Queen's, Madame Emilienne the elderly fitter, Ivy the matcher, and a detachment of lesser fitters and milliners wheeling along a mobile clothes rack on which swung the clothes covered in rustling tissue paper. A footman led the way to the lift, and on the first floor they were met by the Queen's page in his jacket of blue cloth and dark breeches, and led along the vast, red-carpeted corridors the width and length of the Mall along which bicycle races could be run – and, indeed, have been – to the Queen's dressing room in the royal living quarters. The Queen's page could be any age between twenty-five and fifty.

The group came to a halt in the waiting room. There Bobo MacDonald, a force to be reckoned with when it came to choosing the Queen's clothes, took over. 'The Queen is ready,' she announced. The vendeuse and a couple of fitters entered the huge dressing room first. It had a plain carpet, wall mirrors on two sides, a dressing table with a skirt. The hairbrushes were in solid gold, and family photographs and bowls of fresh flowers were everywhere.

Eventually the designer and the rest were also let in. Bobo MacDonald fussed dourly about looking for scarves, gloves and accessories as the Queen requested them, and reacting to the clothes in the plural, as if she and Elizabeth would both be wearing them – 'Too tight for us,' she would grumble. No-one could ever accurately gauge her influence on the Queen's taste in clothes, but her stern Scottish nature reacted against anything frivolous. In conversation she invariably referred to the Queen as 'My Little Lady', and spoke her mind to her employer with the licence of a life-long retainer. The Queen liked her to position herself in the crowd during royal visits, knowing that Bobo would give her an unadorned account of people's comments. She was certainly blamed for the Queen's preferences for solid, sensible shoes chosen because she spends a good deal of time on her feet. As the dressers knelt around her, the Queen made a suggestion here, a comment there. She twirled and moved about in the ball gowns, stretched the arms of the jackets. And meanwhile several corgis roamed around the dressing room snappily waiting for their chopped liver at 4.30 p.m.

In due course, the completed wardrobe, carefully wrapped, was packed in hanging steamer trunks labelled 'The Queen' for the journey, along with the bottled Malvern Water, the English spring water Elizabeth always drank – and still does – at home and abroad, and a large number of pairs of white nylon and cotton gloves (on a royal tour, the Queen can wear four pairs a day), and a collection of the clumpy handbags that invariably hung from her left arm. As always, she paid for the clothes, scrutinizing the bill and occasionally protesting mildly that a particular dress cost too much.

The Queen and Prince Philip took off for Nigeria in January 1956. In Lagos, the entire population seemed to line the streets. Behind the crowd on the royal route new corrugated iron fences eight feet high gleamed in the sunlight hiding vast slums where a large proportion of the city's black population lived. At Kaduna racecourse, they watched a durbar – a gathering of princes – the first ever in Africa. More than two thousand caparisoned horsemen charged at the royal box in waves, each gaudier and more dashing than the one before. Their chiefs saluted, and then the group moved on to make room for the next. So while a crisis loomed at home over the Suez Canal which Egypt's President Gamal Abdul Nasser was threatening to nationalize, the Queen received the homage of the Rwang Pam of Birom, the Atta of Igala, the Tor of Tiv, the Etsu Nupe, and the Och of Idoma.

Back in Britain the crisis intensified, but the flow of visitors resumed. Nikita Khrushchev and Nicolai Bulganin, respectively Soviet Party Secretary and President of the Soviet Union, came to tea at Windsor Castle. When the Duke of Edinburgh casually mentioned that he had always dreamed of seeing Leningrad, Khrushchev told him, 'It would be easy for us to make this dream come true,' and later issued an invitation through Eden. 'Khrushchev pressed very hard indeed,' said the Foreign Office report of the meeting with the Prime Minister. The Soviet leadership welcomed a royal visit for obvious reasons of prestige, but the Foreign Office strongly discouraged it, and two years later, when it somehow leaked out in the American press, denied that such an invitation had ever been made. The British government felt that the presence of the Queen in Moscow would have suggested a higher level of cordiality between Britain and Russia than was actually the case.

What is interesting is that British officials have always told journalists that the royal family ruled out a visit to the Soviet Union because of the massacre of Tsar Nicholas and his family by the revolutionaries. The assassination of the Romanovs has always been a sensitive subject with the House of Windsor. King George V had refused to give refuge to the Tsar who was his cousin, for fear that Britain would be implicated in the revolution. On this occasion, however, Prince Philip – also a great-great nephew of Tsar Nicholas – dropped the broad hint which resulted in an invitation, and he was not likely to have done that without prior consultation with his wife. Still, the Soviet leaders departed with a message that 'Her Majesty regrets . . . ' issued on her behalf by the British government. The Queen did, however, keep the visitors' present for her thirtieth birthday – a horse. The British government would continue to block subsequent invitations, until thirty-three years later when another Soviet leader Mikhail Gorbachev would ask the Queen directly and she would accept. Even so, 10 Downing Street immediately qualified her acceptance, saying the visit could not take place in the immediate future.

The episode underlined the degree to which the Queen's travels to foreign states are an extension of British foreign policy. The suggestion of a specific trip comes from her ministers, and sometimes the Queen has to be persuaded. A visit by the Queen is generally a purely protocol affair and as such offers limited political scope. But as a way of cementing bilateral relations, there is no better icing on the cake than royal icing, no more effective final touch than the regal touch. What's more, a royal presence often also boosts trade by generating an interest in things British. In this respect the Foreign Office is the Queen's travel agent and chaperon, making the arrangements, planning the programme (in conjunction with the Palace), and writing most of the speeches. But it isn't just the Queen's foreign visits that require government approval. The Foreign Office once intervened in her plans to spend an evening at the ballet at Covent Garden.

Elizabeth, who has never been much of a ballet fan, had initially decided not to go to the Covent Garden 1956 Bolshoi Ballet season, the Russian company's first ever visit to Britain. Eight-year-old Prince Charles, however, was taken to see the Bolshoi's performance of *The Fountain of the Bakhchisaray*, an action-packed ballet full of fireworks, including onstage fighting. Charles was clearly thrilled, and his excitement evidently piqued the Queen's interest because a few days later Covent Garden received word from the Palace that the Queen wanted to see it too. Result: consternation! The prima ballerina, Galina Ulanova, did not appear in *The Fountain of the Bakhchisaray*, and if the Queen came to a Bolshoi performance, it had to be one in which Ulanova danced. 'Bolshoi protocol, nay decency and common sense demanded it,' the Queen's cousin the Earl of Harewood, artistic director of Covent Garden, stated with scant common sense but great conviction. In reality, Ulanova demanded it. The Queen could come and see her dance *Giselle*.

Back came the reply from Buckingham Palace. The Queen wanted to see *The Fountain of the Bakhchisaray*, men fighting onstage and all. The chairman of Covent Garden wrote officially inviting the Queen to a performance of *Giselle*. The Palace wrote back: not *Giselle*: *The Fountain of the Bakhchisaray*. Harewood explained the situation to his cousin, but appeared to make very little impression. Then Harewood appealed for help to the Foreign Office, which pointed out to the Queen that, given Ulanova's standing in Russia as the prima ballerina of the Bolshoi, the situation had the makings of a diplomatic incident. Bolshoi protocol won over royal preference. The Queen reluctantly went to a performance of *Giselle*.

The episode can hardly seem to have mattered in the climate of crisis and concern over the Anglo-French invasion – backed by Israel – of the Suez Canal Zone, nationalized by Nasser on 26 July 1956. How much Eden had revealed to Elizabeth about the weeks of secret talks with France and Israel and of military preparations was unclear. Eden himself told an earlier biographer of the Queen that he kept the monarch informed of developments and that she had not been anti-Suez, nor could he say that she was pro-Suez. But for Eden to imply that the Queen had no view either way on the planned aggression was disingenuous. Although the Queen no doubt asked questions as usual without voicing an opinion on the Prime Minister's answers Eden could hardly have been misled into thinking that she did not have one or that she favoured an offensive. Mountbatten – who himself had offered to resign as First Sea Lord on the eve of the allied landing at Port Said, but Eden rejected his resignation – has said she was strongly opposed to the aggression when it came, but had been unable to prevent it. As soon as Eden's intentions became clear she did warn him that – secret talks or no – if the Cabinet was resolved upon a military solution, the Prime Minister should inform the Leader of the Opposition.

When the offensive began the Queen was spending three days at Goodwood for the races, a long-standing engagement but one which made her seem to be distancing herself from Eden's activities in London. Eden needed her signature on a royal proclamation calling up army reservists, and Adeane had to drive down to Goodwood with it, get the Queen's approval and telephone confirmation to the Prime Minister's office so that it could be put into effect.

The Suez War was brought to a humiliating halt under the combined pressure of a United Nations Security Council call for an end of the invasion, and American threats to let the pound collapse. The Queen's reaction was one of anger at a divisive and costly venture. To the British people the setback was a devastating shock. A crucial turning point in the postwar era, almost overnight, a people realized it no longer had the capacity for manipulating its global destinies in the imperial manner of the past. Moreover, the conflict produced a deep and bitter national schism between those who felt that withdrawal had been a mistake and those who branded the action as folly from the start. When Eden's health went to pieces under the strain, the country had never felt more despondent, bewildered, and uncertain of the future. The picture was of a Britain thoroughly menaced, alienated from America, estranged from several Commonwealth countries.

Out of the debris, quite unexpectedly, there suddenly emerged Harold Macmillan, Chancellor of the Exchequer in Eden's government, to succeed the sick and vanquished Prime Minister. For the Queen it was the start of an association that was to endure to their mutual satisfaction for six years.

XI

Philip at Sea

Anthony Eden was Prime Minister for twenty months from April 1955 to December 1956. During that time he can hardly be said to have established a good working relationship with his sovereign. Martin Charteris was to tell Paul Martin, the Canadian High Commissioner in London, that Eden 'was not free of tension during weekly audiences.' Yet the Queen came to London from Balmoral to receive his resignation, thus saving a sick man the complications of a journey to her Scottish home. She also created him an earl and a Knight of the Garter, both in recognition of his long service as Foreign Secretary and also – it was said – as a consolation prize for achieving his ultimate ambition too late, at the wrong time and in failing health.

With Eden gone she was again required to exercise the royal prerogative and appoint a successor. One strong candidate was R. A. Butler – and for the same reason that Eden had been after Churchill: Rab Butler was the Deputy Prime Minister as well as the Home Secretary. Butler possessed the most brilliant mind in postwar Conservative politics. He was a statesman of depth and vision. He was charming and scholarly with a quiet line in irony. Physically, he looked like a fighter who in his youth had been in the ring once too often, in sharp contrast to the plummy, patrician features of his Tory colleagues, who seemed to be just one step away from their own portraits and sculpted busts in the dusty halls of their London clubs.

The Queen knew him because following Eden's collapse he faced the task of cleaning up the Suez mess and came to the Palace for the regular Tuesday Prime Minister's audience. But another important connection for her was the fact that as a young parliamentarian, he had written speeches for her father. The Tory Party admired his abilities, but regarded him as too indecisive. Backbenchers felt he lacked the killer instinct they admired in a leader. When the Queen asked Eden for his views on the succession, he suggested that she should seek the advice of a senior Tory peer, such as Bobbety Salisbury, thus avoiding making any specific suggestions. Bobbety mentioned the name of Harold Macmillan. The Chancellor of the Exchequer was also Winston Churchill's choice. Macmillan was sixty-three – more than double the Queen's age. Much was made in the press of the fact that he was the great-grandson of a poor Scottish crofter, and while this was true, the Macmillan family fortunes had advanced so spectacularly that, aside from his political career, the new Prime Minister was the owner of a leading London publishing firm. He was also married to Dorothy Cavendish, the family name of the Duke of Devonshire, and Chatsworth, the magnificent Devonshire ancestral home, was Dorothy Cavendish's family home.

Crofter ancestor or not, Macmillan had the looks and manners of the classic top-drawer Englishman. He seemed to have stepped out of the pages of a novel by Anthony Trollope. A great raconteur, he responded to an appreciative audience and he found it in the men's clubs of which he was an habitué (he belonged to at least five). But whether he was telling a political anecdote in his club or delivering a statement in the Commons, his timing was impeccable, and this natural skill made him an effective performer on the emerging news medium of television. His unflappable manner was so convincing that it was only after his death that most people learned that behind the façade he was prone to occasional panic, self-doubt and depression. His escape from the cut and thrust of party politics was reading. Once, years after Macmillan left office, the author travelled in the same train compartment with him. He was re-reading Plato's *Republic* in Greek.

The Queen's consultations showed a split in the party, with some backing Rab Butler and others Harold Macmillan. Faced with the impasse, Bobbety Salisbury and Lord Kilmuir conducted a survey of the members of the Cabinet. The two Tory grandees sat in the office of the Privy Council and as each cabinet minister entered in turn Salisbury, with his aristocratic lisp, asked, 'Well which is it to be, Wab or Hawold?' Kilmuir wrote down the preferences. The result – a surprising majority for Macmillan – was taken to the Queen. Michael Adeane then unobtrusively tested the parliamentary reaction to Macmillan and reported widespread acceptance among Tory members. The Queen sent for the winner on 10 January 1957, and asked him to form a new Conservative government. Macmillan warned her, 'half in joke, half in earnest, that I could not answer to the new government lasting more than six weeks,' and she was to remind him of this at an audience six years later.

The selection process by which Macmillan had floated to the surface was neither comprehensive nor democratic. Salisbury's soundings of cabinet ministers was not a vote. There is no question but that Butler was then widely perceived to be the better man. In fact, only one London newspaper had named Macmillan as the likely prospective Prime Minister, the rest having predicted that Butler would be chosen. But it would have taken considerable reserves of determination and self-assurance for the young Queen to question the choice of senior Tories whom she knew and respected.

Butler was bitter about Macmillan's appointment, but he stayed in the Government, to be passed over a second time when Macmillan himself resigned in 1963 – and to be widely regarded as the best Prime Minister Britain never had.

At first, Macmillan found his Tuesday audiences with the Queen 'somewhat difficult' and the dialogue forced. In other words, there was a period of mutual adjustment, the Queen to a new prime minister, and Macmillan to the challenge of dealing with a woman as head of state. Macmillan did not communicate very well with women, possibly as a result of his own unhappy marriage. For nearly thirty years, his wife had carried on an affair with another Tory parliamentarian, Robert Boothby. This was common knowledge in court and political circles, but Macmillan played the complacent husband and looked the other way.

When Boothby – the affair long over – asked to be made a peer, Macmillan obliged. It was an honour that astonished those in the know, a remarkable act of magnanimity towards a man who had caused him so much suffering. But whatever pain resulted from his wife's infidelity was effectively screened behind his languid, wryly amusing public manner, and he sought refuge in his work and in the camaraderie of London's clubs.

To improve the level of discussion at his weekly Palace audiences, Macmillan initiated a procedure whereby he sent the Queen an advance agenda of the points he wished to raise, and this gave her the opportunity to do her homework and frame her own views. For the first time since her accession, the Tuesday audience was beginning to take on the aspect of serious business. Elizabeth responded to the stimulation of these working sessions. Before long, as her confidence increased, the agenda procedure underwent a significant refinement. Instead of the Prime Minister setting the list of topics for discussion, it was drawn up jointly by his Political Secretary and the Queen's Secretary. Besides his audiences, Macmillan also wrote the Queen detailed reports on particular events or situations – a summit meeting with Kennedy, talks in Moscow, a cabinet shake-up. It was a far cry from the 'fun' with Churchill, or the formal, stilted encounters with Anthony Eden.

And Macmillan found – as did everyone – that Elizabeth II was a quick study. He was impressed with the assiduity with which she absorbed the vast mass of documents passed to her and by her instinctive feel for politics. Rab Butler – standing in for Eden – had been struck by her keen interest in political gossip. She seemed fascinated by Parliament – who was rising, who falling. She wanted to hear about how the Government was affected by particular situations but – Butler said – 'Like all clever women she was very interested in personalities.' It was one of Adeane's tasks to keep her up-to-date on such political undercurrents and goings-on. Because he was self-effacing, unchallenging, and monumentally discreet politicians confided in him. An American embassy telegram called him 'efficient and conscientious ... with a passion for anonymity', and a senior French diplomat said he was so unobtrusive, you could look at him and see though to the wall. But in his discussions with her, Macmillan did not neglect the personality side of politics either. When he replaced Heathcoat Amory as Chancellor of the Exchequer, he confided to the Queen that Amory 'had lost his buoyancy and resilience and entered into a permanent quietism more suitable to a monastery than the busy life of every day. I do not say he was defeatist. He just seemed overwhelmed.'

Elizabeth was alone in London when Macmillan replaced Eden at 10 Downing Street. On 15 October, her husband had left on the royal yacht *Britannia* on a tour that set tongues wagging. In the summer of 1956, with the Suez offensive imminent, Philip had begged the Queen to let him return to active service in the Royal Navy. Elizabeth had just signed a royal decree calling up navy reservists with combat experience like himself, and he saw this as an opportunity to return to the life he had loved best. The Queen refused to allow him to go back into the Navy, and Eden had endorsed her refusal, fearing his loss in action or capture. Philip's resentment at having had to give up his naval career had been slowly building up since his wife's accession. The Queen's veto effectively ended his prospects in that direction and there was tension in the royal living quarters at Buckingham Palace.

The Duke's main refuge from the Court was the royal family's luxurious new yacht *Britannia*, sometimes known as 'Philip's Folly' because of his close personal involvement in her construction. He would take the ship out on short cruises in British waters trying to recapture something of his carefree days at sea. But his scheduled tour in October was anything but a short cruise. In fact he was to be away for four months, visiting New Zealand and Australia (where he presided over the opening of the Commonwealth Games in Melbourne), besides some of the most outlying parts of the Commonwealth, including Antarctica, Darwin's Galapagos Islands, and the Falklands. The domestic atmosphere at Buckingham Palace was still tense when he sailed from Britain. He sent Elizabeth white roses on their ninth wedding anniversary plus a photograph of two iguanas with their arms around each other, and spoke to her and the children at Christmas from the Falklands, but otherwise his contact with the family was limited. People who had dealings with the Queen at this time frequently found her edgy and irritable. Her differences with Philip, compounded by the fallout from Margaret's broken romance were taking their toll.

An additional aggravation was the crisis over Michael Parker's divorce. When the *Britannia* sailed to the Gambia on its return voyage Parker learned that his wife had filed for divorce in London on grounds of adultery. The Queen was said not to have been a fan of Parker's, and on the basis of the stories about him and Philip such an attitude would have been understandable. Faced with charges of infidelity, he resigned before the *Britannia* arrived home. In any case, Parker could hardly continue to work for the royal household. Under Elizabeth II 'guilty parties' in divorces were not even invited to Buckingham Palace. But Parker's divorce, compounded with Philip's long absence, fuelled rumours of discord in the royal marriage. Pressed by reporters Adeane issued a denial: 'It is quite untrue that there is any rift between the Queen and the Duke of Edinburgh.' Adeane's statement was clearly inadequate to the situation and did nothing more than increase the speculation. It would have been more effective had he explained Philip's long absence at sea in the context of the Duke's continued perception of himself as a naval officer. Sailors and their families become accustomed to long separations. But Adeane disapproved of Philip almost as much as Tommy Lascelles had and privately looked upon the long cruise as self-indulgent.

Philip, for his part, continued to feel no great admiration for his wife's Court. Mike Parker's departure left him deeply upset and in need of another secretary. In preference to consulting the household, he sought his uncle's help in finding a suitable candidate. He knew the risk he was running, and warned Mountbatten: 'I should be a bit careful about discussing this problem because I'm sure you realize what fun some people would have if they thought you were involved in choosing my staff.' The *Britannia* arrived in London too late for Philip to accompany the Queen on her visit to Portugal, but he flew to Lisbon privately to join her. In Antarctica, he had grown a beard, and so the royal welcoming group, which included Foreign Secretary Selwyn Lloyd (but not the Queen), at Lisbon Airport all wore false beards. The Portuguese officials present were astonished. The schoolboy prank confirmed all their traditional suspicions that the English were mad. But it served to lighten the mood of a potentially awkward reunion with the Queen, and Elizabeth was to remind Lloyd of it at subsequent meetings.

Returning to London on 2 March 1957, Elizabeth made Philip a prince. He was already a Greek prince, but now he would have 'the style and titular dignity of a prince of the United Kingdom of Great Britain and Northern Ireland.' In light of the preceding storm Elizabeth's desire to honour her husband took on the characteristics of a reconciliation, a public signal that all was well between them. It also made a handsome advance gift to Philip for their tenth wedding anniversary in November. In practical terms, however, the wrapping was finer than the gift. He would henceforth be styled His Royal Highness Prince Philip Duke of Edinburgh, adding Prince Philip to his former title. He was, therefore, acquiring the designation suggested by Mountbatten to the King before his marriage to Elizabeth ten years earlier. But his position as a peripheral figure in Elizabeth II's official life remained unchanged. He had neither advanced, nor retreated. Everything came to Philip too late, or in the wrong circumstances.

On one of the evenings of Ascot week Elizabeth took her houseguests to the theatre in nearby Windsor. In the interval, the Queen Mother, the Queen and Princess Margaret spotted Noël Coward sitting in the audience and, to his sheer delight, summoned him to the royal box. To his even greater delight, the Queen Mother commiserated with him because he was getting a bad press. 'We have been most angry on your behalf,' she told him, the plural presumably referring to herself and her two daughters. 'For the press to attack your integrity after all you have done for England both in the country and out of it is outrageous, but don't let it upset you, and remember that we too have had our troubles with the press.' Coward returned to his theatre seat almost hysterical with pride in his royal connections. His troubles with the press were the result of a court action by the British tax authorities charging that one thing he had not done for England was pay his taxes. He was tried, found guilty of tax evasion, and fined. Shortly afterwards he became a 'tax exile' by making Jamaica his permanent home.

Coward was one of the Queen Mother's circle of gay men friends, and in later years Labour Prime Minister Harold Wilson would occasionally receive hints via Buckingham Palace that it would be nice if he would approve a knighthood for the playwright. Wilson would refuse. To him, Coward personified those wealthy Britons who preferred to live somewhere with plenty of sunshine and hardly any taxes rather than in their own country where things were the other way around. In fact, Wilson would describe them contemptuously as taking 'the coward's way out': pun intended. But the royal ladies' sympathies were with Coward both as a longtime friend and also because of their shared suffering at the hands of the press.

The Peter Townsend episode had significantly enlarged the boundaries of what Fleet Street considered publishable about the private lives of the royal family. After Townsend, there was no going back to the old deference. The same new boldness characterized its stories on Elizabeth and Philip's marriage. What the royal family wanted was deferential attention: what they were increasingly getting was intrusive brashness. If Princess Margaret wanted to marry a commoner, then why treat her, or for that matter the rest of the family, as royalty? Queen Victoria would not have exposed herself thus to comparison with mere mortals. Indeed, for a large part of her reign she did not expose herself at all, shutting herself away reclusively inside Windsor Castle.

The wider context was the postwar shift in public attitudes towards leadership and authority in an era dominated by the

United States, with its democratic ideals and presidential system. A national poll late in 1956 showed that 58 per cent of the British population felt the Queen was doing a good job. Seen from the opposite perspective that, of course, meant that 42 per cent did not, reflecting vague but widespread dissatisfaction with the way the monarch functioned. There were other indications, too, such as an expressed commitment to republicanism by a minority section of the opposition Labour Party, raising questions about what might happen if Labour came to power. In the same year, at the Royal Court Theatre in Sloane Square, John Osborne's play *Look Back in Anger* expressed, for the first time, working-class rage. The Queen did not see the play, but she could not have been unaware of its resonance. The old social encrustations were under attack.

In the summer and autumn of 1957, this dissatisfaction was articulated in print with a directness unprecedented in the twentieth century. Four critiques were published in rapid-fire succession. Two were basically reasoned, well-intentioned efforts by monarchists aimed at helping the Queen to survive. The third was a level-headed discussion of the role of royalty. Only the fourth was a nasty attack on the institution, but the cumulative effect was to leave the royal household thoroughly rattled.

The first salvo came from an unlikely source. Lord Altrincham, who was thirty-three, was a Conservative peer and the son of a Tory politician who had been a junior minister in Winston Churchill's war cabinet. Writing about the character and function of the monarchy in the August issue of *The National and English Review*, an obscure publication of which he was the editor, he roused the ire of the British public and the press by criticizing the inadequacies of Elizabeth II's education (' "Crawfie", Sir Henry Marten, the London season, the race-course, the grouse-moor, Canasta, and the occasional Royal tour – all this would not have been good enough for Elizabeth I'), her speaking voice ('a pain in the neck'), and her speeches ('the personality conveyed by the utterances which are put in her mouth is that of a priggish schoolgirl, captain of the hockey team, a prefect, and a recent candidate for Confirmation'). If Altrincham's derogatory comments about the Queen were meant to grab the public's attention for his concrete proposals, the strategy worked too well and his real purpose disappeared in the explosion of public indignation.

One question he raised was whether the conception of the monarchy should change more in the direction of the Scandinavian rulers, where subjects offer respect but no adulation, where the monarch went bicycling unaccompanied down the main streets and did his or her own shopping in the local stores. He also stressed the importance of the Commonwealth and observed that royal tours were an unsatisfactory substitute for periods of residence in Commonwealth countries. 'Residence,' Altrincham wrote, 'need not be confused with perambulation.' Further, Altrincham hoped that Elizabeth would 'have the wisdom to give her children an education very different from her own' by sending them to a state-run primary school. He criticized 'public functions, such as Presentation Parties, which are a grotesque survival from the Monarchy's hierarchal past . . . they pander to snobbishness and give the Queen the appearance of standing at the apex of an aristocratic and plutocratic pyramid.' He pointed out that the Court 'had remained a tight little enclave of British ladies and gentlemen' which did not reflect the complex, multi-racial character of the British Commonwealth.

The United States embassy duly dispatched a copy of what it called 'Altrincham's free-wheeling but not undeserved criticisms' to Washington together with a lengthy confidential commentary. In the twentieth century, said the embassy report, the British monarch remained aloof from party politics and took no position on any public issue without the approval of the Government. 'In return for abandonment of the right to voice an opinion of its own,' it went on, 'the monarchy, according to accepted usage, has earned the right to exemption from public criticism. So powerful is this feeling today that any attack on the Queen approaches the sacrilegious.' The Scandinavian approach was 'more honest and rational,' the embassy report noted, but the British people '*want* their monarch to have certain of the attributes of a British super-man, to be a little larger than life-size, in effect to be the prefect and the captain of the team. They *want* their monarch to represent social virtues that are British and not those exotic but suspect qualities found in India, Pakistan or Ghana, about which the average Briton has little knowledge or interest.'

Another critic who publicly supported Altrincham was the Marquis of Londonderry. In his long article in the left-wing weekly periodical the *New Statesman* he said his fellow peer deserved public backing because 'only by plain speaking . . . can the social squalor of the upper classes be removed from the monarchy and a true democratic monarchy be raised from the social slough it has fallen into.' A newspaper opinion poll showed that 35 per cent agreed with Altrincham and 52 per cent disagreed, with young people tending to be among the former. Altrincham's critics, led by the right-wing League of Empire Loyalists ('a rowdy crew of Teddy Boys,' according to the American embassy report), were considerably more active than his supporters. A League member slapped him as he was leaving a television studio and its representatives denounced him at public meetings.

There was no public comment from the Queen, except that when the League sent her a telegram of loyalty, Buckingham Palace replied that 'Her Majesty much appreciates the loyal sentiments which you express,' which was several notches above a routine Palace reply and, by inference, an expression of disapproval of Altrincham's article.

Another faction of critics came from the ranks of that phenomenon of the late 1950s, the Angry Young Men, the intellectuals who attacked the lack of moral values of the affluent society – and the Angry Old Men. Among the former was John Osborne; and the latter, Malcolm Muggeridge, whose salvo appeared in the 19 October issue of the *Saturday Evening Post*: 'Does England Really Need a Queen?' The piece had made little impact when it was first published the previous year in *Punch*, which Muggeridge edited. But in the atmosphere of controversy generated by Altrincham, its reappearance in the United States raised hackles at home. Yet though Muggeridge is scathingly critical of the royal household, his conclusion is that 'the British monarchy does fulfil a purpose. It provides a symbolic head of state transcending the politicians who go in and out of office . . . It expresses the continuity which has enabled Britain to survive three great revolutions – the American, French and the Russian – and two ruinous and destructive world wars, without being torn by civil conflict.' To be useful, the Queen 'must be put across . . . as a unifying element in a society full of actual and potential discord' and this her present advisers and courtiers are not capable of doing. She needs 'new men around her – men who understand what the mid-twentieth century is about, and what is the role of a constitutional monarch at such a time.'

The real vitriol against what he termed 'the royalty religion' came from the playwright John Osborne in the monthly *Encounter*. Looking both back and forward in anger, Osborne called royalty 'the last circus of a civilization that has lost faith in itself.' His objection to the royal symbol, Osborne wrote, 'is that it is dead; it is the gold filling in a mouthful of decay.' Because royalty was deprived of active political power, he went on, and therefore the necessity to make 'moral, or any other, decisions, it is presented with a staggering power that gives it a greater grip on the public imagination than any other single institution.' Yet it deserved to be 'laughed into extinction'. *Encounter* was an anti-Communist magazine of the Cold War edited in Britain by Americans with Central Intelligence Agency connections. At the time, it was subsidized by the CIA, and ironically its editors received a stern rebuke from Washington for publishing Osborne's diatribe.

If the Queen and her household were previously in any doubt, the spate of criticism will have confirmed that the coronation 'honeymoon' was over, for not since Edward VII had the monarchy been discussed with such lack of deference. While the members of the royal household had borne the brunt of adverse comment, Elizabeth was at least the indirect target if only because she had a totally free hand in choosing her staff, and government approval, where it existed, had been reduced to a formality. There were no significant staff changes as a result of Altrincham and Co. Sir Michael Adeane, who was at least ex officio at the centre of the controversy, remained in place. In some political circles, it was felt that the thrust of Altrincham's criticisms of the royal staff was directed at him. In Whitehall and at Westminster, Adeane was regarded as worthy, courteous and affluent, but narrow and unimaginative. Years later, Anthony Wedgwood Benn, a left wing Labour cabinet minister, would ask him whether the royal family felt any embarrassment in dealing with their German relatives who had fought against the British in two world wars. Adeane replied, 'Oh, but the German royalty are all very decent chaps.' If his advice to his sovereign was on that level, there was much for Altrincham to be depressed about.

Yet, though the bad press shook the Palace the reality was that the monarchy was already changing – but as imperceptibly as leaves change colour on a tree. Within the traditional framework and the timelessness of the Queen's role, shifts were taking place, some so subtle as to be almost invisible to the naked eye, others less so. But what would otherwise be regarded as change was perceived in the Palace as revolution. The Queen adopted several of the proposals in Altrincham's critique, not as a direct result of his article, the Palace insisted, but because the Queen and her household had reached the same conclusions.

Shortly after publication of the article, Prince Charles, aged nine, entered his father's old preparatory school, Cheam, as a boarder. But that decision had more to do with Prince Philip

179

than Lord Altrincham. The Queen also decided that the formal Presentations at Court in March 1958 would be the last. No longer would débutantes resplendent in white ballgowns, elbow-length white gloves, and a headdress of three white feathers mark their entry into society by performing a deep curtsy to the monarch in the Throne Room of Buckingham Palace, while somewhere in the background the Guards orchestra played a little light music. Few mourned the death of the annual ritual. No longer subject to rigid Victorian protocol, its social prestige was undermined by the blue-blooded dowagers who supplemented their income by hiring themselves out as Presentation sponsors for the daughters of the nouveaux riches – and the Americans. The London Season went on very well without Presentations.

In their place, the Queen increased both the number and size of the Buckingham Palace garden parties, and put her occasional lunches with leading businessmen and others on a more regular footing. Elizabeth also tackled the problem of her public speaking voice. In anticipation of the first televised Christmas message in 1957, the BBC was asked to provide a voice coach, who diagnosed the problem as microphone nervousness. He made her do voice exercises, and sought to build up her confidence by asking her to record poetry, articles from newspapers, and old speeches and then playing back the results and analysing them with her.

A simple, everyday illustration of the transition from a 'hier-archical' to a 'popular' monarchy was the increasing frequency with which the Queen and Prince Philip drove their own cars on the public roads. George VI had rarely been seen behind the wheel of a car, and the Queen Mother almost never. But both Elizabeth and Philip enjoyed driving – Philip with more panache than caution. One afternoon in the spring of 1957, Philip and the Queen were making their way to Windsor, where she was to give a dinner for the Commonwealth heads of government, gathered in England for their annual conference. Philip was at the wheel, and beside him the Queen, holding her breath as usual. On the way they collided with another car, but fortunately the accident was not serious and the royal couple arrived at Windsor with clear consciences and in time to change for dinner. Earlier in the day, the Prince had addressed a meeting of the Automobile Association on safe driving. Some years later, while posing for her second Annigoni portrait, the Queen mentioned another traffic accident in which her husband was driving. 'A few evenings ago,' she said, 'a taxi ran into my car and made a large scratch in it. Taxis are sometimes too pushing. Philip was driving the car and he especially doesn't like being pushed.'

When it came to dealing with the press the royal family were slow to formulate a response to the changing times. The Queen was poorly served by her Press Secretary, Richard Colville, who saw his job primarily as preventing information from reaching the media. But the root of the problem was conditioning. It was King George V who first adopted as a convenient philosophy Bagehot's study on the constitutional role of the monarchy. Bagehot was drummed into Elizabeth by Sir Henry Marten. Later, Prince Charles was to be so well schooled in the famous late-nineteenth-century text that he could quote chunks of it from memory. Bagehot warned against 'letting too much daylight in upon the magic' of the monarchy. So the Queen and her family maintained a policy of being parsimonious with information about anything touching on their private lives.

The year's trials and tribulations could not have been eased for Elizabeth by her involvement in the aftermath of Suez, which came in the form of two state visits – to Paris and to Washington. In the case of the former, the Queen was 'persuaded' to visit the French capital to express Britain's appreciation to a nation she did not particularly like for its support in a conflict to which she had been opposed. But in the British popular mind France had never stood so high. Moreover, the royal visit had been part of a deal which the British government had made with Paris in an attempt to dissuade the French from launching a second attack on Nasser, the Egyptian president. The Queen's speeches contained no reference to Suez, but she spoke of French troops fighting alongside the British in the Second World War, and at a state banquet hosted by President René Coty she said, 'Our nations are each the complement of the other. Our peoples understand one another.' This was a piece of wishful thinking she could hardly have believed since no two other neighbouring nations could possibly achieve the same level of mutual misunderstanding.

The American trip was originally planned as a visit to the Jamestown Festival in Virginia in the autumn. Jamestown was celebrating the 350th anniversary of the first English settlement in North America. But Elizabeth and the Eisenhower administration had reckoned without the Suez crisis. In its wake, the trip became part of Macmillan's effort to repair the damage done to the Anglo-American special relationship. Protocol required that the acceptance came before the invitation was extended to avoid the embarrassment of a possible rebuff. The Queen signalled her acceptance in principle in January, but because British opinion polls showed America's popularity to be at an exceptionally low ebb, the White House was asked to hold off announcing the visit 'for several months'. Nevertheless planning was begun in secret of a ten-day itinerary with an arrival date in the middle of October. Besides Jamestown and Washington, the Queen was also to visit San Francisco and Chicago.

Within weeks news of the impending royal visit had leaked in Washington and a storm of protest came tumbling down on the Queen and on Macmillan's government. Opposition to the visit was led by the Suez 'rebels' in the House of Commons, right-wing Tory backbench parliamentarians who had supported the Suez action. Faced with the outcry, the Palace said talk of an American visit was premature, and Downing Street denied it altogether. Elizabeth considered postponing the trip indefinitely, but Macmillan felt it was vital to British interests, and the consequences of shelving it potentially very damaging. While continuing to insist that the White House treat the matter as secret, Palace and government hastily arranged to add Canada to the Queen's tour, thus giving the American visit the appearance of a side trip. When the trip was finally announced in both London and Washington in June 1957, a Canadian leg had been added, and the American visit had been cut from ten days to five to include only Jamestown, Washington and New York. The Palace, the American embassy wired Washington, 'will seek to play down questions on who made decision regarding length of US visit. However, if pressed strongly, Palace may add that the Queen felt she could not spend more than five days . . . in the US.'

Eisenhower was disappointed; the Canadians annoyed. The later inclusion of their country almost as an afterthought of the American tour deeply offended Canadian susceptibilities. It was seen in some quarters as an indication that even the Queen was not immune to considering them poor relations to the United States. Concerned at upsetting a Commonwealth country, the Queen insisted on spending double the amount of time in Canada as in the United States, and that boiled down to cutting back the American visit.

This time, there were no British voices raised in protest. While the Suez rebels in the Commons may still have harboured resentment against the United States, the embassy reported that 'they were inhibited from expressing such sentiments because

Princess Elizabeth and the Duke of Edinburgh on a rustic bridge over the Sagana River in Kenya, following the news of King George VI's death, walking together, not touching, back and forth along the bank.

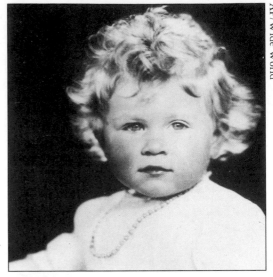

'A little darling with a lovely complexion and pretty fair hair' was how Queen Mary described her granddaughter, Elizabeth of York, shown here aged two.

Lilibet walking with her mother, Elizabeth, Duchess of York

The Duke and Duchess of York and their daughters, Elizabeth and Margaret Rose, in carefree, pre-Abdication days. The Duke wanted his daughters to look upon their childhood as a golden age.

An early appearance by Princess Elizabeth on the balcony of Buckingham Palace, on the coronation of her father, King George VI, 12 May 1937. Elizabeth's balcony appearances were associated with some of the happiest moments of her life.

The House of Windsor

To commemorate the
accession to the throne
of Their Majesties

KING GEORGE VI
QUEEN ELIZABETH

A store window decoration in London on Coronation Day showing the new King and his family. His older daughter rests her hand familiarly on her father's shoulder.

Lilibet, aged ten, walking one of her early corgis. When the Princess was seven the Yorks acquired two of these stumpy-looking, snappy Welsh dogs, Dookie and Jane, and before long a dynasty was started.

The teenage princesses attend a London concert. Elizabeth could be over-responsible. Indulged by a doting father, Margaret was talented but precocious.

Watched rather forlornly by her father, Princess Elizabeth and her husband wave to cheering crowds after their wedding on 20 November 1947. 'I felt I had lost something very precious,' the King wrote to her.

Elizabeth and Philip looking at wedding pictures on their honeymoon at Broadlands, home of Philip's mentor and exemplar, Earl Mountbatten of Burma.

Just the wife of a British naval officer on the Mediterranean station - Princess Elizabeth dancing a Scottish reel with her husband in Malta in 1951.

Three generations of the House of Windsor pose together at Sandringham in 1951. Prince Charles stands beside his grandmother; Princess Anne is in the baby carriage. The evidence of his illness is etched in the King's features. A few months later, he was dead.

The coronation of Queen Elizabeth II in Westminster Abbey, 2 June 1953. A dazzling choreography of clergy and coroneted nobles.

Following her coronation, the Queen and her husband set off on a marathon six-month visit to Commonwealth countries.

In Brisbane, Australia, the mascot of an Australian infantry regiment, a miniature Shetland pony, attracts the Queen's attention.

On the rear platform of the royal train during Elizabeth II's whistle-stop tour of Australia during the Commonwealth trip.

Queen Elizabeth in one of her chivalric regalia, in this instance the Scottish Order of the Thistle, leaving an investiture in Edinburgh.

Queen and heir. The Prince of Wales in the robes of a peer of the realm listens to his mother reading the speech from the throne at the Opening of Parliament in 1970.

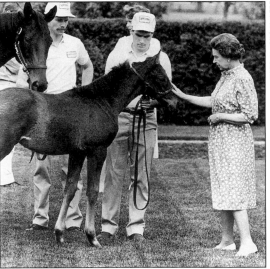

The Queen doing what she has always liked doing best - looking at thoroughbreds - on a visit to Kentucky.

On her first visit to the United States as British monarch in 1957, the Queen met Vice-President Richard Nixon.

When the Queen and Prince Philip lunched with President Ronald Reagan and his wife Nancy in California in 1983, severe storms put a damper on the visit. 'Don't you have anything to wear besides that horrible old mackintosh?' Princess Margaret telephoned the Queen from London.

Three decades after their first commonwealth trip and still on the go. The Queen and Prince Philip at the Great Wall in China in 1987.

Dressed for warmth and comfort in headscarf and raincoat, Elizabeth II watches horse trials with her daughter Anne.

On 29 July 1981, the Prince of Wales married Lady Diana Spencer. The crowd shouted 'Kiss her!' – and he did.

Members of the Windsor family crowd onto the balcony at Buckingham Palace following the wedding of Prince Andrew, the Duke of York, to Sarah Ferguson.

Tim Graham/Sygma Photo

Tim Graham/Sygma Photo

For her meeting with Pope John Paul II at the Vatican, the Queen made a rare appearance wearing black, the traditional colour for non-Catholic queens and princesses at papal audiences.

In 1983, the Queen revisited Treetops. But the hotel built in the branches of a giant wild fig tree had been burned down and a massive new one stood on the site.

... Prime Minister has his backbenchers under tight control and would strongly resent criticism of the Queen's visit for which [he], of course, was responsible.'

No sooner was the trip announced than invitations to the Queen began flooding into the White House from all over the United States. Princeton University wanted to give her an honorary degree, but Dulles had to tell his Alma Mater, 'It is Her Majesty's practise not to accept honorary degrees.' The University of Chatanooga hoped she would visit the campus, however briefly. Not a hope, replied the State Department: the programme had been planned well in advance of the announcement and there was no more time available. Other universities, churches and organizations received the same reply. As the American and British planners of the visit held their meetings in Washington to finalize the crowded programme which was going to require split-second timing, Mr Muirhead of the British embassy solemnly informed them that the Queen shook hands at the rate of ten hands a minute.

The Queen and Prince Philip went first to Canada, where the Prime Minister, John Diefenbaker, had just lost an election and been replaced by the Liberal Lester Pearson. In Ottawa, Elizabeth II, wearing her white satin coronation gown with the Commonwealth emblems woven on the skirt, opened the new session of the Canadian Parliament. She read the Speech from the Throne twice, first in English and then in French. In a further attempt at soothing ruffled Canadian feathers she declared on television, 'When you hear or read about events in Washington and other places, I want you to reflect that it is the Queen of Canada and her husband who are concerned in them.' With that the Queen of Canada and her husband crossed the border to the United States. After attending the Jamestown celebrations, she went to Colonial Williamsburg, where she was presented with the files of the British army headquarters in America during the revolution, 107 leather-bound volumes that had been in the Williamsburg archives. 'This,' she declared, 'is one of Williamsburg's most charming and most imaginative restorations.'

On 14 October 1957, the royal couple arrived in Washington to a warm welcome from the Eisenhowers. The Queen's relationship with President Eisenhower went beyond the formal courtesies between two heads of state. Here was a figure from her wartime youth, a link with her late father, who had liked and admired him and by whom he was liked and admired in return. The personal ties were reflected in Eisenhower's insistence that Elizabeth and Philip should stay at the White House and not at Blair House. However, to avoid setting a precedent for other distinguished foreign visitors who might also expect to stay at the White House, James Hagerty, the White House spokesman, was instructed to say that this departure from usual practice had been necessary because the official guest house was being redecorated. In fact, Blair House had been refurbished from top to bottom the previous year, but shortly before the Queen's arrival workmen moved in and looked busy.

Elizabeth occupied the Rose Room, while Philip had the Lincoln Room, which contained Abraham Lincoln's four-poster bed. The atmosphere was relaxed and friendly, but the schedule very strenuous. When the Queen regretted not having time for a long chat, Eisenhower took it as an oblique criticism of the arrangements and blamed the British embassy for setting a pace 'that would have killed anybody but two people as young and vigorous as [Elizabeth and Philip].' He later told Macmillan that he would have fired any aide who dared set up a similar programme for him. The Queen did find time to give the President her views on Nikita Khrushchev, and to express 'shock at how much hysteria there was over here about Sputnik. It died out at once in Britain.' The Russian launch of mankind's first space satellite, Sputnik I, had prompted a spate of criticism of American technology before the Queen's visit pushed it off the front pages. On the Suez crisis, she told him that her father would have known instinctively how to handle the situation, as he had known how to deal with problems in the Second World War.

Aside from being violently ill from eating sweetbreads for the first time ever when they were served at a White House lunch, the Queen bore the five days with a smile, shaking hundreds of hands at her rate of ten a minute at a gallimaufry of events ranging from opening an exhibition of William Blake engravings at the National Gallery to sitting in the University of Maryland stadium puzzling over the mysteries of American football. More to her liking, she made a quick dash to the Upperville area of Virginia to see the horses so popular in the region. Three decades later, she was to become a regular visitor to the stud farms of Kentucky and Wyoming.

Some Washingtonians were just as bemused by the thirty-one-strong royal entourage. The Countess of Euston was one lady-in-waiting, and the Lady Rose Baring the other. Then there were Sir Michael Adeane, Private Secretary, Colonel Sir Martin

Charteris, the Assistant Secretary who had advanced the visit, Captain the Lord Plunket, equerry, and Commander Richard Colville, Press Secretary. After that came Bobo MacDonald, the Queen's dresser, plus a second dresser; John Macdonald, Prince Philip's footman; the Queen's Page; the Queen's Footman; the Sergeant Footman; the Yeoman of the Baggage; two more footmen; the Queen's hairdresser; and, three Scotland Yard detectives. The clothes she wore on each occasion were mostly Hartnell designs. Her daytime wardrobe tended to be matronly for a woman just turned thirty-one, but on formal occasions wearing a dazzling array of jewellery which she carried with remarkable ease, she was a radiant figure. At the dinner for the Eisenhowers on 19 October at the embassy, she wore a diamond tiara with a drop emerald in each circle, with matching necklace, bracelet and earrings. Left to her by Queen Mary, the tiara was known in the royal family as 'Granny's fender'.

One of the oddities of the royal couple's American itinerary was that they spent the night of 20 October on a stationary train parked in a military base outside Washington. At 11.20 p.m., Elizabeth and Philip were seen off at Union Station by Vice-President Richard Nixon. The royal train then left for New York City followed by a press train, but shortly before midnight, both trains came to a halt at Camp Kilmer, Maryland. In the morning they set off again, arriving at Stapleton, Staten Island, at ten. The Queen took the ferry to the Battery and then went in a motorcade to City Hall for the start of a sixteen-hour day in New York ending with a ball at the Park Avenue Seventh Regiment Armory given by fifty-eight Commonwealth societies and attended by five thousand people. The couple drove directly from the ball to New York's Idlewild Airport for the flight home. From the British point of view, the Queen's visit was a spectacular success, giving the special relationship a boost and contributing to Britain's diplomatic rehabilitation after Suez. It was also the start of Elizabeth II's own close personal association with the United States and successive American presidents. As the British ambassador, Sir Harold Caccia, put it in his report on the tour, 'She has buried George III for good.'

Back home she and Philip marked their tenth wedding anniversary with a small dinner party at Windsor. It seemed the most appropriate celebration in a year of turbulence, if not crisis. But in one important and consoling respect 1957 had been a spectacular year, and that was in horse racing. She was once again leading owner. She had nearly thirty horses in training during the season, including two home-bred colts, Doutelle and Agreement. The former was her favourite racehorse and contributed two of the season's seven major wins (not to mention several minor wins and placings). When Doutelle died seven years later, the Queen wept.

Another first was her televised Christmas message from Sandringham, requiring endless rehearsals, and makeup experiments. In her words, 'The first time my white skin and broad jaw made my face come out like a huge white plate with dark cavities containing black boot buttons; my hair was parted in the centre and [the parting] looked like a white line down a main road. It had to be blacked and yellow paint daubed on my cheeks and the tip of my nose.' But the Sunday after the broadcast, outside Sandringham Church there were ten thousand people, ten times the usual number. She had become more than a Queen. She was a television personality.

XII

Into the Second Decade

In March 1958, a visit to the Netherlands by the Queen and Prince Philip was overshadowed, at least as far as the British media were concerned, by Princess Margaret and . . . Peter Townsend. Back in London after a world tour lasting almost a year, Townsend telephoned Margaret, who invited him to Clarence House. The Queen was not told in advance of their meeting and it rang alarm bells both in the family and among Court officials. A ghost they had thought removed for good had returned for a second haunting. But it turned out to be a false alarm. The flame had gone out in the romance, and they were 'two old and devoted friends' who 'despite their sentimental past, had decided to go their own way.' If they believed their affair could be re-cycled into friendship without attracting attention, they were mistaken. Margaret met her former suitor a few more times but – as Townsend put it rather ingenuously – 'our hopes that our meetings would no longer be news were dashed.'

By the summer, Princess Margaret's most frequent companion was Dominic Eliot, an affable advertising executive and a member of one of England's leading families. Eliot was a houseguest at Balmoral when President Eisenhower spent twenty-four hours there on his 1959 tour of Europe. Britain had been added to Eisenhower's itinerary at the last minute to please Harold Macmillan, who was facing a general election and wanted to show his close ties with other world leaders. To overcome Eisenhower's considerable reluctance to extend his already full tour schedule Macmillan used the Queen's gambit: if the President came to Europe and failed to visit Britain,

187

the Prime Minister warned, it would be an insult to the Queen. Far from being insulted, Elizabeth was not about to break off her summer holiday and return to London. Apart from her 1957 visit, she had seen the President and Mamie Eisenhower again briefly in October 1958, when she visited Canada to open the St Lawrence Seaway. On that occasion she had spent a day in Chicago. So Eisenhower was received informally in Scotland. It was an unusual departure from protocol, but Eisenhower welcomed the break.

On 29 August the Queen drove him in a Land Rover over the rugged, heather-covered hills of the estate to visit the Queen Mother at Birkhall. Then, at a very informal lakeside picnic tea on a cold afternoon, Elizabeth cooked drop scones over a charcoal burner for ten guests, who also included Bobbety Salisbury, and Eisenhower acted as waiter. Prince Philip (rather moodily, Eisenhower thought) sailed a boat alone up and down the lake in a stiff breeze. Charles and Anne were his shore helpers.

Eisenhower admired the scones and, in due course, the Queen sent him the recipe. She had seen a newspaper photograph of him at a barbecue, the Queen wrote from Buckingham Palace, and had remembered a promise to send him the recipe. Enclosed with the note in her own handwriting was a Palace menu card with the recipe copied down in detail. She used golden syrup or treacle which could be very good instead of sugar, she wrote. And the mixture needed a lot of beating and shouldn't stand too long before cooking. She had followed Eisenhower's strenuous trip, she added, and would never again be able to claim that she was being made to do too much on future tours. Eisenhower replied, 'You will understand my rather woeful ignorance of culinary practises when I tell you that I did not recognize the term "caster" as a type of sugar. But when I called the British Embassy for help, the problem was promptly solved for me.'

The following year, Eisenhower was succeeded by John F. Kennedy and a new age dawned and briefly flourished across the Atlantic. As it happened, the newly elected president was another figure from Elizabeth II's childhood but a less familiar one than Eisenhower, for she was ten when the brash teenage son of the American ambassador had gone to tea at Buckingham Palace and – as he put it – 'made time' with the heir to the English throne. In 1961, Jack Kennedy returned to the Palace, this time for a dinner at which he and his wife were the guests of honour. The evening itself went splendidly even though the planning of it had been overshadowed by the drama (for Jackie) of Elizabeth's initial refusal to invite the First Lady's sister, Lee Radziwill.

Lee and her husband, Prince Stanislas (Stash) Radziwill lived in London, and were on the list of proposed guests for the Queen's dinner submitted to Buckingham Palace for the Queen's approval by the White House staff. When the list came back from the Palace, however, the Radziwills' name had been crossed off it. It had not escaped the Queen's vigilance that both Lee and her Polish-born husband had been previously married and divorced. Divorcees were not invited to Buckingham Palace except in an official capacity, and the Radziwills were not members of the visiting American party (in fact, Stash Radziwill was not an American at all).

It would hardly have been in character for either Jackie Kennedy or her sister to have accepted this royal ruling passively, and they did not. For Princess Lee Radziwill, going to the royal dinner meant reaching the summit of social acceptance in her adopted country. Not going raised and left unanswered awkward nagging questions, particularly as the Kennedys were to be her houseguests. For Jackie Kennedy, forcing the Queen to reverse the Palace rules amounted to a demonstration of her new, savoured power as First Lady.

London was to be a private stopover after the President's Vienna summit with Nikita Khrushchev, which was turning into a disaster for the American leader. Khrushchev had come out of his corner fighting and Kennedy was completely overwhelmed by the Russian premier's ruthlessness and savagery. Meanwhile, Jackie was having problems of her own with the press, whose aggressiveness was making her own stay in the Austrian capital unpleasant and miserable. (Complaining about the press to Harold Macmillan later, Kennedy asked him, 'How would you react, if somebody should say "Lady Dorothy [Macmillan] is a drunk?" ' To which Macmillan said, 'I would reply, "You should have seen her mother." ')

Jackie Kennedy was exasperated: her presidential visit to Europe was turning into something of a débâcle. She dispatched the State Department's chief of protocol, Angier Biddle Duke, to Britain. His mission: to try to reverse the Palace decision on the Radziwills. In London, Biddle Duke naturally turned for help to David Bruce, the United States ambassador, and the latter appealed directly to the Palace. 'Major Millbank came from the Palace to talk about the Radziwill matter,' Bruce wrote in his diary. 'I explained that the Radziwills would be the President's hosts and he was coming primarily to see them, and to act as godfather to their newborn daughter . . . I think this vexatious little problem will be solved after Millbank has a chance to discuss it with the Queen.' While Ambassador Bruce was exerting his considerable talent for diplomatic persuasion on the Palace, however, he received a message from President Kennedy himself for relay to the Queen. '[Kennedy] wanted to make it clear that for his part he had no feeling about this incident,' Bruce recorded. 'Any decision on the guest list must be the Queen's.' Clearly, Kennedy was anxious to distance himself from his wife's efforts on her sister's behalf, perhaps regarding it as a *faux pas*.

But Elizabeth did change her mind and the Radziwills were somewhat belatedly 'commanded' to the Queen's dinner on 5 June in honour of President Kennedy. True, they were seated a considerable distance away from the principal guests and closer to what was known by the equerries as 'Starvation Corner', but at least the embarrassment of being excluded altogether had been avoided. Jackie herself sat between Prince Philip and his brother-in-law Prince Kraft von Hohenlohe-Langenburg. In the span of eight years, she had progressed from photojournalist covering Elizabeth's coronation to dining at the Queen's table.

Though there was always talk of rivalry between the two sisters, Jackie Kennedy used her considerable influence as the President's wife to try to create opportunities for her sister to meet the Queen. The objective was to establish Lee Radziwill as a leading London hostess in the same league as, for example, Emerald, Lady Cunard, in King Edward VIII's day. At the instigation of the First Lady, David and Evangeline Bruce gave a dinner for Elizabeth and Philip the sole purpose of which (at least from Jackie Kennedy's point of view) was to provide an opportunity for Prince and Princess Radziwill to establish proper contact with the Queen. The Radziwills did become a fixture in London social life, but entrée to the royal circle eluded them. In 1962, Jackie Kennedy again visited London in the course of an extensive world tour and the Queen invited her to lunch. On that occasion, David Bruce sat beside the Queen and 'talked almost entirely about horses, in which her interest is passionate.' Horses were also a topic of her conversation with her principal guest. Elizabeth and Jackie had each been given a horse by the President of Pakistan, and they compared notes about the excitability of their respective mounts.

It was not just David Bruce's persuasiveness that prompted

the Queen to bend the rules for Jacqueline Kennedy and the Radziwills: there were other considerations as well. She liked what she had seen of the United States and hoped to be invited to see more of it. But she was also very much aware of the importance of the Anglo-American special relationship. Her interest in American affairs extended to sending a message of condolence to the President following the death of J. Edgar Hoover, the legendary director of the Federal Bureau of Investigation: it is safe to assume that there would have been no such message to a European head of state at the death of his chief of internal security.

Yet another possible consideration was the rapport that flourished between Jack Kennedy and Harold Macmillan. In Western Europe an older generation of statesmen was in power: Macmillan in Britain, Konrad Adenauer in West Germany, Charles de Gaulle in France, and in the Vatican the eighty-two-year-old Pope John XXIII. However, it was with Macmillan that the much younger American President established his closest relationship among foreign leaders. He was perhaps not as impressed by Macmillan's seasoned political judgement as the Prime Minister thought he was. But he liked and respected the British statesman, and moreover regarded Britain as America's principal ally in Europe. The Prime Minister admired Kennedy's energy, found that he lacked experience in foreign affairs, but acknowledged his decisiveness.

A further ingredient in this exceptional personal bond was the advent of the 'two Davids' – David Ormsby-Gore, the British ambassador in Washington, and his American counterpart in London, David Bruce. Ormsby-Gore combined ability and a close friendship with Kennedy with the advantage of being the Prime Minister's nephew by marriage. David Bruce was an urbane, highly experience diplomat, with excellent lines of communication to both the British government and Buckingham Palace. But Macmillan never became complacent about the special relationship, to which he attached great importance. So anxious was he to maintain it, he once made the highly unusual suggestion to the Queen that she in effect become Kennedy's pen pal.

In his personality sketch of Kennedy, written for the Queen, the Prime Minister told her, 'He likes presents . . . he likes letters, he likes attention. If I might venture to suggest it, Madam, I think he would welcome very much an occasional letter from you on any matter of partly international, partly political, and partly more personal interest.' The Queen did not rush to her writing desk, but five months later – following her lunch with Jackie – she did write just such a letter to the President, in her own hand, giving their friendship her endorsement. It was 'a great comfort' to know that he and Macmillan were so close, and that the two leaders had confidence in each other's judgement and advice, she said.

She was glad, she added, to hear from the Prime Minister that her Ambassador and his wife were getting on so well. David (Ormsby-Gore) was very highly thought of in London so it was excellent news that he and Cissie were making their mark in Washington. At the time, Prince Philip was in Canada and was due to visit the World's Fair in Seattle and then go to New York for an official dinner engagement, and Elizabeth said she envied him the chance of being in the United States again. The letter was signed 'Your sincere friend,' which became the form for all her subsequent letters over the years to American presidents.

The following year, Kennedy was assassinated. On hearing the news at the house of friends where she was a weekend guest, the Queen telephoned Michael Adeane in London and drafted a telegram to the President's widow expressing her deep sorrow. Kennedy's death must have reminded her of her own vulnerability to such attacks, yet royal security remained low key. The almost perfunctory level of protection provided for the Queen has always surprised visiting Secret Service men on the American presidential detail. During the famous Kennedy dinner at Buckingham Palace a Secret Service man asked one of the royal bodyguards what kind of 'piece' he was carrying. The latter pointed two fingers at his American counterpart and said, 'You're dead,' to indicate that he wasn't carrying a gun at all.

It worked both ways, of course. The Queen was always bemused by, not to say slightly contemptuous of, the protective screen surrounding American presidents, a marked contrast to her own pair of Scotland Yard detectives. Her view was – and has remained – that security must not restrict her activity and that a reasonably acceptable risk goes with the job. 'If someone really wants to get me it is too easy,' has been her usual comment – a truth that would later be brought dramatically home. Perhaps she also shared her husband's view that too much protection was as bad as too little because would-be assassins were tempted by the challenge. 'If it hadn't been for all the security,' Philip once told his official biographer, 'Kennedy wouldn't have been shot.'

Security was not the Queen's only worry in the early 1960s.

In later years, Macmillan was to tell a story about arriving at Sandringham for an audience to be greeted by the Duke of Gloucester, very agitated. 'Thank Heavens you've come, Prime Minister,' said the Duke. 'The Queen's in a terrible state; there's a fellow called Jones in the billiard room who wants to marry her sister, and Prince Philip's in the library wanting to change the family name to Mountbatten.' Late in 1959, Peter Townsend wrote to Princess Margaret to let her know that he planned to marry a young Belgian woman, Marie-Luce Jamagne. That week, Princess Margaret broke the news to the Queen that she wished to become engaged to Antony Armstrong-Jones, a stylish young London photographer much in demand by the glossy fashion magazines. An assignment to take an informal portrait of Margaret had rapidly led to friendship and even more rapidly to talk of marriage.

The situation must have given the Elizabeth a disconcerting sense of *déjà vu*. Like Peter Townsend, Armstrong-Jones was a commoner. Unlike Townsend, he was not divorced, but his parents were. His father was a London barrister and his mother Anne, Countess of Rosse, having married as her second husband the Earl of Rosse. The gossip columnists had a field-day with the fact that Princess Margaret's fiancé's step-mother was a former airline stewardess several years his junior and that Margaret's predecessor in Tony Armstrong-Jones's affections was a Hong Kong-born film starlet named Jacqui Chan. Inevitably, the prospect of the Queen's sister marrying a commoner raised constitutional questions which the Cabinet had to look into. But in February 1960, the Queen had given birth to her third child, and Margaret consequently slipped down to fourth place in the succession after Charles, Anne, and the infant Prince Andrew. In addition, Palace officials argued that times had changed in the intervening five years since Margaret had renounced her plans to marry Peter Townsend. What this boiled down to was that the Establishment realized it no longer had the clout to mount the same offensive even if it wanted to.

The Queen dropped her initial reservations after Margaret made it plain that this time she was determined to marry the man of her choice, and her engagement was announced a week after the birth of the Queen's baby. The problem of Armstrong-Jones's being a commoner was easily overcome: Elizabeth offered him an earldom, a solution he accepted after some hesitation. (Thirteen years later, her own daughter's husband-to-be would refuse to be ennobled at all, preferring to remain Captain Mark Phillips.) Elizabeth gave her sister a lavish wedding – incidentally, the first major royal event since the Coronation seven years earlier. On the night of 4 May, there was a dazzling pre-wedding ball at Buckingham Palace – 'The lovely rooms and pictures, the preponderance of red brocade and glittering chandeliers; the fabulous jewels and the excellent lighting and the whole atmosphere of supreme grandeur.'

The wedding two days later – indeed, the marriage – brought together two worlds in a celebration of the brash, lively new decade, the Swinging Sixties. The Establishment rubbed shoulders with the new London élite – the designers, television personalities, and media figures from the bridegroom's world: Mary Quant, her restaurateur husband Alexander Plunket-Green, comedian Peter Sellers, David Frost. Dozens of others. There was a last-minute hitch when it emerged that the bridegroom's choice of best man was not acceptable because detectives had unearthed his homosexual past, and Armstrong-Jones quickly had to find a substitute. His second choice also turned out to be gay, and a third had to be picked. But the service in flower-filled Westminster Abbey went without a hitch. Noël Coward, who was present, thought the music 'divine and the fanfare immensely moving.'

To Coward, 'The Queen alone looked disagreeable; whether or not this was concealed sadness or bad temper . . . nobody seems to know, but she did scowl a great deal.' The newlyweds drove back to Buckingham Palace through streets lined with banners with the entwined monograms *M* and *A*. After a wedding breakfast, they set off for their Caribbean honeymoon – with the Queen and her mother running beside the car as it was moving along the inner quadrangle. A trendy photographer was not the partner that immediately sprang to mind when Elizabeth II and the Queen Mother thought about a husband for Margaret. But then neither of them had expected her to make a conventional choice, either. Despite their occasional differences, strong bonds of affection linked the three Windsor women, and what was important was that, at thirty, Margaret had found someone with whom she could share life and happiness. Following the honeymoon, the couple moved into an apartment in Kensington Palace, leaving the Queen Mother the sole occupant of Clarence House, and alone for the first time in the eight years since King George VI's death.

The Queen continued to telephone her mother daily, and made a practice of seeing her at least once a week. The older Elizabeth had always been her daughter's closest confidante after her husband, and Princess Margaret's marriage had brought them even closer together. With her outgoing personality and common touch, the Queen Mother was and remains a good influence on her reserved, serious-minded daughter. The Queen looks up at the sky in mock exasperation when she hears such stories as the Queen Mother, in an allusion to the number of homosexuals employed by the royal households, telephoning down to the kitchen: 'I don't know what you old queens are doing down there, but this old queen up here wants a gin and tonic.' But Elizabeth had come to accept, and even envy her mother's common touch and reserves of humanity and humour which had endeared her to the nation. One shared passion, of course, is horses: the Queen Mother had a racing news ticker installed at Clarence to help her with her betting. In 1961, 4 June was a red letter day: for the first time in her life she had three winners on the same day.

One subject which the Queen is hardly likely not to have discussed with the Queen Mother was the Duke of Gloucester's other concern in Macmillan's story, namely, changing the family name to Mountbatten. Among the sermons, prayers, and tributes occasioned in churches throughout Britain by the birth of the new royal prince, a homily by Dr Bloomer, the Bishop of Carlisle, made national headlines. He did not like to think of a child born in wedlock being deprived of the father's family name, the Bishop declared. Dr Bloomer had been persuaded to make this point by Lord Mountbatten. With Queen Mary safely dead and buried, Prince Philip's uncle was renewing his campaign to bring fresh glory to his family name by making it that of the reigning house. The Queen had little enthusiasm for declaring the total extinction of her own dynastic surname, but, once again, the dispute placed her in the middle of a simmering family conflict. On the one hand were members of her family upholding the late Queen Mary's argument that King George V had founded the Royal House of Windsor in perpetuity. On the other was her husband, understandably bitter that his children had not been allowed to bear his name. With the impending christening of her new baby threatening to revive the argument, Elizabeth consulted the Prime Minister. What she presumably sought was a more reasonable solution than her husband's blunt request in 1952 that the Royal House of Windsor should become the Royal House of Mountbatten and Churchill's equally blunt refusal.

Faced with what he called the 'Queen's Affair', Macmillan proposed a compromise: combine the two names and call her family Mountbatten-Windsor. He recalled that when the Marlborough family had changed its name to Spencer-Churchill, the Spencer very soon disappeared. If the family were to be called Mountbatten-Windsor, he confidently predicted that the first part of the name would soon be dropped in public usage and the family would be back where they started. So the Queen notified the Cabinet of her wish to incorporate the name of Mountbatten into the surname by which her descendants would ultimately be known, but said she wanted to do so 'on advice'. This meant that the Cabinet, and not the Queen herself, would seem to be instigating the change, and would be accepting constitutional responsibility. 'She clearly indicated', R. A. Butler, the Deputy Prime Minister, wrote to Macmillan (who was by now touring Africa), having discussed the matter with Elizabeth, 'that the 1952 decisions had been reached, and that she accepted them, but she did not indicate that she accepted them in spirit. She stressed that Prince Philip did not know of the present decision, on which she had absolutely set her heart.'

A disapproving Cabinet argued the Queen's request at great length, and Butler reported that 'several of our colleagues expressed serious regret that this step had to be taken but, while recognizing the dangers of criticism and unpopularity, particularly attached to [Prince Philip], none felt that the Queen's wishes should be refused.'

Thus, almost ten years after it was first broached by Prince Philip, and nine years since the death of Queen Mary who, according to many, had been its main opponent, the change was announced by the Queen in time to avert a fresh eruption of the old argument. She specified that the switch should take effect in the third generation: 'While I and my children will continue to be styled and known as the House and Family of Windsor my descendants . . . shall bear the name of Mountbatten-Windsor.' Buckingham Palace gilded the lily by adding that Elizabeth had 'always wanted, without changing the name of the Royal House established by her grandfather, to associate the name of her husband with her own and his descendants. The Queen has had this in mind for a long time and it is close to her heart.' Her enormous relief at resolving this point of friction within the marriage and the family was made clear by her message of 'special gratitude' to Macmillan. She wanted him to know, she said, that the decision 'had taken a great load off her mind.'

With a little help from Mountbatten the change in surname came into use much sooner than the third generation. Shortly before Princess Anne's marriage in October 1973, he wrote to Prince Charles: '[Anne's] marriage certificate will be the first opportunity to settle the Mountbatten-Windsor name for good . . . If you can make quite sure . . . that her surname is entered as Mountbatten-Windsor it will end all arguments. I hope you can fix this.' Charles – or someone else – did. Though she signed the register 'Anne', the Princess's names were filled in by the registrar as 'Anne Elizabeth Alice Louise Mountbatten-Windsor'.

Philip was no doubt gratified by the Queen's announcement, but whether he regarded the manner of achieving the change as quite the same as obtaining it as his own right and through his own efforts was another matter. In many ways, he remained an outsider, and his brand of intelligence and obvious administrative talents were still not fully appreciated in Court and Establishment circles. The new Archbishop of Canterbury, Michael Ramsey, a somewhat eccentric cleric picked by Macmillan for his spirituality and theological scholarship, had difficulty dealing with the royal family as a whole but especially the Duke of Edinburgh whom he found 'awful'. In retirement, Ramsey would admit, 'Yes, it's perfectly true, I didn't give my mind to the royal family. The Duke of Edinburgh thought I was very donnish. Well I am. And I thought he was very boorish, and he is.'

The Archbishop claimed that in order to show how much he despised him, Prince Philip had read a book throughout Prince Charles's confirmation at which Ramsey had, of course, officiated. Philip's short fuse and blunt manner were a source of constant irritation to officials. He was regarded as an over-protective husband who scrutinized his wife's travel schedules and – with much profanity – took a blue pencil to them when he thought the Queen was being overtaxed. Elizabeth's affection for her husband was standing the test of time and she was equally over-protective towards him – in her own fashion. Two foreign ambassadors' wives who were in London in the 1960s assert that hostesses planning dinners for the Queen and Prince Philip learned not to include pretty young women on the list of guests because their names were almost invariably crossed out when the list was submitted to Buckingham Palace. An attractive young American woman who was studying at Oxford wrote to Prince Philip mentioning that she was a direct descendant of the tsars and therefore his cousin through his paternal grandmother. The woman was duly invited to a royal garden party with instructions to make herself known to an equerry on arrival. Within minutes of being in the crowded Palace gardens, she found herself in the Queen's tea tent engaged in lively conversation with Prince Philip and his Uncle Dickie, while Elizabeth II stood some distance away occasionally glancing in their direction. Then Philip said, 'Before you go, you must meet my wife' and led the young American girl to the Queen. To explain the relationship Philip had to trace Russian and German royal genealogy back through several generations. At the end of it there was a pause and Elizabeth said dryly, 'Well, that doesn't seem like much of a relationship to me.'

Elizabeth was very feminine, even girlish despite being thirty-five years old and the mother of three children. Her complexion was clear. Her remarkable blue eyes sparkled. She kept fit by riding regularly and walking every day. Rain or shine she tramped through the grounds of Buckingham Palace, or Windsor Great Park, or the heather-covered hills around Balmoral, or the Norfolk beach near Sandringham, her ever-present corgi dogs trotting in her wake. A light diet, moderate drinking, and no smoking helped her stay remarkably healthy. She was known to have missed only one public engagement through illness, a royal garden party in 1958 because of a sinus condition.

She had made some progress in conquering her awkwardness with people, but found communicating with women a bigger problem than with men. She lived in a male world. She had not appointed any women to senior posts in the Court. A retired senior military officer held the post of Master of the Household in charge of the day-to-day administration of her domestic staff of several hundred footmen, pages, maids and dressers, but she took a personal interest in the management of her various homes. Half an hour of the Queen's time was set aside each morning to discuss menus with the Palace chef, and all redecoration required her personal approval. It was said that she had chosen the fabric for every cushion on every couch in Buckingham Palace. Yet she never set foot inside a shop: the shop came to her. She liked to relax watching television, but rarely read a fashion magazine. She lacked the small talk which she felt was the topic of conversation with women: weightier subjects were to be discussed with men. Formidable women she tended to steer clear of if possible. Once, after a Covent Garden gala concert, she was working her way along a presentation line that included the soprano Maria Callas. She had something to say to each performer in the line until she reached La Callas. She shook hands with the singer and promptly moved on without a word. Callas was not pleased at receiving the royal silent treatment and demanded to know why. So Lord Harewood, then artistic director of Covent Garden, made discreet enquiries through cousinly channels. The Queen, he was told, just couldn't think of anything to say to her.

In the 1980s, the Queen was to regard another formidable woman – Margaret Thatcher – as the least companionable of her Prime Ministers, breaking a pattern of smooth, harmonious relationships begun with Winston Churchill. Such problems were a long way off, however, and certainly not in evidence with Harold Macmillan, whom the Queen always treated as the valued counsellor that he was. He was punctilious about keeping her thoroughly briefed on his government's activities. His weekly Tuesday audiences continued to be supplemented with detailed written reports on foreign trips and important developments. She was attentive and learned a great deal, stockpiling knowledge and experience, and developing her knack for asking intelligent, well-informed – and for any unprepared Prime Minister, awkward – questions. She was also not taken in by his theatricality and his bouts of self-pity. Once, returning in a black mood from addressing the United Nations General Assembly in New York, where Khrushchev had heckled him by banging his shoe on the table, he talked to her about resigning: he noted that she did not show much concern at the prospect. She had acquired a sense of her own permanence.

The atmosphere was formal and businesslike, but unstuffy: monarch and Prime Minister neglecting state business and borrowing a transistor radio to follow reports on the United States' first orbiting spaceman John Glenn (space exploration fascinated her: the previous year, she had invited Soviet cosmonaut Yuri Gagarin to a family lunch); Macmillan amusing her with his description of the Indian Prime Minister Jawaharlal Nehru as a parody of Churchill, complete with his imitation of the Indian accent of which he was proud.

But they also faced some tough decisions, such as the Queen's very risky state visit to Ghana in November 1961 in the teeth of vigorous concern in Britain for her personal safety. With a few weeks to go before her departure, serious political unrest threatened the regime of Ghana's autocratic, left-wing President Kwame Nkrumah and several bombs had exploded in the capital, Accra. No-one expected the Queen to be attacked, but an assassin's bullet meant for the President could hit her. In addition, Nkrumah was showing distinct signs of hostility towards Britain. Following a trip to Moscow, he had thrown out all his British officers and most of his non-left-wing British advisers, and the London press were asking, Is this a suitable climate for a royal visit?

It wasn't just the press: John Morrison, the powerful chairman of the Tory backbench group, the 1922 Committee (whose daughter Mary Morrison was to become one of the Queen's ladies-in-waiting), urged the Prime Minister and the Palace to persuade the Queen to call the trip off. But the Queen wouldn't hear of it. In her view, cancellation would have amounted to telling Ghana it was not wanted in the Commonwealth. 'How silly I should look if I was scared to visit Ghana and then Khrushchev went and got a good reception,' she said. Macmillan confided to his press spokesman, Harold Evans, 'She had been indignant . . . at the idea of having the trip called off. The House of Commons, she thought, should not show lack of moral fibre in this way. She takes her Commonwealth responsibilities very seriously, and rightly so for the responsibilities of the UK monarchy have so shrunk that if you left it at that you might as well have a film star' and 'she is impatient of the attitude towards her to treat her as a woman, and a film star or mascot.'

Five days before her departure on 9 November, another bomb exploded in Accra. As Commons hostility intensified Macmillan sent Colonial Secretary Duncan Sandys to test the water. Sandys persuaded Nkrumah to drive over the royal route with him in an open car, and when Sandys came back unscathed, Macmillan advised the Queen to make the trip. Meanwhile, he had taken the precaution of securing the postponement of a White House decision – which was imminent – on whether or not to provide massive American funds for Ghana's multi-million-dollar Volta Dam project. He telephoned President Kennedy with the request that if the final decision was not to aid the project, would Washington wait until the Queen was safely home before making the announcement? Kennedy would. In the event, the visit was an outstanding success. Cheering crowds packed the streets and no would-be assassin would have dared. The local press pronounced Elizabeth II 'the greatest Socialist monarch in the world.'

When she returned to London highly praised for her courage, Macmillan telephoned Kennedy to say, 'I have risked my Queen; you must risk your money!' Kennedy's reply was that gallantry demanded that he match the Queen's 'brave contribution' with his own, and in December the United States formally announced its participation in the Volta project.

A year later, the British government's decision to apply for membership of the newly formed European Economic Community, the Common Market, stirred another controversy in the Commonwealth. The old Dominion countries – New Zealand, Australia and Canada – opposed British entry into the Common Market because it threatened their privileged access to the United Kingdom market for their foodstuffs. Elizabeth could scarcely have been called a committed European, even if she recognized the political and economic arguments in favour of joining. In her view, Europeans were foreigners, the people of the Commonwealth were not. And the central question was whether it was worth undermining Commonwealth unity in order to establish close ties with France, Germany, Italy, Belgium, the Netherlands and Luxembourg. Her lack of enthusiasm for the French cannot have been diminished by de Gaulle's remark to Macmillan during the early round of entry negotiations, which Macmillan duly relayed to her, that 'France can and must lead Europe . . . the Anglo-Saxons are not sufficiently sympathetic to . . . the traditions of Europe.'

At the annual Commonwealth Conference in London in September 1962, Macmillan appealed for understanding but got 'a broadside attack', with one Commonwealth prime minister after another accusing the British of desertion and treachery. Macmillan's argument was that British membership of the Common Market would 'not be incompatible with the Commonwealth, the two associations being complementary.' With Britain in the European Community, new markets would open up for the whole Commonwealth, but if Britain stayed out, isolation would follow, and Britain's general political influence would inevitably diminish. It was not a line of reasoning that gained many converts among the Commonwealth leaders. They had only one immediate concern, and that was the prospect of immense loss of trade.

Although Elizabeth did not attend the conference sessions she kept track of things through her meetings with individual prime ministers. Based on these conversations she told Macmillan she was 'worried about Commonwealth feeling.' But the Prime Minister repeated his belief that if Britain were economically weak, the Commonwealth would fade away. It was one instance of her multiple role bringing her close to a conflict of interests. As Queen of England, she was committed to her government's policy of joining the Common Market, but as Queen of Canada, Australia, and other individual Commonwealth countries, she could not act against those countries' interests. While tempers frayed all round and it looked as if the conference could collapse, the Queen was calmly wining and dining each prime minister in turn at Buckingham Palace, and it was partly due to her persuasive efforts that they grudgingly accepted a British commitment that the Commonwealth would not be forgotten when talks for Britain's entry into the European Community were resumed.

But the whole vexing argument became moot because negotiations were not resumed. Early in 1963, de Gaulle closed the door into Europe with his veto of Britain's entry, accusing Britain of being the Trojan horse for American interests, and the door would remain closed for a decade. 'No great rush to let us in, is there?' the Queen remarked to Macmillan. The dryness was the farthest Elizabeth usually came to expressing anger: but there were occasional outbursts of royal rage. In 1961, the Queen visited Nepal and the British ambassador prepared a speech for her praising the Nepalese king as one of the greatest and wisest since (approximately) Solomon. Buckingham Palace, balking at the ambassador's lavish praise, reduced the speech by about a quarter and removed the reference to the King as a divinity. The Queen delivered the shortened version, but by accident the British ambassador's uncensored text was released to the press. There were delighted comparisons. The Queen was furious and demanded the ambassador's immediate removal. But the outcry died down, and the ambassador remained in place.

A sure way to arouse Elizabeth's anger was to ill-treat her corgis. They enjoy a privileged position at the Palace. When a policeman on duty was bitten by one of them, he instinctively lashed out with his foot and the heavy police-issue boot hit its mark. The next morning there was a polite 'request' from the Queen to please refrain from kicking her dogs. At that one brief moment when the policeman had taken punitive action the Queen had been looking out of the window. The corgis' food bowls were lined outside the Queen's study and she was often on hand for their once-a-day feed at four-thirty in the afternoon. But the corgis had an unofficial feeding time during the Queen's lunch, when they stationed themselves under the table and she gave them bits from her plate; or during her periodic group lunches when she put aside scraps on a side plate. As she led her guests in for coffee and liqueurs after the meal, she tossed the food behind her along the corridor and the dogs following fought noisy battles in her wake. The Queen's dogs were not forgotten in death. The grounds at Sandringham, the usual burial ground, are dotted with plaques and tombstones of past favourites. One wall tablet reads: 'H.M. the Queen's F.T. CH[Field Trial Champion Labrador] SANDRINGHAM SYDNEY (4.5.70–2.8.82.). Sydney was an honest worker, a faithful champion and will be missed by all.' The labrador had been named Sandringham Sydney by the Queen because he was born while she was travelling in Australia.

XIII

A Normal Childhood

One area where Prince Philip's influence was the dominant one was the education of the royal children. He was determined his sons should go to the same schools as himself. The Queen, on the other hand, had to be convinced that school was better than being tutored at the Palace, as she had been. When the headmistress of Benenden, Princess Anne's boarding school, was explaining to her the state public examination system in force at the time, the Queen halted her, saying, 'You'll have to explain that a little more fully. Remember, I never went to school.' Schools inevitably raised problems of security, and of exposure to the press as well as to the public. But Philip won the argument and Charles led the way, going first to the London day school Hill House, then to Cheam preparatory school in 1957, and four years later to Gordonstoun.

When Charles started at Cheam, he was so harassed by the media that the Queen's press secretary had to summon the editors of the London newspapers and warn them that if the young prince was not left alone, the Queen would be forced to take him out of school and have him educated at Buckingham Palace. The Queen's persistent message to the press was that she wanted her children to grow up 'as normally as possible'. Her vision of normal meant good teatime manners and thrift: 'bread and sandwiches to be finished at tea before the cakes were attacked, hems let down, elbows patched, two shillings and sixpence a week pocket money, and servants instructed to call the children by their first names when young and not "Your Royal Highness".' It meant Prince Philip roaring, 'Let him do it himself, he's not a bloody cripple,

204

you know,' whenever a servant went to open the door for one of the young princes. And it meant hand-me-down clothing from the older to the younger children – and not just during the war.

As normally as possible. Before starting school, Charles did lessons in the Buckingham Palace schoolroom with his devoted governess Miss Catherine Peebles, a Scotswoman (naturally) known as Mispy. When the time came for Charles to leave for Cheam at the age of seven, separation from Mispy was harder than from his mother. Mispy herself was heartbroken. She continued to teach Princess Anne, but her heart wasn't in it and no love was lost between her and the Queen's pushy, boisterous, strong-willed daughter. Some years later, Mispy was found dead of heart failure in her room at Buckingham Palace. Charles was inconsolable. Anne, by her own admission, was not.

As normally as possible. Two other girls, Susan (Sukie) Babington-Smith and Caroline Hamilton, granddaughters of senior members of the royal household, shared Anne's lessons, and indeed her young life. They were taught in the Buckingham Palace schoolroom, and outside the classroom they were inseparable. They went to Wimbledon together, to the cinema, to horseshows. In 1963, it was Anne's turn, at thirteen, to go to boarding school. The Queen picked Benenden, the girls' school in Kent. Anne's parents asked her if she wanted to go away to school and she said yes. Just as well, she has said, because 'it wouldn't have made any difference no matter what I said.' But there was one decision about which she was not consulted. Neither of the two girls who had been her constant companions of seven years were allowed to go to the same school as herself. At least one of them believes they were separated on the Queen's instructions, presumably to prevent them from becoming cronies and forming a clique. But at the time 'it seemed rather brutal'. They never wrote to each other after leaving the Palace. There was no farewell party. 'There was no contact'. Just the abrupt closing of a chapter in a young girl's life.

Like any mother, the Queen carried out a detailed inspection of all her children's schools before they were enrolled. 'You won't be able to jump up and down on *these* beds,' she said to her son as they surveyed the hard pallets in his dormitory at Gordonstoun for the first time. After that, Charles and Anne – and later Andrew and Edward – were occasionally visited by the Queen and Prince Philip, but usually not on school 'open' days to avoid becoming the focus of attention. (The Queen's daughter-in-law, the Princess of Wales, active in the upbringing of her sons, attends all their school functions.)

As he put on his make-up and costume in the dressing room backstage for a school production of *Macbeth* in which he had the title role, Prince Charles heard the orchestra play the national anthem and knew that his mother had arrived to watch the performance. 'Oh dear,' he observed to his bodyguard. 'My mother will be nervous.' Indeed, the Queen tended to be uneasy when watching one of her children performing on stage or competing in a sport. Her own pantomime appearances as a teenager at Windsor Castle were private affairs for her parents, friends and royal retainers. But her oldest son, the heir to the throne, appeared before a wider audience both at school and later at Cambridge University, seemingly indifferent to the risk of ridicule; and his fondness for amateur dramatics bolstered his self-confidence as a public speaker. A fine horsewoman since her teens, Elizabeth had never competed in a riding event. Her daughter, on the other hand, began riding in competitions (mainly three-day events) when she left school at the age of eighteen. Press photographs of every mishap she had tended to obscure the fact that her riding was Olympic competition standard.

As a boy Charles was solemn and introspective. Winston Churchill, who had a long conversation with him at Balmoral, later told the Queen, 'He is young to think so much.' Charles was six at the time. He loved his mother, but their relationship appeared strained and distant. In front of others, her manner towards Charles and Anne could be brisk. When Harold Wilson, Labour prime minister in the late 1960s, informed her that he was going to Australia to attend the memorial service for that country's premier, Harold Holt, who had drowned in the sea while swimming, she proposed that he should take along Prince Charles. Wilson agreed, and Charles, who was then in his teens, was called in. 'Charles,' said the Queen, 'the Prime Minister has very generously said that he will take you to Australia. Now you will do exactly what he tells you. If he says go to bed, you just go to bed even if you have to break off in the middle of a sentence.'

Charles's biographers portray his relationship with his father as blustery. Prince Philip would have liked to see a more decisive manner in his son. But the reverse was true of Princess Anne's ties with Philip. Anne's outspoken, assertive character mirrors her father's, and he is the parent to whom she has always been closest. She was barely out of her teens when she declared, 'They'll have a job marrying me off to someone I don't want. I'll marry the man I choose no matter who he is or what he is.' When romance bloomed between Captain Mark Phillips of the Queen's Dragoon Guards and the Princess, her mother recognized their shared interest in equestrianism (Phillips was an Olympic competitor) but she was also fully aware that opposition would lead to useless family tension. No doubt the Queen remembered the futility of her own parents' objections to her own marriage.

What is sometimes referred to as the Queen's 'second family' was completed in 1964, with the birth of Prince Edward. Elizabeth and Philip had by then been married for eighteen years, and the gap separating the two pairs of royal children (a decade between Anne's birth and Andrew's) was said to be the result of Elizabeth's decision not to increase the size of her family until she felt comfortable with the pressures of the monarchy. The Queen set aside more time for raising her two younger sons than she had in the case of Charles and Anne. She would spend the evening with her two new babies when she had no engagements, and the increased attention is reflected in the boys' relationship with their mother, which is closer than that of either Charles or Anne. Prince Edward was to become her favourite.

In the early half of 1963, the news was dominated by the Profumo affair. Its central character was John Profumo, the Secretary of State for War, responsible for the Army, whose affair with Christine Keeler, a stunning nineteen-year-old London call-girl, was threatening to bring down Macmillan's Conservative government. Profumo met Keeler in 1961 during a naked frolic around Lord ('Bill') Astor's swimming pool at Cliveden. But the minister's sexual adventures became a serious problem for the Macmillan government when it was revealed that Keeler was at the same time seeing the Soviet naval attaché. The scandal thus acquired security implications. It also spawned a wave of wild rumours and innuendo. Macmillan complained that 'more than half the Cabinet are being accused of perversion, homosexuality and the like.' On 30 June, Ambassador Bruce recorded in his diary: 'Fantastic stories are afloat. It is open season for the irresponsible... There are hints of peccadilloes in the royal family.' Bruce was no doubt aware of an 18 June FBI report on the affair filed from his embassy. It said there were 'some thorny problems involved [in the Keeler affair] inasmuch as there are indications that Prince Philip . . . may be involved.'

If Prince Philip's name did not surface in the stories, it was mentioned in the sub-text. Christine Keeler's pimp, Stephen Ward, combined his activities in London's *demi-monde* with those of a fashionable osteopath and amateur portraitist. The Queen's husband met him in the 1940s and later posed for him for a portrait. It was also widely reported that the judge appointed by Macmillan to investigate the affair, Lord Denning, had interrogated Philip's former secretary, Michael Parker. In the fetid atmosphere of the time, that was enough for Philip's name to be whispered with those of other highly placed personalities. There was no evidence that there was more to it than that, but Philip was once again vulnerable to rumour.

Profumo denied having had an affair with Christine Keeler, first to Macmillan and then in a statement to the House of Commons. When, however, investigators established that there had indeed been a relationship, he was in effect caught in a lie to the House and was forced to resign. Macmillan was painfully embarrassed about raising the Profumo affair with the Queen, not only because of his concern that the royal family was being dragged into the gossip, but also because, as he put it, he felt he 'ought to apologize for the undoubted injury done by the terrible behaviour of one of Your Majesty's Secretaries of State' not just to the Government, but 'perhaps more serious, [to] one of the great Armed Forces' (in other words, to the Army). In retrospect, he wrote, he felt he had been too trusting in accepting Profumo's denials at face value, but 'I had of course no idea of the strange underworld in which other people, alas, besides Mr Profumo have allowed themselves to become entrapped.'

Sensing his mortification, the Queen wrote back sympathizing with him for 'the horrible time' that he was having and supporting his view of the need to act justly. She realized, she told him, how hard it was for people with high standards to suspect colleagues of unworthy conduct.

Though Elizabeth did not spell out her personal view, the scandal was clearly as repugnant to her as it was to the Prime Minister. If Macmillan was clearly out of touch with the excesses of the permissive society, she was no less so. But she was by now experienced enough to be aware, too, that the political fallout from the combination of possible security leaks and the minister's attempted deception could spell disaster for Macmillan. Profumo was driven from public life and devoted a great deal of his time to social work; Stephen Ward, who was tried and found guilty of living off the earnings of prostitution, committed suicide. But political observers predicted that Macmillan's days were also numbered. There was no suspicion of a government cover-up, but as Ambassador Bruce reported to President Kennedy, 'A sacrifice is increasingly demanded here, and the appointed lamb for the altar is the Prime Minister, who must already have appreciated the sad truth that no ingratitude surpasses that of a democracy.'

By the summer of 1963, Macmillan had reached the nadir of his political popularity. One poll showed that only 23 per cent of the country felt he ought to continue. Incredibly, the Prime Minister who four years previously had led his party to one of the greatest election victories had been brought to the brink of collapse by the peccadillo of one of his junior ministers. It was a sad fate for a statesman of formidable skill who had weathered the tension and high drama of President de Gaulle's veto of British entry into the European Common Market, and – more particularly – the Cuban missile crisis. Macmillan had briefed the Queen at length on the missile situation and found her 'as usual, calm and sympathetic'. The following day, General Lauris Norstad, the NATO Supreme Commander, had lunched at Buckingham Palace. 'The Prime Minister fears there's an even chance that we could be at war by this time next week,' she observed to the American general. Well, replied Norstad carefully, Khrushchev's mind was very hard to read. 'Let's hope that he finds us equally inscrutable,' countered the Queen.

The sense of relief following the crisis had been short-lived because of the Profumo scandal which was already the topic of whispered discussion at a mammoth reception given in April by the Queen and Prince Philip to celebrate Princess Alexandra of Kent's coming marriage to the Hon. Angus Ogilvy. It was one of the biggest parties the Queen had given and was never repeated on such a scale following public criticism of the cost. About two thousand guests filled the reception rooms of Windsor Castle, where some of the finest pictures in the royal collection were on display. The guests danced in a room full of paintings by Lawrence. In an adjoining hall, an endlessly long buffet with lobster, mounds of cold meats and champagne was heavily patronized. David Bruce noted that 'most of the Royalties seem to be congregated in one room, where many of them engaged in what did not seem to be a wholly successful enterprise to entertain each other. There was one king (Norway), five queens or ex-queens, and princes and princesses galore.'

In September, to Elizabeth's evident distress, Macmillan informed her of his intention to step down before an election in 1964. Though the news could hardly have come as a surprise to her, the prospect of his departure was not a welcome one. She appreciated Macmillan's experience, unflappable manner (at least outwardly, for he was subject to bouts of insecurity), and his humanity. They had a long discussion about what Macmillan later described as the 'various possibilities', his euphemism for possible successors, and it was clear to the Queen that the succession was by no means clear-cut.

She told him it was important to respect the royal prerogative – her right to hold consultations and make her own decision on whom to ask to form a new government, and not necessarily accept a *fait accompli* – another euphemism for leaving the choice to the Tory Party. After all, she said, if she asked someone to form a government and he failed, what harm was done? In the nineteenth century, more than one Prime Minister who received the mandate from Queen Victoria came back to report he had failed to form a government. It was clear to Macmillan that the Queen was determined to safeguard one of the few powers left to her as a constitutional monarch.

Privately, her reference to 'revolving door' politics, which he associated with other democracies less well established than Britain's, did not go down well. That may have been a factor in the second thoughts he began to have almost immediately after his 'irreversible decision'. It may also have strengthened his resolve not to close the door, at sixty-nine, on almost seven years as prime minister before his party settled on a successor whom the Queen could 'send for' to form a new Tory government, just as he had himself emerged as a candidate from Bobbety Salisbury's summary canvassing of cabinet members. But on 8 October 1963, what he had planned to set in motion as a gradual process suddenly acquired a new urgency. Word reached the Palace that the Prime Minister had been hospitalized in considerable pain with a tumour in the prostate gland.

The following day, convinced the tumour was malignant and that he was suffering from cancer, Macmillan wrote to the Queen confirming his resignation, and drafted a letter to be read to the Conservative Party's annual conference, which had started in Blackpool. In his message to the assembled Tories he stated that it was 'impossible' for him to continue. On 10 October he underwent surgery for removal of the tumour. It turned out to be benign. Had he acted too hastily in stepping down?

Always a bit of a hypochondriac, Macmillan remained sure he was gravely ill and faced a slow, uphill battle to recovery – a conviction not shared by his personal doctor, who informed all and sundry that the Prime Minister would soon be well enough to resume his responsibilities if that was what he wanted to do. But the Profumo affair had sapped a great deal of Macmillan's spirit: he was a tired man. At that moment – though perhaps not in the subsequent two decades of his life – he wanted to give up. Concerned about his condition – and perhaps his state of mind – the Queen telephoned him three times on the day of his operation, and the Queen Mother once. But Macmillan said, 'It has been a bad day, and I can't understand what they are saying.'

For a party that traditionally prided itself on dignity and restraint, the battle within the Tory Party to pick Macmillan's successor was an unseemly scramble. Starting with five candidates, the contest rapidly narrowed down to a battle between Rab Butler and Lord Hailsham. A law passed that year making it possible for members of the House of Lords to renounce their titles enabled Hailsham to enter the lists as plain Mr Quintin Hogg. The latter had Macmillan's initial support against Butler, who the Prime Minister still felt lacked the indispensable forcefulness for the leadership. But at the party conference Hailsham's campaign was so aggressive, with 'Q' for Quintin badges and chanting supporters, that, as one Macmillan aide put it, 'the Establishment reacted with curled lips.' When Hailsham brandished his year-old child in the air and mixed baby food in front of the television cameras Macmillan's backing for him began to waver.

By the time the conference ended the party was still leaderless and in turmoil, and the power struggle shifted to London. A consensus – prompted by Macmillan – was growing among senior Tories to draft Lord Home, the mild-mannered Foreign Secretary. From his sickbed at King Edward VII's Hospital for Officers, Macmillan assigned different prominent party figures to sound out the Cabinet, the House of Lords, the Tory parliamentary group, as well as a sampling of the grass roots. The overall result showed a party deeply divided over the succession, with strong support for Hailsham and Butler, but also opposition to both that was equally violent. On the other hand, there seemed to be broad acceptance of, and above all no strong feelings against, Lord Home as a compromise candidate. As Macmillan saw it, the two main contenders would inevitably create internal dissension and undermine party unity, and only Home could rally the majority and prevent a serious split. So Macmillan secretly made the decision to advise the Queen to send for Home and prepared a memorandum for her outlining his reasons. The written statement

211

was for posterity and for her records for she had already told him she would visit the hospital to consult him.

When news that Macmillan favoured Home leaked to the party, there were frantic attempts by other prominent Tories to reach the Queen with counter-proposals, but they were fended off by her Private Secretary. Hailsham, who was Lord President of the Privy Council, asked to advise her on the matter, but Adeane's reply was that the Queen still had a prime minister to give her advice. There was also the proposal that the Queen should call in the main contenders and preside over their negotiations until a choice was made. To that, Adeane's answer was that the Queen had no intention of becoming involved in the Tory party's leadership problems. So, the smoke was still thick in the political back rooms, and the political manoeuvring had by no means subsided on the morning of 18 October when Elizabeth arrived at King Edward's Hospital for the most unusual formal resignation of a Prime Minister in English history. Because his room was very small Macmillan had been wheeled down to the hospital boardroom for the audience. Over a silk shirt, he wore one of his well-worn sweaters. As he described the scene later, 'The bed covers were down, and concealed underneath the bed was a pail with a tube full of bile coming out of me.' Beside him was a bell, and a nurse stood by outside in case he summoned help while the Queen was there. Sir Michael Adeane accompanied her but waited outside the boardroom while she saw the Prime Minister alone, as she had done so often during his Buckingham Palace audiences.

The Queen was in an unusually emotional state. Waiting outside in case of an emergency, Macmillan's doctor Sir John Richardson noted that her voice could hardly be heard – 'There were in fact tears in her eyes, and perhaps why I could not hear was because her voice was not very steady.' In the Prime Minister's often quoted laconic description, 'She was moved; so was I.' Elizabeth told him 'how sorry she had been to get my letter of resignation.' She asked him, 'What are you going to do?' To which he replied, 'Well, I'm afraid I can't go on.' At which, Macmillan has said, 'She was very upset.' Then she asked him, 'Have you any advice to give me?' He said, 'Ma'am, do you wish me to give you any advice?' When she said yes, he gave her the memorandum, which, with great difficulty because he was in pain, he also read to her.

The Queen accepted his advice to send for the Earl of Home, and then left for the Palace. Thus, Rab Butler, the man disappointed in 1957 and the natural prince *héritier* if ever there was one, found himself defeated in his second (and last) attempt at what Macmillan once called 'the final ascent', and this time by someone widely believed to be less able, though honourable. Macmillan's illness had not dimmed his whimsical humour: 10 Downing Street had supplied an outsize envelope in which to put the memorandum. On leaving, the Queen handed this to Adeane. Glimpsing the scene through the open door of the boardroom, Macmillan thought it 'made [Adeane] look . . . like the Frog Footman.'

When the Queen wrote, two days later, to express her appreciation of his years as prime minister she thanked him for having been her guide, supporter and instructor through the maze of international affairs, and she told him that she had not offered to make him an Earl because she was aware of his 'disinclination'. But she wanted him to know that he could have his peerage on her authority (that is, not at the instigation of the government of the day) whenever he changed his mind.

She had readily agreed to Home's appointment in part because she probably approved of the choice: he was a known quantity not only as Foreign Secretary, but also as a landed Scottish peer. (Like Hailsham, the fourteenth Earl of Home had to relinquish his title in order to become prime minister and he was known as Sir Alec Douglas-Home: like Hailsham, he returned to the House of Lords after receiving a peerage some years later.) The other reason for her acceptance was that Alec Home was Macmillan's choice and she had come to respect Macmillan's judgement. She would certainly have agreed with Macmillan that Home represented 'the best of the old governing class.' But beyond that, Macmillan was the first prime minister with whom she had been able to establish a working relationship. He had guided her to maturity as a monarch, and she was saddened by his departure. There was every reason to believe she would miss his seminars and chatty letters on the major issues of the day.

Decades later, Tory politicians were still replaying those final moves leading to Home's victory in an attempt to determine whether Macmillan had checkmated not just his party but the Queen as well by overriding the royal prerogative. His critics maintain that once Macmillan had announced his resignation the correct behaviour for him would have been to withdraw to the sidelines and let the Tories select a new leader, and the Queen to decide whether or not to choose that leader as her next prime minister. Recent practice suggests the Queen was certain to send for the party leader to form the new government. In theory, however, the Queen can pick whomever she likes, and it is part of the constitutional ritual that the choice is not certain until the monarch makes it.

Far from leaving centre stage, Macmillan continued to hold all the strings in his hand until the very last minute, orchestrating Alec Home's candidacy from his hospital bed. And in light of Elizabeth's reliance on him, any successor bearing his imprimatur had a distinct advantage over his opponents. But Macmillan considered himself still prime minister until he went through the formal act of resignation (and apparently so did the Queen), and he was determined to avoid what he saw as the danger of political 'chaos' resulting from Tory Party squabbles over the succession. He might have nodded pleasantly when the Queen talked of one prime minister after another trying to form a government in a replay of Victorian politics, but he was not about to allow such a state of affairs to come about as a result of his resignation.

Near the end of Macmillan's lengthy premiership, the Queen had begun to worry aloud about changing attitudes towards the royal family. The problem was not unpopularity but boredom. It had come as something of a shock when the tenth anniversary of her coronation had produced a vast outpouring of public indifference, and even the birth of two royal princes had failed to cause much of a stir. The most disconcerting development, Elizabeth remarked at a private lunch about this time, was the fact that the monarchy seemed to be making no impression at all on British teenagers. The *Sunday Telegraph*, the Conservative and ardently royalist paper, lamenting this development, said 'most people care much less [about the monarchy] than they did – particularly the young, many of whom regard the Queen as the arch-square. They are not against in the sense of being for a republic. They are quite simply indifferent.'

In a rapidly changing society, the royal family appeared to be paying little attention to the problem of their public image. In theory, of course, the Queen was above such concerns: all that mattered was that she should be seen to be carrying out her duties. But in a democracy some concessions had to be made to the electronic age. This was especially important at the time because in 1962 the operating costs of the royal household (as opposed to the Queen's personal finances) began running an annual deficit. As an interim measure, the shortfall was covered from a reserve fund set up ten years previously during the Government's last review of the Civil List. Government departments were also picking up

214

various costs: in 1964, for example, Post Office subsidies to the royal family for postage and telephones totalled nearly £58,000. But it was estimated that the reserve would be exhausted before 1970, and it was therefore a matter of time before the question of a substantial increase in the appropriation to the royal household would have to be considered, focusing unwanted attention on the controversial subject of the Queen's personal wealth.

One area of royal public relations which Macmillan felt urgently needed improving was the Queen's Christmas broadcast. Televising the speech had shown how dated and ineffective the pattern of the broadcasts really was, and he dispatched his spokesman Harold Evans to discuss improvements with Sir Michael Adeane. At first, Adeane seemed unwilling to discuss the topic at all, and when he eventually identified the main problem the reason for his initial reluctance was clear. The root of the trouble, it seemed, was that the Queen was acutely camera shy.

The Palace tried each year to get some freshness into the broadcast, said Adeane, and women had been drawn into the drafting, but television had ruined the whole thing. Television? The Queen was cheerful and relaxed beforehand, he went on, but in front of the cameras she froze and there was nothing to be done about it. When the Downing Street visitor suggested that other members of the royal family should be brought into the broadcast and a more informal approach be tried, Adeane was horrified at the proposal. He ruled out any idea of a family scene around the fireside. Five years later, however, a television crew would spend the best part of a year at work on a film that would break new ground with its intimate portrait of the Queen and her family. But by then Adeane would be gone.

One successful innovation which would certainly come under the rubric of good public relations was the opening in 1962 of the Queen's Picture Gallery at the south-west corner of Buckingham Palace adjoining the Royal Mews. What was once the royal chapel where the Queen herself was baptized, before it was destroyed in a German air raid, had been rebuilt as a gallery. Here pictures from the Queen's vast and priceless art collection were put on public view. Nearly a quarter of a million people flocked to the first exhibition, 'Treasures from the Royal Collection', and later ones with different themes would be equally well attended.

Elizabeth II enlarged the collection in both size and scope. Her

215

father's interest in the royal pictures focused on royal portraits, in other words, pictures of his relations and ancestors. Elizabeth has taken a broader view. Her own taste in art has always inclined towards the traditional, with a particular fondness for her hundred or so sumptuous Canalettos, brought into the collection by King George III. But as an investment Prince Philip also acquired a trickling of works by established modern artists – a Francis Bacon, a couple of Jackson Pollocks, and a David Hockney. By 1965 Elizabeth had sat for more than twenty portrait painters, and her conversations during sittings had increased her knowledge about art which helped in her acquisitions. She approached art-buying with the same determination with which she did everything else. The National Gallery in London once found itself competing with her for a small eighteenth-century portrait they both wanted, the Gallery for the national collection, she for the royal one. After the Gallery had bettered her price offer, it received a broad hint from the Palace that the Queen was determined to buy the painting and attempts to outbid her were merely pushing up the cost – and royal annoyance. The National Gallery suddenly lost interest in the painting, leaving the field clear for the Queen.

The creation of the public gallery at Buckingham Palace was largely the work of Sir Anthony Blunt, her cultivated Keeper of the Queen's Pictures, who had inadvertently drawn her close to the murky secret world of espionage. For besides being a former wartime senior intelligence officer, and a distinguished art expert specializing in Italian Renaissance painting, Blunt also happened to be a self-confessed Russian spy.

By 1957, when the Queen appointed him to the post of curator of the largest accumulation of artistic works in private hands in the United Kingdom, he was already under suspicion of having spied for the Soviet Union before, during and immediately after the Second World War. Guy Burgess and Donald Maclean had fled to Russia. The net was closing around Kim Philby. The country's secret apparatus had been shaken to its foundations. Yet British counter-intelligence agents were aware that it was not over. They knew Moscow had recruited at least one more agent at Cambridge University, and it was their belief that Anthony Blunt was the fourth man. But as Harold Macmillan would tell his official biographer years later, '[We] had nothing to arrest the man on. No proof,' even though 'we did suspect that Blunt was a wrong 'un.' With such a thin case, an American intelligence officer familiar with Blunt's case said, 'Nobody dared tell the Palace.'

Then, in 1964, the case against Blunt was strengthened when the Americans handed British investigators fresh indications of Blunt's activities as a double agent. A wealthy American, Michael Whitney Straight, confessed to the FBI that at Cambridge, Blunt had persuaded him to spy for the Soviets just as he, Blunt, had been recruited himself. But, before taking things further, the security services faced the tricky problem of breaking the news to the Queen.

In April, Sir Michael Adeane met Roger Hollis, the director of MI5, who briefed him on the organization's intentions. Adeane was told that MI5's plan was to question Blunt under conditions of immunity. There were obvious practical advantages to working out an accommodation with Blunt. He was the sole member of the Cambridge quartet of spies whom the authorities were going to have the opportunity to interrogate; and the theoretical possibility of gaining valuable information about what secrets had been passed on to Moscow, and perhaps about the extent of Moscow's infiltration of the intelligence service, was preferable to the embarrassing alternative of going public with another spy scandal – to say nothing of arresting the Keeper of the Queen's Pictures as a traitor to his country. For MI5 there was also the danger that Blunt himself might decide to go public if he were exposed, revealing the service's negligence and ineptitude to its full damaging extent.

Adeane, unfazed as ever, asked the key question: If Blunt did confess, what action did MI5 advise the Queen to take? Hollis was ready with the answer: the Queen should not dismiss Blunt, otherwise Moscow might suspect that their agent had been exposed. In addition, Hollis felt that even if a convincing excuse were found to cover up Blunt's dismissal by the Queen – for example, ill health – his departure from his exalted position might tip off other spies whom Blunt might name, thereby robbing MI5 of the element of surprise. When Adeane asked for an estimate of how long the Queen would be expected to retain Blunt under these conditions, Hollis avoided committing himself.

Ironically, Hollis himself has long been the centre of a debate among intelligence specialists over whether he was or was not a Soviet mole in the British secret service. The case against him has never been conclusively proved – but then, neither has the case in his defence. If Hollis really was a mole, the arguments against Blunt's dismissal from royal service had little value because Hollis himself was in a position to nullify its advantages. Senior American intelligence circles never believed that Hollis was a double agent. In the view of one veteran CIA officer, Hollis was, firstly, not considered clever enough to manage the complex duality of being a top counter-intelligence officer and a Soviet mole. Second, his suspicious behaviour was explained by the fact that he was indeed leading a double life, but of a different kind: he had for years carried on a secret affair.

When Adeane reported his conversation with Hollis to the Queen, including the MI5 director's recommendation that she should continue to harbour a former Soviet spy as a member of her staff, she was angry at Blunt's deceit, at the ineptitude of the security services, and at their gall for making such a proposal. The whole idea ran counter to her nature, her dislike for deviousness, and her deep patriotic sense. However, she reluctantly agreed to accept the advice and retain Blunt in the national interest. In short, she was stuck with him. Or, put another way, the Queen was used as an accessory to protect the reputation of MI5.

Confronted with Straight's allegations, Blunt at first denied them, but when he was offered immunity from prosecution, he thought for a long time, poured himself a drink, and confessed. His interrogators suggested that he might find a pretext on which to resign as Keeper of the Queen's Pictures. But, as expected, Blunt played back MI5's own reasons for wanting him to stay put. And stay put he did. Blunt continued to have access to the Queen's priceless picture collection, and occasionally to consult her about exhibitions for the Queen's Gallery and other related questions until his retirement in 1974, highly respected in the art world, knighted by the Queen for his services, and with his secret intact. Everyone, it seemed, wanted it that way.

What is less easily explained, however, is that the Queen then approved another royal post, that of Adviser for the Queen's Pictures and Drawings. He was still ensconced in an office at Windsor Castle when his past came home to roost and he was warned that he was about to be identified as the fourth man in a book about the Burgess–Maclean–Philby case. The Palace had to face the inconvenience of dealing with the truth.

The reason for Blunt's continued survival in royal service may have had less to do with MI5's interrogation, and more with the royal family's desire to keep secret an earlier mission undertaken by Blunt on their behalf. This surfaced in a conversation at Buckingham Palace in the spring of 1964 between Adeane and Blunt's designated interrogator, Peter Wright. There was a whiff of *Alice in Wonderland* about the conversation, which began with Adeane assuring Wright that the Palace was willing to cooperate with his enquiries. 'The Queen has been fully informed about Sir Anthony,' Adeane went on, 'and is quite content for him to be dealt with in any way which gets at the truth.'

Then came the warning. 'From time to time, you may find Blunt referring to an assignment he undertook on behalf of the Palace – a visit to Germany at the end of the war,' Adeane said. 'Please do not pursue this matter. Strictly speaking, it is not relevant to considerations of security.' Now, a tough intelligence officer, as Wright subsequently made himself out to be, would presumably have replied that MI5 was the best judge of what was or was not relevant to considerations of security. But such is the awe in which Buckingham Palace is held that few bureaucrats would have made that point to the Queen's Private Secretary.

No-one outside the Palace was told the precise nature of Blunt's assignment, for which he was said to have received his instructions from King George VI himself, and Blunt kept the secret. The mission was undertaken in 1945 when he was an MI5 officer. He was accompanied by the archivist at Windsor Castle and had a letter from the King to his cousin Prince Manfred of Hesse at Marburg Castle, which was in the American Zone and was being used as a storehouse for captured German documents. He was reliably believed to have been instructed first – with the Prince's help – to recover from the German files letters from Queen Victoria and other documents of historic importance to the royal family. George VI wanted to put them in safekeeping in the royal archives at Windsor.

But Blunt was also believed to have been charged with bringing back any papers he might find relating to the Duke of Windsor's dealings with the Third Reich. Reports and photographs of the former king's contacts with the Nazi leadership in the months before the outbreak of the Second World War had deeply embarrassed the royal family at the time, and they lived in fear that documents might surface containing nasty surprises about the extent of his involvement with Germany. According to one British authority on the security services, Blunt was specifically looking for memoranda of the Duke of Windsor's conversations with Hitler and other top Nazis, and for German transcripts of telephone calls made by the former king during his visit to Germany. Blunt searched the captured records and – over the objections of the female American army officer in charge – virtually helped himself to whatever papers seemed to fit the description, delivering them in several large boxes to Windsor.

In 1947, Blunt was made a member of the Royal Victorian Order, a decoration awarded for personal service to the monarch. A couple of years later, he entered the royal service first as conservator of drawings and engravings, and then as keeper of the royal collection. After he was formally named as the 'fourth man' by the Prime Minister in 1979, he was stripped of his knighthood and the Royal Victorian Order. He took refuge in his villa in Tuscany until his death four years later.

For a while, following Blunt's unmasking by Straight, the Central Intelligence Agency regarded the royal household with a new interest. With British help, a check was made for other possible Soviet moles, but none was found. Prince Philip had already received at least a passing glance from the CIA during the Profumo affair when his name had surfaced in the gossip. At the express request of John McCone, the Agency's austere, straitlaced director, the London station chief Archibald Roosevelt had kept his boss supplied with 'Eyes Only' reports covering every conceivable detail of the Profumo affair as it unfolded. Roosevelt left no stone unturned, no matter what sordid titbit lurked underneath and no matter how far-fetched was the gossip. It was not prurience that had prompted McCone's request. There was the security aspect, of course, but there was something else as well. The two girls in the scandal – Christine Keeler and Mandy Rice Davies – had visited New York, where McCone had reason to suspect that they had met President Kennedy, and if that information emerged, he wanted to be the first to know.

Even royal travel in the turbulent sixties seemed less problem free. In 1964, the Queen and Prince Philip sailed for Canada in the royal yacht *Britannia* to a welcome marred by separatist opposition. It had been five years since Elizabeth's last visit, a period during which Québecois separatism, long a latent presence in Canadian politics, had forced itself to the surface as a violent militant movement. Before her arrival there had been threats on the Queen's life, and with the memory of President Kennedy's assassination still fresh, the security forces were keyed up wherever the royal couple went. Early in the tour the police noticed Prince Philip pressing the buttons to lower the shatter-proof windows of their limousine so that the crowds could get a better look at the

Queen. He was warned to 'leave the buttons alone', otherwise 'the wires leading to the opening mechanisms would be severed.'

So it was with the windows firmly shut that Elizabeth, looking grim and unsmiling, drove through unfriendly streets, thick with police, in Quebec. There was no assassination attempt, but the crowd booed her. They shouted '*Chez vous*' – Go home – and held banners saying '*Québec aux Québecois*'. To someone accustomed to cheering crowds wherever she went, the first hostile public reception of her life must have come as a profound shock. Loyalists explained that the protest was less against the Queen herself than what French-Canadian activists perceived to be Ottawa's use of her to assert its federal authority in Quebec, an authority they fiercely rejected. And indeed, in the English-speaking part of the country she received the expected enthusiastic welcome. But Quebec clearly rankled, and her anger had not subsided when she discussed it with the Canadian Prime Minister Lester (Mike) Pearson. The Liberal leader was sympathetic, but told her frankly that in the long term he did not think Canada would remain a monarchy. He did not say when he thought the change would take place.

In hindsight, however, the visit was a watershed in royal tours because of its early signs of a shift in public attitudes towards the monarchy in the old, established Commonwealth countries from adulation to a healthy, but occasionally critical, respect. Immigration from postwar Europe to Canada, Australia, and to a lesser extent New Zealand, was diluting the English character of those countries and altering the nature of the relationship with the monarchy. This distancing would happen more rapidly in Canada, perhaps because of its closeness to the republican United States. On her Canadian trip the Queen had joined in singing Canada's new national anthem. Within five years, Canada would have switched from its old 'Dominion' flag incorporating the British Union Jack to the new maple leaf emblem.

Also troublesome, but for different reasons, were the ten days that the Queen spent the following year in the Federal Republic of Germany. Bonn, the federal capital, was full of reminders of Queen Victoria's frequent trips to Germany to inspect her vast network of European relations. Elizabeth did not share her great-great-grandmother's fondness for travelling in Europe: she preferred touring the Commonwealth. But the British government needed the state visit as a makeweight to Britain's relations with the emerging industrial power in the European Community. This was the first visit to Germany by a reigning British monarch since 1913, and the Queen had to contend with the residual memory of two wars. In West Berlin, where the Wall was four years old, the rhythmic roar of tens of thousands of German throats chanting 'E-liz-a-bet, E-liz-a-bet' left her shaken and unsettled: it was too close to the sound of Hitler's rallies in the same city. In Hanover, she was shown a less jarring link with the past – an historic letter written to the Elector Prince George by a group of English nobles, as Queen Anne was dying, pressing him to come to London and claim the throne as quickly as possible in order to prevent the Jacobite pretender from attempting to step into the void. George obliged, thus paving the way for the House of Windsor.

The year had begun on a sad note with the death of Winston Churchill. Another link with Elizabeth's youth – and with her father – had been broken. After the state funeral she gave a lunch for the distinguished foreign mourners, an occasion that hit between wind and water, restrained but not formal. She met each visitor without ceremony: the historic giants of the war, Charles de Gaulle, Dwight Eisenhower; royals like King Constantine of Greece, and Queen Juliana and Prince Bernhard, Churchill's surviving generals, Montgomery, Ismay. Charles and Anne wandered casually about. Baby Prince Andrew was brought in for a quick tour. Eisenhower went from group to group, sought after and liked by all – a contrast to President Lyndon Johnson, who had dithered over coming until the last minute. The White House deluged the American embassy and Buckingham Palace with queries and requests, including whether the President could bring his own chair to sit on during the Westminster Abbey service. Then word came from Washington that Johnson wasn't coming after all. He was to be the one American president whom the Queen did not meet while in office.

The New Crowd

Shortly before six in the evening on Thursday, 4 November 1964, Harold Wilson, the new Prime Minister, was driven to Buckingham Palace in his official limousine and deposited outside the Privy Purse door. There he was met by an equerry who escorted him to a lift operated by a footman in white knee breeches. On the second floor an official of the royal household rejoicing in the splendid title of Gentleman Usher in Ordinary was waiting to guide him along a marble corridor lined with paintings by Old Masters. A child's bicycle was propped up underneath one of them. At the stroke of six they arrived at a pair of double doors which the Gentleman Usher threw open. 'Your Majesty, Your Majesty's Prime Minister,' he said. Wilson bowed, not from the waist but, as tradition dictates, with a quick lowering of the head at the neck. The Queen rose from behind her Chippendale desk and settled in an armchair beside the fireplace. She motioned to the Prime Minister to take the chair opposite.

A new era was beginning for the Queen, as well as for Britain. For the first time in Elizabeth II's twelve-year reign the Prime Minister sitting opposite her at the regular weekly audience was not a member of the Conservative Party. Fourteen days earlier, Wilson had led Labour to a narrow victory in the October elections, and his four-seat majority in the House of Commons ended twelve years of Conservative government. After three old Etonians in a row (Eden, Macmillan, Home) the head of the new government was a one-time Cambridge University economics lecturer with a middle-class background and a grammar school education. Gone were the plummy tones of the English upper-class voice: Wilson spoke with the familiar burr of his native Yorkshire.

It was not just a social difference. The left wing of Wilson's party included a sprinkling of republicans, and a larger group who were determined to wring out of the monarchy what was left of its political role, and then to shake it vigorously until its wider social influence also fell out, leaving only its purely ceremonial function clinging to the fabric of royalty. Even before the Labour victory at the polls, the party's left wing was talking of 'mood changing measures' such as Labour ministers refusing to wear black tie at Buckingham Palace functions. Anthony Wedgwood Benn, the party's left-wing gadfly – himself a former peer who had renounced his title – urged the Government in which he was a cabinet minister to abolish the twice yearly Honours List for knighthoods and other decorations submitted to the Queen. And when the members of Wilson's cabinet were sworn in by the Queen, Richard Crossman, one of the party intellectuals and also a minister, found it 'terribly degrading' to have to kneel in front of the Queen, pick up her right hand, which was resting on the table, and kiss it.

It is reasonable to assume that after all the talk of change by the new Government, the Queen was at first on the defensive. Her father had made no secret of his dislike for the socialist cabinet of his day (although he had found some Labour ministers personally agreeable). So, given his influence on his daughter, the antecedents were not favourable. Then Wilson got off to a poor start in his first weekly audience. He had assumed that the meeting was a social occasion – a formal ritual – and, as a result, was unprepared to deal with the Queen's usual flow of intelligent questions and informed conversation. But he quickly got the message that the Queen expected the Prime Minister to have done his homework. Things improved after that, and Wilson soon established a good rapport with her, perhaps better than any other prime minister before or since. Charteris told Paul Martin the Labour prime minister was liked 'at the top'. Another courtier would later recall that 'a mutual affection existed between [the Queen and Wilson].' A moderate socialist, Wilson turned out to be her best protection against the changes demanded by the radical left.

At forty-eight, Wilson was closer to the Queen's age than his four predecessors. That was one reason why they got on so well; but she also appreciated his imperturbability, his formidable intelligence and lively conversation. In addition, Wilson was comfortable with women – and a bit of a gossip; and the Queen was an avid collector of political gossip. She could not, in short, have chosen a more effective way of showing that she was truly above party politics than to establish good relations with her first Labour prime minister. Unlike an American or a French president, she identifies with no particular ideology. By upbringing and inclination she certainly was, and remains, a Conservative, but her sense of distance from the parties is ingrained. At the wedding reception for Crown Princess Beatrix of the Netherlands she found herself sitting next to the Shah of Iran. He talked: she listened. As he expounded on the political problems of Iran and his plans for reform he suddenly asked her which of the British political parties gave more support to the Crown? She was taken aback by the question. British party politics, she explained, were quite separate from the Crown.

It was soon obvious that the left's intended assault on royal privilege did not have the party's full support, and certainly not that of the Prime Minister. But before this reassurance took shape there were some shocks. A private member's bill proposing to abolish all titles, introduced in the House of Commons by a Labour Member of Parliament, Emrys Hughes, brought the royal household to the verge of panic.

Government ministers assured the Queen that party support for the measure was minimal. Provided no attempt was made to prevent it being debated in the House, they confidently predicted it would soon fade away for lack of interest. On the other hand, if any attempt was made to stop the debate, the left would have a *cause célèbre*. Support for the measure would increase. The Queen, influenced by alarmed courtiers who saw their titles on the verge of disappearance, dispatched Adeane to the Prime Minister with what amounted to a plea to 'do something'. On the eve of the debate on what was listed as the Abolition of Titles Bill, Wilson instructed the party whips to cancel it. Fortunately for the outcome, it was too late to alter the Commons Order of the Day, and no more than three or four members were in the chamber for the debate. The next day, the Queen searched anxiously through the papers for accounts of the Commons discussion and found nothing. By being fortuitously too late to take any action at all, the Government had, in fact, buried the issue.

The real challenge came from less drastic proposals for change. Wedgwood Benn, the Postmaster General, once advanced the sacrilegious idea of omitting the Queen's portrait from a new issue of stamps. As the originator of postage stamps, the United Kingdom is the only country whose stamps do not bear its name but have always carried the sovereign's image, usually in profile. On 10 March 1965, here was Wedgwood Benn kneeling in the Queen's sitting room holding up for her consideration enlarged designs for a proposed issue of stamps commemorating the twentieth anniversary of the Battle of Britain. In a double departure from the usual practice the words 'Great Britain' appeared on each design, and the Queen's profile was conspicuously missing from all except one of them. The designer, Benn explained to her, had found it difficult to fit her head into the existing design. Was it true that she had always refused to consider this omission in the past? Elizabeth was 'clearly embarrassed' at the direct question, Benn noted, and said she had no personal feelings about it at all.

As the Postmaster General was leaving, Adeane appeared at his side and told him 'out of the blue' that the Palace had never given any indication of being against non-traditional stamps, but 'I think that the monarch's head has to be on all stamps.' This encounter led Benn to assume rightly or wrongly that the Queen's room was bugged and the Queen's Secretary 'had been listening via a microphone during the audience.'

Some time later, Benn received word from Adeane that the Queen was 'not too happy' with the designs of five out of the six Battle of Britain stamps. The solitary stamp that met with her approval was the one with her portrait. But had she not said she had no personal feelings about it? The headless-stamps saga was a good illustration of the Queen's organic aversion to direct confrontation. There has, however, never been any shortage of people willing to play the heavy on her behalf and communicate the sovereign's displeasure. As part of a Palace pincer movement, Sir John Wilson, Keeper of the Queen's Philatelic Collection, which had been built up by her grandfather and (to a lesser extent) her father, passed the word unofficially to the Post Office that the Queen would never accept stamps without her head on them.

Wedgwood Benn tried to fight the Queen's refusal by putting the issue on the level of ministerial advice but Adeane cut him off at the pass. The Queen's Secretary prevailed upon Wilson to stop his Postmaster General from designing any more headless stamps. What it boiled down to, Wilson told Benn, was that the Queen could 'reject the advice of her ministers' under certain circumstances. This was one such circumstance. 'Wilson's intentions are to be more royal than the Tory party,' grumbled Benn not without justification. The controversy was finished, but it was not quite over. The persistent Benn came up with a compromise proposal. When the monarch's portrait did not fit into a design, a silhouette or cameo would be used instead. Designs were submitted for a new issue of stamps with a minute silhouette incorporated in one corner. The idea was not rejected out of hand, but Martin Charteris wrote back, 'The Queen was not at all satisfied that the small cameo was sufficiently significant.'

Another early source of concern to the Queen was the Labour Party's plan to reform the House of Lords, which Harold Wilson defused and eventually shelved. During the election campaign the left had, in fact, declared that the upper chamber would be abolished altogether. Wilson's government, however, had gradually steered the reform into less radical waters. Greatly reduced in scope, its main elements included cutting to a handful the number of hereditary peers created by the Queen, thinning down the Anglican episcopal presence from twenty-six to sixteen, and increasing the number of life peers nominated by the government of the day, so that the latter would ultimately be the dominant element in the Lords. But in a fit of pique against his left wing, Wilson postponed even these scaled-down changes, and they would not be revived for another decade. The truth was that no politician would willingly dismantle a spoils system as finely honed as the Honours List, and Wilson was a very clever politician. Far from abolishing the Honours and the House of Lords, he made full political use of them to reward friends, neutralize enemies, and create vacancies in his government by kicking people upstairs. The Honours List remained a corner-stone of the English social system – a system in which an honour is not without profit in its own land. The call for 'mood-changing measures' was now a faint, forgotten echo. Disappointed by Harold Wilson's compliance with the Queen's wishes, Wedgwood Benn observed hopefully, 'I doubt whether he is so foolish as to be taken in by the smiles from the Queen and the flunkeys at Buckingham Palace.' Perhaps he was not. But the Queen had no cause for concern.

Wilson would sometimes remark to senior members of his staff that the three things the Queen cared most about were, in order of importance, the Commonwealth, horses and dogs. Everything else came lower down on her scale of priorities. The Prime Minister knew next to nothing about either horses or dogs, but his office staff had instructions to notify him whenever one of the Queen's horses did well so he could mention it at his weekly audience.

There was no shortage of developments in the Commonwealth, especially in such problem areas as Rhodesia, Cyprus and Malta.

In 1965, Ian Smith, Prime Minister of Rhodesia's white minority government, unilaterally declared his country's independence in defiance of Britain. In lengthy negotiations, the Wilson government had been insisting that the black African majority receive the vote as a pre-condition to granting Rhodesia full independent status, but Smith had forced the issue. When Wilson refused to recognize this settler country as anything more than a British colonial responsibility, right-wing Tory backbenchers friendly to Smith tried to enlist the Queen's help to secure British recognition of the Rhodesian government. The Prime Minister, however, had acted with Elizabeth's approval: she was not about to jeopardize the loyalty of the black African Commonwealth countries by supporting Smith's white supremacists. The question was what to do about Rhodesia's secession? Wilson was under pressure from his own party, and from those same African countries, to restore British control in Rhodesia through military intervention if necessary. But Elizabeth felt the use of military force against white Rhodesians, most of whom were of British origin, would create divisions at home, and her opposition was a strong element in Wilson's decision not to send in troops. Instead he imposed economic sanctions, which were to remain in force until 1975.

About the same time, Harold Wilson's government was also involved in lengthy bargaining with Malta over compensation for a planned substantial reduction of British military installations on the island. The cutbacks in Malta were part of a broader policy of reducing defence spending and scaling down Britain's military commitments around the globe, but the military was one of the island's major employers and the reductions were inevitably going to lead to loss of jobs on a worrying scale. Despite this the government of the island, which had become independent in 1964, was getting nowhere in securing what the Maltese considered adequate British help to build up a non-military economy. While the island seethed over Britain's apparent lack of gratitude and a replay of the coronation coach crisis loomed, the Maltese prime minister, George Borg Olivier – the same one who had ridden in the coach in the coronation procession – flew to London and appealed directly to the Queen. Shortly after a long audience doubtless full of nostalgic reminiscences and news of old friends, Wilson and the Maltese government reached an interim settlement of the cash question together with a slow-down in the time-table of British withdrawals.

Another recurring topic of discussion between the Queen and her Prime Minister was the further education of the heir to the throne. The approaching end of Charles's school days had started an occasionally heated family debate to plot the next phase of his life, and in this the Prime Minister acted as adviser and occasionally as referee. Strictly speaking, of course, Charles's future was preordained: as heir apparent he was being trained for kingship. What was open for discussion was the nature of that training.

Charles, who was seventeen, had from all accounts infuriated his father and perplexed his mother by announcing that he wanted to go to university. Neither parent had attended college, and Charles was to say later that he 'had to fight' to be allowed to go himself. A brief spell at Oxford or Cambridge was not considered unsuitable as part of his preparation, but that was not what he had in mind. He wanted to follow regular courses and sit for his degree like any other college student.

The Queen questioned the wisdom of exposing the young, impressionable Prince to continuous contact with the general public for three years. There was also the security aspect to consider; to say nothing of the embarrassing possibility of failure in his examinations. Moreover, there was something distinctly unroyal about his chosen courses. Future kings studied history and constitutional law, not anthropology and archaeology (Charles eventually switched to history). Prince Philip dismissed the idea outright: Charles was going to follow the family tradition of service in the Royal Navy and like it. Wilson's advice, however, was that one phase could be made to serve the other since Charles could enter the Navy as a graduate instead of going to naval college.

On 22 December 1965, the Queen collected a brains trust to consider the problem of the Prince of Wales's future education over dinner at Buckingham Palace. Besides the Queen herself and Philip, the gathering included the Prime Minister; Earl Mountbatten; Sir Charles Wilson, chairman of the University Vice-Chancellors' Committee; the Archbishop of Canterbury, Dr Michael Ramsey; and the Dean of Windsor, the Revd Robin Woods. Ramsey had been included in the group mostly out of a sense of obligation, for the Queen found communication with him difficult. She was, after all, a woman and no intellectual, and Ramsey had little time for women, horses or corgis. The Dean of St George's Chapel, Windsor, which is what is called a Royal Peculiar, and stands outside the jurisdiction of the Church of England, is effectively the Queen's local vicar; and that dimension of his responsibilities is always kept very much in mind when choosing him. 'Your job, you know, will be to look after us,' Elizabeth told Dean Michael Mann when she telephoned him to offer him the post in 1976 and by *us* she meant the members of the royal family. Officially the Prime Minister advised the Queen on the appointment, but the final selection was left to her. She screened each candidate personally, assisted by her mother and sometimes by Prince Philip. One former dean said that what the Queen looked for were 'people who will fit in. I would describe my own interview as forty-five minutes of social intercourse.'

The interview was only part of the screening process. Each prelate was required to preach a sermon for the Queen Mother and Elizabeth II, and then as the ultimate test each candidate had lunch with them both. In 1989, one candidate was tactless enough to preach a sermon on the subject of old age in front of the eighty-nine-year-old Queen Mother. The Dean of Wells, on the other hand, preached a eulogy on the virtues of George VI and was immediately offered the post.

It was therefore as family chaplain that Dean Robin Woods attended the Buckingham Palace dinner. The decision taken that evening that Prince Charles should go to Cambridge University was hardly surprising given the preponderance of Cambridge men around the table. Harold Wilson had been to Oxford, but both Mountbatten and the late King George VI had spent some time at Christ's College, Cambridge. Ramsey was a former Cambridge don, and Robin Woods was a Trinity man with two sons at the college. So the final choice fell on Trinity College where Dean Woods could act as go-between for the Queen with the college authorities. Oxford hadn't stood a chance. The Prime Minister thought that Charles should also spend some time at the University of Wales, and this did take place in due course. From Cambridge the Prince was to go into the Royal Navy as had his great-grandfather and grandfather, his Uncle Dickie, and his own father.

Meanwhile, Harold Wilson learned that the post of Master of Trinity was one of the many positions 'in the Queen's gift' (in other words, the Queen could appoint its occupant), and as it was becoming vacant he suggested offering it to Rab Butler. When he approached the Tory opposition politician on the Queen's behalf, perhaps hinting at the peerage that eventually went with it, the suggestion was accepted with alacrity. Such thoughtful acts explain why Wilson enjoyed such a favoured relationship with the Queen: having Butler as master of her son's college went a long way to calming her worries about Charles at university.

The notable absence from the dinner was, of course, Prince Charles himself. While the Queen and Prince Philip were deciding his future in London, he was in Australia at Timbertop, more of a survival course than a boarding school, away in the forest two hundred miles north of Melbourne. He had been sent there before his senior year at Gordonstoun to give him practical experience of living in a Commonwealth country. 'I absolutely adored it,' he said of the experience. 'In Australia, there is no such thing as aristocracy or anything like it . . . You are judged on how people feel about you.' They felt he was a 'pommy bastard', a high form of acceptance. Having finished school, he was equally happy at Cambridge. Shortly before his arrival, his mother visited his rooms, met the college housekeeper, and discussed her son's health with the nurse in the college infirmary. His father, who was never fully reconciled to the notion of Charles spending three years at university, glowered when Charles took up the cello, and was disappointed that the Prince did not share his own keen interest in cricket.

At Cambridge, Butler became Charles's mentor. The Master kept three-quarters of an hour available for advice every evening should the Prince want it, and gave the Prince a key to a side entrance to the master's lodge. The door gave access to a private staircase that led to Butler's study. The experienced politician helped the student Prince to avoid some potential booby traps. 'May I join the Labour Party?' Charles asked one evening. In the revolutionary atmosphere of the 1960s it would have been surprising if Charles had not shown an interest in the left. But the Master replied 'no': it would be unconstitutional. Small wonder the Queen was worried about Charles at college.

At the lodge Charles met, and was smitten by, Lucia Santa Cruz, daughter of the Chilean ambassador in London, who was helping Rab with research on his memoirs. And according to Butler's biographer, Charles's friendship with the envoy's daughter – which was not discouraged by the Master – 'may have led to a certain cooling in Rab's relationship with the Palace.' But the Queen must have known she was only at the beginning of the long road of Prince Charles's dalliances, affairs and liaisons.

Anyway she was perhaps distracted by having reached her own emotional landmark of forty.

She had been Queen for fourteen years, visited forty-two countries – several of them twice – and journeyed hundreds of thousands of miles. Her oldest son and heir was eighteen years old, but she was the mother of a two-year-old infant – Prince Edward, a child whose placid temperament reflected her own dent-proof calm. Every year she met thousands of people, yet outside her immediate family her true personality seemed like an unfinished portrait, some parts fully painted, others coloured in, but with the detail missing, and whole sections still little more than the artist's sketchy charcoal outline. Perhaps this was because of her own apparent uncertainty about herself. 'One doesn't know oneself,' she told Annigoni when he showed her his second portrait of her in 1968.

Cabinet ministers, officials, and others who dealt with her regularly over a long period generally found her hard to talk to. Some called it shyness with strangers, others reticence, others just plain boredom. Richard Crossman, the Lord President of the Privy Council in Harold Wilson's government, describes the problem in a scene that followed a meeting of the Privy Council at Balmoral. They walked into the drawing room together, 'I was carrying my papers and she was carrying hers . . . Somebody tried to take them off her and she said, "No, I must go and get rid of them." But she stood there for three minutes without a drink, with the papers in her hand and with nothing to say. If one waits for her to begin a conversation nothing happens. One has to start to talk and then suddenly the conversation falters because both are feeling, "Oh dear, are we boring each other?" '

Yet David Bruce noted '[The Queen] is considered by foreign ambassadors in London to be almost the best briefed person in the United Kingdom. Since she is bilingual in French, it makes her conversations with many members of the diplomatic corps easy . . . I always find her conversation interesting and informative.' And one Italian ambassador of the time found her 'a good talker' who seemed to have grasped the essentials of his country's convoluted politics better than many Italians had. It is tempting to conclude that, though she clearly did not have her mother's gift for small talk, Elizabeth's incommunicability was partly because her own diffident subjects sometimes found it hard to talk to *her*.

That dealing with her was not always sweetness and light

was well known to officials. She did not throw tantrums, but Archbishop Ramsey had a word for her way of expressing displeasure – 'governessy', a pun on the fact that the Queen is Supreme Governor of the Church of England.

Royal protocol requires the Prime Minister and senior cabinet ministers to be 'in attendance' to see the Queen off at Heathrow Airport when she leaves the country on official business, and to be there to greet her when she returns. On one occasion when she arrived back from a Commonwealth tour, the Labour cabinet had arranged in advance to welcome her instead at Buckingham Palace, thereby saving the time of the drive to and from the airport in the middle of a busy day. Though the Queen agreed to the change, it did not go down well. As she was greeted by the line-up of ministers at the Palace she observed dryly, 'It's odd to be welcomed into one's own home.'

The late Lord Stewart of Fulham, a former Foreign Secretary, said that the first time he heard her rebuke one of her corgis he thought the tone sounded familiar. Then he remembered: he had heard her complain to a high government official in the same voice on one of her foreign trips. It was Stewart who once complained to the wife of visiting White House adviser Nicholas deB. Katzenbach at a Windsor Castle dinner that he had 'never been able to converse with the Queen except on the subject of her corgi dogs.' And Richard Crossman recalled telling her that a certain controversial reform bill was likely to be successful. By negotiation? asked the Queen. Yes, said Crossman. 'Well, that will be a surprise. It's not something one expected of you.' She said it, Crossman observed, 'in a rather tart way with a rather nice little smile.'

When Eisenhower died, the Queen asked Earl Mountbatten, as one of his former senior colleagues, to represent her at his funeral in Washington. On hearing this, the State Department tactfully sent word to London that several heads of state planned to attend, including Charles de Gaulle, the Shah, and King Baudouin of Belgium. In turn, the Foreign Office equally tactfully asked her to consider raising the level of representation and sending Prince Philip. But the Queen said no, Mountbatten was going. One can only speculate on her reasons. Most likely, Mountbatten had already been notified and she did not want to disappoint him. Moreover, with her sense of occasion, she might have felt that as a wartime colleague, Mountbatten was more suitable.

She could be equally sharp with the household staff. The Queen has always been meticulous about being punctual for appointments. Punctuality is a Palace fetish. Sometimes, however, it can become a parody of itself, as in this story: she is sitting on the verandah deck of the *Britannia* having breakfast and Bennett, her page, appears. The captain of the royal yacht wants to know if she would mind leaving for shore at 0953 instead of 0955. That's nonsense, she replies. She will go when she's ready.

Her frugality was already legendary. She went around instinctively turning off the lights in empty rooms at Buckingham Palace. And the story of her telling Prince Charles, when he was a boy, to return to the garden to look for a lost dog leash because 'Dog leashes cost money' has found its way into half a dozen books about the royal family. While Pietro Annigoni was painting his second portrait of Elizabeth he used a tailor's dummy supplied by the Palace whenever she was not available for sittings. On the head was a wig replicating her own hairstyle and colour. One day, the artist commented on the remarkable resemblance. 'Yes,' the Queen agreed, 'it's an excellent imitation and it also cost a great deal of money.' Clock-watching offended her sense of duty. 'I'm looking at the gardeners down there,' she said on one occasion, looking out of a Palace window. 'They've put everything down and off they go. They simply look at their watches and go off at half-past three. Not because they've finished what they have to do, but because it's half-past three.'

There are many stories of Elizabeth II's carefulness with money, but frugality is a Windsor family trait, even unto the next generation. Her daughter admits to being mean with money, and the Prince of Wales is not known to be a spendthrift either. Pay scales in royal service were still low. Ladies-in-waiting, for example, are unsalaried, receiving only their expenses, but there is never any shortage of aspirants. Harold Wilson, who was soon to be caught in the cross-fire of a debate over increasing the Queen's civil appropriation (which he was in favour of doing), grumbled to his Cabinet, 'Most rich men feel that part of the job of a rich man is spending a good part of his wealth for charitable and public purposes. It takes royalty to assume that all their private income is to be kept to themselves and accumulated and that they are not obliged to spend any of it on seeing them through their public life.'

The quality of her entertaining was invariably faultless but not over-abundant, whether it was a lunch for twelve at Buckingham Palace or the dinner for forty at Windsor Castle for Katzenbach in April 1968. On that occasion, the guests assembled in one of the family rooms, where they were offered drinks. The Queen, Prince Philip and Princess Anne appeared promptly at 8.30 p.m. to make the rounds, everyone having been posted in advance by the officials of the household who remembered all the names for the presentation. Afterwards there was a general mêlée with another round of drinks, and then the guests sat down to a menu of *Goujonettes Panachées, Emince de Volaille à la King, Asperges au Beurre – Sauce Mousseline, Soufflé aux Manges*. The wines – served with restraint – were Forster Ungeheuer 1961, Château Palmer 1952, Louis Roederer 1953 and Sandeman Port 1934. An orchestra of the Welsh Guards played musical comedy tunes, and then a single kilted piper twice made a round of the tables.

Elizabeth's small circle of intimate friends had altered little since her youth: Henry Herbert Lord Porchester (Porchy), her racing manager and the great-grandson of Lord Carnarvon, the discoverer of Tutankhamen's tomb; the Duke of Beaufort, known with slight irony as Master Beaufort because he was Master of the Queen's Horse and also Master of the Beaufort Hunt and seemed to dismount only for meals and to sleep; the Earl of Westmoreland, who would eventually succeed Beaufort as Master of the Queen's Horse when the latter died; and Lord Rupert Nevill, once considered a potential suitor and Lord Plunkett. Among the women were Debo Devonshire, Elizabeth's first cousin Jean Wills, and Lady Susan Hussey, a vivacious brunette who was one of her regular ladies-in-waiting.

A handful addressed her as Lilibet in private, but to most she was Ma'am (to rhyme with harm). Hardly anyone in her life has ever addressed her by her real name. To the royal household Queen Elizabeth was the Queen Mother: Elizabeth II was simply the Queen, Her Majesty, 'HM', or 'the Sov'. Members of her inner circle would mention her humour and sense of fun, but that was a side of her the world did not see. In public, she allowed herself only the occasional sardonic one-liner. In 1968 she visited the new cathedral at Coventry, rebuilt on the site of the old one destroyed by enemy bombers in the Second World War. Dean and chapter waited to greet her at the door wearing magnificent new copes which – unusually – were made from yellow material. The royal limousine arrived, and the Queen emerged wearing a coat the same colour. As she came forward, hand outstretched to the Dean, she said, 'Touché.'

Bobo MacDonald continued to be a favoured retainer and therefore a power in the Palace even after her retirement in the late 1970s. Bobo was far from being the favourite among the Palace staff that she was with the Queen because, aside from an overbearing manner, she had a tendency to appeal directly to the Queen to get what she wanted. Palace lore has several instances of the Queen's intervention on behalf of her former nursery maid and dresser. After every visit by a foreign head of state the Queen, in recognition of the extra work involved, traditionally gives each member of the Palace staff either a full-sized or a half bottle of champagne, depending on their rank. On one occasion, Bobo MacDonald – then already in retirement – complained to the Queen of receiving a mere split when she felt she was entitled to a whole one. Immediately, the Queen sent down an order to the Master of the Household: give Bobo a full-size bottle of the very best French champagne. Bobo once requested pâté de foie gras with her tea and was told the Palace kitchen was clean out of pâté. Again, she called the Queen, and within twenty minutes a Harrods delivery truck was at Buckingham Palace with a fresh supply of pâté de foie gras.

Labour cabinet ministers invited to Balmoral were astonished to see the Queen playing 'The Game', or joining in one of her sister's piano sing-songs. On one occasion during a shoot at Broadlands, the Mountbatten family home, William Evans, Mountbatten's young valet, was helping Her Majesty off with her boots. He knelt down and gripped the mud-covered boot. He tugged at the slippery surface. 'The next thing I knew a hand had been placed on the top of my head as she sought to keep her balance. "Haven't you got a lovely curly head of hair?" she said . . . I always felt strangely honoured about that occasion.'

When she is making a speech, and she is afraid of getting a fit of the giggles the frown appears, making her look bad-tempered. She also frowns when she is inwardly moved or touched and trying not to show it. She frowned a great deal during Prince Charles's investiture as Prince of Wales at Caernarvon Castle on 2 July 1969. Doubtless, it was an emotional moment, but she was also remembering the laughter at their rehearsals in the Buckingham Palace garden. The investiture area had been marked out, with five cords stretched on the ground to indicate the steps, and the Queen and Charles had to lift their feet as if the steps were really there. When the moment came for Elizabeth to practise placing the coronet on her son's head, the golden band turned out to be too large and – amid much hilarity – rested on his ears.

One of her amusements was watching television, especially at the weekend at Windsor Castle where the television room was a small, cosy sitting room along the great long corridor which George III had constructed. An enormous coal fire and an oversize television set dominated the room. Here the Queen watched the weekly wrestling programme which she found 'tremendous fun', and her favourite soap opera at the time, *Coronation Street*. Her other indoor amusement was doing jigsaw puzzles, at which she was an expert. Crossman had a demonstration of how expert when he saw her at work on an enormous jigsaw at Sandringham: 'She was standing there talking to the company at large, her fingers were straying and she was quietly fitting in the pieces while apparently not looking around.' The bigger and the more complicated they were the better she liked it, and to increase the challenge, she sometimes hid the illustration and assembled them 'blind'.

Her ruling passion remained horse racing and breeding; she was in constant touch with her stables, and read the daily racing press with her breakfast. She was by now immovably fixed in her rich-countrywoman persona, never happier than when she was tramping the Scottish hills with her dogs. In reality, this was only a partial portrait. For all her love of country pursuits, nearly forty weeks of the year were actually spent in the city, in residence at Buckingham Palace, or travelling abroad.

Her travels and contacts exposed her to the unrest and dissent of the 1960s which she found unsettling. Mountbatten noted that she was worried 'about the parlous state of the nation.' And at lunch in the owners' box at the Goodwood races some weeks after 'The Events' of May 1968 in France she voiced her concern to David Bruce 'about violence, especially amongst young people throughout the world.' With the Prince of Wales still at Cambridge, discontent at British universities seemed doubly worrying. 'I presided over the inauguration of a new university a few days ago,' she told Annigoni during one of her portrait sittings, 'a modern building with courts like the traditional ones, only larger. The students weren't satisfied. They said they felt like prisoners.' The students' attitude clearly puzzled her. Annigoni mentioned that sit-ins had become an epidemic at French and Italian universities. The Queen's comment was, 'I don't know about Italy, but in France I believe the discontent is justified. A niece of mine, belonging to an obviously traditional family, has returned from the Sorbonne where she has been studying, with completely revolutionary ideas.'

At a time of political protest and agitation on a mass scale – of anti-nuclear marches, anti-Vietnam War rallies, university campus sit-ins, factory strikes – of challenge to authority in all its forms, of conventions turned upside down, of old established values questioned as they had not been since the Marxist revolution, Elizabeth II may have occasionally gazed down the Mall from her study window and wondered if the day might come when it would be filled with hostile crowds marching on Buckingham Palace. This was, of course, extremely far-fetched, yet the royal family was not totally immune from the mood of the times. The Queen was cruelly lampooned in the popular television satirical programme *That Was The Week That Was*. It was the first time she had been made the target of humour in the mass media.

More significant, because it came from a traditionally loyal quarter, was a pamphlet calling for the state allowance to the royal family to be determined on the basis of need and productivity rather than according to tradition. The pamphlet was published by the Bow Group, a study unit reflecting the views of the liberal wing of the Conservative Party. Its team of four authors said they were supporters of the monarchy, but felt that a higher level of disclosure was needed from the royal household on its use of funds voted by Parliament – 'national control of public expenditure on the monarchy is essential.'

These developments were not lost on the royal family. Prince Philip pressed his persistent campaign for modernization to ensure the monarchy's continued relevance to modern Britain. So while the Court repeated the incantation that Elizabeth II's sole interest was in being herself, not in changing her image, the royal family did what any senior management with a company image problem would do, they engaged a public relations firm. The step was taken unobtrusively and – typically – indirectly, but the end result was the same.

The maybe-stage that preceded the possibly, that came before the official denial that served as a smokescreen for the *fait accompli* seems to have had its origins in the appointment of two men to the royal household who had two things in common. One was their middle-class background, and the other their high level of intelligence. In 1960, a bright young Australian civil servant named William Heseltine had spent a year working in the Palace press office on secondment from his post as private secretary to the Prime Minister of Australia, Sir Robert Menzies. Six years later, at Prince Philip's urging, he was brought back as Richard

Colville's assistant and eventually – on the latter's retirement in 1968 – successor. Described by a journalist with long experience in covering the royals as 'congenitally programmed to do no wrong,' Heseltine was to rise to the top job in the Queen's service as her Private Secretary.

The other new face was that of Royal Air Force Wing Commander David Checketts, appointed as the Prince of Wales's first equerry. Checketts was an acquaintance of Nigel Neilson, founder of a successful London public relations firm, Neilson McCarthy, and folklore has it that one day Neilson had the bright idea of approaching Prince Charles's newly appointed equerry out of the blue with an offer of help. At which point the royal family clapped a hand to a collective brow and, uttering some variation of 'Of course, why didn't we think of that?', hired Neilson McCarthy.

In fact, Checketts and Heseltine were appalled at the gap between reality and public perception and decided that some professional help would be useful. There was never any Palace announcement about Neilson McCarthy, and the firm's connection with the royal family remained unofficial. But David Checketts joined its board of directors at a nominal salary as a ready source of advice on its work for the royals. Another director was Major Ronald Ferguson, a top-ranking polo player who played with the Duke of Edinburgh and was then teaching the finer points of the game to the twenty-year-old Prince of Wales. Eighteen years later, Ferguson's daughter Sarah was to marry Prince Andrew. Ferguson had served as commander of the Sovereign's Escort of the Household Cavalry. In ceremonial processions such as the state opening of Parliament he rode immediately behind the royal coach on the Queen's side with his company of the Life Guards following behind him. On one such occasion, Ferguson's horse advanced too far forward, so that he drew level with the coach, blocking the crowd's view of the Queen. Whereupon the Queen, still waving and smiling, shouted above the din out of the open window, 'It's me they've come to see, Ron, not you.'

The public relations company's first assigned task was to help 'launch' Prince Charles as a key royal figure in advance of his investiture as Prince of Wales. 'Here was a first class chap, a first class product, being criminally undersold,' Neilson would say later. '[There was] far too much nonsense in the press about the chinless wonder, and his ears that are no different from anybody else's.' Product. Undersold. The royal family had embraced modern marketing and image-making techniques. It was a tacit recognition that just being there was no longer enough. In another age, George V could reign as the august, remote ruler; George VI was the wartime king, an inspiration to his people of courage and devotion to duty. The Queen had to be seen as fulfilling a role, of being an integral part of Britain's social framework, not hovering above it as a royal icon or, worse, as one of history's irrelevant leftovers.

The selling of Prince Charles included two press cocktail parties at which newsmen could meet and talk to him. The gamble paid off, as the public relations strategists knew it would. The press found him a thoughtful, articulate young man with an engaging line in self-deprecating humour. Then, carefully briefed and rehearsed, he gave a lengthy BBC radio interview to a veteran broadcast journalist, Jack de Manio, who happened to be another director of Neilson McCarthy. But the real unveiling came with his first television interviews. The Prince was an immediate hit with the British public. He was at ease before the cameras, and was launched as a royal superstar. Clearly his appearances in undergraduate theatricals had helped boost his self-confidence.

The next, and tougher challenge was to 'sell' the Queen herself. Although, in recent years, there had been a marked improvement in the delivery of the Christmas speech, appearing on television was still an ordeal to her. But Heseltine was fashioning a media policy that favoured television over the Fleet Street press. Television, which anyway had greater impact, was easier to control both because it needed access, and because the BBC has always worked closely with the Palace (there is a Palace liaison officer at Broadcasting House), and the newly formed rival Independent Television Network had slipped into the same pattern. The Queen had liked a television documentary about the life and times of Earl Mountbatten made by his son-in-law, film producer Lord Brabourne, and the latter now encouraged her to allow a similar venture about herself and her family.

The Queen needed strong persuasion to submit to such wholesale scrutiny. It had been only five years since – through Michael Adeane – she had flatly refused to allow the cameras to film cosy family scenes round the fireside. Adeane and the Palace old guard still questioned the wisdom of letting the arc lights in upon the magic, but Prince Philip was convinced television would give the royal magic a much needed boost. In the end Philip's view – buttressed by Heseltine – prevailed over the traditionalists and the Queen gave the BBC the green light to make the film. But first there were lengthy negotiations – with Philip in the chair – to examine the film-makers' plans and establish the ground rules. Some scenes were vetoed, others modified. Philip tried to bar close-ups of the Queen, as he had successfully done in the television coverage of the Coronation, but Richard Cawston, the BBC head of documentaries, stood his ground: if the camera was kept at a respectful distance the sought-after intimacy would be lost. And in fact the filming was to extend the boundaries of the permissible beyond the BBC's wildest hopes.

Initially, the Queen was tense: overconscious of the camera, and of the miniature microphone pinned to her bosom. But as the crew followed her on her daily schedule she got to know them and relaxed. She learned about lighting and would even make suggestions. The crew accompanied her on a royal tour to Chile, where they filmed her in intense heat and bright sunlight. When she visited a government ministry they waited hidden behind some trees in order to be as unobtrusive as possible, and tracked her as she walked to her car. Dave Gorringe, the cockney electrician, cursing the heat, crouched in the bushes. From the car came the Queen's unmistakably clear tones: 'You certainly won't need your lights today, Sparks!'

From time to time the Queen would invite Cawston to lunch and ask him, 'Why won't you allow me to see the rushes, Mr Cawston?' Because seeing themselves on the screen makes people self-conscious. They begin to correct imaginary faults, and to worry about their good side. This was accepted philosophically. In all, the crew spent seventy-five days with the Queen and her family, and shot forty-three hours of footage. This was edited to the one-hour-and-forty-five-minute documentary called *Royal Family*. Under normal circumstances any television documentary producer who filmed twenty times more footage than he needed would have enjoyed a short career. But, of course, this was no ordinary documentary assignment. Hours of early footage were discarded either because the Queen, or someone appearing with her, was self-conscious or because of some technical hitch. Just as the royal family needed time to become accustomed to the television crew, the crew needed time to get used to them, and to the (literally) palatial setting.

At the BBC the project had been treated as top secret from start to finish. The corporation was taking a gamble because the film's release hinged on obtaining the Queen's approval, and that was far from a foregone conclusion. But when the Queen saw it for the first time at Broadcasting House, in the spring of 1969, she was pleased with what she saw and approved it for release with a few minor changes.

When *Royal Family* was shown on television in the United Kingdom some weeks later, it was a turning point in public perceptions about Elizabeth II and her hitherto private world. The BBC audience research report on the film said, 'The norm is for broadcasts to reinforce existingly held opinions.' *Royal Family*, on the other hand, changed opinions, and 'a new and different image was adopted.'

The first surprise was the revelation that Elizabeth's voice was not the high, tight, neigh of her public pronouncements, and the second was her evident sense of humour. The cleverly conceived opening sequence starts at the barrier where the public view of the Queen stops: at the gates of Buckingham Palace. It shows Elizabeth II returning to the Palace at the end of the annual Trooping the Colour review on her official birthday. For the first time, she is riding Burmese, a seven-year-old black mare given to her by the Royal Canadian Mounted Police. The camera enters through the main Palace gates, then follows the Queen into the inner courtyard, where she dismounts. She is heard telling the groom to give Burmese extra oats because the mare had behaved perfectly. The film shows a hardworking, sensible and close-knit family. There are hitherto unseen glimpses of them at Balmoral. There were also amusing moments: 'How are you settling in?' she asked Walter Annenberg, the United States ambassador, who was filmed presenting his credentials. He had the misfortune to be heard making the following reply: 'We're in the embassy residence, subject, of course, to some of the discomfiture as the result of a need for, uh, elements for refurbishment and rehabilitation.' The British press never forgot it. The Queen nodded inscrutably, but Wedgwood Benn reported her telling him later that the film might have to be cut for showing in the United States because the American ambassador had 'used very long words and made himself look ridiculous.'

The film achieved what it set out to do, namely, to show the human face of royalty. Screened shortly before the Prince of Wales's investiture, it created a significant juxtaposition – the royal family as real people, and then at the investiture in their hierarchal role as symbols of authority and majesty. Amid the chorus of praise for *Royal Family* some critics voiced fears that

242

the television genie, once released, would be hard to put back in the bottle. The film had set a precedent for the television camera to act as an image-making apparatus for the monarchy, but these critics observed that every institution that attempted to use television to popularize or aggrandize itself had been trivialized by it.

The public at large, however, found the new openness of the royal family preferable to the old, closed order. Right or wrong, the House of Windsor was at least prepared for the new decade, and it was no coincidence that the 1970s would begin with a battle for more public funds to cope with rising costs.

Elizabeth looked good on television, good complexion, trim, well groomed rather than elegant, the 'flawless mirror' of what the English feel themselves to be, as the poet laureate Ted Hughes put it. But to the painter Annigoni in mid-1969, comparing her with the young sovereign who sat for him in the Yellow Drawing Room more than a decade earlier, 'Everything about her seemed smaller, in some ways frailer, in some ways harder.' The sixties had been a troublesome, iconoclastic decade.

XV

Money Talks

In February 1969, Richard Nixon was Elizabeth II's guest at lunch at Buckingham Palace and invited her to visit the United States. But the Labour government, which had to contend with strong opposition to the Vietnam War from its left wing, advised the Palace against a trip because it could be read at home as a sign of British support. The Queen was disappointed. She had mentioned to Nixon her interest in visiting California and the Kennedy Space Center. She had also listened with sympathy to what he had to say about America's lonely role in South East Asia, although judging from her later reaction to the news of the My Lai massacre, she considered the American approach to the war rather naïve: 'Poor Americans! They do have their problems. And they believe they're so perfect, or at least that they do things better than anyone else . . . Yes, they do many wonderful things. On the other hand, there is so much puffing up and political speculation, even in this story of the massacre: as if there can be war without cruel and horrible incidents.'

But though the Queen was not to add California to her travel schedule for a number of years, Prince Philip did visit the NASA space centre in November. *En route* he saw Nixon at the White House before going on to New York, where he appeared on NBC's weekly programme *Meet the Press*, and complained about the parlous state of the royal family's finances. He said the royal family would 'go into the red next year and might have to leave Buckingham Palace' for a smaller residence. This, he said, was because the Queen's Civil List allowance was 'based on costs of eighteen years ago.'

244

His revelation was no impulsive outburst. He may have spoken with deliberate exaggeration, but his purpose had been to force the issue out into the open. In the past eight years of rising inflation the Queen's annual allowance from the Civil List had consistently failed to cover the costs of the royal household, and with the reserve fund dwindling, the Queen faced the immediate prospect of dipping into her own private resources to cover the shortfall. She already covered the considerable cost of her large wardrobe. Prince Philip was, in effect, issuing the challenge to the Government that she could not issue herself. The bombshell detonated across the Atlantic in Britain. Many resented the fact that the Queen's husband had gone public in a foreign country instead of first raising the problem at home; others were concerned that the Government was neglecting the Queen's difficulties.

Deeply embarrassed because he was fighting a battle to keep down wages, and preparing for a general election, Harold Wilson was forced to acknowledge in the House of Commons that the Queen needed what he had been denying the trade unions – a raise. (Never mind that it was an increase not in salary but in her operating budget; what it looked like was that a Labour government seemed prepared to give more money to the Queen but not to the workers.) Wilson explained to the House that the Queen's annual grant of £750,000, which had been fixed by Parliament in 1952, had a supplementary provision of £90,000 which was supposed to accrue against later deficits. Until 1961, the royal household had operated in surplus. But from then on, an annual deficit had begun to eat into the reserves, which were expected to run out in 1970.

Wilson added defensively that government ministries had been helping to keep the deficit down by covering more and more of the Queen's expenses: the Government was meeting the cost of maintaining the royal castles; and in 1964, the Post Office had paid nearly £58,000 in subsidies towards the royal family's postage and telephone charges. Wilson promised to set up a select committee of the House of Commons to consider the merits of the case for an increase.

These were widely seen to be irrefutable, and before Prince Philip's comments, the expectation had been that a discreet and respectful inquiry would eventually be set up and would end in agreement on a higher royal budget. The Prince had forced the issue, but in the process had also exacerbated the argument. In addition, on 19 June 1970, to most people's surprise – including the

Queen's – the Labour Party was defeated in the general election. She told Earl Mountbatten that he was 'almost the only person who gave her any indication that there was a good chance that the Conservatives might win.' But win the Tories did – with a comfortable majority of thirty-four seats – and it was the new Tory government that set up the select committee in 1971. Unhampered by the restraints of government, the left was freer than before to voice its resentment at the monarch's wealth.

As Queen of England, Elizabeth II enjoys the most fantastic perquisite next to immortality: she is exempt from paying taxes. That distinction lies at the heart of a self-perpetuating controversy about her personal wealth. As a non-taxpayer she need never set forth an accounting of her income and belongings, and at Buckingham Palace there is a reticence bordering on coyness about how much Elizabeth II is really worth. As a result, cataloguing her wealth is not easy. Clearly, some of the possessions associated with her belong to the institution of the monarchy. The crown jewels and the three main residences – Buckingham Palace, Windsor Castle and Holyrood House in Scotland – are the Queen's only because she is Queen. She resides in them for life, unless she abdicates in favour of the Prince of Wales which, in the standard Palace response to such a possibility, 'is not on the agenda.'

In 1971, the issue of the Queen's finances was brought into the full glare of public curiosity for the first time since her accession, and she became increasingly irritated with the speculation about the size of her private fortune. The Lord Chamberlain, Lord Cobbold, told the committee that 'Her Majesty has been much concerned by the astronomical figures which have been bandied about in some quarters suggesting that the value of [her private wealth] may now run into fifty or one hundred million pounds . . . She wishes me to [say] that these suggestions are wildly exaggerated.' Court officials said the figure was closer to three million pounds, but there has always been a sizeable gap between the Court's estimate and that of knowledgeable outsiders.

The contents of the jewel room at Buckingham Palace alone would have covered a sizeable portion of that figure: fourteen crowns, eleven tiaras, plus an enormous quantity of diamonds, rubies and emeralds. The Fabergé collection included two of the famous Easter eggs. In addition, the Queen's art collection is one of the largest in private hands in the world: nine hundred drawings by Leonardo da Vinci, a hundred Canalettos, twenty-six Van Dycks, a dozen Holbeins, works by Michelangelo, Raphael,

Rubens, Rembrandt. But all of this inherited opulence reflected the taste of her acquisitive predecessors, and is generally considered to be held in trust for the nation. Elizabeth revealed herself more in her unquestionably private assets, the ones her hirelings buy, sell and manage.

Her land holdings included – as they still do – the 52,000 acres of the Duchy of Lancaster (the Duchy of Cornwall revenues provide a handsome income for the Prince of Wales), which ranges from grouse moors in Yorkshire to the land under the Savoy in London, and which in 1970 generated an untaxed rental income of £770,000. In the United States, she inherited, and was said to have added to, sizeable land holdings in Manhattan cutting across the East Side midtown shopping area. Through her German great-great-grandfather Prince Albert she also has large land holdings in Germany and northern France. In Britain, of course, there is Sandringham House, a mansion with two hundred and seventy-four rooms, bought by Edward VII and deeded over to George VI by his brother together with Balmoral Castle.

Her estates were Prince Philip's overall responsibility and run at a profit. The Sandringham estate had fifty acres of blackcurrant bushes under contract to a British soft drink company. Her farms did more than supply unpasteurized Jersey milk to Buckingham Palace in green-topped bottles bearing the cipher ERII underneath a crown. They also contributed to the coffers. Elizabeth also had stock portfolios. The Queen reads the *Financial Times* regularly, checking her shares. Her portfolio had long been managed by London brokerage firms, but a committee of Royal Trustees provided advice, and Elizabeth II's stockholdings were estimated by City analysts to be worth no less than £50 million.

Then there were all the Queen's racehorses, not to mention all the Queen's racing pigeons. Her two hundred or so grey birds with their ER gold ring performed consistently well in competitions. But after the spectacular successes of the first decade of her reign, the Queen's horse-racing interests faced a lean period in the late 1960s. There was no outstanding winner in her stables: Aureole died in 1973 at the age of twenty-three, and from 1968 to 1970 Elizabeth had only five wins in British racing. She still had at least fifteen mares at two studs, and about twenty horses in training, but her racing interests had recently been reorganized following the recommendations of a committee of inquiry which she had set up in 1967 under Lord Porchester. The committee's report suggested that she needed both a racing and a breeding

247

manager. The same year, Porchester took over as the latter and Michael Oswald assumed control of the Royal Studs, and between them they ushered in a gradual reversal in fortunes. So the best in racing profitability was yet to come.

The Queen did not herself appear before the all-party parliamentary committee, officially called the Select Committee on the Civil List, but senior members of her household presented estimates and gave evidence. Though the discussion did not focus on her private wealth, the question loomed over the proceedings. The sensitivity of the issue was reflected in the seniority of the committee's members. Harold Wilson himself led the Labour group; the Liberal Party leader, Jo Grimond, was also a member, and the Government's representation included two cabinet ministers.

Sir Michael Adeane provided them with a detailed study of the Queen's increased work load compared to her immediate predecessors (for example: she personally read the two hundred letters she received every day; she travelled more than any other British monarch had ever done before; etc.). The Comptroller of her household showed how Palace wages had risen dramatically in the past decade. The cleaning and maintenance problems were, of course, immense. Buckingham Palace has about six hundred rooms which were thoroughly cleaned three times a year, and an army of maids had to be engaged for the purpose. The committee had a field day questioning the courtiers on their bookkeeping (Why did the 1969 annual garden party at Holyrood House cost fifty pence more per head than in the previous year?) but showed little inclination to force a confrontation on the thorny question of taxing the Queen's private assets. Labour members on the committee pressed mildly for more details, but their opposition was largely intended to protect their flanks from the left, and the Palace team's tight lips on the Queen's personal wealth were accepted only with a murmur of protest. Wilson was too much of a monarchist to try to make political capital out of the situation.

But the tranquil scenario of its hearings was disturbed from time to time by an irreverent salvo from outside. Richard Crossman, now editor of the New Statesman, the left-wing weekly, wrote a highly critical editorial entitled 'The Royal Tax Avoiders'. ('One has to admire her truly regal cheek'.) The Queen was angry. Following Labour's 1970 defeat, Crossman had come to the Palace to take his leave as minister. He had detected a slight note of regret in their leave-taking. He had asked her if she minded elections. She said, 'Yes, it means knowing a lot of new people.'

Just when she was beginning to feel comfortable with one group of politicians, another group replaced them and the process was begun all over again. Crossman's attack did nothing to improve her view of the political class.

But Mountbatten advised Elizabeth and his nephew that the Crossman article could not go unanswered, that a strong reply was a more effective defence than dignified silence. 'Unless you can get an informed reply published . . . the image of the monarchy will be gravely damaged,' he wrote to Prince Philip. 'It is true that there is a fortune, which is very big, but the overwhelming proportion (eighty-five per cent?) is in pictures, *objets d'art*, furniture, etc., in the state-owned palaces. The Queen can't sell any of them, they bring no income.' What was needed, he said, was an authoritative article presenting the Queen's side of the picture in *The Times*, which would in turn be picked up by the world's press. If something along these lines was not attempted, he said, public resentment at having to pay more while the Queen amassed a fortune would continue to grow. 'So will you both believe a loving old uncle and NOT your constitutional advisers and do it.'

The Queen continued to weather the storm in silence, and in 1972, a new Act of Parliament increased the Civil List to £1,500,000, roughly double the amount voted in 1952. It was, however, a problem that refused to go away. In 1975, a heated Commons debate took place over a proposed £450,000 increase in the Civil List to cope with rocketing inflation. The House heard that three years after her most recent budget increase the Queen needed an additional £650,000 to meet the 44 per cent price rise, but as a compromise solution she had agreed to contribute £220,000 from her private funds. Despite this concession the debate turned into another running attack on the Queen's tax immunity – an aspect of the issue on which the Government benches remained conspicuously silent. There was the accompanying fusillade of hostile press comment all over again and the counter-offensive from the dedicated monarchists. In the end, the House approved the increase by an overwhelming vote of 427 to ninety. But the number of no's was twice as many as had been forecast, in spite of a warning from the Prime Minister that any member of the Government who voted against the Queen was risking his job. The Prime Minister was again Harold Wilson, the Labour Party had been voted back into office in 1974.

For a woman who had never uttered a public word on the subject, the Queen's side of the taxation argument was remarkably well publicized. As usual, there were always people willing to take up her cause. The historical background was an agreement reached between King George III and the Government whereby the King turned over to the national exchequer all revenue from Crown lands (except the Duchy of Lancaster) in return for a yearly allowance fixed by Parliament. So the Government was already getting several quid for its quo. Besides, were the Queen and her successors to be forced to pay – for example – inheritance taxes, there was the danger that within a generation what had become a valuable part of the national heritage in palaces and art would have been broken up to meet the bill.

But George III's agreement, of course, pre-dated the introduction of income tax and the left felt that the monarch's refusal to submit to taxation while at the same time collecting a state subsidy set her above her own laws. It was the ultimate arrogance: let them eat tax forms. It could be argued that successive governments had been able to hold down the size of the Civil List allowance because of what amounted to the hidden subsidy to the Queen of continued tax exemption. What this meant in practice, however, was that the monarchy's exact cost to the nation was not known; and quite a number of parliamentarians thought it would be a more orderly arrangement – and one that dampened down controversy – if the Queen agreed to full disclosure of income and received a realistic allowance, even on the lavish side, to do her job.

To the Queen, the taxation and disclosure issue was simply a non-starter. No government could justify matching what would be an enormous tax assessment and everyone knew it. So, for one thing, she would be seriously out-of-pocket. But was it just the money? Beyond that there was a determination that this was one battle the politicians were not going to win. It was her last ditch. The point beyond which no government would go. So far, no government has tried to.

The Queen and Prince Philip celebrated their silver wedding on 20 November 1972. The official photograph, by the Queen's cousin Patrick Lichfield, showed a relaxed couple, the Prince in an open-neck shirt, the Queen in a simple pink blouse, with the inevitable single strand of pearls round her neck and pearl earrings. A couple to whom time had been kind, if perhaps not overgenerous. Philip, who six months earlier had turned fifty, retained the lean, healthy good looks of an outdoorsman, though his hair was thin and receding. In these days when proper care and attention can postpone the ageing process, it is surprising to see

Elizabeth look more than her forty-six years. The lines around the mouth are heavily etched, and deep ridges surround the eyes. But the ease in the relationship is unmistakable. Whatever their difficulties, they are in the past. They have the look of a couple who have grown up together.

Throughout the sixties Philip had burned up his surplus energy by going on long trips without the Queen. For example, between 1960 and 1970 he made seven solo visits to the United States, including a six-week trip in 1966 to Miami, Houston, Dallas, Palm Springs, Chicago, Los Angeles and New York, a visit to the Seattle World's Fair in 1967, and his NASA visit in 1969. In addition, he toured Asia, and accompanied the Queen on her royal visits. For a great deal of the time theirs was a long-distance relationship, although he was meticulous about keeping in touch with his family by letters. Now he was spending more time at Buckingham Palace. He seemed more philosophical about his marginal position, thinking of himself as 'an unofficial Ombudsman'. Not in the usual sense that people brought him their grievances (although many did), but more because he felt that he spoke for people who could not speak for themselves, or whose interests had been ignored.

His 1969 New York interview on the family finances was one instance of his raising an issue which his wife could not. The intriguing question was how to know when he was speaking for his wife. They often argued over issues, Philip putting his point forcefully and the Queen making her points in her usual calm manner. The Prince had come down firmly on the side of the Rhodesian whites when Ian Smith unilaterally – and illegally – declared his country independent. The Queen, on the other hand, had backed the Prime Minister, Harold Wilson, in his refusal to come to terms with the white supremacist regime. But also during that period, Lord Stewart, who was spending the weekend at Windsor Castle, was asked by Philip why the British government was opposed to Spain joining the North Atlantic Treaty Organization. General Franco was still in power at the time but the United States had long advocated admitting Spain to NATO, so that here too Philip was voicing a well-known right-wing opinion.

His views were a curious blend of ultra-conservative and radical. He told one Labour minister that he felt the House of Lords should be abolished and replaced by an elected upper house. He also said he believed that British opinion was opposed to Britain joining the European Economic Community, and that the Prime Minister's weekly audience should be broadened to include other ministers who could explain things to the Queen. But that wouldn't help the monarchy, the minister replied. Philip said he was thinking of the national interest. If the monarchy failed to meet the national interest, he would opt out altogether. The importance of clinging to relevance if the monarchy wants to survive has always been one of Philip's favourite themes. As for the Commonwealth, the Queen should stop being Queen of the Commonwealth because 'They don't want us.'

On one occasion, following a Privy Council meeting at Balmoral, the Queen was chatting with some of the cabinet ministers when Philip boomed in. He sat down beside the Queen and 'for over half an hour monopolized the conversation.' Then he looked at his watch and said to the Queen, 'Well, they ought to be going now.' And out they went. The Queen tended to accept his overbearing manner placidly. Unless he overstepped the mark, when he found himself quickly reminded of his place. Harold Wilson returned to Downing Street from his weekly audience one evening and told a member of his staff that Prince Philip had suddenly burst into their meeting unannounced. He immediately began complaining about a domestic problem. The Queen – according to Wilson – said nothing but 'froze him with a look.' Prince Philip muttered what might have been an apology and left. The prime minister's audience is with the Queen alone.

That was a far cry from Prince Albert's active participation in Queen Victoria's audiences with her successive prime ministers. The Court's – and particularly Tommy Lascelles's – insistence on keeping Philip – and through him Lord Mountbatten – away from state business had endured. So, for that matter, had Philip's resentment against his early treatment by his wife's parents, which doubtless helped set the tone for the Court, and he could be 'very savage' at private dinner parties about the 'uppity' attitude of King George VI.

Foreigners who expected him to be grave and dignified were sometimes put off by his tendency to crack jokes, which made him seem flippant. But humour, like travel, was one of his safety valves, a device for easing the tension. On a royal tour of Brazil, he told one audience the following joke: when God, during the creation, was distributing natural resources to various parts of the earth he lavished riches of every kind on Brazil – minerals, forests, the Amazon River. After a few days of this divine generosity, his advisers warned him that he was lavishing too much on Brazil

252

and there would be little in the way of good things left for other lands. But God explained, 'Tomorrow, I shall create the Brazilians.' Joke-telling ran in the family, particularly the stories involving (usually) bad puns. The Queen and Philip made up a joke based on something that happened when Princess Margaret visited Tanganyika. A tribal chief was preparing to receive her in his village and ordered a throne brought out of storage. But the throne had not been used since his grandfather's time. It was weak and wobbly and fell to bits, proving that people who live in grass houses should not stow thrones. One of Princess Margaret's favourites was about the members of the Basque pelota team who all tried to get through a hotel revolving door at once, resulting in several injuries. The moral of the story: never to put all your Basques in one exit.

The Queen 'simply adores him', according to a friend who saw them in private at the time. She called him 'darling'; he had a variety of affectionate nicknames for her, occasionally 'Sausage'. Yet, in public, she was more relaxed when her husband was not with her, possibly because it removed the suspense of not knowing when he was going to have a tantrum – or flirt with a good-looking girl. Unlike their children, they have never been seen exchanging as much as a peck on the cheek. Signs of affection were limited to the occasional warm smile. In 1970, Elizabeth II was watching both Charles and Philip playing polo when her son was knocked down and heavily rolled on by his pony. But Charles got up and carried on playing. In the next chukka, Philip collided with another player, came down very heavily, and lay quite still. As the doctor ran out to her husband, Elizabeth leaned forward, craning her neck and frowning slightly: she allowed herself no other sign of the anxiety she must have been feeling. Any urge she might have had to rush to her husband's side was held in check by her habitual iron self-control.

Prince Philip was helped to his feet and off the field. It was evident that he was in pain and the doctor would not let him go on playing. Mountbatten, who was present, urged her to make sure that an X-ray was taken and that Philip stayed in bed. Elizabeth's reply was to 'wish me luck to see if I could stop him,' Mountbatten wrote. Shortly afterwards, Philip began to suffer from arthritis in his hands and had to give up polo altogether – to the Queen's intense relief.

Despite his lurking impatience and challenging hawkishness, he was an indulgent father who found it difficult to be stern for very long with his children. Queen Elizabeth, on the other hand, had no difficulty in that respect. But it was with Philip that the children discussed their problems, and there was never any question who was head of the family. When the children were in their early teens, he established the practice of the annual family meeting at Balmoral, which had the dual purpose of reviewing problems and having a vacation. This Victorian custom was to continue, unbroken, even after three of the children were married and parents themselves. The summons came from Philip in the weeks just before Christmas. The Prince of Wales, Princess Anne, Prince Andrew and Prince Edward converged on Balmoral, but they stayed at Craigowan House in the hills above the castle. The Queen was never present. The respective spouses were not asked either. None of the participants ever spoke about this private get-together, and equally, none ever missed a year.

At their 1972 gathering, the young royals had much to talk about. The Duke of Windsor had died in Paris – a family ghost in life, he was not going to be exorcized by his death. And Princess Anne planned to marry the man of her choice the following year.

By May 1972, the former King Edward VIII was a dying man, stricken with cancer in the tonsils, which were impossible to remove owing to the proximity of the carotid arteries. Since his exclusion from the coronation, there had been little change in his estrangement from the royal family. He had visited London four times, and in 1967 was for the first time invited to be present at a minor royal ceremony with the Duchess – this was the dedication of a plaque in memory of Queen Mary outside Marlborough House. The Windsors sat in the front row together with the Queen and Prince Philip, the Queen Mother and other members of the family, and the ceremony lasted exactly fifteen minutes, giving the Duke his wish for a 'once only meeting of a quarter of an hour' between Wallis and the royal family for which he had pleaded in the 1940s in order to make the Duchess more respectable. His income had been restored to him and the Queen had also offered him an office in Buckingham Palace for his exclusive use, the unspoken understanding being that the Duchess was not welcome to share the privilege. Then in 1968, the Duke asked for permission for himself and the Duchess to be buried in the royal family's private cemetery laid out lovingly by Queen Victoria at Frogmore, near Windsor, for her mother, Prince Albert and herself. Over a year later, the Queen agreed to this in a letter to her uncle in August 1970, largely because Adeane convinced her that to refuse would be carrying the family ostracism of her uncle beyond what was either reasonable or decent.

But these concessions were not a prelude to reconciliation, and the Duke of Windsor's impending death had loomed awkwardly over a four-day visit which the Queen was scheduled to make to Paris. The trip had been 'sold' to her by the government as a French invitation designed to mark the agreement on Britain's entry into the European Economic Community. In reality, however, it was the brainchild of Sir Christopher Soames, the ambassador in Paris, who had also told the French that Elizabeth was eager to come. The French had agreed to the visit without much enthusiasm. As the date drew closer, however, the attitude of President Georges Pompidou's government suddenly switched from routine attention to energetic effort. Perhaps Pompidou hoped that some of the supra-political and sovereign magic of the monarchy might rub off on himself. There were indications that the Queen was equally unenthusiastic, but had been persuaded with the promise of an afternoon at the Longchamps races.

The cliffhanger was the question of her moribund uncle. The most recent complications to the Duke's condition were such that he was liable to die quite suddenly, without warning. So when Martin Charteris advanced the trip in January, a contingency plan was worked out with Soames in the eventuality of the Duke's death. If he died before the visit began, then it was to be cancelled. If he died while the Queen was in Paris, it would go on, but the big embassy ball would have to be cancelled. If he was still alive on day three of the royal visit, the Queen would call on him. Soames also set up a daily telephone call with the Duke's doctor. At 6.00 p.m. every evening, Soames rang the doctor to ask, 'And how is our friend today?'

The Duke was still alive on 15 May when the Queen arrived for her four-day stay. The aircraft of the Queen's Flight taxied to the appropriate place where President Pompidou and his wife were waiting on the tarmac. The door opened. And for a full two minutes nothing happened. The Queen was not ready. 'If they want me here all that much,' she said, 'they can wait a bit.'

On the first evening Pompidou entertained the Queen at Versailles, which was like a dream of its vanished royal splendours – dinner at the Palais du Grand Trianon, a ballet, and a reception in the Hall of Mirrors. The following day the Queen gave a dinner at the embassy, the tableware having been brought over from Buckingham Palace for the occasion. Christopher Ewart-Biggs, the minister at the embassy who had drafted the speeches for the Queen's Paris visit, was appalled at the Palace rewrite of her after-dinner speech. 'We sent to the Palace a speech for the Queen of England on a great occasion,' he complained. But what she read was 'something in the style of a dowager opening a conservative fête.' Having to read plodding speeches was a frequent complaint by Elizabeth II herself. She found her annual opening-of-Parliament speech prepared by the Government particularly heavy going. 'This morning, I made the dullest and most boring speech of my life,' she told Annigoni in 1969. 'It dealt with such dry material. One tries to put a little expression into one's voice, but it's not humanly possible to produce anything remotely lively.'

The embassy also noted that she was not listening to other dignitaries' speeches made to her. When this was pointed out to Adeane he dared not tell her, and said he was 'thinking of speaking to the Queen Mother [about it].' After dinner, the party set off for the Champ-de-Mars to watch an equestrian performance – in the relentless rain – by the Cadre Noir of the French Republican Guard.

The following day the Queen went south to meet Prince Charles, who was now in the Navy and whose ship was at Toulouse. On the return trip she stopped at a country château for tea with a French aristocratic family, who were surprised to have been supplied in advance with a case of Malvern Water with which to make the brew. That afternoon, the Queen, Prince Philip and Prince Charles called on the Duke of Windsor at his house on the Bois de Boulogne. The Duke, who had insisted on receiving the Queen sitting up, fully clothed, was seated on an armchair in the sitting room which separated his bedroom from that of the Duchess. He wore a double-breasted blue blazer, shirt and tie with the famous Windsor knot at the throat. Emerging from the back of his shirt collar was a long tube attached to the Duke's fluid flasks, which were concealed behind a screen near where he was sitting. The Queen was received by Wallis, who took her up to the Duke alone and then left them together. When she entered, the Duke stood up with great difficulty and slowly bowed to his niece.

The conversation was stilted, and for the most part limited to small talk. They discussed the Queen's Paris visit, and the race meeting she had attended at Longchamps. However, the Duke did ask for, and received, Elizabeth's reassurance that both he and his wife would be buried at the family burial plot at Frogmore. Philip and Charles then entered and the talk turned to the Royal Navy. But the meeting had sapped what little energy the Duke could muster, and when his visitors rose to leave, he seemed very moved, but was unable to stand up.

The Queen herself was frowning her inscrutable frown when she left the Windsors. It must have been clear that – barring a very large miracle – she would not see him alive again. The man responsible for radically changing her destiny was on his deathbed. Twelve days later he would be dead. Perhaps she had thought it ironic that the frail old man in the elegant, very French drawing room should be suffering from the same disease that had struck down her father twenty years earlier. Or possibly the visit had revived dim memories of an uncle whose handsome, youthful presence had filled her nursery. Practical woman that she was, she could have been worrying about the problems of the funeral. But she had little time to contemplate the sadness of the occasion. The visit had to go on. At the French president's dinner in her honour that evening, she was all smiles. The French did not want to see a gloomy Queen.

The subsequent embassy report to the Foreign Office in London captured the essence and purpose of the Queen's visit. The Queen, it said, was for the French exactly what they wanted and expected of her, 'a figure of magic and fascination, of royal mystique that is at the same time miraculously human. It was this that enabled the visit to accomplish its essential political purpose.' To the Queen, it seemed, it was all in a day's work. It did not make her any fonder of the French. Visiting London shortly afterwards, the French Foreign Minister Maurice Schumann, who spoke perfect English, addressed her in French. Some time later, the new French ambassador, also an English-speaker, did the same. She concluded that it was deliberate policy not to speak English, and it annoyed her. And when Ewart-Biggs mentioned in the course of a later audience that he thought Paris was beautiful, she said, was it? All she had seen was the British embassy and the Elysée Palace. From the audience, Ewart-Biggs 'got the strong impression that . . . the French [were] not very close to her heart.'

The British flags had hardly been taken down from the streets of Paris when Dutch flags were put up for the visit of Queen Juliana on 28 June. After the city's ecstatic welcome for Elizabeth II its reception for the Dutch queen was cold beer. As the Dutch royal visit had been scheduled first, Juliana was said to have let Elizabeth know how much she resented being upstaged. Moreover, it was not the first time that the royal houses of Britain and the Netherlands had found themselves with conflicting visit schedules. In 1957, the White House had to choose between inviting Queen Elizabeth II or Queen Juliana, and chose the former.

It was left to Pompidou's successor, President Valéry Giscard d'Estaing, to make the return state visit to Britain. The Queen, Ewart-Biggs observed, 'showed little enthusiasm for Giscard' and found the visit a tiresome experience from arrangement to conclusion. In May 1973, she complained to a visitor about how difficult the French president was being about his schedule, first suggesting a visit to Scotland, and then changing his mind. Giscard suggested making an evening arrival in London by helicopter, but the Queen, whose dislike for helicopters was well known, vetoed the idea. Then, at Giscard's dinner in her honour at the French embassy, she asked for a window to be partially opened because the room was hot. But with a Frenchman's fear of *courants d'air* – draughts – the French president had ordered it closed again.

The Duke of Windsor died on 28 May, twelve days after the Queen's visit, and an aircraft of the Royal Air Force was dispatched to Paris to transport the former king's body to Britain for the funeral. Wallis was supposed to accompany the coffin, but the flight was made without her. At the last minute, she had collapsed under the strain of her intense grief – compounded by her apprehension at having to confront the whole royal family without her husband. The Paris embassy was instructed to approach her with a personal message from the Queen that another plane would be sent to bring her to the funeral – a gesture that was made after Mountbatten's warning to the Palace that if Wallis missed the funeral, 'the impact on public opinion here would be disastrous.'

The royal family seemed determined to bury the Duke with as little fuss as they could get away with – perhaps partly to avoid being accused of hypocrisy. Unable to praise him, the Queen and her family said nothing. But the BBC told Mountbatten, whom they asked to broadcast a tribute to his dead cousin, that both the President of France and the President of the United States had released statements, and the royal family's silence was becoming embarrassing. When Mountbatten sought Palace approval, the Queen's first reaction was negative. The royal family would not break their silence, she said. When Mountbatten rehearsed the

BBC's arguments, she finally agreed provided – as Mountbatten put it – 'I spoke about him in a balanced way.' Mountbatten took this to mean that he should be sparing in his praise of the man, and critical of his decision to abdicate.

Mountbatten was also on hand to greet the Duchess when she arrived in London, frail but controlled. 'Your sister-in-law will receive you with open arms,' he said to reassure her as they drove to Buckingham Palace. 'She is so deeply sorry for you in your present grief and remembers what she felt like when her husband died.' She was taken to see her dead husband lying in state in St George's Chapel, Windsor. An officer of the Guards in full dress stood at each corner of the bier. (When King George V died, princes of the royal house – including the Duke of Windsor – had stood guard.) Wallis, heavily veiled, stood gazing at the coffin and said, almost in a whisper, 'He was my entire life. I can't begin to think what I am going to do without him, he gave up so much for me and now he has gone. I always hoped that I would die before him.'

At the funeral service on 5 June, Wallis Simpson, the woman who had brought shame and tragedy to the Royal House of Windsor, sat beside three generations of Windsor women: the Queen, the Queen Mother and Princess Anne. Then came lunch in the castle. The Queen stood in the family drawing room looking through a crack in the open door, which she would occasionally open to call in a passing guest. 'I'm trying to avoid too many people coming in here,' she told one relation as she ushered him in, 'the rest are going down to the Green Drawing Room.'

In the House of Commons, the Government introduced a motion of condolence to the Queen on the death of her uncle. By prior arrangement with the Palace, it made no mention of the Duchess; and it was left to a backbencher to propose an amendment in which the House also offered condolences to the widow. Parliament did not adjourn on the day of the funeral of the former monarch. Two days earlier, the Trooping the Colour ceremony had also taken place as scheduled. The Queen had reluctantly been on the point of cancelling it. 'She realized what a disappointment this would be to all the troops on parade, and to the thousands of people who bought tickets, as it could hardly be laid on again later,' Mountbatten recalled. But he suggested turning it into a tribute to the Duke of Windsor, with the drums draped in black, officers in black armbands, and a special roll of drums in his memory. 'She thought that was a wonderful idea.'

XVI

The Queen Goes Walkabout

'**A**s you know, we have a wedding next week. My being here is the best possible arrangement for a happy family relationship.' So said Prince Philip in Perth, Australia, in the spring of 1973, while at home in London his daughter prepared for her nuptials. When a daughter was about to be married, he went on, the best place for a father to be was 'out of the way'. Her marriage to Mark Phillips was the natural outcome of their consuming interest in riding and especially eventing. An accomplished rider, Mark, the son of a Wiltshire farmer, was a member of the British Olympic team in 1972. No less so, Anne had won the European championship the previous year on Doublet, a horse originally bred by the Queen as a polo pony for her husband.

Off his horse, this young, good-looking officer was unassuming and easygoing. Caught in the full panoply and ceremonial of a royal wedding, he was somewhat overwhelmed. Though designated a 'family' rather than a state occasion, which meant that the Queen was footing the £140,000 bill, the wedding had all the accoutrements of a major royal event – the state coach, the Household Cavalry, sixteen trumpeters, the military bands and, of course, the cheering crowds. On what was for Mark the long walk from the altar to the Abbey door Anne asked him a number of times if he was all right, and as they emerged into the open she told him, 'Be ready to acknowledge the crowds on the way back.' Mountbatten sneaked a look at the marriage register and was consoled to see that the bride's entry was Anne Mountbatten-Windsor.

At Buckingham Palace, the Queen rounded up the members of the family for the wedding photograph, and positioned them according to a chart prepared in advance. The wedding breakfast was a cheerful affair. The guests included Princess Grace of Monaco, who sat between Prince Charles and Mountbatten ('Anne had placed her there out of love for us both', wrote Mountbatten). Prince Philip began his speech, 'Unaccustomed as I am to public speaking,' which got a laugh. So he said, 'I will start again: Unaccustomed as I am to speaking at breakfast.' Mark's reply was spoken in such a low voice that a lot of guests could not hear what he said.

After the couple had lived for some time at Sandhurst, where Mark Phillips was an instructor, the Queen bought her daughter Gatcombe Park, in Gloucestershire, from Rab Butler for £485,000. 'The royal family, you know, drive a very hard bargain,' Rab was heard to say on more than one occasion. The Queen was prepared to make Mark Phillips the gift of a title, but – somewhat to her annoyance – Phillips, staunchly supported by his wife, preferred to remain a commoner.

As one royal marriage was launched, however, another was tossing on stormy seas. By 1972, Princess Margaret and her husband, Lord Snowdon, were estranged and leading separate lives. At first, Snowdon had opened up a new world of show business and media friends to her, and this appealed to the artistic side of her nature. There were dinners at their Kensington Palace apartment mixing the friends from her background with the likes of Peter Sellers, Sean Connery and Peter O'Toole. But Snowdon chafed at the constraints which made it hard for him to pursue the work he refused to see relegated to a pastime. On the other hand, Margaret had led too royal – and perhaps too sheltered – a life to allow her to mix easily in different worlds, some of which were less inclined to be reverential. Their disagreements became famous in the royal family. They even had different views on vacation homes. Margaret loved Les Jolies Eaux, her summer home on the Caribbean island of Mustique; 'Tony' Snowdon hated it. To the Queen, a divorce in the royal family, and so close to the throne, was unthinkable: her advice to her sister was to work out a *modus vivendi*. So, with their two small children – Viscount Linley and Lady Sarah Armstrong-Jones – the couple continued to live under the same roof amid persistent rumours of a break-up of their marriage.

Meanwhile, Mark Phillips may have got away with not accepting a peerage, but this did not absolve him from exposure to the rigours

261

of being a royal. As soon as the honeymoon was over, he and Princess Anne joined the Queen and Prince Philip on board *Britannia* bound for a visit to New Zealand. At rehearsals for the ship's concert – a regular feature on most royal yacht trips – he watched in astonishment as his mother-in-law gave members of her staff a demonstration of how to dance the haka, a Maori grass-skirt dance. Then she went off to consult the encyclopedia of New Zealand (no yacht should be without one!) for the correct words of the haka chant.

Royal tours are meticulously advanced by the Palace: a team usually consisting of an Assistant Secretary to the Queen, the Press Secretary and a member of the police security team, known as the Royal Protection Squad, visits the country in question and collects as much information as possible about each proposed event, and it is on the basis of this visit that the final schedule is worked out with the Queen and Prince Philip at Buckingham Palace. Despite the advance planning, things do go wrong, and the Queen has had some nasty shocks on her travels. One of the worst was the exhibition of 'land diving' she witnessed during this tour at Pentecost Island in the New Hebrides.

The Queen and the royal party watched from a platform as young men swarmed up to eighty-foot-high diving boards, attached a strong length of rope to each foot, and then – to a background of frenzied chanting from the crowd – leapt into the air as if they were diving into the sea, or a swimming pool. Beneath them, however, was a bank of soft ground: the carefully measured ropes, when fully stretched, were supposed to shorten their fall so that they just touched the ground. The third jump ended in disaster as both ropes broke and the man disappeared into the earth up to his shoulders. They pulled him out unconscious, and carried him quickly away, but no attempt was made to stop the jumping. As jump followed jump, Elizabeth watched with mounting apprehension, dreading having to witness an even worse, possibly fatal, disaster. But there were no further mishaps. She sent Prince Philip to enquire after the injured man. He was told the man had been hospitalized for a week. In fact, he died the next day.

Some surprises were less traumatic. Lord Mountbatten once visited Malacca with the Queen and Prince Philip when they watched two weddings: a traditional Malay wedding, and a traditional Chinese one. The Malay bride wore a magnificent dress full of gold brocade and embroidery. Both brides were attended by a professional marriage broker, an elderly woman, who helped to officiate the ceremony. The Queen, fascinated, asked to meet the newlyweds. In the course of the conversation one couple said they had been married for five years, and the other for two. They were merely re-enacting their nuptials for the Queen's benefit.

By now a new procedure had become a standard feature of all royal tours. The walkabout was first tried out in New Zealand in 1970 after much thought. When the Queen, after visiting a school in Christchurch, deliberately approached the delighted crowd and began slowly walking along chatting with individuals, she crossed a psychological barrier. Plunging into crowds was the style of politicians, not royalty. But the exercise in humanizing the Queen and her family begun with the television film *Royal Family* had gone into a new phase. William Heseltine's idea, walkabout – an Australian noun as in 'going walkabout' – was under discussion for some months at the Palace before the Queen agreed to try it. The New Zealand tour was chosen because it was thought to offer fewer security problems than tours to other countries.

The crowd outside the school had not been expecting to do more than glimpse the Queen at a distance. Seeing her close up, talking to individuals, generated a tremendous excitement. 'How long have you been waiting?' Elizabeth asked. 'Do you work here?' 'From Birmingham? Goodness, you are far away from home!' Children? School? Weather? The Queen and the people now knew what each other looked like, the sound of each other's voices, accents. They were suddenly real to each other. It took some time to register, but when children began standing in the crowd with posies to give to the Queen, the royal household knew the new idea had caught on and become firmly rooted.

When the Queen was in New Guinea, a political crisis at home forced her to cut short her trip and fly to London. The results of the 28 February 1974 general election had given Edward Heath's Tory government only 297 seats in the House of Commons out of its total of 635. Labour, with 301 seats, had a lead but not an overall majority. Instead of resigning, Heath dug in and attempted – without success – to remain in office by forming an alliance with the Liberal Party, led by Jeremy Thorpe. The Queen summoned him to the Palace and let him know that it was her interpretation of the constitution to call the leader of the single largest party in the new House – that is Harold Wilson – to try to form a government.

Wilson formed a minority government. The hypothetical question looming over the situation was what the Queen would do if Wilson asked for a follow-on election. Would she have been justified in refusing him a second dissolution of Parliament in the interests of national stability? In the absence of a written constitution, the issue had experts arguing about what her decision should be. But Wilson did not put the Queen to the test. He managed to continue until the autumn, when a second election gave him a small working majority.

The Queen had not succeeded in establishing a rapport with Wilson's predecessor, Edward Heath. He was a new breed of Tory politician with a middle-class background quite different from that of the party aristocrats she knew. Moreover, he was a bachelor with few social graces, and painfully shy with women. Paul Martin reported being told by Martin Charteris that 'Heath was rigid' during his weekly audiences. So, it may well have been a relief for the Queen to once again have to deal with Harold Wilson. They slipped easily into their old relationship. And although several prime ministers have stated that no alcohol is served during the Tuesday audience, a senior Downing Street official remembers Wilson returning from the Palace 'half cut because the Queen had wanted to go on drinking and gossiping.' One of the Queen's conversational gambits was to ask the Prime Minister whether he had seen a particular news item in the late edition of the London *Evening Standard*. Quite often he had not and, Wilson recalled, 'this small advantage used to please her.'

On one occasion, it was the Queen who had not read the *Evening Standard* and therefore had missed a story from Paris about President Giscard d'Estaing. This said that he was in the habit of cruising the streets of Paris at night in a non-government car looking for prostitutes. A week later, Wilson told her that he would be visiting Paris briefly for Common Market talks with the French president. 'Ho, ho,' said the Queen meaningfully, clearly remembering the Paris news story. Wilson had dinner with Giscard at the Elysée Palace, and then went back to the British embassy, where he was staying, and went straight to bed because, in his words, 'I was as sick as a dog.'

On his return he made his report to the Queen. 'How did it go?' she asked him. Wilson briefed her on his talks with the French president. 'And what about ho, ho?' she said. Wilson replied, 'Madam, there was no ho, ho.' He told her about feeling unwell after, or perhaps as a result of, his dinner, 'and she was terribly disappointed.'

That kind of saucy banter reflected a relaxed self-confidence in her ability to handle the burden of responsibility. We are a long way from the diffident girl who dealt with Anthony Eden and Macmillan. Asked by Wedgwood Benn, with his usual bluntness, 'What would happen [to the Queen] if you were knocked down by a bus?' Michael Adeane replied that he thought 'she could just about manage now.' It was a backhanded compliment at best, implying that she had progressed under his guidance. Adeane had then been her Private Secretary for more than a decade. But a whole string of realistic, sophisticated and experienced statesmen, politicians and diplomats were impressed by Elizabeth's grasp of facts, figures and ideas, even her ability to 'over-trump' them on occasion. Henry Kissinger, who was Secretary of State when she visited the United States for the 1976 bicentennial celebrations, summed up the feelings of a lot of Americans when he described her as 'a very interesting lady with a lot of savvy.'

The answer lay in her relentless application to the copious briefing papers which landed on her desk twice daily in the red leather boxes. She did not have her father's gift of a photographic memory, but she mastered briefs rapidly and was good at grasping essentials. Moreover, she had lost any youthful hesitancy to make her views and desires known. Roy Jenkins, the former Labour cabinet minister, visiting her in his capacity as President of the European Community, found her quite outspoken on some leading figures in the Community. 'Her Europeanism does not extend to an uncritical acceptance of the major European leaders,' he wrote. 'She got Giscard right, but underestimated Schmidt.'

She was not intimidated by senior figures in the Establishment. When Crossman was absent from a Privy Council, she relayed her strong objection through Adeane. At the next Privy Council, Crossman made a little explanation and half-apology. 'She didn't relent, she just listened.' In 1974, when Archbishop Ramsey retired, the Queen had to be prodded by the Duchess of Kent to give him a farewell lunch. 'It was a nice lunch,' Ramsey used to recall. 'The Duke of Edinburgh wasn't there, just the Queen and the corgis.' But he made the mistake of referring to new legislation he had successfully introduced, which restored to the Church of England the right to revise the liturgy, thereby reducing the state's latitude to intervene in Church affairs. The Queen had clearly not appreciated this reduction of her powers as head of the Established Church. 'I shouldn't have mentioned it,' Ramsey recalled. 'Her face went all governessy.'

Ramsey was made a peer on his retirement. The scandal would

have been too great had he not. Yet, although the honours system has long been a way of rewarding service and repaying favours done for the Prime Minister and his government or party, and the twice-annual Honours List was compiled by the Government, the Queen's approval was anything but a formality. She could question nominations, and even refuse them. In 1974, she raised an eyebrow at some of Wilson's nominees for honours, and especially his intention of granting a peerage to his personal assistant, Marcia Williams. Clearly believing that the Prime Minister had trivialized the institution of the peerage and the House of Lords by some of his nominations, she sent word that it was not too late for him to have second thoughts. But, to the Queen's annoyance, the Prime Minister was determined to ennoble Marcia Williams, who became Baroness Falkender. When Wilson retired as Prime Minister two years later, the Queen attended a farewell dinner at 10 Downing Street at which Lady Falkender was present. According to another senior Wilson staffer, the Queen said, 'Mr Wilson, I will, of course, speak to Lady Falkender if you want me to.'

Equally, the Queen sometimes overrode the Prime Minister's resistance to giving honours to individuals she considered to be deserving. When Noël Coward was seventy, she went to a birthday lunch given by the Queen Mother, gave him a cigarette case, and asked him whether he would 'accept Mr Wilson's offer of a knighthood.' Coward kissed her hand and 'said yes in a strangulated voice.' There had been no change in Wilson's view of Coward as a tax dodger, but the royal family, after years of broad hints that had no effect, had requested a knighthood for the playwright.

While the Queen and Prince Philip were in Indonesia they were shaken by the news from the other side of the world of an attempt to kidnap Princess Anne. It was the most serious attack the royal family had ever had to face, and it led to a sober reassessment of their security arrangements. The Princess and Mark Phillips were being driven to Buckingham Palace after a film première when a small car squeezed the royal limousine on to the pavement, forcing it to stop less than a hundred yards away from the Palace itself. Before anyone could do anything the driver had leapt out and opened fire on the Princess's car with a .22 calibre pistol. In quick succession, the attacker shot at point-blank range the Princess's detective, the Palace chauffeur, a passing policeman, and a journalist who stopped his taxi to aid the royal couple. There followed a frantic tug-of-war with the gunman trying to drag Princess Anne out of her car by one arm while her husband had hold of the other. What did he want? the Princess asked him coolly. The man replied, 'I'll get a couple of million for this.'

What Ian Ball, a twenty-six-year-old Englishman, got was a court sentence committing him indefinitely to a mental hospital. When police reinforcements arrived and captured Ball, he was found to be carrying a bizarre ransom note to the Queen demanding millions of pounds for the return of her daughter: he had apparently planned to leave it in the car. Miraculously, no-one was killed in the attempt.

It was five o'clock in the morning in Djakarta when Prince Philip was woken up to take his daughter's call, and she told him the story in her own laconic way. Once he had been reassured that the Princess was safe and well, he told the Queen about the incident. Typically, he made a joke about it, saying that he pitied the man who succeeded in kidnapping his feisty daughter. But as a result of the attempt the Queen agreed to an escalation of security around her and the members of her immediate family. Scotland Yard grouped the royal detectives into the Royal Protection Squad and they received training from the élite special forces unit, the Special Air Service (SAS).

The SAS were also given detailed plans of the internal arrangements of each royal residence: the position of the doors, windows, open fireplace, even the furniture; and royal homes were supposed never to be rearranged without advising the SAS. Knowing the exact layout of a particular room was obviously helpful in an eventual hostage situation. All the royal cars were fitted with electronic homing devices so that each vehicle's movements could be tracked at Scotland Yard from the moment it left Buckingham Palace. The days when the Queen could walk among her people protected only by the comforting presence of an unarmed detective were over.

She accepted the new strictures reluctantly and she enjoyed getting away from her escort whenever possible. Once, when Harold Wilson was spending the annual Prime Minister's weekend at Balmoral, she suggested they have tea with the Queen Mother at Glamis Castle, her family home. 'You don't need your detective, let me drive you over,' said the Queen, and they set off with Elizabeth at the wheel, and without their respective bodyguards – who, needless to say, followed at a discreet distance.

The Balmoral weekend was intended to bring the Queen and her Prime Minister together in a more informal setting than their weekly meetings at Buckingham Palace. Not that the meeting was free from ritual. Sometimes, the Queen took Wilson and his wife, Mary, to a little chalet in the rambling grounds of Balmoral for tea. On these occasions, she invariably brewed the tea and afterwards washed up the dishes. It was Elizabeth II's scaled down version of Queen Marie Antoinette's dairy farm at Versailles. More than one visiting Prime Minister found himself either a spectator or a participant in this domestic interlude, which Wilson recalled from his September 1975 Balmoral weekend: 'The Queen filled up the kettle and Mary helped her to lay the table. After a most agreeable tea, the Queen passed an apron to Mary, put on one herself and they both proceeded to wash up the crockery.'

Wilson chose this informal moment to advise the Queen that he intended to honour his previously declared intention to step down the following year midway through his term. He had announced his retirement plans during the 1974 general election campaign, but few people had taken him seriously at the time, perhaps including the Queen herself. Elizabeth's reply, Wilson said, left him 'with the impression that she had enjoyed our two-way seminars over the years and that I might still have second thoughts on the matter.' Wilson did not change his mind, and on 16 March 1976 he astonished the political world by resigning from office. The cascade of information began at 11.30 a.m. when he made his announcement in the Cabinet. By the afternoon, his departure and the appointment of James Callaghan as his successor dominated the news, and a brief statement from Buckingham Palace announcing the legal separation of Princess Margaret and her husband Lord Snowdon was hardly noticed.

The couple were parting as a result of irreconcilable differences. The Queen was 'naturally very sad,' said the announcement. 'There has been no pressure from the Queen on either Princess Margaret or Lord Snowdon to take a particular course.' There was no mention of divorce. Thanks to Wilson, the sixteen-year marriage which had been the subject of gossip and the butt of insider jokes for more than a decade had come to an end not with a media bang, but with a whisper.

When the Queen first approached Wilson regarding the marriage it was to obtain cabinet approval for a legal separation. By 1973, Margaret and Lord Snowdon's marriage had shifted from the public squabbling stage to estrangement, and they were leading separate lives. Snowdon had returned to his career and was a top photographer for *The Sunday Times*. A visit by the couple to the United States gave rise to speculation about a reconciliation, but it was short lived. Back in London, Margaret was seen in trendy night-clubs with different escorts, as was Snowdon.

The final break-up came when Snowdon opened his paper one morning and saw photographs of Margaret with an aspiring pop singer named Roddy Llewellyn, who was thirteen years her junior. Llewellyn had been one of her frequent companions for more than two years, but this was the first time they had been photographed together. Snowdon pressed for an end of the marriage. 'According to [Snowdon's] friends,' wrote Nigel Dempster, one of Margaret's better informed biographers, 'Roddy was the first of the Princess's lovers to get to him, and from that moment he was determined to get out of the marriage.' The Queen was advised that a legal separation now seemed in the royal family's best interests. Of course, divorce was a possibility. But divorce was always such a touchy subject with the Queen, it would need longer consideration.

In 1967, Elizabeth had given her consent to the divorce of her cousin, Lord Harewood, from his first wife Marion Stein, so that he could marry the Australian-born musician Patricia Tuckwell. But Harewood was eighteenth in line to the throne, Margaret was fifth. Moreover, following his divorce, Lord Harewood became a non-person as far as Buckingham Palace was concerned and was barred from the royal family's official functions, including the funeral of his uncle the Duke of Windsor. (Ironically, Lord Harewood's mother, the Princess Royal, had been the first member of the family to extend the hand of reconciliation to the former monarch, her brother, in 1937, and of all the Windsors had remained in closest touch with him throughout the rest of her life.) On the other hand, the emotional and practical implications of shutting out Princess Margaret in the same way Harewood had been shut out were considerable. For example, there was the question of whether Princess Margaret, as a divorced woman, would be able to continue to share the load of official commitments. If she was not, then the burden would be the greater on the Queen and the other members of the family.

Having obtained cabinet 'advice' on a separation, however, the Queen's first consideration was to lessen the impact of the announcement. This time, there was little danger of another explosion of what Noël Coward had called the 'pseudo-religious claptrap' of the Margaret–Townsend era. Social and moral attitudes had become more liberal since the 1950s, and the alarums and excursions of the past on that score were now viewed as archaic. Still, from the Palace's viewpoint, the less clamour the better.

This was when Harold Wilson came in. He urged the Queen to time the announcement for the morning of his resignation. That way, the media would have two competing major news stories on the same day and each would lessen the impact of the other. Ultimately, Buckingham Palace delayed release of the statement until the afternoon and Wilson's ploy worked almost too well. By the time the story of the forty-five-year-old Princess's irreconcilable parting from her husband surfaced, Wilson's 'surprise' resignation had gained so much momentum that the royal separation story received short shrift. The latest drama of Margaret's ill-starred personal life was an unwelcome fiftieth birthday present to her elder sister, but there was more to come.

The separation was still fresh in the memory when the Queen and Prince Philip joined the Americans in their bicentennial celebrations in July of that year. State Department confidential briefing papers to President Gerald Ford and the Kissingers warned that the separation had 'embarrassed the royal family' and that it and the Duke of Windsor's abdication 'are sensitive subjects for the Queen.'

The royal family did not, of course, have a monopoly on sensitive subjects to be avoided in conversation: the American president who had invited Elizabeth and Philip to the United States in the bicentennial year had resigned less than twelve months earlier in order to avoid possible impeachment following the Watergate scandal. The Queen did not need to be told that Richard Nixon's fall from grace was not a topic for polite conversation. All the same, her main speech in the United States did not ignore the divisions Watergate had created among Americans. 'The gift I would most value next year,' she declared, 'is that reconciliation should be found wherever it is needed.' The Queen had sailed to Philadelphia on *Britannia*, visited Washington and the University of Virginia, Monticello, rejoined the royal yacht at Newport, Rhode Island, and briefly set foot in New Jersey and New Hampshire. The last two states were hurriedly added to the schedule to give the trip a bicentennial focus. Elizabeth had thus visited seven of the original thirteen states, and this diverted attention from the fact that, despite earlier talk of it, she had not included California in her itinerary. The official word from the Palace to the Americans was that a western side-trip would have made the tour too tiring. But the fact that Nixon – her original host – had taken refuge in California following his resignation would have been an additional deterrent. By staying on the east coast, the Queen side-stepped the embarrassing question whether or not to receive the disgraced president.

In Washington for the first time since 1957, the Queen attended a White House dinner given by the Fords. As the Queen and Prince Philip sat with the President and his wife, Betty, in the second-floor living room having a pre-dinner drink, the lift door opened and Jack, the Fords' eighteen-year-old son burst in, still fiddling with the unfamiliar shirt-front studs of his rented evening tails. He had not been told that the royal couple had already arrived and stood there, mouth open, gaping awkwardly at the four of them. Elizabeth II turned to Betty Ford and smiled. 'I have one just like it at home,' she said. It was a reference to Prince Andrew, not known for his finesse. Guests at the dinner included the comedian Bob Hope, and Telly Savalas, the television police detective. The latter's show *Kojak* was a royal favourite, and the Queen had asked to meet him. The entertainment included the highly popular couple The Captain and Tennille. They sang something called 'The Muskrat Love Song'. 'Many deemed it unsuitable entertainment for Queen Elizabeth,' Betty Ford was to comment later, 'although she seemed to enjoy it thoroughly.'

In Britain, the embarrassing gossip about Princess Margaret refused to die down – and no wonder. Once the separation from her photographer husband was announced, Princess Margaret's friendship with Roddy Llewellyn became more visible. Photographs appeared of the Princess and Llewellyn – complete with long blond hair and trendy clothes – at her house on Mustique. The Queen refused to receive her sister's boyfriend at any of the royal residences, but when she and Prince Philip visited Margaret on her island in 1977, Llewellyn was with the Princess and a meeting was inevitable. The gossip about her affair caused concern in the royal family. 'The Princess Margaret problem continues to receive attention,' noted Paul Martin, Canada's well-informed High Commissioner in London. '[The Duke of] Edinburgh has spoken within family circles quite strongly. The Queen is said to have urged her sister to modify her private role ... Private affairs belong privately. If, however, the public person's private affairs become a matter of public concern, then they form part of the public judgement, whether one likes it or not.'

Martin was referring to the stories of a family conference at Windsor at which Prince Philip bluntly confronted the Princess with the consequences of her behaviour. The stories about her, he said, had a knock-on effect and were harming the Queen. Elizabeth herself spent sleepless nights pondering the problem in search of a solution that would not unduly penalize her sister. Margaret's defence was that things looked worse because she was not divorced from Snowdon. She had been put at a tremendous disadvantage. Margaret's friends – according to one of her biographers – were also worried about her drinking. On 10 April 1978, she went into hospital in London where she was found to be suffering from gastro-enteritis and alcoholic hepatitis. The same week her divorce from Lord Snowdon was granted, with the Queen's consent. As soon as he was free to do so, Snowdon married Lucy Lindsay-Hogg, a BBC television producer, but there was a widely held belief that Margaret had promised not to remarry for a number of years.

In one of those ironic juxtapositions of the public façade and private tensions, 'the Princess Margaret problem' had unfolded against a background of Commonwealth-wide celebrations marking the Silver Jubilee of Elizabeth II's accession, in which the Queen chose to stress her attachment to family values whenever possible. When Mountbatten asked her why she had looked so cross and worried as she knelt beside her husband at the Jubilee thanksgiving service at St Paul's the answer was probably already obvious to him. But the Queen made light of it, saying that she was thinking 'how awful it would be' if Idi Amin, the oversize, despotic President of Uganda, were to reverse his initial refusal to join the Commonwealth heads at the service and suddenly appear. In that eventuality, she told Mountbatten, she had decided that she would take the City of London's pearl-handled sword, which was lying on a velvet-covered table in front of her, and 'hit him hard over the head with it.'

The Jubilee produced a vast outpouring of public affection for the Queen. Letters of loyal greetings arrived at Buckingham Palace by the sackful. Following the thanksgiving service, the Queen and Prince Philip walked through the packed streets to the nearby Guildhall for lunch with the City authorities. Out of the cold and rain, a great roar went up when she appeared, and suddenly she smiled. 'Oh dear, did you get awfully wet?' she asked solicitously. When they said, 'Yes, but it was well worth it to see you!' she threw back her head and laughed. One secretary told her, 'We've come here because we love you.' To which the Queen replied, 'I can feel it, and it means so much to me.' Faced with such warmth and affection from a normally undemonstrative people, her only sign of being deeply affected was a little tremor in her neck.

In the Commonwealth, there were scattered signs of a more sceptical attitude. In Sydney, Australia, there were Aborigine protesters, a few 'Queen Go Home' placards (where in the past there had been none), and eggs thrown at her car by left-wing radicals. In Canada, there was the opposition of French separatists, whose party had in 1976 for the first time won control of the provincial government, and also Prime Minister Pierre Trudeau's plans to amend the Canadian constitution to remove the last traces of dependence on the British parliament. In the process 'all power and authorities' belonging to the sovereign as Queen of Canada were transferred to the Governor-General, her representative in Ottawa – but now appointed by the Canadian government.

The Queen had made it plain to Trudeau that she was not anxious to be divested of her powers, which included procedural functions such as signing Canadian ambassadorial appointments and signifying agreement to the appointment of foreign ambassadors to Canada. Caught in the crossfire between Buckingham Palace and Ottawa, Paul Martin observed, 'The Queen is a politely determined woman who doesn't easily conform against her views as to what should be done.' The proposal might have run into less opposition had it come from a Canadian premier who was more popular at Buckingham Palace. Based on some of his public utterances, the Queen was worried that the Crown 'had little meaning for him.' Not only was his commitment in some question, so was his behaviour. His bursts of flamboyance brought frowns of disapproval from the Palace. The Queen was not present when he slid down the highly polished banister at Windsor Castle, but she had read about it in the press.

In an attempt to overcome royal objections, Trudeau flew to London to explain his government's proposed changes in person, which he did at lunch with the Queen and Prince Philip. His main point was that the change did not involve any alteration in her status as Queen of Canada and sovereign. On the contrary, the role, status and fact of the monarchy would be enshrined for the first time in Canada's statutes. The Queen seemed reassured, but then he upset her again by revealing to her, out of the blue, his choice as the new Governor-General. The Queen did not like to be taken by surprise.

The Commonwealth picture was not all setbacks, however. The Queen registered a personal triumph in the successful Commonwealth heads of government conference in the Zambian capital of Lusaka in 1979. After fourteen years of white supremacist rule in

Rhodesia the African Commonwealth members were determined to force a showdown, and the advance talk was that the Africans were threatening to quit the Commonwealth if Britain remained unable or unwilling to achieve a settlement. With Rhodesia in the throes of a fierce civil war, the British Prime Minister had advised the Queen that it was too risky for her to attend the conference. The constant threat of what the Foreign Office referred to euphemistically as 'activity' made a royal visit extremely hazardous. But the Queen was extremely irritated by the Government's attempts to cancel her trip. When black nationalist guerrillas under Robert Mugabe and Joshua Nkomo stepped up their border activities in the days before the conference, and the Prime Minister again pressed the Queen not to come, a serious row blew up between Buckingham Palace and 10 Downing Street.

The message from the Palace was that it was not the Prime Minister's decision whether the head of the Commonwealth attended the conference. Elizabeth's role as comforter and counsellor at every Commonwealth Conference since 1973 was not going to be swept away because of a few terrorists. Not only were the Queen and Prince Philip going ahead with their trip as scheduled, they were taking Prince Andrew. Downing Street's pressure was doubly irksome to the Queen because the newly elected Prime Minister seemed not to appreciate Elizabeth II's special attachment to the Commonwealth and her profound knowledge of its workings and personalities. Moreover, the Prime Minister who was advising the Queen to stay at home was herself a woman. Relations between the Queen and Margaret Thatcher had not got off to a particularly good start.

Mrs Thatcher was predisposed to a solution, but her reputation among the African states was not calculated to create a suitable climate for negotiation. On the contrary, what was known of her character and what had been read into her speeches almost guaranteed that the talks would break down. Into this tense setting stepped the Queen the day before the conference opened and immediately began a series of private meetings with the key Commonwealth leaders, notably Kenneth Kaunda, the President of Zambia, and President Julius Nyerere of Tanzania. Was this the way, she said, to start a conference, with all the acrimony and threats of a walkout? The thing to do was to go on talking. The government-controlled Zambian press became less aggressive almost overnight, and an agreement was cobbled together which led to Rhodesia becoming Zimbabwe.

The deal was Thatcher's deal, but the Queen used the full weight of her experience and influence with African leaders to warn them not to go too far. Although, as usual, she attended none of the conference sessions, by its end she had had a tête-à-tête with every one of the forty or so leaders present. Sir Shridath Surendranath (Sonny) Ramphal, the Secretary General of the Commonwealth, said, 'She has a way of knocking people's heads together without appearing to do so.' Possibly her part grew in the telling, but the Queen herself was not unaware that she had helped avert a serious crisis. When Paul Martin saw her nearly three months after her return, she 'spoke of Lusaka and cleverly injected the importance of the Crown in that situation,' he wrote. 'She didn't minimize her contribution in outlining her conversations with the various prime ministers at luncheons and similar gatherings. She had talked quite frankly to them.' Dealing with the Commonwealth, the Queen was in her element: British prime ministers tended to regard their government's institutional commitment to a multi-racial cluster of Third World countries as a bit of a nuisance. For the Queen the Commonwealth was an important extension of her influence beyond the United Kingdom. She had known many of the leading figures since her accession – longer than her British prime ministers, in some cases – and she identified with it. 'What holds the Commonwealth together?' Prince Charles asked a Commonwealth diplomat, and before the latter could reply, he said, 'The Queen.' And there is no reason to believe that Elizabeth II herself thought differently.

The Queen returned to London on 5 August and went straight to Balmoral for her annual Scottish holiday. She had cause to be satisfied with her African excursion, which, besides Zambia, had taken her to Malawi, Botswana, Kenya and Tanzania. There were many memories to savour, and typically, there was much amusement over a remark she had heard one African chief whispering to another as she moved along the presentation line-up, 'My God, the Queen is a woman.'

But on 27 August the laughter faded as tragedy struck the family. The Queen was told that Dickie Mountbatten had died in Sligo, Ireland: an IRA terrorist bomb blew up his fishing boat, also causing the death of one of his twin grandsons, his son-in-law's mother, Lady Brabourne, and a young Irish boat boy.

This time it was the Queen who broke the news to her husband, just as he had broken the news of her father's death on the banks of the Sagana River. Like her parents, Elizabeth had once been somewhat suspicious of Mountbatten, but she had come to admire his drive and buoyant spirit. She listened to his advice, and entrusted him with delicate missions. Philip was deeply shaken by the death of his uncle, who was also his friend – and above all a father figure who had seen him through the insecurity of the early years. Without Dickie Mountbatten's strong backing and encouragement his initiation into the House of Windsor (assuming it would have taken place at all) would have been tougher and his position as consort harder.

Charles was devastated. His 'honorary grandfather' had been his guide and mentor, and a sympathetic counterweight to his domineering father. On the day of the scheduled state funeral according to Mountbatten's own directions, the family had met beforehand at Broadlands, and it was clear that Charles was in an emotional state. The story goes that Prince Philip began to lecture his grief-stricken son, and expressing his disappointment at Charles's decision to leave the Navy, which he had done two years earlier. It has been said that a row developed between father and son in which Charles broke down and wept, and the belief was that Prince Philip had forced the fight deliberately in an attempt to avoid Charles breaking down in public.

Thousands of people lined the streets to see plumed helmets and veterans' medals glitter as the funeral procession of perhaps the greatest of Britain's pro-consuls, christened in the arms of Queen Victoria but very much a twentieth-century man, moved to muffled drumbeats. At the service in Westminster Abbey, Charles spoke a poignant tribute to his great-uncle: 'I adored him . . . I still cannot believe that I am standing here delivering an address about a man who, to me, always seemed reassuringly indestructible.'

In the train carrying the coffin to Broadlands, there was a reversal of the usual roles; it was the Queen, sitting opposite her husband, who kept up a light, sensitive patter of conversation so that the family would not give way to grief while there was a crowd watching on the platform.

Mountbatten's assassination left Prince Charles bereft, disconsolate and confused. There was no-one now in whom he could confide: with whom to discuss his aspirations and ideas, as he could not with his father whose outlook on life was so different from his own, or his mother, burdened by her many responsibilities. One of the two girls who attended lessons at Buckingham Palace with Princess Anne recalled that the Queen never came to the Palace schoolroom. 'If she wanted to know how we were getting on she would send for our notebooks.' It was no different with Charles: the Queen kept the same distance during his school days. His father was a major influence, but not always a happy one. In his desire to mould a son of a different temperament into his own image, Philip sometimes did little more than undermine Charles's emerging self-confidence. It was his 'honorary grandfather' who filled the emotional void.

Somehow, Mountbatten was always there when needed – whether it was to play on the beach with a small boy in Malta, or to deputize for Prince Philip when Charles graduated from naval basic training, having come top of his year in navigation and seamanship. As a schoolboy, Charles looked forward to visiting Broadlands, where the atmosphere was cheerful. Buckingham Palace could sometimes be tense, and was always formal. And as he grew older he came to appreciate the Mountbatten home even more both as a refuge and as a stimulating and relaxing place to be. Prince Philip pressured, and sometimes goaded. Mountbatten advised and encouraged. There are ethnic overtones here. Prince Philip – perhaps unwittingly – had a lot of the traditional Mediterranean father figure in his makeup: stern, expecting the highest standards and unquestioning obedience from his children. Mountbatten had a more relaxed, Anglo-Saxon approach to the younger generation.

Charles greatly admired him, wished to emulate him, and desired deeply not to disappoint him. Mountbatten saw Charles's potential, but he also saw his faults. He had detected in him a stubborn streak. He felt it could develop into an unwelcome trait of selfishness and thoughtlessness, and warned him of the danger of ending up a carbon copy of his Great Uncle David. But there were also serious discussions, in which Mountbatten listened to Charles's ideas – something few others seemed willing to do. In this he was probably the single most important influence on the young Prince.

The loss could not have come at a worse time for Charles. At thirty-one he was beginning to realize fully the nature of his predicament. In his historic role he was living on the uncomfortable edge between the way things were, and the way they might become. Now he was alone: and it is reasonable to speculate that the loss of his closest confidant pushed him towards a decision he had so far avoided – to look for a wife.

XVII

A Bride for Charles

On 15 November 1977, there was an unusual occurrence at Buckingham Palace: the Queen was late for an appointment. An investiture was due to start in the state ballroom at eleven in the morning, and as the minutes ticked away the waiting recipients and their friends and families began muttering among themselves. Eventually, ten minutes late, the Queen entered the ballroom and announced, 'I apologize for being late, but I have just had a message from the hospital. My daughter has just given birth to a son.' There was a hesitant silence, and then, encouraged by the Lord Chamberlain, Lord Maclean, the assembly applauded. With the arrival of Peter Mark Andrew Phillips, Elizabeth was a grandmother at the age of fifty-one, and the succession was secure into the next generation, but only indirectly. Her oldest son, and the heir to the throne, showed no signs of settling down.

The Prince of Wales scarcely lacked contact with the opposite sex: in fact, he can be said to have had a roving eye and a zest for female companionship. But now that he was twenty-nine the Palace – if not himself – was giving thought to a suitable marriage. He was not unaware of his duty in that direction. Once, in a box at Covent Garden Opera House, he asked Lady Susan Hussey, the Queen's lady-in-waiting who had accompanied him, 'Will I ever be able to choose the girl I want to marry?' He was then in his teens and marriage seemed a distant prospect. Lady Susan, who had been unofficially assigned to help with the selection of suitable girls for him, gave his hand a comforting pat and said, 'We'll see.' The real answer was, of course, that it depended on whom he chose. His natural charm and good looks, as well as who he was, meant that young women were never in short supply, but not all would be described as suitable choices for marriage.

His women friends came in two categories: the marriageable daughters of leading English families, and the ones who raised Palace eyebrows. The former included Lady Jane Wellesley, whose father is the Duke of Wellington; Amanda Knatchbull, Lord Mountbatten's granddaughter; Victoria Legge-Bourke, a school friend of his sister's; and Camilla Shand. Their relationship ranged variously from friendship to something more intimate. At least one high-born young woman with whom he discussed marriage declined, refusing to pay the inevitable price in loss of personal freedom. The other group included women from many walks of life encountered in the course of his travels as a naval officer, on royal visits, on the international polo circuit, and elsewhere. This mixture was in evidence in his two guests at the dinner for sixty given by his mother at Windsor Castle to mark the Queen Mother's seventy-fifth birthday. On one side of him sat Amanda Knatchbull, and on the other a glamorous young starlet named Tanya George. When Charles visited Atlanta in 1977, President Jimmy Carter arranged for a young Georgia girl to be included among the guests at a small reception given by the Governor. In an ecstatic letter to Carter, she mentioned talking to the Prince over brandy until three in the morning. 'The Prince's equerry insisted that I let him know when my plans for a trip to Europe are finalized,' she went on.

Inevitably, the royal family's view of Charles's bachelor life was conditioned by the memory of his great uncle the Duke of Windsor, who was held up to the young Prince as a dire example of the sticky end reserved for those who persist in leading a profligate life. 'I thought you were beginning on the downward slope which wrecked your Uncle David's life and led to his disgraceful abdication and futile life for ever after,' Mountbatten admonished him after an escapade in the West Indies.

In 1978, in Deauville, France, Charles met a woman at a polo tournament who influenced many of his attitudes. A striking former actress, she was ten years Charles's senior. In a Mayfair attic she introduced him to her Indian guru, Master Chiran Singh, with whom Charles spent an hour discussing Christianity and the Bible. She half converted him to vegetarianism and claimed that he temporarily stopped hunting and fishing. Their relationship was kept quiet from the press, and the family did not acknowledge her existence. Once on a weekend at Windsor when the Queen and Prince Philip were in residence, Charles and his friend had dinner in the seclusion of his small former nursery – served by a footman in breeches.

But the Queen had her own sources of information on her son's activities and – regardless of their durability or lack of it – the alarm bells that friendships of this kind must have set off in the royal family can only be imagined. One November afternoon, Charles was entertaining the same woman in his rooms at Buckingham Palace, when his valet Stephen Barry entered with the message that the Queen was unwell and had cancelled her scheduled dinner with him. Charles was clearly upset at this last-minute cancellation, which seemed to be a message of disapproval. Shortly afterwards, the friendship waned.

In 1980, when Charles was thirty-two, out of the Navy, and still very much a bachelor, the royal family – apparently increasingly nervous about the Duke of Windsor's ghost – took a determined hand in the search for a future queen. The field of European royalty was considered, but the list of possibles quickly narrowed down to Princess Marie-Astrid, daughter of the Grand Duke of Luxembourg. A small cabinet committee was formed under the chairmanship of the new Conservative Prime Minister, Margaret Thatcher, to consider the implications of the Prince of Wales marrying a Roman Catholic princess, and the extreme anti-Catholicism displayed by the Prime Minister suggested that its response would not have been enthusiastic.

Moreover, the Queen Mother was in favour of the Prince of Wales finding a wife in the United Kingdom. She had herself been a singular exception – and a singularly successful one – to the practice of royal sons and daughters marrying into the royal houses of Europe. What was more, with the help of her longtime lady-in-waiting and friend, Ruth, Lady Fermoy, she had a suitable candidate.

Lady Diana Spencer was the twenty-year-old third daughter of the eighth Earl Spencer. In a sense, she was the girl next door: her family home, Park House, less than half a mile from Sandringham, had a swimming pool in which the younger royals used to frolic. Not Charles, though. He was already at Gordonstoun while Diana was still in her pram. In a match inspired – if not orchestrated – by the Queen Mother a number of people conspired to bring Charles and Diana together. They first met in Silver Jubilee year, by which time the Spencers had moved to the family house at Althorp in Northamptonshire and Charles was invited by her sisters to shoot. Here Charles and Diana agreed they had met each other for the first time, 'in a ploughed field.'

The combination of Diana Spencer's magic, Charles's own romanticism, plus the influence of his grandmother, for whom he had a great affection and whose judgement he trusted, eventually led to an engagement being announced on 24 February 1981. The Queen had been very much on the sidelines of the courtship. Whatever she felt about Diana as a wife for her son, it was ironic that Charles's choice should fall on the child of divorced parents. Earl Spencer (then Viscount Althorp) had been divorced by his wife when Diana was six – and divorced very messily at that. In the wake of Princess Margaret's divorce some of the royal strictures were having to be rethought. But the Queen's personal distaste for divorce was well known, and she could not have derived much comfort from admitting more of it into the family.

Elizabeth was also noticeably out of the picture in the euphoric days of the announcement and Diana's first captivating public appearance at Prince Charles's side. This was seen as a desire on her part to leave the limelight to her son and his future bride. Nevertheless, some people who saw it at first hand felt that the Queen warmed to Lady Diana Spencer rather slowly. One day, shortly before the marriage, the Queen produced the key to the jewel room at Buckingham Palace, gave it to Lady Diana, and asked her to pick her own wedding gift. It was not the most personal way of choosing a gift for her future daughter-in-law; however the Queen was said to have also given them a more domestic gift later.

But the Queen would shortly face a trauma of her own – what looked like an assassination attempt while she rode to her birthday Trooping the Colour the month before the royal wedding. Dressed in the scarlet uniform of the Coldstream Guards, she was riding erect on Burmese. Behind her rode Prince Charles and Prince Philip, trotting into the narrow approach to Horse Guards Parade as the bands played military marches and the crowds sat in tiers of silent anticipation. Suddenly, the Queen saw, ten feet away, a man raise a black revolver and point it at her, and – as she told the royal family afterwards – the realization suddenly came to her that she was to be the target of an assassination attempt. Nobody rode in front of her or beside her. Never in her life had she seemed so close to death. There were six shots, two spaced and the rest bunched. Her horse shied and tossed its head. The Queen, though pale, kept steady as they were fired.

She knew she was alive, but 'I didn't know what had happened to everyone behind.' As she turned to look at her son and husband, they had already ridden and closed in beside her. 'Are you all right?' they muttered. 'Fine,' said the Queen, calming her horse as the crowd vented its fury on seventeen-year-old Marcus Sarjeant – who had fired what turned out to be blank cartridges from a toy pistol – as he was taken away by police. There was a reassuring smile from Philip, a pat for Burmese, as the Queen made it clear that the parade would go on. Ironically, a hundred yards away several hundred of her crack troops were waiting in parade formation. When the Queen Mother heard the news she was so shaken, she stumbled and hurt her leg badly on a step. As she rode past the balcony overlooking the parade ground where her mother and other members of her anxious family were watching, the Queen gave a slight wave and a reassuring smile. At no point had her face betrayed the slightest hint of the fear and distress she must surely have felt.

The following day was Sunday, and in the nation's Anglican churches the usual prayers for the Queen at the end of the service took on real meaning. Elizabeth was in the royal family pew at St George's Chapel at Windsor, where the Dean thanked God for her survival. The Queen's faith was – and remains – genuine, if straightforward and unquestioning. No other area of her responsibilities better reflected her watchfulness for any encroachment upon her prerogatives and her ultra-diligence in fulfilling her official obligations than her position as head of the Established Church. After the apparently unnerving experience of dealing with one eccentric intellectual Archbishop of Canterbury, she was said to have taken matters firmly into her own hands, and royal approval in the appointment of his two next successors was not the usual formality.

To follow Ramsey she picked the other extreme. Donald Coggan was a down-to-earth, practical cleric. As Archbishop of York, he was the senior Anglican prelate and – in the absence of an outstanding candidate – the obvious choice. But Paul Martin noted that 'most of those who were making private recommendations . . . had recommended another personality. It was the Queen herself who made the decision to appoint Coggan.' Or, as Ramsey once put it more colourfully, 'Against all advice, the Queen dug her little toes in and said "We'll have this one!" ' After the elaborate texture of Ramsey's mind, Coggan was good, plain velvet. But he was generally regarded in the Church as a caretaker archbishop and retired after only five years. It was said at the time that by the end even the Queen found him too gung-ho.

She also had a say in the choice of Robert Runcie, who was a man of an entirely different stamp. As a tank commander in the Scots Guards in the Second World War he was known throughout the regiment as 'Killer Runcie' because of his toughness in battle. As a churchman, however, his views were moderate, and this fact made him something less than an ideal candidate to Mrs Thatcher's Tory government. But the Queen wanted him, and it was Runcie, not Downing Street's choice, who was installed at Lambeth Palace, the Archbishop's official residence in South London.

In 1983, Elizabeth visited Exeter Cathedral and, raising her eyes from the hymn book, beheld a sight which aroused the royal anger. The Dean and the canons were wearing . . . scarlet cassocks. The Queen said nothing at the time, but shortly afterwards a letter arrived from Buckingham Palace conveying the Queen's displeasure and reminding the Exeter Cathedral Chapter that only the chaplains appointed to the royal household (and bearing such ancient titles as Chaplain of the Closet) and the clergy of Westminster Abbey and Canterbury Cathedral were entitled to wear scarlet. Accordingly, the Exeter Cathedral clergy was requested to change colour. Similar messages went to the cathedrals of Leicester, Ripon and Winchester, where the clergy was also found to be wearing scarlet cassocks.

As it turned out, the canons of Exeter and Ripon preferred to fight than switch. Both chapters unearthed documents indicating that the monarch had no right to tell them what to wear. The Dean of Ripon came up with a reference to the cathedral clergy in the fifteenth century wearing *bloodii* coloured cassocks: close enough to scarlet. The Queen was not impressed. She instructed the Lord Chamberlain and the Bishop of Bath and Wells to negotiate the change, and in a compromise agreement, reached after considerable resistance from the chapters involved, she consented to pay out of her own pocket for new cassocks for the Dean and clergy of each cathedral.

At the same time she was careful not to offend Anglican sensibilities. For example, she received the Revd Billy Graham, the American revivalist preacher, at Buckingham Palace on more than one occasion, and even invited him to preach for the royal family at Windsor. But then Graham – who attracted huge audiences on his English tours – invited her to one of his big public meetings in London. The approach was made through the American embassy, and the reply was that after consulting the Archbishop of Canterbury the Queen declined the invitation.

Prior to the Prince and Princess of Wales's visit to Rome in 1985, Charles had expressed an interest in attending mass celebrated by Pope John Paul II. Aside from his interest in the rite itself, Charles viewed his presence at mass as a gesture towards Christian unity. It took nine months of three-way discussions involving the Vatican, the Archbishop of Canterbury's office and the Prince of Wales's office, before attendance of the Pope's daily mass by Prince Charles and Princess Diana was finally pencilled into their Rome schedule. This is the mass the Pope celebrates for his staff and a handful of special guests at eight o'clock each morning in a small private chapel in the papal apartment. At Prince Charles's request the Home Office had supplied a ruling that the issue raised no constitutional complications, and it had even been established that the Church of Scotland had no objection. But Charles had reckoned without his mother's veto. Though the Anglican Church and Archbishop Runcie had given Charles's request full backing, when the Queen learned of it Buckingham Palace overruled Lambeth Palace. Elizabeth felt that the idea of the future head of the Established Church at mass, and in Rome, of all places, would not be well received by many English Protestants. Prudence before innovation: the mass was omitted from the Wales's programme.

The Queen's grim expression at the wedding of the Prince of Wales and Lady Diana Spencer on 29 July 1981 was attributed by members of her Court to aftershock, and it is easy to believe that the incident six weeks earlier had left some residue of anxiety about public exposure. And this was exposure: more than 600,000 lined the route from Buckingham Palace to St Paul's Cathedral, with the police on duty facing the crowd instead of the royal procession for the first time in history. The attempt on the Queen had added a frisson of danger to the general excitement, but nothing happened – except that an unknown twenty-year-old girl instantly found a place in the affections of the nation. 'Here is the stuff that fairy tales are made of,' said the Archbishop of Canterbury, Dr Robert Runcie, in his sermon during the service. He had captured the essence of the moment.

But the Queen's expression – the mouth a thin, stretched line, the severe eyes, the brows knit in a slight frown – was also her family wedding face. The one that stops her showing emotion when the young bride pledges her troth to 'Philip Charles Arthur George', in her nervousness transposing her husband's first two names, and when the bridegroom endows his bride with 'thy worldly goods' instead of his own. Or when the bride sinks into a graceful curtsy in front of her on the way out of the cathedral on her new husband's arm, the future king and queen of the United Kingdom. The Queen stood perfectly still. She was looking at her past and her future. Whatever anxiety the royal family might have had over Charles's bachelor life, it was now a closed chapter. There was no mistaking the couple's happy glow. Charles had fulfilled the first of his dynastic obligations with flying colours: there seemed little likelihood that he would shirk the second, which was to produce, as the saying went, 'an heir and a spare'.

The wedding had been very much his show: his choice of St Paul's was partly so that he could turn the marriage service into a splendid musical event, with three orchestras, a famous choir, and the equally famous soprano Kiri te Kanawa to sing the solos. Hardly the kind of musical scope his mother would have considered. It was his idea – enthusiastically endorsed by his bride – that she did not promise to 'obey'. The traditional appearance on the Buckingham Palace balcony was also in a sense his show, even though he and his bride were surrounded by the Queen and the family. When the crowd that packed the Mall shouted, 'Kiss her!' the Prince of Wales gave his wife a lingering kiss. The other royals looked on incredulously. No-one had ever before gone further than the marionette-like regal wave.

Yet for all the euphoria, the wedding also produced a couple of instances of the Queen's hidebound rigidity, or at least her inability always to countermand royal protocol when it seemed counterproductive. Because it was a family wedding, and not a state occasion, royal guests were invited to the wedding breakfast, but foreign heads of state and of government, including Nancy Reagan, who was representing the President, were given lunch by the Prime Minister, Margaret Thatcher. This segregation of royals and mere commoners was, of course, announced in advance, causing some foreign governments to downgrade the level of their delegations because of what they understandably saw as an implied snub.

King Juan Carlos of Spain also took it as a snub when the Palace announced that the newlyweds would be flying directly to Gibraltar to board the royal yacht *Britannia* for their Mediterranean honeymoon cruise. The idea was to avoid three days at sea in uncertain Atlantic weather conditions, but the decision created a chill between the royal houses of Britain and Spain, because of the historic ownership dispute over Gibraltar.

Juan Carlos, who like Elizabeth was a great-great-grandson of Queen Victoria, had good family relations with his English cousins – good enough for him to telephone Prince Charles. The King made the point that given the national sensitivity over the Gibraltar issue, he did not think he and Queen Sophia could attend the wedding if the newly married couple went there immediately afterwards. As an alternative, the Spanish monarch suggested a diplomatic compromise: Charles and Diana would fly to Cadiz, on Spain's Atlantic coast, where he, Juan Carlos, would be on hand to welcome them, and then go on to Gibraltar. But Buckingham Palace balked at this proposal, with its implied recognition of a link between Spain and its tiny British appendage. So in a further call, Charles explained that the Foreign Office had advised him to stick to the original plan. The result was a boycott of the wedding by the Spanish royals, and much resentful press comment in Madrid.

The puzzle was that senior Foreign Office diplomats told Spanish officials – according to the latter – that the Palace had not sought official advice. On the contrary, the decision had been made within the royal household with little regard to its political implications.

The irony was that when, some years later, the two countries agreed to disagree over Gibraltar, a real friendship blossomed between the new Princess of Wales and the Spanish royal couple, and she and her two sons, Prince William and Prince Harry, would spend a few weeks each summer as their guests in Majorca. Moreover, the Princess's official visit to Spain in 1987 was one of her most successful foreign trips. But by then she had long since popped out of the chrysalis of her wedding dress and had become Princess of Wales, megastar.

Initially, Prince Charles and his wife moved into the former's bachelor apartment at Buckingham Palace because renovation work on their Kensington Palace apartment had not been completed. The Princess of Wales did not find it easy to start married life under the same roof as her mother-in-law. At first, she upset the protocol-minded Palace staff by doing things herself instead of asking the page or footman assigned to look after her, such as suddenly appearing in the Palace kitchens to ask for an apple or to request a cheeseburger or her favourite baked beans because she did not care for the Palace cuisine, which she found 'too French'. Having listened to several complaints from the royal chef, a figure of both bulk and power in the Palace, the Queen sent for the Princess of Wales and asked her to stay out of the kitchens. The Princess left the Queen's presence in tears like an admonished schoolgirl. Nor was that the only tearful exit, and the new Princess's distress became the subject of Palace staff jokes.

Yet it soon became clear that the arrival of Diana in the staid ranks of the royal family was like a gust of wind blowing through an open window. With her natural elegance and her refreshingly open manner she was as different from the rest of them as a visitor from Mars. Prince Philip would watch her with sardonic amusement, perhaps wondering where on earth the son of whom he could be so critical had found the good sense to make such a choice. The Queen regarded her with wry acceptance, the Queen Mother with quiet satisfaction (the Princess had spent some time living at Clarence House learning the ropes from her), and the rest of the family with varying degrees of wariness.

Following the most famous royal wedding in history, watched on television world wide by over 800 million, the explosion of her popularity was inevitable. Yet the extent of it caught the royals by surprise, nor was it entirely welcome, from several points of view. In a rare public display of temper, the Queen had shouted angrily, 'Go away, and leave us alone!' at reporters trailing after her shooting party at Sandringham hoping for a glimpse not of the monarch but of the new Princess. The royal family regarded Sandringham as their holiday home and off-limits to the press. Some months after the wedding, both the Queen and the Princess of Wales were at the same concert at the Royal Albert Hall. The photographers crowded round the new bride, virtually ignoring the Queen. 'Well, I think I might be going on upstairs,' Elizabeth told one photographer. 'They don't want me, do they?' It was said with good humour and it would be hard to pinpoint indications that the Queen felt any personal animus at having the limelight stolen from her by the younger woman, but their joint public appearances quickly stopped. Resentful or not, it was not good policy for the Queen to be seen constantly in her daughter-in-law's shadow.

In December the Princess of Wales was pregnant, and the press's Dianamania showed no signs of abating. In February, two Fleet Street tabloids published a photograph of Diana on a beach in the Bahamas. Taken from a distance with a telephoto lens, it showed the Princess in a bikini – and very pregnant. When the

Queen's Press Secretary, Michael Shea, protested to the two papers that the Queen was 'very, very upset' both papers published a tongue-in-cheek apology ('We thought our readers would want to share her joy.'). Clearly, the time had come for action.

Elizabeth instructed Shea to summon the editors of the main London newspapers and television companies to Buckingham Palace and to read them the riot act. It was a highly unusual step, so unusual that when the twenty-one editors gathered in the white and gold 1844 Room, so called because of its occupation that year by Tsar Nicholas of Russia, they recalled that such a gathering had not been convened for twenty-five years. The Queen, Shea told them, was worried about the invasion of the royal family's privacy: the Princess of Wales in particular felt beleaguered. Citing the most recent offence from that very morning's tabloid newspapers – a photograph of the Princess of Wales in jeans leaving the local village shop near her country home in Gloucestershire, having bought sweets – as an example, he said she was increasingly despondent at the idea that nowhere was she safe from photographers. She was having a difficult pregnancy, more than usually affected by morning sickness 'because of her [young] age and build,' and she was entitled to a private life.

Shea accepted the argument that Britain was living through an economic depression and stories about Diana provided happy, welcome relief. But if anything the Princess did was 'good news' for newspaper readers, the attention of the press was hardly good for her, and she was suffering from media claustrophobia. One of the editors present quoted Shea as saying, 'The people who loved and cared for her were growing anxious for her immediate happiness and her long-term attitude.'

There was a lengthy, awkward discussion about what was public and what was private, and the editors made vague commitments to exercise self-restraint, which they would have a hard time honouring in the highly competitive news business. Then they were led to the Carnarvon Room, hung with Goya pictures of Spanish guerrillas in the Peninsular War against Napoleon, and in came the Queen with Prince Andrew.

No-one mentioned the earlier conference, but the subject hung over the gathering like the dark clouds in the Goya paintings. The editor of *The Times* talked to the Queen about Leonid Brezhnev and Henry Kissinger's recently published account of what he said about peace when they were both hiding in a tree on a bear hunt. Then one tabloid editor, bolder than the rest, challenged the Queen point blank. 'If Lady Di wants to buy some sweets without being photographed, why doesn't she send a servant?' The semi-circle of editors froze, and then there was nervous laughter as the Queen said, smiling, 'What an extremely pompous man you are!' After that royal put-down no-one else dared raise the subject again.

Yet the editor had a point, though perhaps not very lucidly put, namely, that the Princess of Wales was not playing to the established royal rules. Neither the Queen, nor Prince Philip, nor the Prince of Wales, walked into a store to buy sweets: the sweets were bought for them. But if the Princess of Wales wanted to retain a degree of freedom of movement not normally associated with the royals, she was running the risk of greater media exposure. In effect, Diana wrote her own rules. As a shopper she possessed enthusiasm and drive. Accompanied only by her personal detective (who had the Duchy of Cornwall credit card), she continued to pop into large department stores to survey the latest fashions, and to try on clothes; she attended the sports day at her sons' school – and ran in the mothers' race; and she had lunch regularly at a trendy London restaurant with girlfriends.

Although the traditionalists in the royal household frowned on such goings-on, the Queen may have remembered her own interlude, living in Malta in the 1950s. However, that was a controlled environment; those were more respectful times. This was the London of predatory media. The ground was thick with lurking photographers with long-range lenses. In time, however, the Princess's version of the royal lifestyle gained acceptance and a *modus vivendi* evolved with the media. But the hysteria had not died down when Diana gave birth to her first son, Prince William Arthur Philip Louis of Wales, second in line to the throne, on 21 June 1982, ten and a half months after her spectacular wedding. Charles drove mother and child home from the hospital, to Kensington Palace where the other residents – their royal relatives – rushed out to welcome them waving handkerchiefs and towels. Then Princess Margaret, the Kents and everyone else went round to the Gloucesters, and Princess Margaret recalled, 'Never has there been such a party.'

In other respects, however, these were the worst of times. On a desolate cluster of wind-blown islands in the remote South Atlantic, Britain was fighting Argentina. The military junta in Buenos Aires had ordered the invasion of the Falklands, and

Margaret Thatcher had responded by ordering a task force to the area, at first with the intention of providing muscle for British diplomatic negotiations for an Argentinian withdrawal and only ultimately to retake the island by force.

One of the ships in the task force was the carrier HMS *Invincible*, with Prince Andrew on board as a twenty-two-year-old navy helicopter pilot. When the *Invincible* sailed from Portsmouth on 25 April, however, there was no indication that the second in line to the throne (as he then was) would be going into combat. For although the Navy sailed for the South Atlantic amid roars of approval from the House of Commons, the peace process was still going on with United States Secretary of State Alexander Haig as its principal agent, and various peace proposals were bouncing back and forth between Washington, London and Buenos Aires. Armed conflict between two such unlikely antagonists still seemed inconceivable: there was a feeling that a political compromise would be cobbled up at the eleventh hour, and the task force would steam back.

The Queen, needless to say, followed the developments closely, carefully studying the contents of her red boxes and questioning visitors. But as the wrangling went on, with the Argentinian generals too weak domestically to make concessions, and the British government pressed by public opinion not to cave in, Mrs Thatcher got tougher. She was not recklessly looking for war, but she felt that this was a gallant expedition for the worthiest of causes, and she became convinced that her destiny was wound up in a confrontation to sweep the Argentinians into the sea and restore British honour.

When British troops finally landed at San Carlos Bay, and the Queen's son went to war, a direct line to the Ministry of Defence was installed at Sandringham so that Elizabeth could have up-to-the-minute news of the fighting on request. From all accounts, she did not share Mrs Thatcher's enthusiasm for military action and for some time raised questions at their meetings about the possibility of a political settlement. The sinking of the Argentinian battleship *General Belgrano* by the British submarine *Conqueror*, in which 368 sailors perished, hugely escalated the war, which until then had been almost without casualties. The task force commander had asked for permission to attack the *Belgrano*, and Mrs Thatcher quickly gave it. Two days after the sinking of the *Belgrano*, HMS *Sheffield* was hit by an Exocet missile: twenty-two lives were lost and many British sailors were injured. The time for political solutions was over.

A banquet for President Ronald Reagan and his wife, Nancy, who were spending the night as her guests at Windsor Castle, gave the Queen an opportunity to praise American support for Britain in the South Atlantic conflict, pay tribute to the British forces, and to combine that with what was for her an unusually outspoken public condemnation of Argentina. 'This conflict in the Falkland Islands was thrust on us by naked aggression and we are naturally proud of the way our fighting men are serving their country,' she declared. The weeks of turbulence and concern for these men – and especially one particular navy helicopter pilot – made her unusually irritable. It was the closest she could have come to the burden borne by her father through the six years of the Second World War.

This was her frame of mind when she set off for what she regarded as a quiet early morning horseback ride with Reagan in Windsor Great Park. But the White House press office had stationed photographers at regular intervals, and the President kept pausing to have his picture taken. That, together with his tendency to ride ahead of her instead of beside her as protocol and, indeed, good manners required, combined to annoy her, and by the end of their ride she showed it.

When the war was over, and the boys came home, the Queen let Mrs Thatcher have her moment of victory. While the Prime Minister exulted in what was very much her triumph, the Queen stayed out of the limelight. What was left undone seemed more significant than what was. The Queen and her Prime Minister did not stand on the balcony of Buckingham Palace, as George VI had done with Churchill on V-E Day. Neither the Queen, nor any other royal was present at the victory parade in the City of London: only Margaret Thatcher. (In the 1945 parade celebrating victory in the Second World War, the King took the salute. Churchill and Labour leader Clement Attlee, by then Prime Minister, were positioned at a discreet distance.) The Queen did attend the service of thanksgiving at St Paul's Cathedral on 26 July. She liked Runcie's emphasis on peace and remembrance of the fallen – on both the British and Argentinian sides. Mrs Thatcher did not.

But the Falklands conflict had established Mrs Thatcher in political leadership. Coming towards the end of her first term, the Falklands victory provided her with the springboard to new elections. After a difficult first term, burdened by rising unemployment as she applied the fiscal measures she was convinced were necessary for eventual recovery, the Falklands gave her a song to

291

sing. And she sang it in June 1983 in her election campaign. In a landslide victory the Conservatives increased their parliamentary majority by 100 to 144.

The summer of the Queen's thirtieth year on the throne will surely stay for ever in her memory, both for the bad news and the good news. July, especially, was a rotten month for the Queen. Lord Rupert Nevill, who had been not merely Prince Philip's Private Secretary but one of her small group of lifelong friends, died suddenly; an intruder broke into the Palace; she suffered a loss of a different kind when Commander Michael Trestrail, the detective who had been her personal bodyguard it seemed for ever, was forced to resign after a homosexual prostitute attempted to blackmail him; a troop of the Blues and Royals Regiment of the Household Cavalry was blown to pieces by an Irish terrorist bomb while riding in full dress in Hyde Park; and for the first time the Queen had to go to hospital – for a wisdom tooth operation.

The intruder came, not in the night, but just before breakfast. He had scaled the spiked wall of Buckingham Palace at six forty-five in the morning, then climbed through an unlocked window into the room containing the valuable stamp collection. A passing policeman who saw him going over the wall had telephoned the Palace police: they made a cursory inspection of the grounds, saw nothing suspicious, and abandoned the search. But the intruder had discovered that the door of the stamp room was locked and left by the same window, setting off the flashing-light alarm in the security control room in the Palace. The police sergeant on duty switched it off, saying, 'There's that bloody bell again – always going off for no reason!'

If what followed were a film, it would be laughed off the screen as too improbable. The intruder shinned up a drainpipe, found a first-floor window open – for it was already hot and muggy on the 9 July morning, and for the second time entered the Palace undetected. He was now in the office of the Master of the Queen's Household. Removing his sandals and socks, he padded up a flight of stairs and found himself on the floor of the private apartments. His intention was to reach the Queen's own bedroom.

Slack security had played its part, but he had also been lucky in finding a temporary blind spot in the Queen's inner defences. The armed police sergeant, always slipper-shod for silence through the long night watch outside the Queen's bedroom, had gone off duty at six in the morning, and the page who was supposed to

292

replace him had not arrived. The posse of corgis – there were by now eleven of them – usually so watchful and snappish, were out with a footman for their morning run in the Palace grounds. So the intruder moved silently along corridors, ignored by the Palace servants as he opened one door after another, looking into the rooms. They thought he was a barefooted workman who had arrived early. He knew he was getting close to his objective when he saw them working as quietly as possible.

In one ante-room he found a heavy glass ashtray. The sight of it had suddenly made him think of slashing his wrists in front of the Queen, so he smashed it, cutting his thumb on the jagged edge. At seven-fifteen he entered the Queen's bedroom. The slamming of the bedroom door first alerted the Queen: it was close to the arrival of her morning tea, but 'I realized immediately that it wasn't a servant because they don't slam doors,' she told police later.

Then the intruder pulled back the curtains – by hand instead of using the cord – and the Queen sat bolt upright in her big four-poster bed. Standing in front of her was a dark, intense-looking young man in jeans and a T-shirt. 'Our eyes met and both of us looked dumbfounded.' Immediately, the self-control mechanism slipped into gear, thereby averting a worse situation, just as it had done a year earlier when Marcus Sarjeant fired his blanks.

'Get out of here at once,' she snapped at him. But the man took no notice and approached the Queen's bed, with blood dripping from his right thumb, and there he sat talking. The Queen pressed the night alarm-button connected to the police control room. Nothing happened. Then she pushed the bedside bell that rang in the corridor. But there was nobody in the corridor or the pantry next to her bedroom. The duty maid was cleaning in an adjoining room, and the footman was still out with the corgis. So she did one of the things she does best – looked interested, guiding the conversation with a skill she had perfected over the years when meeting the tongue-tied, the inhibited and the shyly inarticulate. He was Michael Fagan, a thirty-one-year-old labourer, and he told her about his unhappy family affairs involving his wife, four children, two stepchildren and parents.

As casually as possible, not knowing how he would react, she reached for the telephone and dialled 222 for the operator. 'I want a police officer,' she said in a perfectly even voice. The Palace operator relayed the message to the police at 7.18 a.m. Six minutes elapsed; Fagan talked about his family. The Queen talked about her own: 'Prince Charles is a year younger than you,' she told him politely. She made a second call: why had there been no response? To her relief, the intruder asked her for cigarettes. This gave the Queen her chance. 'You see I have none in this room,' she said, 'but I will have some fetched for you.' And she went out into the corridor and called in a chambermaid, Elizabeth Andrew. When she saw the Queen's barefoot visitor comfortably settled at the foot of the bed, she said, 'Bloody 'ell, Ma'am, what's 'e doing in there?' Despite the tension, Elizabeth relished the moment and later did very good impersonations of the girl's Yorkshire accent.

The Queen and the maid managed to lure Fagan out of the bedroom with the promise of cigarettes in the pantry. By this time the footman had returned with the corgis. The former grabbed Fagan by the arm and gave him cigarettes while the Queen had some difficulty in keeping away the indignant dogs; for Fagan was now becoming hysterical. As she confronted the situation with a chambermaid and a footman for support Elizabeth was becoming increasingly angry.

Suddenly, she saw a swarm of perspiring policemen charging down the corridor to rescue their Queen. The young one in the lead remembers how he got to the top of the stairs and, catching sight of the Queen's head looking out of a doorway, automatically started to straighten his tie. 'Oh, come on, get a bloody move on,' shouted the Queen, relief giving way to irritation. Fagan was led away by the deeply embarrassed police. The law of trespass did not permit him to be prosecuted for his unauthorized audience. However, he confessed to having previously broken into Buckingham Palace on 7 June, almost five weeks before the bedroom incident, perhaps to reconnoitre, and on that occasion had drunk half a bottle of wine. So he was charged with burglary, but acquitted by the jury of seven men and five women. The whole episode, said a relative in court, was in no way directed against the Queen, whom he admired. 'It was a cry for help.' He was sent to a mental hospital. (He was discharged on 20 January 1983.)

At his trial, Fagan pointed out the good news wrapped in the bad, the silver lining in a very dark cloud. 'It might be that I've done the Queen a favour,' he declared. 'I've proved that her security system was no good.' There was a grim undeniability about that statement. It was a nightmarish way to make the discovery, but the Queen's predicament could have been worse had her visitor been a terrorist, or someone with more violent intentions than uttering a cry for help.

It emerged in the investigation that the police had not hastened to her room because the Queen had sounded so 'calm'. Within a few hours of the incident she was officiating at an investiture, and those attending were none the wiser. It was not until some weeks later that she took the full impact of the aftershock. At the family gathering for the christening of Prince William, she was tense. 'The Queen is very strained,' a member of her household admitted, 'almost in a state of shock.' She cancelled her annual visit to the Goodwood races, and was ordered to rest by her doctors.

Her greatest distress was at the intrusion into her own privacy. An irritating side issue was the unwelcome press speculation about why Prince Philip was not on hand to deal with Fagan. But the Queen and Prince Philip occupy separate bedrooms and have always done so.

Elizabeth had always accepted the element of danger attached to her public appearances as part of the job. But in her apartment she expected to be secure. She left Mrs Thatcher in no doubt on this point when the Prime Minister came to the Palace – three days after the incident. 'It could have been a terrorist,' the Queen told her.

The Government's initial response failed to impress the Queen. In the middle of the Falklands conflict, its collective mind a long way off in the South Atlantic, it seems to have done virtually nothing until 12 July when banner headlines – INTRUDER AT THE QUEEN'S BEDSIDE – shocked the nation. Then William Whitelaw, the Government's shambling Home Secretary, confirmed the news to a shocked House and made a flustered attempt to explain the ineptitude of the Palace security, admitting – to hollow laughter – that, despite recent improvements, Palace security was still 'not satisfactory'.

A commission of inquiry into the incident was quickly set up by the police and the Royal Protection Squad. Some heads rolled, others were 'transferred'. At the same time, security procedures were tightened up. But the inquiry produced an unexpected casualty unconnected with the Fagan break-in. Commander Trestrail had been the Queen's personal bodyguard for nine years. Her safety inside the Palace was not his problem, but events were to build up catastrophically for him. He had always provided just the sort of protection the Queen liked: subtle, swift and courteous, but never obvious. Lean and looking very much the part of the administrative side of the household, he had a genuine affection for the Queen. His own mother had died when he was very young. A cultivated man, he could discuss plays, films and books with the Queen. 'We thought the dialogue was a bit false, a bit too toned down,' he said of a play the Queen had seen (with himself in the party) shortly before Fagan's break-in. 'We know people don't talk like that.'

It was when the Queen was at an unaccustomed low ebb that she heard Trestrail had resigned. The inquiry had brought to light his affair with a male prostitute three years earlier. He had actually offered to resign after the intruder incident, but the Queen would not hear of it. However, the clamour over the security at Buckingham Palace had prompted the prostitute, thirty-six-year-old Michael Rauch, to offer to sell the story of his relationship with the Queen's personal bodyguard to a Fleet Street tabloid. The paper alerted the Palace and Rauch ended up at Scotland Yard. Trestrail's subsequent confession that his former lover had attempted to blackmail him automatically classified him as a security risk and his removal became inevitable.

Elizabeth tried to persuade her detective to resign on health grounds as a face-saving exercise. But in the end even she could not save him. She was notified of his resignation by Scotland Yard. Through his lawyer he apologized to the royal family for the distress he caused them. The Queen never saw Trestrail again: once he had fallen from favour, he was out, finished. Instead, the rug for her knees would be handed into the car by his replacement, Superintendent Chris Hagon.

Then came the Irish terrorist bombing atrocity in Hyde Park. The bomb was detonated as the troop of the Blues and Royals trotted past, killing five troopers and their horses. When the Queen appeared at one of the summer garden parties following a week that had combined the outcry surrounding Trestrail's departure and the sadness of the Knightsbridge bombing she looked strained and tense and there were fewer smiles.

The final blow, and the one that made the Queen burst into tears, was Rupert Nevill's death. They had grown up together, he had become a trusted courtier, and since 1976 he had been Prince Philip's Private Secretary. In his tribute to Lord Rupert at the memorial service in Westminster Abbey, Philip said his late Secretary could mix martinis better than anyone he had ever known. The congregation tittered nervously, but it was Philip's attempt to lighten the heavy atmosphere of the occasion. It was after Nevill died that the Queen was advised by her doctors that she needed a complete rest.

Fortunately, it was time for the yearly migration to Balmoral, briefly interrupted in September to welcome home her helicopter pilot son on board the aircraft carrier HMS *Invincible* after five and a half months in the Falklands. The reunion took place in a cabin on the carrier, but the Queen's happiness was evident as she joined the other waiting relatives and girlfriends on the quay at Portsmouth and filmed the 'Welcome Home Our Heroes' banners. From time to time she quickly brushed her right eye, then quickly recovered and pointed things out to Prince Philip and Princess Anne. But in December, she took a seven-week winter break, the longest of her reign. It had been an emotional year.

XVIII

Queen and Prime Minister

One issue on which the Queen and her Prime Minister were in agreement was the importance of the special relationship between Britain and the United States. Mrs Thatcher's leading biographer called the Prime Minister's collaboration with President Ronald Reagan 'the most important foreign relationship Margaret Thatcher formed as prime minister' and 'the most enduring personal alliance in the Western world throughout the 1980s.' In 1982, the Reagans had been the Queen's overnight guests at Windsor Castle. At lunch, the Queen Mother and Ronald Reagan had discovered that they shared a favourite poem, which was 'The Ballad of Dan Magrew', and had proceeded to recite it, each alternately speaking a stanza. Reagan was the seventh United States president whom the Queen had met at least once, including Harry Truman, her host during her 1947 Washington visit as heir presumptive.

Somewhere between the poetry and riding in Windsor Great Park the Reagans had invited the Queen to visit their mountaintop California Rancho del Cielo (the Ranch in the Sky), in Santa Barbara, and so in February 1983 the Queen made her long-considered, but long-postponed trip to the western United States. This was short notice by the standards of the Palace, but the royal visit to Reagan's own state had suddenly acquired a *raison d'être* as Britain's way of expressing gratitude for America's extensive help in the Falklands War. In her formal address at Los Angeles City Hall, the Queen said, 'The support of your government and of the American people touched us deeply and demonstrated to the world that our close relationship is based on our shared commitments to the same values.'

298

The Reagan administration saw the Queen's visit as a welcome balance to growing opposition in Britain to Washington's decision to deploy medium-range Cruise and Pershing nuclear missiles in Western Europe. 'In Britain, public confidence in US leadership has been declining,' Secretary of State George Shultz wrote to Reagan in a confidential memorandum on the Queen's visit, 'and there is considerable opposition building to key aspects of our policy, particularly on defense.' Though the Queen had no direct role in government, she was popular and widely admired. This made her visit 'politically important as it will underscore the strong bonds of friendship, common heritage, and shared values of the British and American people.' Shultz urged Reagan 'to state your appreciation' of British support for American security policy (in other words, missile deployment).

But from the start, the Queen's visit was Nancy Reagan's show. This was never publicly stated, but when Mike Deaver, the senior White House gnome and at the time her closest associate, was put in charge of the arrangements over the heads of the State Department protocol team, it was clear that Nancy Reagan had assumed personal control of the programme. State, with its talk of improving Anglo-American relations, had been pushed into the background. In her eyes, the visit had but one underlying purpose, and that had to do with enhancing the Reagans' image and prestige.

To say Nancy Reagan was a fan of the British royal family was putting it mildly. As the wife of the President of the United States, her own manner could be quasi-regal, but according to Joan Quigley, the astrologer she frequently consulted before either she or the President made any important decision or travel plans, her attitude towards the genuine article – Queen Elizabeth II – was 'worshipful'.

The British royals were one of Nancy Reagan's fixations. When she met the Queen for the first time at the wedding of Prince Charles and Princess Diana, the State Department had established in advance that the First Lady would not curtsy, but she practically had to be restrained from sinking to the ground in the traditional obeisance. She devoured information about the Queen, and a visit to Washington by a member of the royal family would trigger a royal name-dropping spree that lasted for weeks. No other foreign visitor came close to matching the Queen's glamour. To have Elizabeth II as her guest in California was one of the high points not simply of her eight years as First Lady, but of her life.

Initially, as an official connected with the planning of the trip recalled, the Palace suggested alternative dates for the visit, and Nancy Reagan consulted her astrologer to determine which was the most auspicious. Joan Quigley has refused to comment, but the widely held view among the American planners was that it was the astrologer who suggested the week of 24 February. Reagan's wife then rallied her California friends to plan an ambitious ten-day programme in the state beginning with the Queen's arrival in San Diego on board the royal yacht *Britannia* and ending in San Francisco, a distance greater than the entire length of England and Scotland. To ensure a big enough budget for the preparations, a committee was formed of rich Californians who had backed Ronald Reagan in the election, including his key campaign money man, Holmes Tuttle, the millionaire Ford distributor in Los Angeles. Frank Sinatra was drafted to organize the entertainment for the Queen's visit to 20th Century-Fox Studios.

The visit seems to have become an obsession for the First Lady. As the date of the visit drew near, one Washington staffer was to remember, 'She went overboard.' Washington aides and Californians involved were bombarded with telephone calls nagging, complaining, demanding – occasionally even encouraging. She wanted this to be a visit the Queen would never forget.

No doubt that the Queen never will, but not primarily for the reasons Nancy Reagan had in mind. The original schedule was a leisurely cruise along the bright, languid, sun-drenched California coast north to San Francisco. But the royal party had reckoned without a week of the worst weather in California's history. Heavy rain, gales, a freak tornado and sixteen-foot waves lashed the coastline – in fact, the whole state – causing the cruise to be cancelled. The Queen's tour became a hectic pastiche of improvisations and adjustments, and the First Lady's elaborately planned schedule looked like the debris of a pile of squashed profiteroles.

Despite the weather, the Queen and Prince Philip fulfilled all their engagements one way or another, and rain-soaked crowds were waiting to see them wherever they went. Fame, especially enduring fame, is the Californian dream, and the Queen was transcendentally famous without really trying, the embodiment of an institution as old and grand as a giant sequoia. Still there were hitches. When the Queen was airlifted from San Diego to San Francisco on Air Force Two, the Palace footman in charge of the royal jewels was left behind at the airport. In his precious suitcase was the diamond tiara the Queen was to wear at a gala dinner, and another plane had to be provided to chase after Her Majesty.

Fox Studios was included in the programme because the Queen had wanted to see a Hollywood studio, and this was the finest old studio still in operation. She dined on Sound Stage Nine, a vast hangar-like building where the *M*A*S*H* television series had been filmed. The area was redecorated with fibreglass and plaster statues and a twenty-foot-high fountain used in *Hello Dolly*, and the historic theme was extended to some of the guests, vintage film actors of Ronald Reagan's generation including Fred Astaire, Roy Rogers, Gene Kelly, Bette Davis, Lucille Ball, Loretta Young and James Mason. The Queen seemed rather nonplussed by Master of Ceremonies Ed McMahon, and sat straight-faced through a medley of songs by Frank Sinatra and Perry Como. Yet this was probably Nancy Reagan's finest hour. As a film actress she had not achieved greatness in Hollywood. Yet here she was playing hostess to the Queen of England in front of her more successful contemporaries.

'Don't you have anything to wear besides that horrible old mackintosh?' Princess Margaret asked her sister on the telephone from London. She had been following Elizabeth's progress through California on television and had seen her – as had the public – permanently encased in an olive-drab Burberry and huddled under an umbrella. Driving around the vast Palm Springs estate of millionaire publisher Walter Annenberg, the former American ambassador to London, she even resorted to a plastic rain hat tied under her chin.

In fact, sloshing through the rain never fazed the Queen. When Nancy Reagan apologized for the weather, Elizabeth replied, 'Don't be silly. It's an adventure.' Which it certainly was. Getting the royal couple on and off *Britannia* was a challenge because water flooded the pier. On one occasion the Americans commandeered school buses from the San Diego naval base nearby, and the Queen and Prince Philip set off in one of them, sitting in the front seat and laughing like children.

With his short fuse, Prince Philip found it harder to cope with the vagaries of the schedule. On one occasion, he was sitting with the Queen in their limousine after a function, but the car didn't move. 'Let's get going,' snapped Philip. The White House official who was escorting them explained that the motorcade was held up because other members of the party were still scrambling through the rain to their cars. Far from accepting the explanation, Philip's agitation mounted. Beside him in the car was a newspaper; he rolled it up and began to poke the Secret Service man sitting in the front seat, shouting, 'Get this fucking car moving!' The Queen sat staring straight ahead, totally ignoring her husband's outburst. She could have been alone.

On another occasion while returning to the yacht in the evening after fulfilling an engagement on his own, Philip noticed a waiting crowd in the street. He turned on the light inside the car so that he could be seen. The Secret Service man asked him to turn it off. 'It makes you too easy a target,' he said. Philip was livid. 'I'm damned if I will! Why do you think these people are out there? They want to see me, and I want to wave to them.' The State Department's Chief of Protocol, Selwa Roosevelt, who had accompanied him, did her best to explain that the Secret Service man was acting on orders. As they reached the royal yacht, the Prince, 'still fuming, tore out of the car and slammed the door in my face, just as I was following him,' she wrote later. 'He could have done me serious injury.' But Philip suddenly turned back, took her hand, and apologized for his tantrum. Later in San Francisco, after shaking hands with five female city officials in a row Philip snapped, 'Aren't there any male supervisors? This is a nanny city.' That was when a member of the travelling household confided to American officials that the Queen tended to be more relaxed when Philip was not present. Yet, between eruptions, Philip could be charming and extremely amusing. On one occasion, he was so attentive to the elegant American Chief of Protocol that 'I felt the Queen was giving us a disapproving glance.'

The day of the Queen's visit to the Reagan ranch, the storm was at its most vicious and the schedule at its most muddled. The planned helicopter trip to the homestead was ruled out, and the whole visit was almost cancelled because of flooding on the seven-mile mountain pass. But Reagan arrived with a fleet of four-wheel-drive vehicles airlifted from Washington and the party made the tricky ascent up the snaking mountain pass for a Tex-Mex feast of tacos and enchiladas, stuffed chilies and refried beans. Shortly after his guests departed the weather cleared. 'Damn it,' said the President. 'I told them it was going to clear.' His aides tried to radio them back, but the Queen and Prince Philip kept right on going.

The Queen liked Ronald Reagan. She was amused by his stories and responded to his charm. However, perceptive American staffers connected with the Queen's visit felt that beneath the surface correctness there was less warmth towards Nancy Reagan.

Elizabeth was said to have found the First Lady assertive and affected, and in private would do a wicked imitation of Nancy's rather breathless voice and her mannerisms.

Reagan's Windsor Castle riding incident had been forgotten, but Nancy's breach of protocol on the same 1982 visit apparently stuck in the royal memory: when the Reagans arrived at Windsor, Nancy had purposefully led Philip inside ahead of the Queen and the President. Then, at the Queen's dinner for the Reagans on that occasion, the President's wife had appeared in a shimmering gold sheath which the royal household considered way over the top for the occasion.

The whirl of changes in the programme kept Nancy Reagan's nerves on edge. But the American team proved adept at improvising, and the Queen equally good at coping with the changes. Due to the cancelled cruise the Queen arrived in San Francisco on the afternoon of 3 March, instead of the following morning. Moreover, with *Britannia* still at sea battling the storm, the Queen was bereft of her usual accommodation. The Reagans were already installed in the St Francis Hotel's Presidential Suite which was bristling with the panoply of presidential power, including the telephone hot line to the Kremlin. So the White House commandeered the second best suite, a rather drab set of rooms whose main saving grace was a magnificent view of San Francisco Bay. Nancy Reagan rushed her interior decorator to San Francisco to redecorate it. Within hours, with the help of furniture borrowed from one of the city's leading antique dealers, the suite was miraculously transformed into passable royal quarters for the night. The Queen's impending arrival was not a sufficiently strong argument for the hotel staff to work after quitting time: union rules prohibited it. So quite senior White House and State Department staffers found themselves cleaning, polishing and moving heavy furniture themselves.

It was the first time the Queen had slept in a hotel since her accession. But this landmark was almost overshadowed by another first in many years – eating in a restaurant. As a result of the altered schedule a gap yawned in the programme. Dinner was the biggest problem since nothing had been planned. So the Reagans took the Queen and Prince Philip and their senior staff to Trader Vic's, a well-known Polynesian restaurant. Seated cosily round the table were the Queen, Prince Philip, the Reagans, Deaver, Sir Philip Moore, Lady Susan Hussey, and one or two other officials. When the time came to open the fortune cookies, the Queen read hers and promptly slipped it into her purse.

In October, the Anglo-American relationship was put to its strongest test since the Suez Crisis, when Reagan ordered the invasion of the Caribbean island of Grenada, a Commonwealth country, without first notifying the British government. When Reagan telephoned to break the news to Margaret Thatcher that American troops had landed on the island, she 'went ballistic' with rage – as one of her aides put it. Not only was the invasion in plain breach of international law, it was a gross affront to British dignity, in particular that of the Queen, as Grenada's head of state. Elizabeth herself could not have been overjoyed. By the end of the Grenada week, with the mission of removing the pro-Cuban militant socialist regime accomplished, the Prime Minister was taking a more pragmatic view, and found it easier to support the outcome while still disapproving of Reagan's methods, and there is little reason to think that the Queen did not share this approach.

Indeed, the Queen was back in the United States in 1984, this time not as monarch but as a leading English racehorse owner. Because of the tensions in Ireland it had long been considered too dangerous for the Queen to send her mares to Irish stud farms. None of the Queen's mares had been 'covered' by any Irish-based horse since 1972. Barred from access to most of the best stallions in Europe, she developed an American connection and by 1984 had up to a half-dozen mares at stud farms in central Kentucky. The American breeding effort – in the words of her racing manager Lord Carnarvon – was designed 'to obtain class speed, to jazz up the stud a little bit . . . Also, the Queen is getting outcrosses that she couldn't get in England.' With nearly a quarter of her mares in the United States, it was inevitable that the Queen would want to come and inspect the farms herself.

The American trip had been 'Porchy' Carnarvon's idea. This was familiar country to him because his wife Jane Wallop was Wyoming born; and on her first visit the Queen stayed at the Carnarvons' house in Big Horn, Wyoming, for half the visit and then moved to Lane's End Farm, the sprawling home and stud farm in Kentucky belonging to William Farish, a leading Kentucky owner and breeder. Farish had stabled some of the Queen's mares for many years, but had never met her before she came to stay at his house.

The red boxes followed the Queen to the heartland of America so that she could remain in touch with developments at home, and a small group of members of the household, American Secret Service men and State Department officials moved into nearby motels.

But writing to Reagan from Wyoming, Elizabeth told him she was spending a holiday 'doing the things I like best – looking at beautiful thoroughbreds and lately walking in the wide open spaces by the mountains.' Except for a quick trip to Normandy in 1981, to visit stud farms in the area, this was Elizabeth II's first private holiday outside Britain. The private nature of the visit raised an intriguing problem: because the Queen holds no passport, the Immigration authorities needed some persuading by a State Department official before they would agree to allow her off the plane and into the country. In the end, a formula was found that satisfied bureaucratic requirements: the Secretary of State undertook to assume responsibility for her presence in the United States, and for her departure.

She brought no doctor either. So the White House arranged for two local doctors to be on stand-by. Robustly healthy as ever, she did not require their services, but her young footman did. He was rushed to the local hospital in Sheridan, Wyoming with a slipped disc. When he was told he needed immediate surgery he fled, and the Queen had to persuade him to return to hospital for the operation.

She drove to the stud farms in a small motorcade, but once there insisted on visiting her mares and their foals alone, walking across the fields by herself for a reunion with such old favourites as Highclere, winner of the French Prix de Diane and the Thousand Guineas at Ascot, Christchurch and Contralto. On the drives between one stud farm and another the often heated three-way conversations between the Queen, Carnarvon and Farish had only one topic – racehorses.

Before leaving she hosted a dinner in an unlikely setting for a royal occasion – the Maverick Supper Club, Sheridan's leading restaurant. Confronted with the long restaurant menu, which in itself may have been a novel experience, she pored over it carefully and then said, 'Well, I suppose I'll have a queen-size steak.'

The White House was told that 'Her Majesty expected a telephone call from the President.' In 1984, Reagan missed the appointed time for the call and telephoned 'right in the middle of dinner.' When Elizabeth returned in 1986, the Palace reasonably tactfully passed the word to the White House that it should not happen again.

There was a lot for the Queen to think about as she tramped the foothills of Sheridan County, Wyoming. News reached her of Margaret Thatcher's narrow escape in an IRA bomb explosion at her hotel in Brighton, and she immediately telephoned the

Prime Minister to express concern and relief. The incident must have reminded her of her own vulnerability to attack. On her official sixtieth birthday in June, she had reviewed the annual parade riding Burmese for the last time. The horse was now judged too old for the long ceremony, but she had no desire to replace him with another. She had decided that she would no longer review the parade mounted and wearing the uniform of the Guards. From next year, it would be an open carriage and civilian clothes. She was, after all, four times a grandmother. Princess Anne had Peter and Zara, and after William, the Princess of Wales had borne a second son, Prince Henry.

But there were indications that the marriage of Charles and Diana was going through a bad patch. The difference in age, and above all in interests, was creating problems between them. The Princess was a rock fan, while Charles preferred opera at Covent Garden. She tired quickly of traipsing through museums and galleries, while he was in his element. In social circles, there were stories of them arriving at balls and parties together, and Charles leaving early to go to bed while Diana stayed on and danced until all hours. When the Princess was seen at a rock concert in the company of the same young man on two successive occasions, the gossip columnists had a field day. The circumstantial evidence of a troubled relationship was strengthened when Charles went alone to Balmoral (which the Princess finds cold and forbidding), and failed to return to London for either his fifth wedding anniversary or his eldest son's birthday.

No-one could fault the Princess of Wales as a mother. Having grown up without one herself she seemed determined that William (Wills) and Harry would not lack a mother's care and attention. She also got full marks for her determined approach to her public responsibilities. When she became royal patron of the National Association for the Deaf, she learned the sign language so as to be able to communicate with the deaf. Having agreed to become president of Britain's marriage guidance organization, she insisted on sitting in as a guidance counsellor herself. But who would counsel the counsellor? Part of the early problem seemed to be that she failed to understand fully the constraints imposed by her royal persona. She wanted her cake, and to eat it. Another part of the problem was that as her popularity increased she began to overshadow her husband whenever they appeared together. It was not jealousy, more the frustrating realization that nobody was listening to his carefully prepared speech because they were too busy taking notice of what his wife was wearing.

As the rumours swirled around the Prince and his wife, the Queen summoned them to Buckingham Palace. The Queen's children did not drop in casually on their mother: because of her schedule, they were either required to make an appointment, or were asked to come. Similarly, the Queen did not drop in on her children unannounced. The Palace telephoned in advance.

Her main concern, the Queen was said to have told Charles and Diana, over tea, was the bad publicity. Whatever the domestic problems, they were of a private nature and would have to be resolved privately. Meanwhile, it was important to maintain a royal façade.

But royal façades were hard for non-royals to acquire – and maintain. In 1986, Prince Andrew, created Duke of York for the occasion, married Miss Sarah Ferguson, daughter of Major Ron Ferguson, by then Prince Charles's polo manager. Buxom, boisterous, extremely friendly, she seemed well matched with Prince Charles's extroverted younger brother, who enjoyed navy life as much as Charles had disliked it. The Queen seemed pleased with the match, and it was likely that her son's outdoorsy new bride, who was a good rider, would appeal to her. Moreover, as commoners went, the new Duchess of York was not an unsuitable choice: she was no stranger to the Court. Her father had lived on the fringes of the royal family for a large part of his life. Even so, the exuberant Duchess of York has had to be reminded several times by the Palace that informality could be carried too far.

But it was also ironic that, like the Princess of Wales, the Queen's second daughter-in-law was also the child of a broken home, her mother, Susie, having divorced Ron Ferguson to marry Hector Barrantes, an Argentinian polo player.

Attention was briefly diverted from the arrangements for the Duke of York's wedding when the accumulation of seven years of rumour about disagreements between the Queen and her Prime Minister bubbled to the surface in a *Sunday Times* newspaper report. Its main point was that the Queen was privately 'dismayed' by the Prime Minister's refusal to consider imposing trade sanctions on South Africa as an anti-apartheid measure. The Queen's outraged concern was that Mrs Thatcher's position was undermining Commonwealth unity. It then went on to say that not only was this the Queen's opinion but she had authorized her advisers to make it known, and thus was intervening in the political process.

Then followed a catalogue of all the Queen's points of difference with the Thatcher government, ranging from her secret anxieties about the fifty-one-week miners' strike in 1984 to her 'misgivings' about the United States bombing of Libya (for which Air Force bombers had refuelled in Britain with Mrs Thatcher's permission).

William Heseltine, of course, quickly denied that the Queen, or anyone speaking for her, had conveyed such feelings. Downing Street also denied the story, but by now the press had the bit between its teeth and was talking of a high-placed mole at Buckingham Palace who had leaked the story.

As it turned out, *The Sunday Times* article did not come from a mole but had its basis in some form of off-the-record guidance from the Palace's spokesman Michael Shea. Briefing the Court correspondents shortly after the story was published, Shea – a former Foreign Office diplomat who wrote mystery novels in his spare time – closed the door with an exaggerated air of secrecy, and told them jokingly, 'I'm now going to reveal the identity of the Palace mole.' Then he put his knuckles against his nose and wiggled his extended fingers like a mole's whiskers. But the American embassy, reporting to Washington on what it termed the 'rift' between the Queen and Mrs Thatcher, did not see the humour of it. 'The question now seems to be,' the embassy stated, 'whether the Queen's press secretary, who is acknowledged to have spoken to *The Sunday Times* in advance of the story, can hold on to his job.' Not long afterwards, the normally sure-footed Shea left the Queen's service.

It seemed unlikely that the Queen would have suddenly turned her back on thirty-four years as a punctilious constitutionalist and authorized her servants to ventilate her opinions through the pages of a newspaper. But the telling point was that such an episode should occur at all after thirty-four years, and that it should be directed against Britain's only woman prime minister. The fact that the story rang true was a reflection of the widely held perceptions of both women and their relationship. The irresistible force from 10 Downing Street had run into the immovable object at Buckingham Palace. Quite a change from the published reminiscences by the elderly gentlemen of the past – Elizabeth and Harold Wilson gossiping cosily over a glass of Scotch; Elizabeth and Macmillan pouring out his problems with the Profumo affair to the young, sympathetic monarch.

Perhaps inevitably, there was a temptation to see the working relationship between two powerful women as an adversarial one, but the reality was that it progressed bumpily from initial wariness to formal correctness and even a degree of mutual respect in spite of the differing viewpoints. But cosy, never. Margaret Thatcher had been brought up a devoted monarchist. Hovering ambitiously on the threshold of public life, she saw Queen Elizabeth's accession as supplying her with a significant role model. As Prime Minister, she was positively reverential to the Queen, and her low curtsies amused the Palace. On one of her annual weekends at Balmoral with her husband, the Queen and Prince Philip took them to their cabin in the woods where the Prince barbecued sausages, and the Queen then did her dishwashing routine. Margaret Thatcher was stunned: the sight of her Queen up to her elbows in dishwater shattered her middle-class picture of royalty.

There was no reason to suppose that the Queen was not equally correct towards Mrs Thatcher. But the early stories about Mrs Thatcher's dealings with the Court suggest an undertone of frostiness, and the Court must have been picking up the vibrations from somewhere. Mrs Thatcher once arrived for her audience wearing the same colour dress as the Queen. To prevent a repetition of this, her office telephoned Buckingham Palace before the next audience to ask what the Queen planned to wear. The Palace replied that the Queen never noticed what anyone around her was wearing. In fact, the Queen does compare notes on what she will wear at specific public functions with the wives of visiting foreign dignitaries. But she was not about to make a habit of it with her Prime Minister. An earlier episode had as its setting one of the summer garden parties in the grounds of Buckingham Palace. When the Queen, with Mrs Thatcher in attendance, arrived at the party there was a burst of applause from the invited guests. Mrs Thatcher waved cheerily at the crowd. The Queen was not amused. When she is present *she* does the waving. Elizabeth turned around and walked into the tea tent, leaving Mrs Thatcher standing alone with her husband, Denis.

Superficially, they were almost too alike: meticulous, well-groomed, hardworking, controlled, informed, and almost the same age (Mrs Thatcher was born in October 1925). But differences in style and outlook overshadowed the similarities. The Queen had the easy matter-of-fact manner of someone who is secure in herself and her role. Mrs Thatcher found it hard to mask her competitive urge even when she was with the Queen. When both were scheduled to speak at the memorial service for the assassinated Earl Mountbatten, they exchanged speeches ahead of time as a courtesy. The Queen's address was an informal, familial tribute; Mrs Thatcher's, which had been drafted for her by Lord Hailsham, was rolling Churchillian prose totally unsuited to her style of delivery. Having seen Elizabeth's text, she cut out all the rhetoric and delivered a low-key address in the same vein as the Queen's. 'They went down about equal,' said a Thatcher intimate familiar with the episode. 'But they otherwise would not have, a comparison the Prime Minister was determined to avoid.'

Though the Queen was a hard worker, Mrs Thatcher was a driven one. Both women can be said to have experienced early difficulties in reconciling the demands of their jobs with family life. The Queen made amends with her 'second' family: Mrs Thatcher never had any more children after her twins. Unlike Mrs Thatcher, the Queen relaxed in many ways, from jigsaws to riding.

Ultimately, however, what separated them was rooted in different views of what was best for their country. These were two women who looked out of different political windows. For years, the Queen had heard from Conservative and Labour prime ministers alike of the importance of a national consensus, the recognition that different branches of society – government, financial, bureaucracy, labour – each had a role to play in modern Britain. They thought there was such a concept as the community which encompassed the very purpose to which citizens of every class and calling should bend their lives.

Then came Margaret Thatcher: like Heath, she belonged to the new breed of Tory leadership, and there was little likelihood of having previously known her on the grouse moor, or weekending at one of the statelier stately houses. But she knew what she wanted – and it was not consensus. Her approach was confrontational from the start. Her aim was to smash the trade unions, not collaborate with them. If she could, she would sink the Labour Party as well. As for community, she once said, 'There is no such thing as society,' meaning that what mattered was the individual and his or her relationship with other individuals, not the abstraction. Soon, at their weekly meetings, the Queen came to represent the old values, the paternalistic tradition in public service, and Mrs Thatcher, the tough new approach, hell-bent on change. 'The Queen still never departed from her formula of asking questions,' was how a knowledgeable Tory put it. 'But these days there were a lot more questions.' By 1985, Britain's prosperity had become the envy of the Reagan administration and Margaret Thatcher's European neighbours. Two years later the Tory government would balance its budget – something Ronald Reagan could only dream about – and was able to make significant cuts in income tax.

Whenever Margaret Thatcher considered anyone for a job she had to fill she would ask, 'Is he one of us?' Meaning, did he share her zeal for radically changing the system? In that sense, Elizabeth II was not 'one of us'. The Queen recognized what her Prime Minister had done to improve the nation's economic well-being. She knew that Mrs Thatcher acted with the best interests of Britain in mind and that they shared an intense patriotism. Her concern was about the long-term effects on Britain of Thatcherism. 'What I worry about,' she said, 'is how this period will look in the history books.'

It was hardly coincidental that *The Sunday Times* story should focus on a supposed disagreement over the Commonwealth, for this was probably the area where the difference in outlook was most clear-cut. Mrs Thatcher felt that anything the Commonwealth as a whole preferred was likely to demand British opposition. But the Commonwealth remained central to the Queen's thinking. Just as it was the Lusaka Commonwealth Conference that led to their first skirmish, the South African sanctions issue enshrined their differences into legend.

But there were other factors. The Queen studiously avoided using the royal 'we' in conversation. Margaret Thatcher used it more and more. When her Texas-born daughter-in-law gave birth to a son, she stopped in front of the television cameras stationed outside 10 Downing Street and announced breathlessly, 'We are a grandmother.' On another occasion, she told a BBC reporter, 'We are in the fortunate position, in Britain, of being, as it were, the senior person in power.' Such *lèse-majesté* did not pass unnoticed at the Palace. Nor did Mrs Thatcher's practice of countering criticism that she was unfeeling by visiting the scenes of major disasters – usually more of a royal than a political initiative – and making sure she got there first. In the winter of 1990, Margaret Thatcher resigned following a party revolt against her leadership, and Elizabeth II found herself dealing with the ninth British Prime Minister of her reign. This was John Major, who shared Margaret Thatcher's middle-class origins, but not her confrontational style. The intrigue surrounding Mrs Thatcher's ouster recalled earlier Tory leadership battles, but on this occasion, the Queen was spared any hint of involvement: the succession was

311

resolved by a vote of the Conservative parliamentary party. When Margaret Thatcher went for her farewell audience Queen and Prime Minister were correct as always, but there seemed to be little residual warmth from their eleven-year collaboration.

XIX

She

There was a small group of people in London whose frequent subject of conversation was a woman referred to only as She. As in, She's determined to go to Russia next year. The woman in question was, of course, Queen Elizabeth II. The avoidance of mentioning her name by members of the royal household, and a tiny coterie of others besides, was a form of a discretion but also an underlying assumption that by now her recognition factor was so high that her name did not even need to be mentioned.

No other face on earth had been known to so many for so long. No-one has been the focus of more film footage, press photographs and television time. Buckingham Palace can rattle off impressive statistics of the number of miles covered and countries visited in her continued effort to keep the British Commonwealth – her Commonwealth – from fracturing, and in her role as her country's leading diplomatic representative.

Not by nature an innovator, she presided over a gradual process of change in the style of the monarchy primarily designed to adapt the institution to the postwar social upheaval in Britain, the rise of the middle class, and the loss of empire and influence – without tampering with the substance. The remarkable achievement of her long reign, seen as it nears its forty-year mark, was not the change but how much remained unchanged. Elizabeth II's place in history was rooted in this. Without the upheaval some had thought necessary she has ensured the durability of the institution. Her grandfather, George V, would find many things different at Buckingham Palace, but none of the essentials. He would also have known his way around much of the royal ceremonial, both public and private. Privy councillors still stood around the table in the monarch's presence for the twenty minutes or so that it took the Lord President to read the titles of the new laws requiring royal approval, and for the Queen to say, 'Agreed' after each title. The Queen still nominates new sheriffs (local officials) by pricking their names on a list with a bodkin, usually a hatpin.

In the process of modernization she was pushed forward by her husband, Prince Philip, who computerized the Palace. But despite the computers and the royal household's pride in its own cost-consciousness and businesslike compactness, the monarchy has retained both its grandeur and formality.

Roy Jenkins, who as President of the Common Market travelled widely in Europe, noted that visiting Buckingham Palace was a more formal occasion than in any other royal house in Europe. Some years earlier David Bruce noted that the 'arrangements for entertaining British royalty in a private house are somewhat complicated. First of all one must submit a list of whom the host and hostess might like to invite. It comes back, usually with a suggestion for the deletion of some names and proposed additions. All the guests must be assembled for the arrival of the Royal visitor, who is met by the host and hostess at the front door, conducted in by the host, who presents any of the guests he or she does not know. After the meal, it seems the custom to bring up the other guests successively for short chats.' Moreover, such dinners were 'advanced' by the Queen's Private Secretary, who briefs the host and hostess about her taste in food and drink, as Charteris did before Elizabeth and Philip dined with the Canadian High Commissioner. Charteris, noted Paul Martin, told him, 'The Queen sometimes likes a dry sherry before dinner, oftentimes a gin-and-tonic and sometimes a good martini in the American and Canadian style. At dinner, a good French red wine always does the trick. The same apparently applies to Philip.'

Elizabeth maintained her stately routine – moving from castle to castle by season, attending the Ascot races, bestowing honours, opening Parliament, and sailing on her yacht *Britannia*.

She travels less these days, and it becomes increasingly difficult to be innovative with the scheduling of a royal visit because she has usually been before. What gave her visit to China in 1986 its added excitement was the novelty of being there for the first time. The Chinese gave her a spectacular welcome. Crowds by

314

the thousands lined the streets to see her, and she responded with exceptional warmth. Before her meeting with Deng Xiao Ping – a chainsmoker – it had been delicately put to the Chinese leader that, in deference to the Queen, he should not smoke, and would he please hide the ever-present spitoon. But after ninety minutes of conversation, the Queen said generously, 'Mr General Secretary, I'm sure you would like to smoke.' Put out of his misery, Deng gratefully lit a cigarette and puffed away through the rest of their talk. Towards the end of the tour Philip produced one of his more amazing gaffes. Did they not worry, he asked British students studying in Beijing, that they might become slant-eyed? The following morning at breakfast, nobody spoke in the royal party.

On royal tours, the grand standard was if anything getting grander. For the Queen and Prince Philip's Pacific cruise in the royal yacht in 1986, her personal entourage numbered forty-eight. The list included two ladies-in-waiting; her Private Secretary, then Sir Philip Moore; and the Deputy Private Secretary, then Sir William Heseltine; the Master of the Household and his deputy; the Press Secretary; the Queen's equerry; her personal surgeon; Prince Philip's Private Secretary and his equerry; the captain of the Queen's Flight; seven 'lady clerks' to various Court officials; three members of the Royal Protection Squad; two assistant dressers for the Queen (Bobo MacDonald was not with her); two maids; the Queen's Page; the Queen's Footman; the Queen's hairdresser; the Page of the Presence; the travelling yeoman (who looks after the baggage); Prince Philip's two valets; the royal chef plus three senior cooks and a pastry *sous*-chef; the dining room supervisor; the deputy sergeant footman; three footmen; two dining room assistants; a kitchen porter; and an orderly. This group travelled on a yacht which already had a full Royal Navy complement of 256 – all equipped for silent running with special-issue rubber-soled shoes. While it is true that the President of the United States' travel team exceeds twice that number, this includes aides from his executive staff, more security than the Queen, and communications personnel. What made the Queen's travelling retinue strikingly different was that the domestic staff predominated.

The woman at the centre of this formal structure is small, trim, with hair that continues to be a warm brown colour into her sixties thanks to a rinse called Chocolate Kiss, and a smile that lights up her face with a direct friendliness. It gives a hint of the personality behind the often remote public exterior. At poignant or human moments her frown hides layers of unexpressed feeling. In Perth little Joanna Bjelanovic presented a bouquet to Her Majesty and asked if she could kiss the Queen. The Queen's reply was 'No, dear, I'm sorry.' The distance is always there. But as Henry Kissinger reassured President Gerald Ford in his briefing paper for the Queen's 1976 American bicentennial visit, 'Behind the facade of seriousness . . . she is a warm and witty person. You will find that she does her homework and will be well briefed on the Ford family.'

She has only been seen to be visibly moved in public on one occasion. That was when visiting casualties in a Welsh hospital following a local dam disaster. She was thirty-two at the time; it was her first encounter with tragedy on a large scale, and she was totally unprepared for the emotional impact. After that the mask of iron control never slipped again. Not even when a teenager fired at her – not with a long-range weapon from some distant window but up close, so that she witnessed the action in slow motion as he pointed the gun and took aim, and then heard six shots. What followed was a typical little set piece in her public reaction to the unexpected – a faint smile of reassurance, a slight tightening of the mouth, and on with the business of the day.

Not over-demonstrative by nature, the English – if perhaps not so much the other peoples that make up the United Kingdom – identify with their monarch's frequently poker-faced expression in public, and would have found an emotive Queen unseemly, and even embarrassing. Just as they found comfort in the fact that Elizabeth 'has little interest in the arts', as Kissinger put it in his confidential briefing paper, perhaps again to reassure Ford, who was no intellectual giant himself. She sees herself as a countrywoman who likes dogs and horses, an image that is understood and appreciated. In a democratic monarchy, maintaining a sustained level of popularity is important not merely in itself, but as a form of protection against parliamentary pressure: it can be a way of appealing to the people over the heads, as it were, of the elected government. When the House of Commons did not press for a rethink of the monarchy's exemption from taxation, it was because there were few votes to gain, and potentially many to lose, from such a policy.

Her great-great-grandmother Queen Victoria was on the throne for sixty-four years, and Elizabeth II's robust health suggests that she will reign 'happy and glorious' – as the national anthem says

316

– past the turn of the century, in the tradition of longevity of English Queens regnant. She is an outstanding advertisement for homoeopathic medicines, in which the royal family have always been believers; for barley water, which she periodically consumes in large quantities to clean out the royal system, thus losing the extra pounds resulting from her sweet tooth; for a non-smoking moderate regimen: and for meticulously avoiding the local water on her wide-ranging royal travels. Malvern Water is not the only food item packed in the luggage. The list includes Darjeeling and China tea, fruit cake, shortbread biscuits, jam, honey, barley sugar for energy, English mint sauce, sausages from Harrods for the royal breakfast and chocolates. All packed into boxes marked with a cross, along with homoeopathic remedies for sleeplessness, hay fever, arthritis, colds and nervous tension. The Queen's enormous wardrobe travels in blue cases and trunks marked 'The Queen' in gold letters.

Fashion trends are relentlessly shut out of that wardrobe. Skirt lengths remained the same, with an almost religious commitment to covering the knees. Pastel colours predominate and bold designs are barred altogether, and the shoes are invariably medium-heeled and sensible, designed for comfort rather than style. The overall effect is not elegance but a kind of streamlined formality that serves a purpose, a little top-heavy when not supported by the right kind of corsetry.

By 1987, *Fortune* magazine was granting Elizabeth II an accolade of her own as the richest woman in the world. Her personal wealth has grown to £4.6 billion. London analysts placed her shareholdings at no less than £2.1 billion. The Duchy of Lancaster, her main real-estate holding in the United Kingdom, generated an untaxed rental income of £1.5 million in 1986. The following year the total estimated value of her art, jewellery, land holdings and horses was £2.6 billion. And 1988 was a good racing year. With thirty-two horses in training, she recorded thirteen wins, twelve seconds, five thirds and nine fourth places in seventy-nine races run, to earn over £75,000. Her Civil List allowance has also increased appreciably, to nearly £4.3 million, but to most Britons the monarchy is still considered cost-effective.

A woman of wealth, then, as well as a subtle and pervasive influence. For though a constitutional monarch reigns but does not rule, Elizabeth II is not nearly the acquiescent rubber stamp monarch she is made out to be. Her constitutional position does not allow her to instruct the Government on how it should act

317

on any matter, but it does allow her to express her views, and it is a right she exercises with vigour. 'You can't cancel Concorde!' she told the Minister of Technology when the Labour government was considering ending the joint Anglo-French supersonic airliner project for a lack of interest from potential customers.

At the beginning of 1979 she was said to have voiced her opinion that Britain should give refuge to the deposed Shah of Iran who had been forced out of his country by a militant Islamic popular movement led by the Ayatollah Ruhollah Khomeini from exile in France. The Shah did not formally ask to come to Britain, but he clearly needed a home and the Queen felt that asylum should be offered in recognition of his past support for British interests in the Middle East. It was said she believed that the state must recognize personal as well as national obligations. Elizabeth's concern was an echo of her father's efforts to restore the Greek and Balkan monarchies after the Second World War. But the Queen's view was discounted by the Foreign Office which advised Margaret Thatcher – who, incidentally, was also sympathetic – against harbouring the Shah because of the obvious security risk, and the possible adverse effect on Britain's relations with the Islamic world. In the mid-1980s, the Government was dragging its feet in devoting funds for an anti-AIDS campaign. At a 1986 Buckingham Palace lunch, the Queen asked the Labour opposition leader, Neil Kinnock, whether, in his view, the Government was doing enough to combat the epidemic. Kinnock said no. Would it help if she had a word with the Prime Minister, she asked. He felt certain that it would. The Queen promised to do so. A month later, the Ggovernment set up a cabinet committee on AIDS.

It would be hard to believe that anyone as in touch with developments, and as alert in defence of her position and prerogatives as Elizabeth II, had not realized that the era of change dramatically ushered in at the end of the 1980s must have an impact on the monarchy. She must therefore be aware that the British monarchy is an institution which needs to develop a strategy for change. There is one scenario in which the Queen could have change thrust upon her. Conservative governments are not calculated to produce any challenge to the continuity of the monarchy. More worrying would be a prolonged period of Labour administration. In the past, Labour had a reassuringly monarchist leadership, but the party can be schizophrenic in its attitude towards the British royal house and a surge of left-wing dominance could mean trouble.

A natural role for the British monarchy in the next century would be as the leading royal house in a united Europe. In terms of its importance this would be conceded, but there are reservations. After little more than a mild interest in Europe for forty years, the Queen hardly qualifies as the symbolic focal point of European unity. Her strong, single-minded commitment to the Commonwealth is rapidly becoming a lost cause, as the grouping of former colonies is broken up by the centrifugal forces of self-interest. If a united Europe is the bus to catch for the year 2000, then it is a bus which Queen Elizabeth, with her corgis and racehorses, can be said to have missed. Whether or not in her heart she would want to be on it is a different question. If she would not, she is out of step with Britain's stated policy which is committed to the integrated Europe of 1992.

Aside from the Commonwealth, the Protestant definition of the monarchy could be a liability in enlarging its European role. There are fewer rigorous Protestants around than there were. The Queen has a large number of Catholic subjects with whom she is forbidden by law to be in communion, at peril of losing her throne. A monarchy which is the leader of the Protestant faith could not assume a role in a Europe that is predominantly Catholic, but a change in the Queen's status as head of the Anglican Church – an alteration of the so-called Act of Settlement which requires the sovereign not merely to be Protestant but also head of the Protestant faith – would psychologically make all the difference.

The Prince of Wales, waiting in the wings for his turn on the throne, would be in a better position to effect this shift in emphasis towards Europe. He has shown a greater enthusiasm for 'the Continent' than has his mother. Following his 1985 tour of Italy he became a regular visitor, staying with an aristocratic Italian family in Tuscany and doing some serious browsing in museums, churches and historic buildings. The Tuscan hills also give him fresh scope to exercise his interest in landscape painting; and he has told at least one friend that he has come to regard Italy as his 'second home', as he put it. A collection of his Italian watercolours was shown in Urbino in 1989. On a visit to Paris with the Princess of Wales, he discovered – probably to his surprise – that his French hosts were as interested in him, and what he had to say in his good French, as they were in his glamorous wife, who spoke no French. Even the Prince and Princess of Wales's annual family vacation with the Spanish royals is a breakthrough. The Queen is not known ever to have crossed the English Channel for a private holiday (although she did once visit stud farms in Normandy).

Before he can develop this European connection Prince Charles will, of course, have to succeed Elizabeth II, which appears unlikely during her lifetime. The Queen remains dead set against abdication. It may have been good enough for Queen Juliana of the Netherlands, who stepped down in favour of her daughter Princess Beatrix, but it is not good enough for the House of Windsor. Like marriage, Elizabeth views kingship as a lifelong vow, as the Queen Mother explained to Paul Martin at the Jubilee celebrations. Her daughter appreciated 'the spiritual quality of the commitment made at the coronation . . . to serve and to reign,' she told the Canadian High Commissioner. Thought of abdication does not fit that mould.

Besides, abdication has sinister overtones in Britain. By their hard-line stand against the Duke of Windsor, the royal family have in this respect painted themselves into a corner. In the early years of his reign, King George VI was haunted by the fear that his brother would return to England and become the focal point for an opposition royalist party. The Duke of Windsor continued to be actively discouraged from residing in Britain long after King George overcame his fear, on the grounds that the ex-King's presence would have been an embarrassment, and his ostracism was perpetuated by Elizabeth II. Michael Adeane once cited to Wedgwood Benn the example of Belgium where – he said – the continued presence of ex-King Leopold made life awkward for his son King Baudouin. (On the other hand, the presence of the Count of Barcelona – formerly King Alfonso of Spain – in Madrid creates no evident awkwardness for his son, King Juan Carlos.) It is therefore possible that Elizabeth had come to identify abdication with exile from Britain, thus making it a doubly unthinkable prospect.

But in the 1980s polls began to show a double novelty: the rising popularity of the Princess of Wales, and a growing public voice in favour of Elizabeth II's abdication. According to a Gallup Poll in December 1988, 59 per cent of those questioned felt that the Queen should step down from the throne to make way for the Prince of Wales. It was the first time the supporters of abdication had risen over the 50 per cent mark. In the same poll Charles emerged as the favourite member of the Windsor dynasty, displacing the Queen Mother from her regular perch at the top of the popularity list. As she gets older, Elizabeth II's determination to stay put is likely to grow rather than diminish, old age being golden for the popularity of royals. There is also the advantage of cumulative experience. But there are also drawbacks, such as the hint of arthritis in the pace of the institution, and the occasional whiff of staleness floating out of the open windows of Buckingham Palace into the changing world around it.

Many British people, it is said, are reassured by the Queen's unchanging approach to the monarchy. To them she is a comfortable example of duty and of an unostentatious British style. Elizabeth II keeps the traditional show on the road. Put another way, she guarantees the status quo. Prince Charles, on the other hand, offers no such assurance, which is both his drawback and his attraction.

Articulate, educated and brooding (he once told a girlfriend that he admired his brother Andrew for his extrovert enjoyment of life), he is a man going through more than the usual midlife crisis of someone of his age. For a Prince-in-waiting the historical antecedents are not encouraging. Edward VII was sixty when he succeeded his mother, Queen Victoria, and by that time he was a wasted man after a life of over-indulgence. Edward VIII was forty-two and also suffered from the combined consequences of a privileged position and under-employment of his energies and talents. So Prince Charles's first challenge is to find a way of preventing an internal rot from setting in.

The second is to find a way to be, as he once put it, 'not the King to be, but the Prince of Wales that is.' Prince Charles has used his position to explore relatively controversial ideas. He has been an outspoken critic of the Thatcher government's cutbacks in Britain's social welfare programme, and he has been actively involved in campaigns to bring help to the inner cities, and to expand job opportunities for school leavers. He has co-written and appeared in a high-quality series of television documentaries based on his traditionalist views on architecture, and has become a champion of environmental causes.

All were worthy issues with which the Queen had no quarrel, but by the 1980s Charles's increasingly high profile seemed to set up a dichotomy within the royal family. The future monarch was asserting his right to a voice in the affairs of his country, and there were signs that the current monarch didn't much like it. An image-rivalry developed between the Queen's household at Buckingham Palace and that of Prince Charles at Kensington Palace, exacerbated by the rapid turnover of the Prince's staff due to a combination of low pay and his reputation for refusing to listen to advice. On more than one occasion, Prince Charles agreed to preside over an official function, or take on a speaking engagement, but Buckingham Palace – for one reason or another – un-accepted for him. His wish to attend mass celebrated by Pope John Paul II was only one example of this conflict.

As heir to the throne, the Queen kept a low profile, remaining in the shadow of her beloved father. And there is no reason to believe that she would have become more outspoken had she waited, as Charles has had to wait, to ascend the throne. With Charles it is different. There has never been much room for him in his mother's shadow, and now he is something of a nuisance. Having objected to being barred from seeing state papers herself, she has taken the issue no further in giving her son access to her boxes. The Prince of Wales sees very few government documents.

In 1988, he had the bright idea of merging his charitable fund, the Prince's Trust, with the Jubilee Trust, a similar fund set up by the Queen a decade earlier. Charles's argument was that the combined resources produced a charitable organization with more scope than two small ones. Moreover, whereas the Queen takes less of a hands-on approach to the work of the Jubilee Trust, Charles is personally involved with the Prince's Trust, of which he is an active chairman. New letterheads were printed and expanded programmes discussed, but there was a snag: the Prince of Wales had taken his mother's approval of the merger for granted. Instead, the Queen refused to allow her charitable organization to lose its identity, and approval was summarily refused.

The Queen's apparent disapproval is only one of Charles's problems. His commitment and concern has met with a mixed response among his future subjects. Some, probably the large majority, respond warmly to his palpable honesty, but there is also polite alarm. A future king with a bent for intelligent criticism is an unknown quantity. For many, therein lies a danger. But Charles is still the House of Windsor's best hope for the renewal it needs to face the next century. If he occupies the throne in time.

*   *   *

In 1983, the Queen and Prince Philip revisited Treetops, the game reserve where she was staying when her father died. The return was more duty than pleasure for the memories it stirred can only have been unhappy ones, but she had promised to go back and, inevitably, there it was in her schedule. Once again she drove to the edge of the clearing near the waterhole where in the early morning of 6 February 1952, she had filmed two sparring rhinoceroses, unaware that her father was dead and she was now Queen. The Treetops she knew, the log cabins built in the giant fig tree, was no longer there. It had been burned down by Mau Mau terrorists in 1954. In its place – on the ground – was a modern thirty-eight-bed hotel. There were no elephants this time, either, and Prince Philip remarked that there were fewer trees compared to thirty-one years earlier. Hungry elephants, he was told by the Kenyans, had eaten them.

As the Queen stood on the hotel's observation deck, the scene at the waterhole sparked her interest. 'Oh look, Philip, a buffalo!' she called to her husband. 'Darling, look, he's wallowing,' as the buffalo obligingly rolled about in the orange mud. But the royal visitors seemed apprehensive and uneasy. After lengthy negotiations between the photographers and members of the Palace staff, a commemorative pose was set up at the waterhole. 'Oh dear,' muttered the Queen as she was guided to the right spot.

It was late in the afternoon when the Queen returned to the hunting lodge at the Sagana River where, on that earlier visit, in the pale dawn hours she had learned her fate. The sky cleared quite suddenly, and Mount Kenya glimmered in the distance. The beautiful stone and cedar country house, which the Queen had given back to the people of Kenya, had been enlarged, but she was able to recognize much of it. She talked to a gardener who had helped her plant two trees, and together they planted another. That evening she dined at the lodge with Prince Philip and a few members of the royal household. Their Kenyan hosts left them alone with their memories.

Source Notes

I
Out of Africa

Page and source

1   A white pillowcase: For description of Elizabeth II at Tree-tops see Eric Sherbrooke Walker, *Treetops Hotel*, pp. 102–13; Elizabeth Longford, *Elizabeth R*, pp. 137–38; Ann Morrow, *The Queen*, p.47.

2   'Oh, look,' and 'I don't want to miss a moment': Morrow op. cit., pp. 47–48.
    'He's like that': Sherbrooke Walker op. cit., pp. 102–13.
    Sealed Accession documents: Morrow op. cit., p.45.

3   A deeply insecure man: see Sarah Bradford, *King George VI*; Sir John Wheeler-Bennett, *King George VI*.
    Tantrums in public: Peter Townsend, *Time and Chance*, p.124.
    Comedian Bob Hope: private information.

4   'One has to be': *Time* magazine, 14 March 1983.
    'Letting too much daylight': Walter Bagehot, *The English Constitution*, first edition, 1867.
    Corbett stood guard: Morrow op. cit., p.48.

5   'My most thrilling experience': Sherbrooke Walker op. cit. p.105.
    'I will come back': ibid.
    'He looked as if': Longford op. cit., p.141.

7   Pulled out of the air: Harold Nicolson, *King George V*, p.321.

8   The marriage arrangement: Bradford op. cit., p.261.
    John, who was epileptic: ibid. p.61.
    Friends of 'Mrs S': Queen Mary to Prince Paul of Serbia, 12 December 1936.

9   'All right, Bertie': Bradford op. cit., p.65.

II
Lilibet

10   The Yorks hated: Bradford op. cit., p.78.
      A breech baby: Longford op. cit., p.28.
11   'A little darling': James Pope-Hennessy, *Queen Mary*, p.238.
      'More like your little mother': Bradford op. cit., p.66.
      'We always wanted': Wheeler-Bennett op. cit., p.209.
      'Noble looking': Marion Crawford, *The Little Princesses*,
      p.11.
12   'There has been no-one': Wheeler-Bennett op. cit., p.211.
      'I have heard': Wheeler-Bennett op. cit., p.210.
      Worn by Queen Victoria's: Morrow op. cit., p.12.
      'Cried so much': Mabell, Countess of Airlie, *Thatched with
      Gold*, p.176.
13   At King George's insistence: Longford op. cit., p.32.
      'Gnashes': Bradford op. cit., p.128. Lionel Logue: ibid.,
      p.130; Wheeler-Bennett op. cit., p.220.
      'More confidence now': Bradford op. cit., p.130.
14   When, as King: ibid. p.135.
      'Your sweet little daughter': Wheeler-Bennett op. cit., p.216.
      'Lilibet always came first'; and 'She made his convalescence':
      Airlie op. cit., p.176.
15   Lady Cynthia Asquith: *Illustrated Weekly*, London 4 April
      1953.
      'I hope you like it' and 'Why Bud?': ibid.
      'Shrunken old man': Bradford op. cit., p.198.
16   'Oh no, Granny': Longford op. cit., p.60.
      'Giving me, at the same time': Osbert Sitwell's diary, quoted
      in Bradford op. cit., p.148.
17   'A golden age': Wheeler-Bennett op. cit., p.263.
      'I had a feeling': Crawford op. cit., p.34.
18   'For goodness' sake': ibid., p.22.
      'That genealogies': ibid., p.54.
19   Prince Henry: Sir Henry Bruce-Lockhart, *Diaries*, p.45.
      With Noël Coward: Noël Coward Diaries, p.230.
      Came dangerously close: Bradford op. cit., p.230.
      Kiki Whitney Preston: ibid.
20   Lascelles . . . Baldwin: Duff Hart-Davies, *In Royal Service*,
      p.4.
      'God forgive me': ibid.
      'Highest moral principles': private information.

325

'Whom do I have the honour': *Time* magazine, 6 November 1935.

22   Permission to terminate: Francis Watson, quoting Lord Dawson of Penn, the royal physician, in 'The Death of George V', *History Today*, December 1986.
Elizabeth met Wallis: Duchess of Windsor, *The Heart Has Its Reasons*, p.225; Crawford op. cit., p.72.
'Who *is* she, Crawfie?': ibid.

23   'What I said': Crawford op. cit., p.72.
He seemed distracted: ibid., p.73.
'An adventuress': Michael Thornton, *Royal Feud*, p.101.
Stepped into the breach: ibid., p.134.

24   On 20 October: Bradford op. cit., p.145.
'Was appalled': Thornton op. cit., p.103.
Three options remained: Bradford op. cit., p.145.

25   Public sentiment rapidly built up: ibid.
'Important people came and went': Crawford op. cit., p.79.
'I think Uncle David': Longford op. cit., p.68.
From a footman: Longford op. cit., p.66.

26   'Does that mean': ibid.

III

Heir Presumptive

27   Residual doubts: Bradford op. cit., p.171.

28   'A lot of prejudice': Airlie op. cit., p.225.
Close association: ibid., p.172.
'This is terrible': Philip Ziegler, *Mountbatten*, p.215.
'A little brother': Crawford op. cit., p.83.
'At 145 Piccadilly': Crawford op. cit., p.84.

30   'A dreadful woman': private information.
'As a child': Pietro Annigoni, *An Artist's Life*, p.270.

31   'Stretch a point': Report from Violet Synge to Chief Guide, Girl Guide archives.

32   Violet Synge noted: private information.
'Day after day': Marion Crawford, *Happy and Glorious*. p.23

33   There was time: private information.
'I leapt out of bed': Longford op. cit., p.71.

35   'The King wants': Bradford op. cit., p.234.
For weeks: *Elizabeth II*, Crawford, p.28.

36   'Stop her, Mummy': Crawford, *Little Princesses*, p.225.
     BBC deleted: *Children's Hour* feature, BBC, December 1988.
     'Crawfie, I saw you': *Elizabeth II* op. cit., p.44.
38   'The princesses': Rose Kennedy, *Times to Remember*, p.248.
39   Once, Elizabeth mentioned: *Elizabeth II* op. cit., p.55.
     Liked Violet Synge: private information.
40   Now she resented: private information.
     'A little leaven': Bradford op. cit., p.178.
41   'Tour made us': Wheeler-Bennett op. cit., p.146.
     'No more high-hat': Bradford op. cit., p.316.
     'I'd offend folks': Airlie op. cit., p.214.
42   'She really does': Harold Nicolson, *Diaries and Letters, 1930–1939*, p.78.
     Lisa Sheridan, *From Cabbages to Kings*, p.96.
     'Ran into Princess': Kennedy op. cit., p.320.

IV
The House of Windsor at War

46   'Rather offhand': Crawford *Little Princesses*, p.134.
     'How good he is': ibid.
     'Stared at him': Earl Mountbatten of Burma, *Diaries*, p.256.
     'It is hard': Ziegler op. cit., p.246.
47   Elizabeth wrote: letter in the Girl Guide archives.
48   For King George VI's reaction to Chamberlain's resignation
     and Churchill's appointment as Prime Minister, see Wheeler-
     Bennett op. cit., p.446; Longford op. cit., p.86.
     'My eldest daughter': Wheeler-Bennet op. cit., p.447.
     'They dug trenches': Longford op. cit., p.88.
49   Learning German . . . and tutorials in American history:
     New York Times, 14 February 1940.
     'Margaret gets': Alexandra of Yugoslavia.
     The King would spend: Nicolson *Diaries and Letters*, op.
     cit., p.358.
50   A bomb fell on Buckingham Palace: Wheeler-Bennett op.
     cit., p.470.
51   The Queen said: ibid.
     'We're dressing': Crawford, *Little Princesses*, p.168.
     'You may go to bed': ibid., p.169.
52   'A worrying time lately': Martin Gilbert, *Winston Churchill*,
     vol.V, p.450

Greek royal circles: private information
Channon, in Greece: Sir Henry Channon, *Chips: The Diaries of Sir Henry Channon*, 7 June 1941.

54 'Always amiable': Prince George to Prince Paul of Yugoslavia, 5 April 1942.
On one occasion: *Elizabeth II* op. cit., p.72.

55 The Canon noted: Aidan Crawley to the author, 1989.
'Lilibet much grown': Alice, Countess of Athlone, *For My Grandchildren*, p.145.

56 A senior officer: Crawford *Little Princesses* op. cit., p.207.
Could do no wrong: John Dean, *Prince Philip*, p.78.

57 Dropped the infant: Bradford op. cit., p.234.
'Another cousin for you': meeting described by Queen Alexandra of Yugoslavia in *Memoirs*, p.139.
'Dressed alike': Channon op. cit., 12 October 1942.

59 'Who do you think': *Elizabeth II* op. cit., p.67.
'The [royal] family': Harold Nicolson, unpublished entry in diaries quoted by Bradford op. cit., p.238.
Determination to be . . . British: Longford op. cit., p.81.

60 'Eccentric' and 'philanders on the Riviera': Channon op. cit., 6 November, 1942.

61 Not popular with the Queen: Ziegler op. cit., p.238.

62 Met Elizabeth and Philip: Queen Alexandra op. cit., p.198.
Frequent meeting place: ibid., p.199; Channon op. cit., 13 May 1944.
Marina replied: Queen Alexandra op. cit., p.201.
'Going too fast': Ziegler op. cit., p.346.
'We both think': Wheeler-Bennett op. cit., p.749.

63 'A wicked little girl': Bradford op. cit. p.411
'Where's Philip': Crawford *Little Princesses*, p.243.
Did not find it easy: ibid., p.243.

V

Marriage and Motherhood

64 Any patrol log-books: Girl Guide archives.

65 'Shy, occasionally': Townsend op. cit., p.125.
'When you go in': Peter Townsend to author.

66 Tick, tick, tick: Townsend op. cit., p.127.
'Found her a rival': Bradford op. cit., p.322.
'I am sure this is': Ziegler op. cit., p.344.

67 Mountbatten walking in the embassy garden with Philip

and King of Greece: Lord Killearn, *The Diaries of Lord Killearn*, p.256.

'Philip entirely understood': Ziegler op. cit., p.335.

'Perpetual currents': Townsend op. cit., p.156.

68   'How could I': Wheeler-Bennett op. cit., p.255.

69   One memorandum . . . excused . . . boot camp: Morrow op. cit., p.135.

70   'You felt a bit silly': Morrow op. cit., p.136.

'Jealous, tiresome': ibid.

71   Behaved like two birds: for the princesses' Victory-night outing, see Longford op. cit., p.100; and the Queen's own account in a BBC broadcast on the fortieth anniversary of the victory in Europe, 8 May 1985.

72   'I suppose I began': Basil Boothroyd, *Philip, An Informal Biography*, p.24.

'Please, I beg' and 'a certain job': Ziegler op. cit., p.347.

Lord Linlithgow: Lord Killearn op. cit., p.354.

'They have been': Airlie, op. cit., p.228.

73   'Yes, it does happen': ibid.

'Believe it or not': Longford op. cit., p.103.

In Australia: Anne Edwards, *Royal Sisters*, p.127.

74   A matter of course: Crawford, *Little Princesses*, p.241.

75   'But he's not English': ibid., p.244.

'Some six months': US Embassy Dispatch No. 1649, 14 July 1947.

76   Prince Philip's change of name: see Ziegler op. cit., p.342; Bradford op. cit., p.265.

77   'It is absolutely': Crawford, ibid., p.246.

Embassy Dispatch from Pretoria, 12 April 1946.

Classified report: Embassy Report 1045, 2 May 1947.

78   'Stories of the good impression': ibid.

'For Heaven's sake': Townsend op. cit., p.219.

79   'You are to follow': Bradford op. cit., p.364.

As George VI spoke: Peter Townsend to the author.

Written by Dermot Morrah: private information.

81   Elizabeth told guests: US Embassy Dispatch No. 1649. 14 July 1947.

Dinner at Lewis Douglas's: private information.

82   'I am not being rude': Ziegler op. cit., p.441.

'Senior to Philip': Wheeler-Bennett op. cit., p.344.

83   'I think the answer': Michael Bloch, *The Duke of Windsor's War*, p.279.

84 The wedding breakfast: Queen Alexandra op. cit., p.190; Alice, Countess of Athlone op. cit., p.204.
'When I handed': Wheeler-Bennett op. cit., p.754.

VI

The Principal Position

87 'The principal position': Boothroyd op. cit., p.49.
Slowly, his evident professional: private information.

89 'She dances': Mountbatten Diaries op. cit., 16 November 1949. This account of Princess Elizabeth in Malta is also based on the author's recollections.
At the sight: J.A. Mizzi, 'Royal Days in Malta', *Malta Life* Magazine, October 1972.

90 The only anonymous telephone call: Ziegler op. cit., p.387.
'You'll have to face': Mizzi op.cit.

91 A group of riders: ibid.

92 Her role: Princess Elizabeth's activities as captain's wife were frequently reported in the weekly Services page of the *Times* of Malta.
'He is too sweet': Wheeler-Bennett op. cit., p.740.

93 'I haven't the faintest': private information.

94 King George VI saw: Bradford op. cit., p.443.
Biblical references: Boothroyd op. cit., p.145.
A deep disappointment: Bradford op. cit., p.447.

95 Hair-raising chases: Mizzi op. cit.

96 'The King has a growth': Lord Moran, *The Struggle for Survival*, p.346.

97 A bizarre meeting: Bradford op. cit., p.456.
'Counteract the closeness': US Embassy Dispatch, 28 October 1951.

98 At first been dubious: private information.

99 Had to be disinvited: White House memo, 1 October 1951.
The homey Trumans: Margaret Odlum, Mrs Truman's social secretary, to author, 11 June 1989.
'As one father': President Truman to George VI, 3 November 1951.

100 When her . . . secretary: Sir John Colville, *Diaries*, p.178.
'She wasn't interested': ibid.

VII
A Death in the Family

101 'It is not . . . easy': George VI to Dwight D. Eisenhower, 7 January 1952.
The King was contemplating: Alistair Horne, *Macmillan, 1894–1956*, p.365.
'His Majesty': Lascelles to Dwight D. Eisenhower, 23 January 1952.
102 'Hyde Park Corner': Bradford op. cit., p.523.
'Seemed much altered' and 'I felt with deep foreboding': Oliver Lyttelton, *Memoirs of Lord Chandos*, p.341.
Chips Channon thought: Channon op. cit., p.462.
103 Lascelles telephoned: Bradford op. cit., p.521.
Ford found Churchill: ibid.
Colville tried to cheer him up: Sir John Colville, *The Fringes of Power*, p.640.
'Mike, our employer's': Bradford op. cit., p.521.
104 John Dean noted: Dean op. cit., p.174.
Filming the . . . mountains: *New York Times*, 8 February, 1952.
'Sent those hearses': Longford op. cit., p.142.
105 'The sight of that young figure': Earl of Avon (Anthony Eden), *Full Circle*, p.40.
'Her old Granny': Pope-Hennessy op. cit., p.619.
'Lilibet, your skirts': Dean op. cit., p.175.
106 'I hope you can': Bloch op. cit., p.306.
She advised him: ibid., p.309.
107 'As if he felt': D.R. Thorpe, *Selwyn Lloyd*, p.162.
'Uninteresting and unintellectual': Channon op. cit., p.463.
108 'Glistened with tears': Queen Alexandra op. cit., p.214.
'Peter had the feeling': ibid., p.214.
Allowance . . . to be discontinued: Bloch, op. cit., p.309.
109 'Ice-veined bitches': ibid., p.312.
Mountbatten now reigned: Colville Diaries op. cit., p.641.
In aeternum: Ziegler op. cit., p.682.
Memorandum from Philip: Colville, Diaries op. cit., p.641.
Saw himself as Lord Melbourne: Sir David Pitblado, Churchill's Joint Secretary, to author.
110 Not Philip's real name: Ziegler op. cit., p.681.
Mountbatten's own explanation: Ziegler op. cit., p.682.
113 'A German princeling': Peter Townsend to the author.
The Thursday Club: Unity Hall, *Philip – The Man Behind*

the Monarchy, p.108.

'I'm just an amoeba': Longford op. cit., p.156.

115   Daphne du Maurier: Michael Thornton, *Observer*, London, 16 April 1989.
'It is difficult': Queen Mother to Eisenhower, 11 March 1952.
Depression of widowhood: private information.

116   Churchill's arterial spasm: Moran op. cit., p.375; Colville Diaries op. cit., p.642.
Churchill's dinner: information from two of those present.
Lascelles: Moran op. cit., p.377.

117   Lascelles felt Churchill's: ibid.

118   'To be lent a villa': Gilbert op. cit., p.759.
To remain Mr Churchill: ibid, p.823.

VIII
New Elizabethans

119   'People are prattling': Channon op. cit., 24 November 1952.
Conservative government decided: Brian Barker, *The Times*, London, 30 May 1983.
'Abbey Happy': Channon op. cit., 24 November 1952.
The day was saved by Queen Wilhelmina: Athlone op. cit., p.235.

120   Alexander Korda: Michael Korda, *Charmed Lives*, p.267.
Bernard, Duke of Norfolk: Brian Barker, *The Times*, London, 30 May 1983.
Coronation Commission: minutes of the Coronation Commission, Cabinet Office Papers, 16 March 1952.
Queen's Commonwealth titles: *The Times*, London, 4 May 1952.

121   Commonwealth official to American diplomat: US Embassy dispatch, 15 December 1952.

122   Speaker to represent the Commons: Coronation Commission minutes, 5 December 1952.
Televising the Coronation: Sir John Colville, *Sunday Telegraph*, 9 January 1983; Coronation Commission minutes, 28 July 1952.
Lascelles against broadcasting: Nicolson *Diaries and Letters* Vol II, op. cit., 5 December 1952, p.62.
Televising the Coronation: Coronation Commission minutes, 5 December 1952.

123 Queen's Coronation route proposals: Coronation Commission minutes, 28 July 1952.
Queen practises wearing crown: Longford op. cit., p.159.
Pile for Abbey carpets: Coronation Commission minutes, 28 July 1952.
Queen tolerated no horseplay: Morrow op. cit., p.50.
'She looks towards it' US Embassy dispatch, 27 July 1952.
'Extraordinary thing': Longford op. cit., p.157.

124 'With all her gracious charm': US Embassy dispatch, 27 July 1952.
Refusal to invite her Uncle David: Bloch op. cit., p.313.
Duke of Norfolk quote, and Lascelles' to Allen: ibid., p.314.
'By the sovereign or ex-sovereign of any state': ibid.

125 'Should be attached by a comb': Earl Marshal's coronation circular to the Diplomat Corps, November 1952.
Elizabeth had gone with Queen Mary: Marion Crawford, *Happy and Glorious*, p.81.
Hartnell's design of coronation dress: Norman Hartnell, *Scarlet and Gold*, p.232.
'Mama is very sick': Bloch op. cit., p.322.

126 Prime Minister George Borg Oliver announced: Malta Legislative Assembly Debates, 11 May 1953.

127 The Colonial Secretary, Oliver Lyttelton: Lyttelton op. cit., p.427; also private information.
The Queen released the horses: Lyttelton op. cit., p.427.
Household Brigade Ball, Colville Diaries op. cit., p.713.

128 'Is all well, Ma'am?': Longford op. cit., p.191.
Noël Coward watching on television: Coward Diaries, 4 June 1953.
William Walton: Susana Walton, *Behind the Facade*, p.131.

129 Senator Jack Kennedy proposed: Judie Mills, *John F. Kennedy*, p.107.
To the photographer Cecil Beaton: Cecil Beaton, *Diaries: The Strenuous Years 1948–1955*, 4 June 1952.

130 'Le Lac des Cygnes': Colville Diaries op. cit., p.714.
Philip's role in Coronation: Coronation Commission minutes, 6 February 1953.
'Oh hullo, did you watch it?': Beaton Diaries, op. cit., 4 June 1953.

131 A record 20.4 million: BBC viewer statistics.
The British government delayed the release: *The Times*, 18 May 1976.

132 'One of the great disasters' Lord Harewood, *The Tongs and the Bones*, p.137.
Noël Coward . . . a performer: for example, at a party given by the Duchess of Kent, 21 June 1953. See Coward Diaries for that date.

133 Sir Michael Adeane . . . approached Harold Nicolson: Nicolson *Diaries and Letters*, Vol.II, p.323.
The Queen's decision to switch jockeys: Longford op. cit., p.192.
The Queen and the prize cup: *Time* Magazine, 17 July 1952.

IX
Margaret in Love

135 Flicking a spot of fluff: Longford op. cit., p.164.
Talked in the Red Drawing Room: Townsend op. cit., p.193.
Queen Mother sympathetic: private information.
Margaret's sister: Longford op. cit., p.150.

136 Under the Royal Marriages Act: Townsend op. cit., p.198.
Those who knew Margaret: private information.

137 In 1948, Townsend accompanied: Longford op. cit., p.148.
Even after a decade: Townsend to the author.
'Under the circumstances': Christopher Warwick, *Princess Margaret*, p.59.
'You must be either mad or bad': Townsend op. cit., p.198.
As Lascelles saw it: private information.

138 The Queen refused: Townsend op. cit., p.149.
Published diary: Colville Diaries op. cit., p.716.
According to Colville's later account: Longford op. cit., p.152.
Prior to the meeting: private information.

139 He said goodbye: Townsend op. cit., p.202.
She shook his hand: Townsend op. cit., p.203.
Torpedo: ibid.
'Welter of psuedo-religious': Coward Diaries op. cit., p.215.

140 Immediate prospect: Gilbert op. cit., p.849; Moran op. cit., p.414.
Churchill told: Moran op. cit., p.472.

141 Bermuda . . . a disappointment: Gilbert op. cit., p.942.
'We have followed': ibid.
Churchill's reply: ibid.

A farewell dinner: Coward Diaries op. cit., p.222.

143 Thereafter decreed: private information.

144 'Not you': private information.
'A programme of excursions': Ziegler op. cit., p.515.
Mountbatten accompanied: ibid.
'The exercise': the fleet's manoeuvre described by Ziegler op. cit., p.515, and J. A. Mizzi (who witnessed it) in *Sunday Times* of Malta, 11 November 1972.
One purpose: the episode described by Mizzi, ibid.

145 'I could not detect': Moran op. cit., p.547.
'Did my father do it': Longford op. cit., p.160.

146 'If I were Mummy' and 'Some awful ordeals': Longford op. cit., p.169.
'As a model': Annigoni op. cit., p.84.
'Sausage': Longford op. cit., p.169.

147 'An African queen': Godfrey Talbot, *Ten Seconds From Now*, p.103.
'A combination': Hansard, 11 November 1953, col. 952.
'A man of genuine': US Embassy Dispatch 488, 27 July 1952.

148 'The weather makes me happy': Annigoni op. cit., p.85.

149 'We said goodbye': Hélène Cordet, *Born Bewildered*, p.101.
'Hot under the collar': ibid., p.165.

X

The End of the Affair

151 When Richard Dimbleby: private information.
Victory at Epsom Downs: Lord John Oaksey, *The Queen*, p.132.

152 Totally exhausted: Gilbert op. cit., p.1083.
After the Tory Party Conference: Colville Diaries op. cit., p.673.
Churchill and Eden agreed: Gilbert op. cit., p.1102.
Churchill . . . put off his resignation: ibid., p.1114–15.
Queen's letter: ibid. p.1126.

153 'Understood the uncertainty': ibid., p.1117.
The Downing Street dinner: Colville Diaries op. cit., p.708.
Churchill offered dukedom: Gilbert op. cit., p.1123–5; Colville, *The Fringes of Power* op. cit., p.710.

155 Townsend meets Margaret: Townsend op. cit., p.213.

156 'Obviously lonely': William Clark, *From Three Worlds*, p.158.
The Queen Mother against: private information.
The Queen's feelings of angst: private information.
'Eden behaved', and Constitutional formula: Clark op. cit., p.158–9.
157 'We rediscovered one another': Townsend op. cit., p.226.
Cabinet met: ibid., p.228.
158 Salisbury threatens resignation: ibid., p.231; Longford op. cit., p.176; Alistair Horne, *Macmillan 1957–86*, p.37; *The Times*, editorial, 24 October 1955.
159 'It's not possible': Longford op. cit., p.177.
Produced an envelope: Townsend to author.
160 Margaret sees Archbishop: Longford op. cit., p.177.
'The drama stands out': Clark op. cit., p.159.
161 Situation disqualified him: Longford op. cit., p.176.
National poll: Nicholas Courtney, *Sisters-in-Law*, p.32.
To make innuendoes: Morrow op. cit., p.209.
The Queen was furious: private information.
162 An understanding: private information.
Her father . . . her grandfather: Nicolson *Diaries and Letters 1945–1962*, p.334.
163 'I often only': Morrow op. cit., p.76.
'Palace days': ibid., p.77.
The vendeuse and a couple of fitters: ibid., p.78.
164 'Too tight for us': private information.
In conversation: Dean op. cit., p.87.
165 Always dreamed of seeing Leningrad, and 'It would be easy': Nikita S. Khruschev, *Khrushchev Remembers*, p.406.
'Khrushchev pressed': *Observer*, 1 January 1989.
Government denies invitation: ibid.
166 Charles at the ballet: Harewood op. cit., p.169.
167 Eden himself told: Robert Lacey, *Majesty*, p.238.
Mountbatten – who himself: private information.
She did warn him: Clark op. cit., p.284.
Eden needed her signature: Clark op. cit., p.285.

XI
Philip at Sea

170 When the Queen: this was Eden's account of how Macmillan surfaced as the front-runner, as told to Canadian High Commissioner Paul Martin eighteen years later. Martin, *The London Diaries, 1975–79*, entry for 17 November 1975.

171 The Queen's Secretary: private information.
'Somewhat difficult': Horne op. cit., p.169.
Remarkable act: ibid., p.83.
Initiated a procedure: ibid., p.169.

172 He was impressed: ibid.
She seemed fascinated: Lacey op. cit., p.243.
Philip begged the Queen: private information.

173 The Duke's main refuge: Lacey op. cit., p.213.
White roses . . . iguanas: Longford op. cit., p.181.
Fuelled rumours of discord: for example, *Baltimore Sun*, 23 May 1957.

174 'I should be . . . careful': Ziegler op. cit., p.576.
All wore false beards: Thorpe op. cit., p.223.

175 Coward and the Queen Mother: Coward Diaries op. cit., p.357.
'Coward's way out' and Coward's knighthood: private information.

176 'A pain in the neck' etc.: see *The National and English Review*, August 1957.

177 'Altrincham's free-wheeling' *et seq.*: US embassy confidential dispatch 13 August 1957.
Newspaper opinion poll: in the *Daily Mail*.

178 Buckingham Palace reply: mentioned in the US embassy dispatch 13 August 1957.
Malcolm Muggeridge: *Saturday Evening Post*, 19 October 1957: 'Does England Really Need a Queen?'
John Osborne: *Encounter*, October 1957, 'They Call it Cricket.'

179 Any embarrassment: Anthony Wedgwood Benn, *Diaries*, Vol I, p.414.

180 A voice coach: private information.
'A taxi ran': Annigoni op. cit., p.86.

181 The Queen was 'persuaded': Clark op. cit., p.192.
American trip planned: John Foster Dulles to US President, 22 May 1956.
'For several months': secret internal US State Department

memos to Secretary of State, 27 March and 17 April 1957.

182 American embassy wired: US embassy telegram, 11 June 1957.
Eisenhower was disappointed: Eisenhower letter to Macmillan, 7 June 1957.
'They were inhibited': US embassy telegram, 13 June 1957.
Invitations to Queen: correspondence in US State Department file on the royal visit.

183 Mr Muirhead: memorandum of conversation, US State Department, 2 July 1957.

184 Later he told Macmillan: Dwight D. Eisenhower, *The White House Years: Waging Peace*, p.213.
'Shocked at ... Sputnik': Piers Brandon, *IKE – The Life and Times of Dwight D. Eisenhower*.
On Suez crisis: private information.

XII

Into the Second Decade

187 'Two old and devoted': Townsend op. cit., p.279.

188 An insult to the Queen: Horne op. cit., p.147.
Eisenhower received at Balmoral: Eisenhower op. cit., p.420.
She had seen: Queen to Eisenhower, 24 January 1960.
Ike's reply: 4 February 1960.

189 Jackie and Lee: incident described in Diaries of David Bruce, 29 May 1960 *et seq.*
'How would you react': Horne op. cit., p.304.

190 At the instigation: private information.

191 J. Edgar Hoover: message in the Johnson Presidential archives.
Macmillan and Kennedy: see, for example, Arthur Schlesinger Jr., *A Thousand Days*, p.233.
Kennedy personality sketch: Harold Macmillan, *At the End of the Day*, p.148.

192 Queen to Kennedy: 14 May 1960.
'You're dead': Michael Varney and Max Marquis, *Bodyguard to Charles*, p.26.
'If it hadn't been': Basil Boothroyd, 'The Prince I came to know rather well', *The Times*, 10 June 1981.

193 'Thank Heavens': Horne op. cit., p.170.

194 'The lovely rooms': Coward Diaries op. cit., p.437.

'Queen alone looked disagreeable': ibid., p.438.

195 'I don't know': Chris Ogden, *Maggie*, p.261.

196 Macmillan proposed: Horne op. cit., p.170.
'She clearly indicated': Anthony Howard, *RAB – Biography of R.A. Butler*, p.276.
Disapproving Cabinet: ibid.

197 'Special gratitude', and 'Taken a great load': ibid., p.277.
Mountbatten to Prince Charles: Ziegler op. cit., p.683.
'Yes, it's perfectly true': Michael De La Noy, *Michael Ramsey*, p.221.
Two foreign ambassadors: private information.
Attractive young American: private information.

199 Maria Callas: Harewood op. cit., p.232.
Macmillan talks of resignation: Harold Evans, *Downing Street Diary*, p.234.
John Glenn: ibid., p.187.
Nehru imitation: Horne op. cit., p.415.

200 John Morrison: ibid., p.398.
'She had been indignant': Evans op. cit., p.311.
Five days before: Horne op. cit., p.398.

201 'I have risked my Queen': ibid.
Commonwealth Conference: ibid., p.355.
'Commonwealth feelings': ibid.

202 Queen wining and dining: private information.
The Queen was furious: John Kenneth Galbraith, *Ambassador's Journal*, p.96.
Ill-treat the corgis: Varney and Marquis op. cit., p.22.

XIII

A Normal Childhood

204 'You'll have to explain': Brian Hoey, *Anne, The Princess Royal*, p.33.

205 Mispy and Anne: ibid., p.29.
Anne's parents . . . 'seemed rather brutal': ibid., p.30.

206 'Charles,' said the Queen: Harold Wilson, *Memoirs*, p.3.

207 'They'll have a job': Hoey op. cit., p.122.
'Fantastic stories': Bruce Diaries, op. cit., 30 June 1963.

208 Macmillan to Queen: Horne op. cit., p.485.
The Queen wrote back: ibid., p.486. Horne calls it a 'charmingly consoling letter.'

'A sacrifice is increasingly': Bruce to President, Bruce Diaries, op. cit., 5 July 1963.

209   Poll quoted by Horne op. cit., p.484.
In September: this interview reported by Macmillan in volume VI of his autobiography, *At the End of the Day*, p.495.

211   Profumo affair had sapped: Horne op. cit., p.542.

212   Frantic attempts: ibid. p.573.
Queen visits Macmillan: Macmillan, Vol.VI; Horne op. cit., p.565.

214   A private lunch: private information.

215   Adeane on the Queen's broadcast: Evans op. cit., p.270.

216   The National Gallery: Annigoni op. cit., p.231.
[We] had nothing': Horne op. cit., p.466.

217   In April: Chapman Pincher, *Too Secret Too Long*, p.366–369; and private information.

218   Senior American: private information.
When Adeane: private information.
Blunt confessed: Pincher op. cit., p.368–369.
A conversation at Buckingham Palace: Peter Wright, *Spycatcher*, p.223.

219   Blunt kept the secret: Bradford op. cit., p.455; Pincher op. cit., p.369; Chapman Pincher, *Mask of Treachery*, p.345.

220   Prince Philip: private information. Philip was mentioned only in passing, and the report said he was not linked to the Profumo affair.

221   He was warned: Longford op. cit., p.259.
'*Chez vous*': ibid.
Discussion with Pearson: Martin op. cit., p.411.

222   Left her shaken: former Foreign Secretary Lord Stewart of Fulham, who was minister-in-attendance for the trip, to the author, 1989.
She met each: Bruce Diaries op. cit., 30 January 1963.

XIV

The New Crowd

224   'Mood changing': Wedgwood Benn *Diaries, Vol.I* op. cit., p.14.

225   An avid collector of gossip: private information.

Government ministers: Richard Crossman, *Diaries, Vol.II*, p.195.

Dispatched Adeane to the Prime Minister: ibid.

226 Benn kneeling: Wedgwood Benn, Vol.I p.232.

Queen 'not too happy': ibid., p.281.

Pincer movement: ibid., p.361.

Adeane cut him off: ibid., p.335.

'Wilson's intentions': ibid., p.364.

227 'The Queen . . . not at all satisfied': ibid., p.408.

The three things: private information.

228 With Elizabeth's approval: royal source to author, 1976.

But Elizabeth felt: ibid.

229 'Had to fight': Prince Charles to newspaper editors, May 1989.

On 22 December 1965: Ziegler op. cit., p.685; Howard op. cit., p.350.

Ramsey had been included: De La Noy op. cit., p.222.

230 Decision taken: Ziegler op. cit., p.685; Wilson op. cit., p.3.

Wilson learned: ibid., p.3.

231 'I absolutely adored': Longford op. cit., p.216.

His mother visited: Varney and Marquis op. cit., p.117.

Butler and Charles: Howard op. cit., p.351.

232 'I was carrying': Crossman Diaries, Vol.II op. cit., p.45.

David Bruce noted: Bruce Diaries op. cit., 15 June 1966.

233 'Governessy': De La Noy op. cit., p.224.

'It's odd': Lord Stewart of Fulham to the author.

'A rather tart way': Crossman Diaries, Vol.II op. cit., p.683.

234 That's nonsense: Mountbatten Diaries op. cit., pp.187–8.

'A great deal of money': Annigoni op. cit., p.185.

Clockwatching: ibid., p.183.

'Most rich men': Crossman Diaries, Vol.III op. cit., p.724.

Dinner for Katzenbach: Bruce Diaries op. cit., 23 April 1968.

236 'The next thing': William Evans, *My Mountbatten Years*, p.79.

Remembering the laughter: Annigoni op. cit., p.176.

237 Mountbatten noted: Ziegler op. cit., p.660.

And at lunch: Bruce Diaries op.cit., 2 April 1968.

239 Neilson MacCarthy: John Pearson, *The Ultimate Family*, p.134.

'Here was a first class': ibid.

240 The selling of Charles: Courtney op. cit., p.45.

Brabourne . . . encouraged her: ibid., p.46.

With Philip in the chair: Morrow op. cit., p.89.

241 'You certainly won't need': ibid., p.90.
Hours of early footage: private information.
242 Audience research: quoted in Courtney op. cit.
243 'Everything about her': Annigoni op. cit., p.172.

XV
Money Talks

244 Nixon lunch: private information.
'Poor Americans': Annigoni op. cit., p.186.
245 Deeply embarrassed: Crossman Diaries, Vol.III op. cit., p.723.
246 'Her Majesty has been much concerned': Lord Cobbold to the House of Commons Select Committee, 1971.
248 Detailed study: Adeane to the Select Committee, 1971.
'Yes, it means': Crossman Diaries, Vol.II op. cit., p.953.
249 Mountbatten advised: Ziegler op. cit., p.684.
251 'An unofficial Ombudsman': Wedgwood Benn Diaries, Vol.II op. cit., p.238.
Opposed to Spain: Lord Stewart of Fulham to the author.
252 Philip boomed in: Crossman Diaries, Vol.II op. cit., p.45.
Harold Wilson returned: private information.
'Very savage': Morrow, ibid., p.242.
253 Watching . . . polo: Mountbatten Diaries op. cit., p.197–8.
255 Largely because: private information.
The brainchild of Sir Christopher Soames: private information.
As the date drew closer: Sir Christopher Ewart-Biggs Diary, 3 January 1972.
Contingency plan: Lady Ewart-Biggs to author.
'How is our friend': Bloch op. cit., p.354.
'If they want me': Ewart-Biggs Diary, 15 May 1972.
256 'We sent the Palace': ibid.
'Thinking of speaking': ibid.
Duke of Windsor meets Queen: Bloch op. cit., p.354.
The conversation: private information.
Foreign Office report quoted by Ewart-Biggs Diary, 26 June 1972.
257 She said, was it: ibid., 18 May 1973.
Queen Juliana: Ewart-Biggs Diary, 28 June 1972.
258 White House had to choose: this is clear from State Department Memorandum to the President, 12 November 1956.

The royal family seemed determined: Mountbatten Diaries op. cit., pp.250–1.

259 'Your sister-in-law': ibid.
'He was': ibid., p.253.
By prior arrangement: Wedgwood Benn Diaries, Vol.II op. cit., p.431.

XVI
The Queen Goes Walkabout

260 'Be ready': Hoey op. cit., p.51.
261 'The royal family': Anthony Howard, *Rab* p.356.
Margaret loved Les Jolies Eaux: Longford op. cit., p.203.
262 'Land diving' at Pentecost Island: Mountbatten Diaries op. cit., pp.280–1.
Malacca wedding: ibid. p.239.
263 The Queen summoned: private information.
264 'Half cut': private information.
'Ho, ho': episode described in Wilson's Memoirs op. cit., p.4–5.
265 'Her Europeanism': Roy Jenkins, *European Diary*, p.130.
Ramsey lunch: De La Noy op. cit., p.224.
266 It was not too late: private information, but Andrew Roth, *Sir Harold Wilson – Yorkshire's Walter Mitty*, p.25, says there was some indication that the Palace returned the whole list of proposed honorees.
'Mr Wilson': private information. Coward Diaries op. cit., p.679.
267 It was five o'clock: Hoey op cit., p.59. Kidnapping attempt episode based on various press and published sources.
SAS were also given: Hoey op. cit., p.62.
268 'The Queen filled the kettle': Wilson Memoirs op. cit., p.6.
270 To time the announcement: Joe Haines, Wilson's spokesman at 10 Downing Street, to the author.
Briefing papers: memorandum to Secretary of State, 2 July 1976, and memorandum to the President from Henry Kissinger, 2 July 1976.
This diverted attention: Kissinger memo.
271 'The Princess Margaret problem': Martin op. cit., p.351.
273 'A politely determined woman': ibid., p.324–36.

274 Into this tense setting: Hugo Young, *One of Us*, p.491; Ogden op. cit., p.265.

275 'She has a way': Quoted in *The Times*, 16 April 1986. 'She didn't minimize': Martin op. cit., p.568. 'My God, the Queen': Morrow op. cit., p.154.

276 The story goes: private information.

XVII
A Bride for Charles

278 'Will I ever': Morrow op. cit., p.70.

279 'The Prince's equerry': letter in Carter Presidential archives. 'The downward slope': Ziegler op. cit., p.686. Charles met a woman: private information.

280 One November afternoon: ibid. A small cabinet committee: Hugo Young, *One of Us*, note to p.288.

281 One day, shortly: private information.

282 'I didn't know': Morrow op. cit., p.130.

286 To telephone Charles: private informatiion.

287 'Well, I think': Morrow op. cit., p.3

288 The twenty-one editors: meeting described by Harold Evans, *Good Times, Bad Times*, p.233. 'If Lady Di': ibid.

289 'Never has there been': Longford op. cit., p.337.

292 'There's that bloody bell': Morrow op. cit., p.231; Longford op. cit., p.5.

293 'I realized immediately': Morrow op. cit., p.232. 'Our eyes met': ibid. 'I want a police officer': press reports.

294 'You see I have none': Longford op. cit., p.6.

295 'The Queen is very strained': Morrow op. cit., p.234.

296 'We thought the dialogue': ibid., p.236. Trestrail's subsequent confession: ibid., p.237; press reports.

XVIII
Queen and Prime Minister

299 'In Britain, public confidence': George Shultz, memorandum to the President, 23 February 1983.

300 The Palace footman: Selwa Roosevelt, Chief of Protocol, to author, 1990.

301 'Don't you have anything?': Selwa Roosevelt to author, 1990. See also Roosevelt, *Keeper of the Gate*, p.203.
'Let's get going': private information.

302 'I'm damned if I will': Selwa Roosevelt.
'Aren't there any male supervisors?': *Time* magazine, 14 March 1983.
'I told them': ibid.

307 Her main concern: *The Sunday Times*, 24 June 1986.
Bubbled to the surface: *The Sunday Times*, 20 July 1986.

308 Briefing the Court: private information.
'The question now': embassy dispatch, 28 July 1986.

309 A devoted monarchist: Young op. cit., p.489.
Prime Minister was stunned: Ogden op. cit., p.261.
The Queen never noticed: Robert Harris, *Observer*, 27 November 1988.
When both were scheduled: Ogden op. cit., p.263.

310 'There is no such thing': Young op. cit., p.490.

311 'What I worry about': Ogden op. cit., p.264.

XIX
She

316 'More formal occasion': Jenkins op. cit., p.130.
'No, dear': Morrow op. cit., p.175.
'Behind the façade': memorandum to the President, 23 February 1983.

317 The richest woman: *Fortune* magazine, 'Shrewd Managers of Regal Riches', 12 October 1987.

317 And 1988: private information.

320 'The spiritual quality': Martin op. cit., p.264.

323 'Oh look, Philip': *The Times*, 11 June 1983.

Bibliography

Unpublished Sources

Bruce, David. Diaries. Virginia Historical Society, Richmond.

Carter, President Jimmy. Presidential Papers. Jimmy Carter Presidential Library, Atlanta, Georgia.

Eisenhower, President Dwight D. Presidential and other papers. Dwight D. Eisenhower Presidential Library, Abilene, Kansas.

Ewart-Biggs, Sir Christopher. Diary. Courtesy Baroness Ewart-Biggs, London.

Johnson, President Lyndon B. Presidential Library, Austin, Texas.

Kennedy, President John F. Presidential Papers. John F. Kennedy Presidential Library, Boston, Massachusetts.

National Archives, Washington D.C.

Nixon, President Richard M. Presidential Papers; Files of the State Department; United States Embassy, London; United States Embassy, Johannesburg; etc.

Paul, Prince of Serbia. Letter and papers. Bakhmeteff Archive, Columbia University Library, New York.

Public Records Office, Kew Gardens, London. Coronation Commission records, and other official documents.

Truman, President Harry S. Presidential Papers. Harry S. Truman Presidential Library, Independence, Missouri.

Published Sources

Airlie, Mabell, Countess of. *Thatched with Gold.* London: Hutchinson, 1962.

Alexandra of Yugoslavia. *For a King's Love: Memoirs.* London, Hodder & Stoughton 1956.

Alice, Princess, Countess of Athlone. *For My Grandchildren.* London: Evans Brothers, 1966.

Annigoni, Pietro. *An Artist's Life.* London: Collins, 1977.

Asquith, Lady Cynthia. *The Duchess of York.* London: Hutchinson, 1937.

Avon, Earl of. *The Memoirs of Sir Anthony Eden: Full Circle.* London: Cassell, 1960.

Bagehot, William. *The English Constitution.* 1st edition: 1867.

Beaton, Cecil. *The Strenuous Years 1948–1955.* London: Hutchinson, 1975.

Benn, Anthony Wedgwood. *Office Without Power, 1968–1972.* London: Hutchinson, 1980.

Benn, Anthony Wedgwood. *Out of the Wilderness, 1963–1967.* London: Hutchinson, 1983.

Bloch, Michael. *The Duke of Windsor's War.* London: Bantam, 1982.

Boothroyd, Basil. *Philip: An Informal Biography.* London: Longman, 1971.

Bradford, Sarah. *King George VI.* London: Weidenfield & Nicolson, 1989.

Brandon, Piers. *IKE – The Life and Times of Dwight D. Eisenhower.* London: Secker & Warburg, 1987.

Bruce-Lockhart, Sir Robert. *Diaries.* London: Secker & Warburg, 1956.

Channon, Sir Henry. *Chips: The Diaries of Sir Henry Channon,* ed. Robert Rhodes James. London: Weidenfeld & Nicolson, 1967.

Clark, William. *From Three Worlds.* London: Longman, 1975.

Colville, Sir John. *The Fringes of Power, 10 Downing Street Diaries, 1939–1955.* London: Hodder, 1985.

Cordet, Hélène. *Born Bewildered.* London: Peter Davies, 1961.

Courtney, Nicholas. *Sisters-in-Law.* London: Weidenfield & Nicolson, 1988.

Coward, Noël, *Diaries,* ed. Graham Payne and Sheridan Morley. London: Macmillan, 1982.

Crawford, Marion. *The Little Princesses.* New York: Harcourt, Brace, 1950.

Crawford, Marion. *Happy and Glorious;* London: Newnes, 1953.

Crossman, Richard. *The Diaries of a Cabinet Minister.* Volume I: *Minister of Housing, 1964–1966.* London: Hamish Hamilton, 1975; Volume II: *Lord President of the Council and Leader of the House of Commons, 1966–1968.* London: Hamish Hamilton, 1976.

De La Noy, Michael. *Windsor Castle: Past and Present*. London: Headline, 1990.

De La Noy, Michael. *Michael Ramsey. A Portrait*. London: Collins, 1990.

Dean, John. *Prince Philip*. New York: Henry Holt, 1954.

Edwards, Anne, *Royal Sisters*. New York: Morrow, 1990.

Eisenhower, Dwight D. *The White House Years: Waging the Peace*. London: Heinemann, 1961.

Evans, Harold. *Downing Street Diary: The Macmillan Years 1957–1963*. London, 1981.

Evans, Harold. *Good Times, Bad Times*. London: Weidenfeld & Nicolson, 1983.

Evans, William. *My Mountbatten Years*. London: Headline, 1989.

Ford, Betty. *The Times of My Life*. New York: Simon & Schuster, 1978.

Gilbert, Martin. *Winston Churchill*, Volume V. London: Collins, 1988.

Hardinge, Helen. *Loyal to Three Kings: A Memoir of Sir Alexander Hardinge, 1920–1943*. London: William Kimber, 1967.

Harewood, Earl of. *The Tongs and the Bones: The Memoirs of Lord Harewood*. London: Weidenfeld & Nicolson, 1981.

Hartnell, Norman. *Scarlet and Gold*. London: Weidenfeld & Nicolson, 1972.

Hoey, Brian. *Anne: The Princess Royal*. London: Grafton, 1989.

Holden, Anthony. *Charles, Prince of Wales*. New York: Simon & Schuster 1979.

Horne, Alistair. *Macmillan*, Volume 1 *1894–1956*; Volume 2 *1957–1986*. of the official biography *Macmillan*. London, 1989.

Howard, Anthony. *RAB: A Biography of R. A. Butler*. London: Jonathan Cape 1987.

Jenkins, Roy. *European Diary*. London: Weidenfeld & Nicolson, 1989.

Judd, Denis. *Prince Philip. A Biography*. New York: Random House, 1980.

Junor, Penny. *Diana, Princess of Wales*. London: Weidenfield & Nicolson, 1982.

Kennedy, Rose. *Times to Remember*. New York: Morrow, 1974.

Khrushchev, Nikita S. *Khrushchev Remembers*, tr. Strobe Talbott. Boston: Little, Brown, 1970.

Killearn, Lord. *The Diaries of Lord Killearn*. London, 1975.

Korda, Michael. *Charmed Lives*. London: Simon & Schuster, 1978.

Lacey, Robert. *Majesty* Elizabeth II and the House of Windsor, London: Sphere, 1986.

Lascelles, Sir Alan. *In Royal Service: The Letters and Journals of Sir Alan Lascelles,* Volume II, ed. Duff Hart-Davies. London: Hamish Hamilton, 1989.

Longford, Elizabeth. *Elizabeth R.* London, Weidenfeld & Nicolson, 1983.

Lyttelton, Oliver. *Memoirs of Lord Chandos.* London: Bodley Head, 1962.

Macmillan, Harold. *At the End of the Day, 1961–1963.* London: Macmillan, 1973.

Marie Louise, Princess. *My Memory of Six Reigns.* New York: Dutton, 1957.

Martin, Paul. *The London Diaries 1975–1979,* ed. William R. Young. Ottawa: University of Ottawa Press, 1988.

Mills, Judie. *John F. Kennedy.* New York: Franklin Watts Inc., 1988.

Moran, Lord. *The Struggle for Survival, 1940–1945.* London: Constable, 1966.

Morrow, Ann. *The Queen.* London: Book Club Associates/ Granada Television, 1983.

Mountbatten of Burma, Earl. *From Shore to Shore: The Diaries of Earl Mountbatten of Burma 1953–1979,* ed. Philip Ziegler. London: Collins, 1989.

Nicolson, Harold. *Diaries and Letters 1930–1939,* ed. Nigel Nicolson. London: Collins, 1966. Diaries and Letters 1945–1962 ed. Nigel Nicolson. London: Collins, 1968. *King George V.* London: Constable. 1952.

Ogden, Chris. *Maggie.* New York: Simon & Schuster, 1990.

Pearson, John. *The Selling of the Royal Family.* New York: Simon & Schuster, 1986.

Pearson, John. *The Ultimate Family.* London: Grafton, 1987.

Pincher, Chapman. *Too Secret Too Long.* New York: St. Martin's, 1984.

Pope-Hennessy, James. *Queen Mary.* London: Allen & Unwin, 1959.

Roosevelt, Selwa. *Keeper of the Gate.* New York: Simon & Schuster, 1990.

Roth, Andrew. *Sir Harold Wilson: Yorkshire's Walter Mitty.* London: Macdonald and Jane's, 1978.

Schlesinger, Arthur, Jr. *A Thousand Days.* New York, 1967.

Shawcross, William. *The Shah's Last Ride: The Fate of an Ally.* New York: Simon & Schuster, 1988.

Sheridan, Lisa. *From Cabbages to Kings*. London: Oldhams, 1955.

Talbot, Godfrey. *Ten Seconds from Now*. London, 1973.

Terraine, John. *The Life and Times of Lord Mountbatten*. London: Hutchinson & Co., 1967.

Thorpe, D. R. *Selwyn Lloyd*. London: Jonathan Cape, 1989.

Thornton, Michael. *Royal Feud*. London: Collins, 1983.

Townsend, Peter. *Time and Chance*. Chicago: Academy, 1978.

Varney, Michael, and Max Marquis. *Bodyguard to Charles*. London: Robert Hale, 1989.

Walton, Susana. *William Walton: Behind the Facade*. Oxford University Press, 1978.

Warwick, Christopher. *Princess Margaret*. London: Weidenfeld & Nicolson, 1983.

Watson, Francis. The Death of George V, *History Today*, London, 1986.

Wheeler-Bennett, Sir John. *King George VI: His Life and Reign*. London: Weidenfeld & Nicolson, 1958.

Wilson, Harold: *Memoirs: The Making of a Prime Minister 1916–1964*. London: Weidenfeld & Nicolson, and Michael Joseph, 1986.

Windsor, Duchess of. *The Heart Has Its Reasons*. London: Michael Joseph, 1956.

Windsor, Duke of. *A King's Story: The Memoirs of HRH the Duke of Windsor*. London: Cassell, 1951.

Wright, Peter. *Spycatcher*. New York: G. K. Hall, 1988.

Young, Hugo. *One of Us: A Biography of Margaret Thatcher*. London: Macmillan, 1989.

Ziegler, Philip. *Mountbatten: The Official Biography of Earl Mountbatten of Burma*. London: Collins, 1987.

Index

351